DATA PROTECTION, PRIVACY AND ARTIFICIAL INTELLIGENCE

This book presents insights from the 2025 CPDP.ai international conference, where leading scholars, policy makers and practitioners examine how Europe's fast-evolving digital frameworks shape global debates. As the EU legislates at unprecedented speed, it not only regulates technologies such as AI, but also defines their governance through rights-based instruments including the AI Act, the Data Act, and the GDPR.

The chapters analyse the consolidation of the EU model of AI and data governance, covering topics such as Fundamental Rights Impact Assessments, proportionality, transparency obligations for companion chatbots, and transatlantic contrasts in AI and health-data regulation. Contributors explore how divergent legal traditions influence accountability and democratic oversight, and how emerging duties – such as the duty of loyalty in data processing – could rebalance power between citizens and infrastructures. Other chapters address data access under the Data Act, empirical supervision of algorithmic profiling, and proposals to strengthen GDPR enforcement.

Opening with 'The World Is Watching', an artistic and philosophical reflection on perception, opacity, and the more-than-human in surveillance societies, the book bridges critical theory and regulatory practice. A dedicated Practitioners' Corner connects real-world governance experience with academic insight, highlighting pressing challenges for the year ahead.

Uniting law, technology, and ethics, this interdisciplinary volume captures Europe's effort to govern AI and data infrastructures – under the close gaze of a watching world.

Computers, Privacy and Data Protection

Paul De Hert (Series Editor)

The *Computers, Privacy and Data Protection* series, now published by Hart, collects multidisciplinary peer-reviewed scientific manuscripts that are the result of papers that have been presented at the international Computers, Privacy and Data Protection conference (CPDP), that takes place every year in Brussels. As a world-leading multidisciplinary conference, CPDP gathers, within an atmosphere of independence and mutual respect, academics, lawyers, practitioners, policy-makers, industry and civil society from all over the world, offering them an arena to exchange ideas and discuss the latest emerging issues and trends.

The series provides cutting edge research on legal, regulatory, academic and technological development in privacy and data protection. The books, which have been published since 2009 with growing success, are comprised of academic research dealing with topics such as recent developments in privacy and data protection law, multidisciplinary and interdisciplinary insights in privacy and data protection, privacy by design, privacy enhancing technologies and emerging technologies such as conversational agents, machine-learning algorithms, internet of things and cloud computing. The book series discusses daring and prospective approaches and serves as an insightful resource for readers with an interest in computers, privacy and data protection.

Previous volumes in this series (published by Springer)

2009
Reinventing Data Protection?
Editors: Serge Gutwirth, Yves Poullet, Paul De Hert, Cécile de Terwangne, Sjaak Nouwt
ISBN 978-1-4020-9497-2 (Print) ISBN 978-1-4020-9498-9 (Online)

2010
Data Protection in A Profiled World?
Editors: Serge Gutwirth, Yves Poullet, Paul De Hert
ISBN 978-90-481-8864-2 (Print) ISBN: 978-90-481-8865-9 (Online)

2011
Computers, Privacy and Data Protection: An Element of Choice
Editors: Serge Gutwirth, Yves Poullet, Paul De Hert, Ronald Leenes
ISBN: 978-94-007-0640-8 (Print) 978-94-007-0641-5 (Online)

2012
European Data Protection: In Good Health?
Editors: Serge Gutwirth, Ronald Leenes, Paul De Hert, Yves Poullet
ISBN: 978-94-007-2902-5 (Print) 978-94-007-2903-2 (Online)

2013
European Data Protection: Coming of Age
Editors: Serge Gutwirth, Ronald Leenes, Paul De Hert, Yves Poullet
ISBN: 978-94-007-5184-2 (Print) 978-94-007-5170-5 (Online)

2014
Reloading Data Protection
Multidisciplinary Insights and Contemporary Challenges
Editors: Serge Gutwirth, Ronald Leenes, Paul De Hert
ISBN: 978-94-007-7539-8 (Print) 978-94-007-7540-4 (Online)

2015
Reforming European Data Protection Law
Editors: Serge Gutwirth, Ronald Leenes, Paul De Hert
ISBN: 978-94-017-9384-1 (Print) 978-94-017-9385-8 (Online)

2016
Data Protection on the Move
Current Developments in ICT and Privacy/Data Protection
Editors: Serge Gutwirth, Ronald Leenes, Paul De Hert
ISBN: 978-94-017-7375-1 (Print) 978-94-017-7376-8 (Online)

2017
Data Protection and Privacy: (In)visibilities and Infrastructures
Editors: Ronald Leenes, Rosamunde van Brakel, Serge Gutwirth, Paul De Hert
ISBN: 978-3-319-56177-6 (Print) 978-3-319-50796-5 (Online)

Previous titles in this series (published by Hart Publishing)

2018
Data Protection and Privacy: The Age of Intelligent Machines
Editors: Ronald Leenes, Rosamunde van Brakel, Serge Gutwirth, Paul De Hert
ISBN: 978-1-509-91934-5 (Print) 978-1-509-91935-2 (EPDF) 978-1-509-91936-9 (EPUB)

2019
Data Protection and Privacy: The Internet of Bodies
Editors: Ronald Leenes, Rosamunde van Brakel, Serge Gutwirth, Paul De Hert
ISBN: 978-1-509-92620-6 (Print) 978-1-509-92621-3 (EPDF) 978-1-509-9622-0 (EPUB)

2020
Data Protection and Privacy: Data Protection and Democracy
Editors: Ronald Leenes, Dara Hallinan, Serge Gutwirth, Paul De Hert
ISBN: 978-1-509-93274-0 (Print) 978-1-509-93275-7 (EPDF) 978-1-509-93276-4 (EPUB)

2021
Data Protection and Privacy: Data Protection and Artificial Intelligence
Editors: Dara Hallinan, Ronald Leenes, Paul De Hert
ISBN: 978-1-509-94175-9 (Print) 978-1-509-94176-6 (EPDF) 978-1-509-94177-3 (EPUB)

2022
Data Protection and Privacy: Enforcing Rights in a Changing World
Editors: Dara Hallinan, Ronald Leenes, Paul De Hert
ISBN: 978-1-509-95451-3 (Print) 978-1-509-95453-7 (EPDF) 978-1-509-95452-0 (EPUB)

2023
Data Protection and Privacy: In Transitional Times
Editors: Hideyuki Matsumi, Dara Hallinan, Diana Dimitrova, Eleni Kosta and Paul De Hert
ISBN: 978-1-509-96590-8 (Print) 978-1-509-96592-2 (EPDF) 978-1-509-95691-5 (EPUB)

2024
Data Protection and Privacy: Ideas That Drive Our Digital World
Editors: Hideyuki Matsumi, Dara Hallinan, Diana Dimitrova, Eleni Kosta and Paul De Hert
ISBN: 978-1-509-97600-3 (Print) 978-1-509-97598-3 (EPDF) 978-1-509-97599-0 (EPUB)

2025
Data Protection, Privacy and Artificial Intelligence: To Govern or To Be Governed, That is the Question
Editors: Eleni Kosta, Dara Hallinan, Paul De Hert and Suzanne Nusselder
ISBN: 978-1-509-98401-5 (Print) 978-1-509-98399-5 (EPDF) 978-1-509-98400-8 (EPUB)

2026
Data Protection, Privacy and Artificial Intelligence: The World is Watching
Editors: Jonas Breuer, Dara Hallinan, Paul De Hert and Manos Roussos
ISBN: 978-1-509-99312-3 (Print) 978-1-509-99314-7 (EPDF) 978-1-509-99313-0 (EPUB)

Data Protection, Privacy and Artificial Intelligence

The World is Watching

Volume 18

Edited by
Jonas Breuer
Dara Hallinan
Paul De Hert
and
Manos Roussos

•HART•
OXFORD • LONDON • NEW YORK • NEW DELHI • SYDNEY

HART PUBLISHING

Bloomsbury Publishing Plc

Kemp House, Chawley Park, Cumnor Hill, Oxford, OX2 9PH, UK

1385 Broadway, New York, NY 10018, USA

Bloomsbury Publishing Ireland Limited, 29 Earlsfort Terrace, Dublin 2, D02 AY28, Ireland

HART PUBLISHING, the Hart/Stag logo, BLOOMSBURY and the Diana logo are trademarks of Bloomsbury Publishing Plc

First published in Great Britain 2026

A catalogue record for this book is available from the British Library.

A catalogue record for this book is available from the Library of Congress.

ISBN: HB: 978-1-50999-312-3
ePDF: 978-1-50999-314-7
ePub: 978-1-50999-313-0

Typeset by Compuscript Ltd, Shannon

PREFACE

Technology should be debated openly, not announced from podiums. The Computers, Privacy and Data Protection (CPDP) conference remains committed to inclusive dialogue on how technology shapes society – and how society must shape technology. As Amandeep Singh Gill, UN Envoy for Digital and Emerging Technology, reminded us: 'AI isn't just about algorithms, compute, and data. It's about power.' At the heart of this debate are fundamental rights. Privacy and data protection may not appear in every constitution, yet they resonate worldwide amid justified concern over power asymmetries. The spread of data protection and AI laws may signal some progress but also reveals uneven rule-of-law standards. European-style data governance, sometimes seen as a global standard, invites scrutiny: who benefits, and who is left out? In 2025, conflict, war, and the establishment of authoritarian regimes deepen concerns, not only about how technology mediates power.

The 17th edition of CPDP, held in Brussels from 22–24 May 2025, brought together over 500 speakers and 1,400 participants from more than 50 countries. With 84 panels, 37 workshops, and a vibrant programme of art, keynotes, and radio programmes, CPDP.ai 2025 created space to question, connect, and collaborate. Under the theme *Data Governance, AI, and Privacy: The World Is Watching* this edition examined the expanding reach of EU digital legislation and its global repercussions. As Europe regulates phenomena such as AI and constructs new frameworks like the European Health Data Space, its influence spreads – but not without tension. The so-called Brussels effect both inspires and unsettles, revealing power asymmetries that shape digital governance worldwide.

Each year, CPDP.ai collaborates with an artist whose work engages with the conference theme: Adam Harvey (2019), David Shrigley (2020), Taietzel Ticalos (2022), Judith Fegerl (2023), and Vladan Joler (2024). The 2025 edition continues this tradition with James Bridle, whose artwork *The World Is Watching* explores perception, opacity, and the more-than-human in surveillance societies. Extending ideas from his works *New Dark Age* (2018) and *Ways of Being* (2022), Bridle's contribution reflects on how human and non-human ways of seeing intertwine within technological, ecological, and political systems. Mireille Hildebrandt continues this book with an introductory chapter based on her Opening Night keynote. She examines how law structures markets and how the material demands of AI infrastructures – energy, water, and rare earths – reshape sovereignty and sustainability. Hildebrandt contrasts the ideology of artificial general intelligence with the European Union's more grounded approach to governing AI as a 'normal technology', setting the stage for the chapters that follow.

It is striking that a conference dedicated to privacy and data protection has become so deeply engaged with questions surrounding artificial intelligence. This shift reflects not a departure from CPDP's mission but shows that AI governance now forms one of the most contested political frontiers, also in relation to data protection and digital rights. The next part of the book gathers peer-reviewed academic papers, many of which take up this challenge by examining the legal, ethical, and technical dimensions of AI as discussed at CPDP.ai 2025. Anna-Julia Saiger opens the part by tracing how the notion of disruption has evolved in debates on Big Tech and artificial intelligence. Oreste Pollicino et al follow with a proposal for a practical framework – the FRIAct – to operationalise Fundamental Rights Impact Assessments for high-risk AI systems. Rachael Olaitan Aborishade identifies a missed opportunity in the AI Act to regulate romantic chatbots.

Gary Hsuanyu Liu takes over and analyses the trans-Atlantic rebalancing of privacy power through health-data governance and AI oversight, while Anže Erbežnik, David E Harris, and Owen Doyle compare EU and US (especially Californian) approaches to AI and personal-data regulation, exposing their growing divergence. Emma Semaan explores the promise and limits of technical standardisation as a regulatory tool when grounded in public oversight. Emanuela Podda et al contribute a multidisciplinary perspective on *data access by design*, linking legal, technical, and ethical dimensions of accountable data infrastructures.

Next, the Practitioners' Corner continues an initiative introduced by Eleni Kosta in the previous volume to give space to non-academic perspectives reflecting the multistakeholder nature of CPDP. This section links practical experience with academic insight, highlighting emerging challenges for the year ahead. Jolien Ghyselinck and Peter Berghmans discuss the evolving role of Data Protection Officers in today's regulatory landscape and what their wellbeing reveals about organisational accountability. Jurriaan Parie and co-authors present the work of their NGO on empirical methods for supervising algorithmic profiling systems, showing how technical tools can reinforce transparency and fairness in practice. Charles-Albert (Charly) Helleputte closes the section with a reflection on General Data Protection Regulation (GDPR) enforcement and the need to rethink its underlying mechanics to ensure consistency and trust across jurisdictions.

As has become a valued tradition, this volume closes again with the Concluding Remarks of Wojciech Wiewiórowski, European Data Protection Supervisor, which were, this time, not fully delivered at the end of the conference. His reflections reaffirm how data protection remains a compass for digital humanism – a framework to place people before technology. He calls for sustained cooperation among regulators and stakeholders to ensure that AI governance strengthens, rather than replaces, existing safeguards for fundamental rights.

Taken as a whole, this book reflects the diverse perspectives shared at CPDP.ai 2025, capturing the essence of the conference and its evolving community of scholars, practitioners, regulators, and artists. It underlines CPDP's mission to advance rights-based digital governance through dialogue and collaboration.

Before concluding, the editors would like to take the opportunity to thank our reviewers: Tal Zarsky, Tjaša Petročnik, Masa Galic, Ine van Zeeland, Marco Bassini, Hiroshi Miyashita, Kristina Irion, Stephanie von Maltzan, Ivan Szekely, Ian Brown, Diana Dimitrova, Simone van der Hof, Valentina Golunova, Michael Birnhack, and Friso Bostoen. Their careful reviews, expertise, and generosity in sharing their time and insight have been invaluable to ensuring the rigour and quality of this volume.

Jonas Breuer, Dara Hallinan, Paul De Hert, and Manos Roussos
12 November 2025

CONTENTS

PART 3
PRACTITIONERS' CORNER

PART 4
EDPS CLOSING REMARKS

CONTRIBUTORS

Rachael Olaitan Aborishade is a technology lawyer and policy researcher based in Nigeria, specialising in AI governance, data protection, and e-commerce. She has served as Research Fellow at the Centre for Artificial Intelligence and Digital Policy and as Graduate Legal Intern at UNIDROIT, contributing to digital-asset policy and soft-law development. She holds an LLM in International Technology Law from Vrije Universiteit Amsterdam and was recognised as a 2025 Lexxion EDPL (European Data Protection Law Review) Arising Scholar.

Peter Berghmans is CEO and trainer at the Data Protection Institute, Belgium, and a member of the Vlaamse Toezichtcommissie. He acts as Data Protection Officer in the healthcare sector, including for the Collaboratief Zorgplatform, and previously taught data protection and security at Thomas More University of Applied Sciences.

James Bridle is a writer, artist, and technologist based in Greece. Their work has been commissioned and exhibited internationally and online, exploring the intersections of art, technology, and society. Their writing has appeared in *Wired*, *The Atlantic*, *The New Statesman*, *The Guardian*, and the *Financial Times*. They are the author of *New Dark Age* (2018) and *Ways of Being* (2022) and wrote and presented 'New Ways of Seeing' for BBC Radio 4 in 2019.

Andrea Cosentini is Head of Data Science and Responsible AI at Intesa Sanpaolo, Italy. With a background in physics and mathematics, he previously led the bank's Center of Excellence on AI and served as Chief Data Officer in the Department for Transformation of the Presidency of the Council of Ministers, where he helped design the National Digital Data Platform.

Giovanni De Gregorio is PLMJ Chair in Law and Technology at Católica Global School of Law and Católica Lisbon School of Law, Portugal, and a member of the Católica Research Centre for the Future of Law. His research focuses on constitutional and digital governance, freedom of expression, and platform regulation.

Owen Doyle is a policy researcher specialising in technology regulation, AI governance, social media, and online information ecosystems. Owen currently works as a policy analyst at Harris Research Group.

Anže Erbežnik is Professor of Criminal Law at the European Faculty of Law, Slovenia, and Advisor to the European Parliament's Legal Affairs Committee. He previously advised the Civil Liberties, Justice and Home Affairs Committee. His work focuses on criminal law, EU law and AI law, and he has published widely in these fields.

Andrea Ermellino is a Data Scientist in the Responsible AI team at Intesa Sanpaolo, Italy. He holds degrees in data science and computer science from the University of Milano-Bicocca, where he is pursuing a PhD in mechanistic interpretability. His research explores explainability and transparency in artificial intelligence.

Dario Fontanella is International Strategic Affairs Specialist at Intesa Sanpaolo, Italy. His expertise covers foreign affairs, international economics, corporate finance, and AI management. He previously worked in corporate finance at ENI and in AI development at Intesa Sanpaolo.

Jolien Ghyselinck is Data Protection Officer at the National Institute for Criminalistics and Criminology, Belgium, and is appointed for data protection of DNA analysis in criminal matters in the public sector. She is a board member of dpo pro, the Professional Union of Data Protection Officers in Belgium, and guest lecturer at the Data Protection Institute. She has previously served as Data Protection Officer for several public institutions and supervisory authorities under the Belgian Parliament.

David Evan Harris is Chancellor's Public Scholar at the University of California, Berkeley, and teaches at the Haas School of Business. He serves as Senior Policy Advisor at the California Initiative for Technology and Democracy, Senior Advisor on AI and Elections at the Brennan Center for Justice, Senior Research Fellow at the International Computer Science Institute, and Senior Fellow at the Centre for International Governance Innovation.

Brinn Hekkelman is Research Fellow in the Data Science and Risk and Regulation programmes at the Netherlands Bureau for Economic Policy Analysis. His research focuses on fairness in selection algorithms and on the economic implications of individual risk accumulation. He holds a PhD in computer science from the Netherlands.

Charles-Albert (Charly) Helleputte is Partner in the data privacy and security practice at King & Spalding, based in Brussels and Paris. He advises clients on cybersecurity and privacy compliance in complex cross-border contexts involving frameworks such as NIS, PSD2, and CTR. He teaches at UCLouvain (Saint-Louis, Brussels) and at the Université Catholique de Lille in Paris, and is a founding member of DRAILS (Data, Robotics, Artificial Intelligence, Law and Society).

Mireille Hildebrandt is Emeritus Professor at the Vrije Universiteit Brussel, Belgium. A leading legal scholar in law, science, and technology, she has been central to the development of the Law, Science, Technology & Society (LSTS) research group and the Computers, Privacy and Data Protection (CPDP) community. Her work focuses on artificial intelligence, data protection, and the foundations of constitutional democracy.

Nicole Inverardi is AI Ethicist in the Data and AI Office of Intesa Sanpaolo, Italy. She focuses on ethical and legal aspects of artificial intelligence in finance and on implementing EU AI Act requirements. Her interests include human autonomy, control, and sovereignty in AI decision-making.

Mark Kattenberg is Research Fellow in the Decentralised Governments programme at the Netherlands Bureau for Economic Policy Analysis. His work covers applied empirical research on the housing market and local government finance. He received his PhD from Utrecht University with a dissertation on the economics of social housing.

Nicola Leschke is a doctoral researcher in the Privacy Engineering and Policy-Aligned Systems group at Salzburg University, Austria. Her work lies at the intersection of computer science and law, with a focus on technical challenges in personal data access. She previously worked as research associate at the Technical University of Berlin, where she obtained her degrees in information systems engineering.

Gary Hsuanyu Liu is a Doctor of Juridical Science (JSD) Candidate at Washington University School of Law and Dwight D Eisenhower/Clifford Roberts Fellow. His research develops fiduciary 'data loyalty' duties and health-data trusts for AI-enabled medicine, integrating statutory design with algorithmic impact and equity audits. His trans-Atlantic lens contrasts the EU AI Act and European Health Data Space with US HIPAA/FTC and First Amendment limits, aiming to rebalance privacy power through enforceable, rights-preserving governance for health AI.

Federica Paolucci is Postdoctoral Research Fellow at Bocconi University, Italy, in the DigCon project financed by the Fondo Italiano per la Scienza. Her research addresses the protection of fundamental rights in the use of artificial intelligence, particularly biometric identification systems.

Frank Pallas is EXDIGIT Professor for Privacy Engineering and Policy-Aligned Systems at Salzburg University, Austria. His research explores the relationship between complex technical infrastructures and legal or policy frameworks. Before joining Salzburg University, he held academic positions at TU Berlin, KIT, and FZI Forschungszentrum Informatik in Karlsruhe.

Jurriaan Parie is co-founder of NGO Algorithm Audit, Netherlands. With a background in mathematics, he works on translating complex algorithmic concepts into accessible language and advancing responsible AI practices. He leads the development of a European knowledge platform for AI bias testing and standards to promote fairness and transparency in digital systems.

Ilaria Penco is AI Ethicist in the Data and AI Office of Intesa Sanpaolo, Italy. She focuses on the ethical and legal implications of AI and on fundamental rights protection under the EU AI Act. She previously worked as legal counsel in strategic finance at Intesa Sanpaolo.

Emanuela Podda is a legal researcher with a PhD in Law, Science, and Technology. She works at the intersection of law and computer science, focusing on the legal challenges of data processing, the design of compliant data governance models, and the interaction between technical and regulatory frameworks. She is also a qualified lawyer with professional experience in European institutions.

Oreste Pollicino is Full Professor of Constitutional Law and AI Law at Bocconi University, Italy, where he directs the Master of Laws in Law of Technology and Automated Systems. He is Principal Investigator of the DigCon project financed by the Fondo Italiano per la Scienza. His work bridges academia and policymaking, with contributions to the European Commission, OECD, and World Economic Forum.

Daniele Regoli is Lead Data Scientist at the AI Delivery Center of Intesa Sanpaolo, Italy. Trained in physics and cosmology, he previously worked in research at the University of Padova and Scuola Normale Superiore in Pisa. He leads teams developing AI solutions across business divisions.

Ylja Remmits is an AI expert at NGO Algorithm Audit, Netherlands. With experience in computer science, policy, and consulting, she leads projects supporting the implementation of the EU AI Act in the Dutch public sector and has previously advised technology companies on Digital Services Act compliance.

Anna-Julia Saiger is a postdoctoral researcher at the Faculty of Law, Freiburg University, Germany. Her research focuses on governance challenges in the digital age and on addressing the triple planetary crises within European and international legal frameworks.

Pierangela Samarati is Professor at the Department of Computer Science, Università degli Studi di Milano, Italy. Her research focuses on data protection, security, and privacy. She has coordinated numerous national and EU-funded projects and published extensively on information protection. She is Institute of Electrical and Electronics Engineers, Assocation for Computing Machinery, and International Federation for Information Processing Fellow.

Emma Semaan is a doctoral researcher at the Faculty of Law, University of Oxford, United Kingdom, where she also teaches at the Oxford Internet Institute. Her research focuses on the regulation of digital technologies from a comparative and interdisciplinary perspective. She is a Fellow at the Open Technology Institute in Washington, DC, contributing to digital privacy and technology policy.

Silvia Tessaro Trapani is Data and AI Ethicist in the Data and AI Office of Intesa Sanpaolo, Italy. She works on aligning AI technologies with European regulatory and ethical frameworks, with a focus on models of human oversight that safeguard fundamental rights in AI-driven decision-making.

Thierry Vandenbussche is Art Director at Privacy Salon, Belgium. He has organised CPDP and Privacy Salon events since 2019 and has curated exhibitions on privacy and data control, including *Festival of Control*. He previously founded the platforms Courtisane, Outlandish, and Stilll, and continues to coordinate Privacy Salon's artistic and curatorial projects.

Birte Vingerhoets is Communication and Production Lead at Privacy Salon/CPDP, Belgium. She works on public engagement around privacy and data protection and holds a Master's degree in Digital Media in Europe from the Vrije Universiteit Brussel.

Wojciech Wiewiórowski has been the European Data Protection Supervisor (EDPS) since the 6 December 2019. He is also an Adjunct Professor in the Faculty of Law and Administration of the University of Gdańsk. Previously, he was Inspector General for the Protection of Personal Data (Polish Data Protection Commissioner) 2010–2014 and the Vice Chair of the Working Party Art. 29 in 2014 and European Data Protection Assistant Supervisor 2014–2019.

PART 1

Introduction

1

The World is Watching: Perception, Opacity, and the More-than-Human in Surveillance Societies*

JAMES BRIDLE, THIERRY VANDENBUSSCHE AND BIRTE VINGERHOETS

Abstract

This chapter introduces *The World Is Watching*, an exploration of perception, opacity, and the more-than-human in surveillance societies. Centred on James Bridle's commissioned artwork for CPDP 2025, it examines how human and non-human ways of seeing intertwine within technological, ecological, and political systems. Drawing on phenomenology, science and technology studies, and critical data theory, it argues that perception is not exclusively human but distributed across living and artificial agents. By engaging thinkers such as Merleau-Ponty, Haraway, Morton, Pasquale, and Shiva, the chapter links sensory diversity, algorithmic opacity, and democratic accountability. It concludes that recognising non-human perception and technological agency is essential to re-imagining governance in an age of pervasive surveillance.

Keywords

More-than-human; Surveillance; James Bridle; Perception; Democracy

In 2025, the Computers, Privacy and Data Protection (CPDP) conference commissioned artist and writer James Bridle to design its cover artwork. Bridle's work, which often interrogates the intersections of technology, perception, and power,

* This chapter gradually grew out of a series of conversations and interviews between artist James Bridle and CPDP organisers Thierry Vandenbussche and Birte Vingerhoets.

was invited to engage with the conference's theme: 'The world is watching'. This phrase, at once evocative and unsettling, serves as a provocation – not only about who watches whom, but about the very nature of watching itself. Bridle's response, as ever, is to turn the question inside out, exposing the multiplicity of gazes that constitute our shared reality: human and non-human, organic and artificial, visible and obscured. His artwork, and the themes it evokes, invites us to consider perception not as a singular, human-centred act, but as a distributed, entangled process involving a vast array of actors, each with their own ways of sensing, knowing, and responding to the world.

This introduction chapter sets the stage for the legal and ethical explorations that follow in this volume. It argues that the more-than-human world – encompassing animals, plants, machines, and ecologies – demands a radical rethinking of perception, knowledge, and democracy in an age of pervasive surveillance.

Image 1.1 CPDP.ai 2025 Visual Identity

I. The More-than-Human Gaze: Perception Beyond the Human

A. Who Sees? The Plurality of Perception

The more-than-human world encompasses all beings with whom we share this planet, not only other humans, but animals, plants, fungi, bacteria, and the intricate systems and ecologies in which life unfolds. To approach this world through the lens of perception raises profound and unsettling questions: Who sees? How do they see? What kinds of perception do we share, and where do they diverge? These questions challenge the anthropocentric assumption that human ways of seeing and knowing are central or sufficient. They invite us to consider the multitude of other forms of awareness and sensation that exist alongside our own.

James Bridle's artistic practice has long been concerned with the limits and possibilities of perception. His works – such as *Seamless Transitions* (2015), which visualises the invisible infrastructures of migrant detention and deportation, or *Cloud Index* (2016), which investigates the relationship between weather and computation – reveal the hidden layers of technological and ecological perception. Bridle's art does not merely document these systems; it renders them sensible, making visible the ways in which human and non-human actors are entangled in networks of surveillance, control, and care.

Yet, as Bridle's work suggests, perception is not the exclusive domain of humans. Octopuses, for example, possess distributed cognitive systems, with neurons spread throughout their bodies, allowing for semi-independent processing in different limbs – a radical departure from the centralised cognition of primates. Cephalopods also detect polarised light, invisible to the human eye, while insects perceive the world through compound eyes, each lens capturing fragments of visual information. Plants, too, sense light and gravity, not with eyes, but with bodies evolved to interpret the rhythms of the earth. These diverse sensory systems challenge our understanding of what it means to 'see'. As Maurice Merleau-Ponty argued in Phenomenology of Perception,[1] perception is always embodied and situated; it is not a passive reception of data, but an active, relational process. Alva Noë's enactive approach to perception further emphasises that seeing is a form of doing, shaped by the body's engagement with its environment.[2]

[1] Maurice Merleau-Ponty, *Phenomenology of Perception*, trans. Colin Smith (London: Routledge & Kegan Paul, 1962), originally published in 1945.

[2] Alva Noë, *Action in Perception* (Cambridge, MA: MIT Press, 2004).

Image 1.2 Collection of sea animal eyes (detail in image 1)

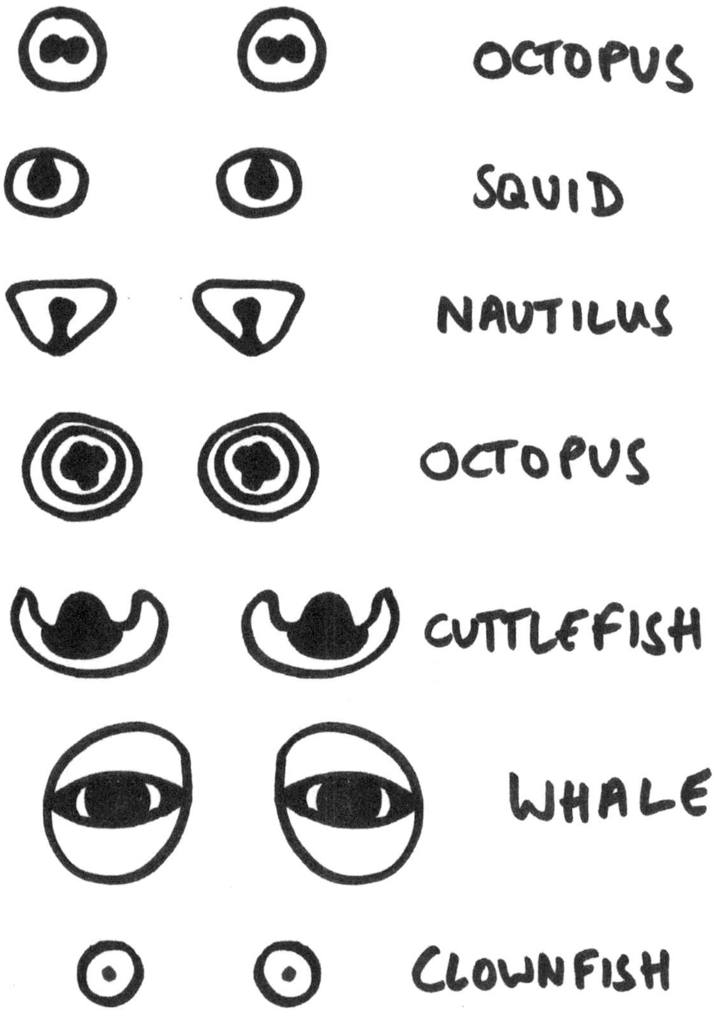

B. The Epistemological Challenge of Non-Human Knowing

To take the perceptions of non-human beings seriously is not just an ethical gesture; it is an epistemological challenge. It asks us to reconsider what it means to see, to know, to relate. As Donna Haraway writes, we must learn to 'think with' other beings, recognising that their ways of knowing are not merely different but often incommensurable with our own.[3] This incommensurability is not a barrier to understanding, but an invitation to humility and curiosity. It suggests that we might have much to learn from the sensory and cognitive lives of non-human beings – about resilience, adaptation, interdependence, and the limits of human understanding.

Timothy Morton's concept of 'hyperobjects' – entities so vast and complex that they defy human comprehension – further complicates the picture.[4] Climate change, nuclear waste, and global surveillance networks are hyperobjects, their scale and temporality exceeding the bounds of human perception. Anna Tsing's work on mushroom ecologies similarly highlights the importance of attending to the 'arts of noticing' practised by non-human actors, whose survival strategies and sensory attunements offer alternative models of knowledge and coexistence.[5]

C. Machines as Alien Perceivers

Alongside biological perception, we must also reckon with the artificial eyes that populate our world: cameras on street corners, sensors in doorbells, drones in the sky. These technologies are not neutral extensions of human vision; they embody distinct epistemologies shaped by the logics of computation, capital, and control. Shoshana Zuboff demonstrates how such systems do not merely observe but actively shape behaviour, extracting value from the prediction and modification of human action.[6] Yet, as James Bridle's work reminds us, these technologies are not just tools; they are actors in their own right, with their own forms of agency and opacity.[7]

Bruno Latour and Susan Leigh Star help us understand how technological systems become 'black boxes' – opaque, taken-for-granted entities whose inner workings are hidden from view.[8] The legal and ethical implications of this opacity are profound. If we cannot see how these systems operate, how can we govern them? How can we ensure that they serve democratic ends rather than entrenching existing power asymmetries?

[3] Donna Haraway, *Staying with the Trouble: Making Kin in the Chthulucene* (Durham, NC: Duke University Press, 2016).

[4] Timothy Morton, *Hyperobjects: Philosophy and Ecology after the End of the World* (Minneapolis: University of Minnesota Press, 2013).

[5] Anna Lowenhaupt Tsing, *The Mushroom at the End of the World: On the Possibility of Life in Capitalist Ruins* (Princeton, NJ: Princeton University Press, 2015).

[6] Shoshana Zuboff, *The Age of Surveillance Capitalism: The Fight for a Human Future at the New Frontier of Power* (New York: PublicAffairs, 2019).

[7] James Bridle, *Seamless Transitions*, digital video, 5:28 min, commissioned by The Photographers' Gallery, London, 2015, https://nomegallery.com/artwork/seamless-transitions-2015/; and *Cloud Index*, digital commission for the Serpentine Galleries, 2016, https://jamesbridle.com/works/cloud-index.

[8] Bruno Latour, *Science in Action: How to Follow Scientists and Engineers through Society* (Cambridge, MA: Harvard University Press, 1987); Susan Leigh Star, 'The Ethnography of Infrastructure'. *American Behavioral Scientist* 43, no. 3 (1999): 377–91.

II. Opacity, Power, and the Crisis of Democratic Agency

A. The Black Box Society

The opacity of technological systems is not accidental; it is a feature of their design. As Frank Pasquale argues, the lack of transparency in algorithmic decision-making undermines accountability and erodes public trust.[9] When people cannot understand the systems that govern their lives, they cannot meaningfully participate in democratic processes. This lack of understanding generates fear, distrust, and alienation – emotions that are reflected in the widespread democratic crises we see today.

Kate Crawford shows how the opacity of machine learning systems is not just a technical issue but a political one.[10] Algorithms trained on biased data reproduce and amplify existing inequalities, yet their operations remain largely inscrutable to those affected by them. This 'procedural opacity', to use Helen Nissenbaum's term, is a direct challenge to the rule of law, which depends on the principle that citizens must be able to understand and contest the decisions that affect them.

B. Surveillance and the Erosion of Autonomy

Michel Foucault famously described the panopticon as a model of surveillance that induces self-regulation through the mere possibility of being watched.[11] Zygmunt Bauman updates this analysis for the digital age, arguing that contemporary surveillance is not just about control but about the commodification of attention and behaviour.[12] In this context, the more-than-human gaze takes on a sinister dimension: not only are we watched by other humans and non-human animals, but by systems designed to predict, nudge, and manipulate our actions.

The legal implications are clear. If surveillance technologies operate beyond the reach of public scrutiny, they undermine the very foundations of democratic governance. As Bridle's work suggests, we must ask: What values do we bring to our encounters with these systems? What kind of world do we aspire to create? These questions are not just philosophical; they are urgent legal and political challenges.

C. Toward a More-than-Human Democracy

The recognition of non-human perception and the critique of opacity point toward a more expansive vision of democracy – one that includes not only human citizens

[9] Frank Pasquale, *The Black Box Society: The Secret Algorithms That Control Money and Information* (Cambridge, MA: Harvard University Press, 2015).

[10] Kate Crawford, *Atlas of AI: Power, Politics, and the Planetary Costs of Artificial Intelligence* (New Haven, CT: Yale University Press, 2021).

[11] Michel Foucault, *Discipline and Punish: The Birth of the Prison*, trans. Alan Sheridan (New York: Vintage Books, 1977; orig. pub. 1975).

[12] Zygmunt Bauman and David Lyon, *Liquid Surveillance: A Conversation* (Cambridge: Polity Press, 2013).

but the more-than-human world. Vandana Shiva and Bernard Stiegler both argue for a politics that acknowledges the interdependence of all living beings and the need for collective stewardship of shared resources.[13] This requires new forms of legal personhood, new rights for non-human actors, and new mechanisms for transparency and accountability in technological systems.

Image 1.3 Collection of technological eyes (detail in image 1)

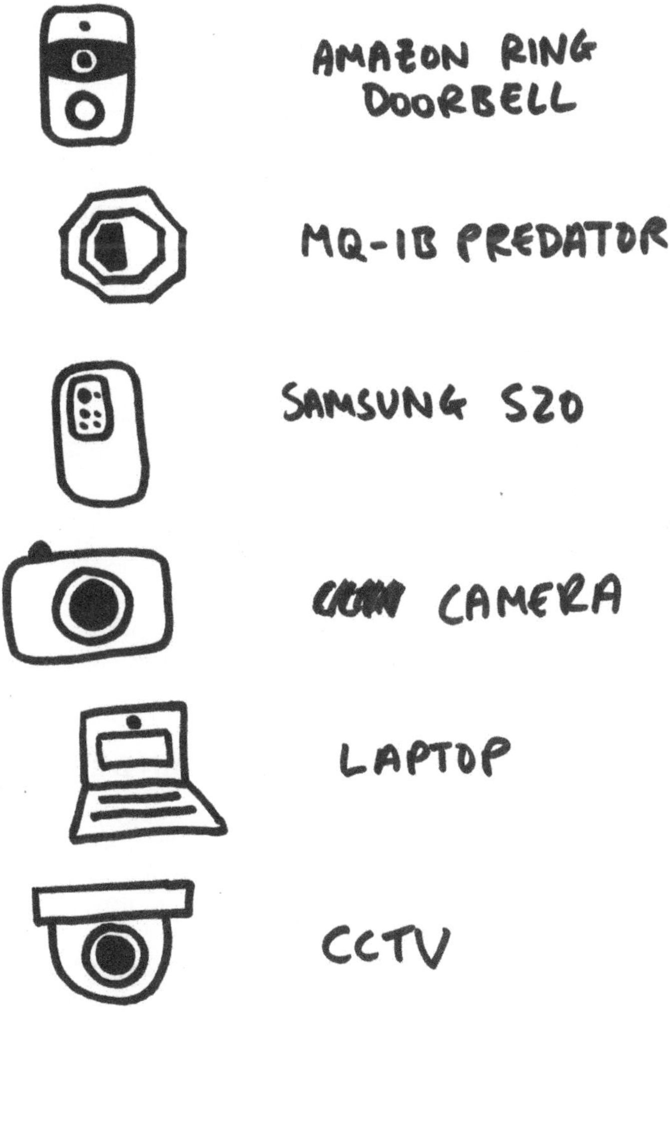

[13] Vandana Shiva, *Earth Democracy: Justice, Sustainability, and Peace* (Cambridge, MA: South End Press, 2005); Bernard Stiegler, *Automatic Society: The Future of Work*, trans. Daniel Ross (Cambridge: Polity Press, 2016).

III. Conclusion: Re-imagining Perception, Reclaiming Agency

James Bridle's artwork for CPDP 2025 is more than a visual provocation; it is a call to action. It asks us to see the world anew – to recognise the multiplicity of gazes that surround us and to confront the opacity of the systems that shape our lives. In doing so, it challenges us to rethink the boundaries of perception, knowledge, and democracy.

The chapters that follow in this volume take up this challenge, exploring the legal, ethical, and technical dimensions of computer, privacy, data protection, and AI governance. They ask how we might design systems that are not only transparent but also responsive to the needs and perceptions of all beings, human and non-human alike. In a world where the more-than-human is watching, the task of law and policy is to ensure that this watching is just, accountable, and life-affirming.

Image 1.4 Collection of animal eyes (detail in image 1)

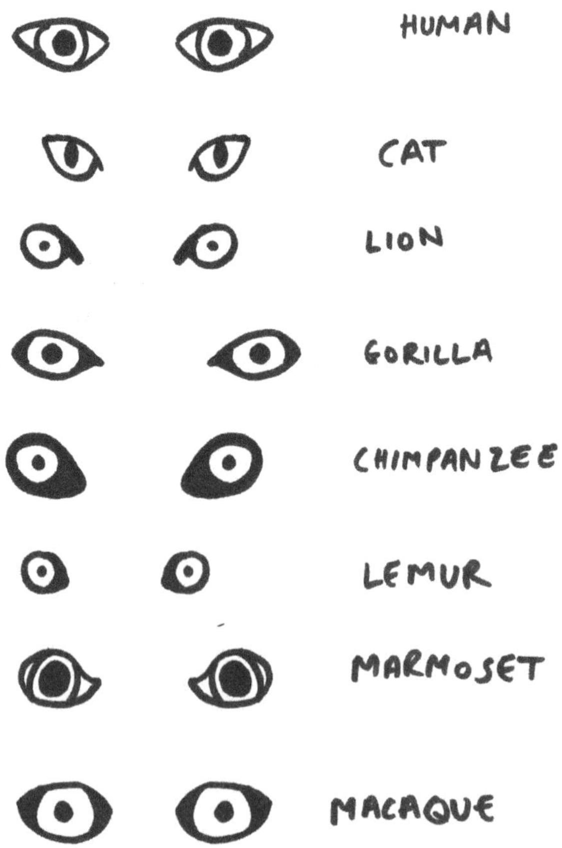

Image 1.5 Collection of eyes (detail in image 1)

This work has come to life through an unfolding series of conversations and interviews between the artist James Bridle, and Thierry Vandenbussche and Birte Vingerhoets of the CPDP organising team, through which the project gradually took form.

Bibliography

Bauman, Zygmunt, and David Lyon. *Liquid Surveillance: A Conversation*. Cambridge: Polity Press, 2013.

Bridle, James. *Cloud Index*. Digital commission for the Serpentine Galleries, 2016. https://jamesbridle.com/works/cloud-index.

Bridle, James. *Seamless Transitions*. Digital video, 5:28 min. Commissioned by The Photographers' Gallery, London, 2015. https://nomegallery.com/artwork/seamless-transitions-2015/.
Crawford, Kate. *Atlas of AI: Power, Politics, and the Planetary Costs of Artificial Intelligence*. New Haven, CT: Yale University Press, 2021.
Foucault, Michel. *Discipline and Punish: The Birth of the Prison*. Translated by Alan Sheridan. New York: Vintage Books, 1977. Originally published 1975.
Haraway, Donna. *Staying with the Trouble: Making Kin in the Chthulucene*. Durham, NC: Duke University Press, 2016.
Latour, Bruno. *Science in Action: How to Follow Scientists and Engineers through Society*. Cambridge, MA: Harvard University Press, 1987.
Merleau-Ponty, Maurice. *Phenomenology of Perception*. Translated by Colin Smith Colin Smith. London: Routledge & Kegan Paul, 1962. Originally published 1945.
Morton, Timothy. *Hyperobjects: Philosophy and Ecology after the End of the World*. Minneapolis: University of Minnesota Press, 2013.
Noë, Alva. *Action in Perception*. Cambridge, MA: MIT Press, 2004.
Pasquale, Frank. *The Black Box Society: The Secret Algorithms That Control Money and Information*. Cambridge, MA: Harvard University Press, 2015.
Shiva, Vandana. *Earth Democracy: Justice, Sustainability, and Peace*. Cambridge, MA: South End Press, 2005.
Star, Susan Leigh. 'The Ethnography of Infrastructure'. *American Behavioral Scientist* 43, no. 3 (1999): 377–91.
Stiegler, Bernard. *Automatic Society: The Future of Work*. Translated by Daniel Ross. Cambridge: Polity Press, 2016.
Tsing, Anna Lowenhaupt. *The Mushroom at the End of the World: On the Possibility of Life in Capitalist Ruins*. Princeton, NJ: Princeton University Press, 2015.
Zuboff, Shoshana. *The Age of Surveillance Capitalism: The Fight for a Human Future at the New Frontier of Power*. New York: PublicAffairs, 2019.

2

A Defining Moment for the EU: Geo-economics, Data Protection, and AI

MIREILLE HILDEBRANDT

Abstract

Based on her keynote at the Opening Night of CPDP 2025, Mireille Hildebrandt (Professor Emerita at the Faculty of Law and Criminology of Vrije Universiteit Brussels and at the Science Faculty of Radboud University in the Netherlands) examines how law structures markets, links to international order, and intersects with the geo-economics of artificial intelligence (AI). The chapter analyses how AI infrastructures – dependent on vast amounts of electricity, water, and rare earth minerals – reshape international law, digital sovereignty, and environmental sustainability, as Big Tech consolidation transforms the political economy of law. Hildebrandt critiques the ideology of artificial general intelligence (AGI) and the techno-utopian visions surrounding it, contrasting them with the European Union's legislative framework that treats AI as a 'normal technology'. She argues that this approach offers a realistic yet fragile path that must be defended and further developed to withstand geopolitical and economic pressures.

Keywords

AI; Law & Economics; Geopolitics; Necessity; Geo-economics; Rule of Law; Political Economy of Law; Rare Earth Minerals; Digital Sovereignty; Ecological Sustainability

I. Law and Economics

For a long time, 'we' have lived under the aegis of the so-called 'Washington consensus',[1] that is the imaginary of the neoliberal world order, based on supposedly sound scientific evidence, grounded in rational choice theory and later behavioural economics. Both share the ideological backdrop of rational choice theory as to how human beings should best make decisions, namely based on a rational – deeply utilitarian – cost benefit analysis.[2] We have seen the US pushing the post-Soviet Union into a raw capitalist system, based on the claimed long-term advantages of shock therapy, creative destruction, and the trickle-down effect.[3] Many have critiqued this neoliberal world order, demonstrating the lack of evidence and the uneven distributive effects.[4] Who would have thought that at the end of the day it is authoritarianism that overrules the neoliberal order, destroying – almost in passing – the institutions meant to correct and reign-in brute capitalism.

Do lawyers, raised on a diet of a supposedly neutral legal positivism, understand the myriad ways that law and the Rule of Law have been instrumentalised by the neoliberal saga?[5] Do we, lawyers, realise, how legal method has been marinated in the dry juices of rational choice theory with its key vocabulary of 'efficiency', 'costs benefit analysis', 'transaction costs', 'externalisation of costs', and the 'Pareto optimal' utopia that allegedly explains legal institutions and/or stipulates how they should be built? And, for that matter, do we, lawyers, realise, how legal method has been diminished as unscientific in the context of another strand of law and economics, called behavioural economics, meant to convince us of an

[1] Douglas A Irwin and Ward Oliver, 'What Is the "Washington Consensus?"', *PIIE Realtime Economics Blog*, 8 September 2021, www.piie.com/blogs/realtime-economics/2021/what-washington-consensus. Note that 'we' concerns both 'the Global North' and 'the Global South', though with different impact.

[2] Philip Mirowski and Dieter Plehwe (eds), *The Road from Mont Pelerin: The Making of the Neoliberal Thought Collective*, 1st edn (Cambridge, MA: Harvard University Press, 2009); Jason Blakely, 'How Economics Becomes Ideology: The Uses and Abuses of Rational Choice Theory'. In *Agency and Causal Explanation in Economics*, ed. Peter Róna and László Zsolnai (Cham: Springer International Publishing, 2020), https://doi.org/10.1007/978-3-030-26114-6_3; Daniel Kahneman, 'Maps of Bounded Rationality: Psychology for Behavioral Economics'. *The American Economic Review* 93, no. 5 (2003): 1449–75. Cp Daniel Engber, 'Daniel Kahneman Wanted You to Realize How Wrong You Are'. *Science, The Atlantic*, 28 March 2024, www.theatlantic.com/science/archive/2024/03/daniel-kahneman-death-psychology/677903/.

[3] On shock therapy and creative destruction (usually attributed to Schumpeter): Greg Rosalsky, 'How "Shock Therapy" Created Russian Oligarchs and Paved the Path for Putin'. *NPR Planet Money Newsletter*, 22 March 2022, www.npr.org/sections/money/2022/03/22/1087654279/how-shock-therapy-created-russian-oligarchs-and-paved-the-path-for-putin. More in-depth: 'Hugo Reinert and Erik S. Reinert, 'Creative Destruction in Economics: Nietzsche, Sombart, Schumpeter'. In *Friedrich Nietzsche (1844–1900)*, ed. Jürgen G. Backhaus and Wolfgang Drechsler (Boston, MA: Springer, 2006), https://doi.org/10.1007/978-0-387-32980-2_4. On the so-called trickle-down effect: Mark Mattern, *The Trickle-Up Economy: How We Take from the Poor and Middle Class and Give to the Rich* (Boulder, CO: Lynne Rienner Publishers, 2021).

[4] Arthur M Diamond, 'Schumpeter's Creative Destruction: A Review of the Evidence'. *Journal of Private Enterprise* 2, no. 1 (2006): 7–26, https://journal.apee.org/Fall2006_7; Eli Cook, 'Efficiently Unequal: The Global Rise of Kaldor-Hicks Neoliberalism'. *Global Intellectual History* 9, nos. 1–2 (2024): 247–69, https://doi.org/10.1080/23801883.2022.2062423.

[5] Katharina Pistor, *The Code of Capital: How the Law Creates Wealth and Inequality* (Princeton, NJ: Princeton University Press, 2019).

anthropological pessimism that is based on a questionable narrative about the cognitive biases inherent in the human condition?[6]

Does the emerging domain of law and political economy (LPE) offer a viable alternative to better understand the complexities and the normative challenges of local, national, and supranational jurisdictions?[7] Can LPE explain and give direction to an analysis of international law,[8] avoiding its colonisation by an oftentimes cynical Real-Politik?[9]

In this contribution, based on my Keynote at the Opening Night of the Computers, Privacy and Data Protection (CPDP) 2025,[10] I want to briefly discuss how law institutes economic markets,[11] how national law depends on international law[12] and where geo-economics matters. I will then investigate how AI infrastructure's need for massive amounts of electricity, water, and rare earth minerals is transforming the playing field of international law, noting that the consolidation of Big Tech corporations has already impacted the political economy of law.[13] Finally, I will discuss the ideology of AGI,[14] and propose that the European approach to legislating, governing, and judging AI as 'a normal technology' is a viable though contested alternative that must be consolidated, defended and further developed to survive geopolitical power grabs by the US, Russia, and China.[15]

II. The Constitution of Economic Markets

Market economies depend on the legal effect attributed to contract and property. Market economies do not grow like grass. They are not forces of nature but

[6] Gerd Gigerenzer, 'The Bias Bias in Behavioral Economics'. *Review of Behavioral Economics* 5, nos. 3–4 (2018): 303–36, https://doi.org/10.1561/105.00000092.

[7] Jedediah Britton-Purdy et al, 'Building a Law-and-Political-Economy Framework: Beyond the Twentieth-Century Synthesis'. *Yale Law Journal* 129, no. 6 (2020): 1784–835, www.yalelawjournal.org/feature/building-a-law-and-political-economy-framework.

[8] Anne van Aaken and Joel P Trachtman, 'Political Economy of International Law: Towards a Holistic Model of State Behaviour'. In *The Political Economy of International Law*, ed. Tomer Broude et al. (Cheltenham: Edward Elgar, 2016), www.elgaronline.com/edcollchap/edcoll/9781785364396/9781785364396.00009.xml.

[9] On the pitfalls of importing so-called interdisciplinary perspectives into law, including their methodological commitments, see Mireille Hildebrandt, 'Digging Deeper: Cross-Disciplinary Research Approaches'. *Brussels Privacy Hub*, 6 October 2025, https://brusselsprivacyhub.com/digging-deeper-cross-disciplinary-research-approaches/.

[10] Available at www.youtube.com/watch?v=PfoFBXD7p-s (starting at 21 minutes).

[11] Simon Deakin et al, 'Legal Institutionalism: Capitalism and the Constitutive Role of Law'. *Journal of Comparative Economics* 45, no. 1 (2017): 188–200, https://doi.org/10.1016/j.jce.2016.04.005.

[12] Mireille Hildebrandt, 'International and Supranational Law'. In *Law for Computer Scientists and Other Folk* (Oxford: Oxford University Press, 2020), https://doi.org/10.1093/oso/9780198860877.003.0004.

[13] Yochai Benkler, 'Political Economy of Technology'. *Law and Political Economy Blog*, 2018, https://lpeblog.org/category/political-economy-of-technology/.

[14] Timnit Gebru and Émile P Torres, 'The TESCREAL Bundle: Eugenics and the Promise of Utopia through Artificial General Intelligence'. *First Monday*, 14 April 2024, https://doi.org/10.5210/fm.v29i4.13636.

[15] Arvind Narayanan and Sayash Kapoor, 'AI as Normal Technology'. *Knight First Amendment Institute*, 15 April 2025, http://knightcolumbia.org/content/ai-as-normal-technology.

affordances of modern positive law. Historically, market economies are a recent phenomenon, built on the performative effect of positive law that institutes specific types of markets, where people who do not know each other can exchange goods and services, trusting that contracts can be enforced and property protected. The fact that markets are instituted by law implies that they can be shaped in myriad ways. In the era of global capitalism and digital hyperconnectivity, economic markets have become highly complex moving targets, continuously adapted by national, supranational and international law, including both private and public law, often liable to competing normativities[16] both legal and other. The point is that capitalism or socialism are essentially contested labels for a diversity of economic practices that ultimately depend on the institutional facts created by the performative speech acts of legislatures, public administration and courts, while admitting that the meaning of such institutional facts will ultimately depend on the consequences they have. And those consequences in turn also depend on how these institutional facts, for instance contract or property, are read and enacted by those addressed by the relevant legal norms.

III. Geo-economics, National, and International Law

Textbooks on international law may buy into the idea that international law depends on the free will of independent sovereign states, which are thus accorded primacy. Instead, as I argued elsewhere,[17] without an international law that demands respect for external sovereignty there would be no internal sovereignty.[18] In that sense international law seems to precede national law and the principle of non-intervention that affords sovereign states the freedom to govern themselves as they wish. The relationship between national and international law should, however, not be seen as causal (one preceding and causing the other) but as mutually constitutive. As international law assumes national law, so does national law assume international law. They are the result of Grotius'[19] and Bodin's[20] work on

[16] Mireille Hildebrandt, 'Text-Driven Jurisdiction in Cyberspace'. In *Transformations in Criminal Jurisdiction: Extraterritoriality and Enforcement*, ed. Micheál Ó Floinn et al (London: Bloomsbury, 2023), www.bloomsbury.com/uk/transformations-in-criminal-jurisdiction-9781509954223/; Chris Reed and Andrew Murray, *Rethinking the Jurisprudence of Cyberspace* (Cheltenham: Edward Elgar, 2018); Mireille Hildebrandt, 'Review of: Chris Reed and Andrew Murray, *Rethinking the Jurisprudence of Cyberspace*, Cheltenham: Edward Elgar, 2018'. *Modern Law Review* 83, no. 3 (2020): 690–94, https://doi.org/10.1111/1468-2230.12491.

[17] Hildebrandt, 'International and Supranational Law'. See also Jeremy Waldron, 'The Rule of International Law'. *Harvard Journal of Law & Public Policy* 30 (2006): 15–30.

[18] Mireille Hildebrandt, 'Extraterritorial Jurisdiction to Enforce in Cyberspace? Bodin, Schmitt, Grotius in Cyberspace'. *University of Toronto Law Journal* 63, no. 2 (2013): 196–224, https://doi.org/10.3138/utlj.1119.

[19] 'Hugo Grotius on the Law of War and Peace: Student Edition', Cambridge Core, Cambridge University Press, August 2012, https://doi.org/10.1017/CBO9781139031233. See also Hildebrandt, 'Extraterritorial Jurisdiction to Enforce in Cyberspace?'.

[20] Jean Bodin, *Bodin: On Sovereignty*, ed. Julian H. Franklin (Cambridge: Cambridge University Press, 1992). See also Hildebrandt, 'Extraterritorial Jurisdiction to Enforce in Cyberspace'.

international law and sovereignty, while the reception of the Peace of Westphalia[21] consolidated the idea of internal and external sovereignty as two sides of the same coin; one cannot have the one without the other.

So, what is the role of geo-economics in the realm of international law and how does it connect with AI and EU Data Protection law? Geo-economics is usually defined as the use of economics strategies to gain geopolitical power,[22] or even 'war with other means',[23] for instance by way of 'trade policy, investment policy, economic and financial sanctions, financial and monetary policy, energy and commodities, aid and cyber. While some function as they have in the past (aid), others are new (cyber) or operate in a different environment (energy)'.[24] It is tempting to invoke the tariff wars currently invoked by the president of the US to demonstrate the role played by geo-economics, but more interesting to acknowledge that it has played a major role in international relations and was actually key to Grotius' seminal *Mare Liberum* of 1609.[25]

In the context of the rise of AI and the challenges it poses to national and international law, including data protection law, it is crucial to understand the role played by rare earth minerals in both geopolitics and geo-economics. Rare earth minerals are minerals that are crucial for batteries and magnets and thus critical for myriad electronic devices (including electrical vehicles and data servers), the defence industry, and notably renewable energy.[26] Where fossil fuels have defined geopolitical relations for over half a century, rare earth minerals are taking over as the scarce resources that determine international relations, geo-economic power play, and digital sovereignty, while creating a volatile environment where both Big Tech corporations and states battle to gain and consolidate access to what they consider the *sine qua non* for growth and independence.[27] The circumstances under which these minerals are mined are devastating, including child labour and other types of exploitation, as well are causing environmental and

[21] 'Westphalia, Peace of (1648)'. *Oxford Public International Law*, https://opil.ouplaw.com/display/10.1093/law:epil/9780199231690/law-9780199231690-e739.

[22] 'Geo-economics, or the application of power politics by economic means, is a contest waged via global trade and investment rather than on a traditional battlefield.' Finnish Institute of International Affairs (FIIA), 'Strategic Intelligence'. *World Economic Forum Strategic Intelligence Platform*, https://intelligence.weforum.org. Or it is defined as 'the use of economic tools to advance geopolitical objectives', Marianne Scheider-Petsinger, 'Geoeconomics Explained'. *Chatham House*, updated 2020, www.chathamhouse.org/2016/12/geoeconomics-explained.

[23] Robert D Blackwill and Jennifer M Harris, *War by Other Means: Geoeconomics and Statecraft* (Cambridge, MA: Harvard University Press, 2016), https://doi.org/10.2307/j.ctt1c84cr7.

[24] Scheider-Petsinger, 'Geoeconomics Explained'.

[25] 'Hugo Grotius' Theory of Trans-Oceanic Trade Regulation: Revisiting *Mare Liberum* (1609)'. *Institute for International Law and Justice*, www.iilj.org/publications/hugo-grotius-theory-of-trans-oceanic-trade-regulation-revisiting-mare-liberum-1609/.

[26] '*The Guardian*, 'What Are Rare Earths and Critical Minerals – Explained in 30 Seconds'. *World News*, 17 October 2025, www.theguardian.com/world/2025/oct/17/rare-earths-critical-minerals-explained.

[27] John Hua Fan et al, 'Geopolitics and Rare Earth Metals'. *European Journal of Political Economy* 78 (June 2023): 102356, https://doi.org/10.1016/j.ejpoleco.2022.102356; *Nature*, 'The Global Fight for Critical Minerals Is Costly and Damaging'. *Nature* 619, no. 7970 (2023): 436, https://doi.org/10.1038/d41586-023-02330-0.

health damage.[28] In the meantime, the role of China as rare earth mineral superpower and the rush to challenge its position may further destabilise what has been called the international 'rule-based order'.[29] In that context, the EU has to navigate a complex web of trade deals, economic sanctions, and retributive counterplay, where both its environmental and its AI legislation are becoming part of the negotiations. It would be easy to assert that the EU should not water down its legislative approach in the face of geo-economic threats by the US, but such assertions may be easier said than done, considering the odds.[30]

IV. The Ideology of AGI

Generative AI has been widely proclaimed as the forerunner of AGI. Though the functionality of large language models (LLMs) in terms of generating, rather than analysing or predicting language behaviour is spectacular, in point of fact generative AI remains locked in the prediction of next-word tokens, based on stochastical inferences. As two of the three founding fathers of the underlying technology (deep learning) and others well versed in computer science have explained, deep learning will not achieve anything like AGI, whatever the PR of the believers.[31]

Most scholars agree that AGI is too vague a term to even mean anything, let alone offering scientific criteria to allow for falsification. The latter would require a theoretical framework from which hypotheses can be deduced that enable falsification by means of empirical testing (which is not the same as deployment of

[28] Centre for Economic Policy Research (CEPR), 'Policy Insight 147: Escaping the Critical Minerals Curse', 15 October 2025, https://cepr.org/publications/policy-insight-147-escaping-critical-minerals-curse.

[29] Marc Trachtenberg, 'The Rules-Based International Order: A Historical Analysis'. *International Security* 50, no. 2 (2025): 7–54, https://doi.org/10.1162/isec_a_01101. Note that some suggest that the term is highly problematic. 'Supplanted casually by its simulacra such as the "rules-based order" or "multipolar world", the international rule of law lies in shambles', see 'Symposium Justitia and Leviathans: The Struggle for the International Rule of Law'. *Open Universiteit*, www.ou.nl/en/-/symposium-justitia-and-leviathans-the-struggle-for-the-international-rule-of-law.

[30] David Meyer, 'Don't Water down Landmark AI Rules to Appease Trump, Key EU Lawmakers Warn European Commission'. *Fortune*, https://fortune.com/2025/03/26/eu-ai-act-code-of-practice-disinformation-election-benifei-trump-appease-tech-lobbying/.

[31] Jason Howell, 'Meta AI Chief Yann LeCun: Human Intelligence Is Not General Intelligence' *Jason Howell's Newsletter* (Substack), 9 April 2025, https://jasonhowell.substack.com/p/meta-ai-chief-yann-lacun-human-intelligence; Anirudh Goyal and Yoshua Bengio, 'Inductive Biases for Deep Learning of Higher-Level Cognition'. *Proceedings of the Royal Society A* 478, no. 2266 (2022): 20210068, https://doi.org/10.1098/rspa.2021.0068; Brian Cantwell Smith, *The Promise of Artificial Intelligence: Reckoning and Judgment* (Cambridge, MA: MIT Press, 2019); Blaise Agüera y Arcas, *What Is Intelligence? Lessons from AI about Evolution, Computing, and Minds*, ed. Benjamin H Bratton (Cambridge, MA: MIT Press, 2025), https://mitpress.mit.edu/9780262049955/what-is-intelligence/; Madhumita Murgia et al, 'AI Pioneers Claim Human-Level General Intelligence Is Already Here'. *Financial Times*, 6 November 2025, www.ft.com/content/5f2f411c-3600-483b-bee8-4f06473ecdc0; *My AI*, 'The GenAI Divide – State of AI in Business 2025', https://my.ai.se/resources/6487.

test data to validate a performance metric).[32] OpenAI has defined AGI as 'highly autonomous systems that outperform humans at most economically valuable work' (note the emphasis on economic value, on human intelligence as the yardstick and on surpassing that yardstick),[33] while Stuart Russell and Peter Norvig defined it as 'a universal algorithm for learning and acting in any environment' (note the suggestion of a 'master algorithm').[34] The key points seem to be that such systems or algorithms are autonomous (functioning without human input) and/or capable of transforming knowledge gained in one domain to another domain (moving beyond one-trick ponies). As to the first point, it is sad to see the hard work being outsourced to Africa;[35] as to the second, it is precisely this point that makes it impossible to test the reliability of an AGI algorithm, because it is not specified in ways that allow for testing.[36]

Amongst the active supporters and funders of AGI, Gebru and Torres have detected a powerful set of billionaires with shockingly extremist views. I invite the reader to study their 2023 paper in *First Monday*, on the TESCREAL background of AGI.[37] The acronym TESCREAL stands for transhumanism, extropianism, singularitarianism, cosmism, rationalism, effective altruism, and longterminism. These 'isms' seek to move enhancement beyond human limitations, towards human-machine merging, sentient AI, mind-uploading, immortality, transformation of the universe, deploying AI to make the world better, while making a better world by deploying AI and, finally, maximising value based on a totalitarian utilitarianism that enables the colonisation of outer space. The authors detect many links to eugenetics and white supremist ideologies and highlight the fact that even if the reader rejects the implied fantastical overreach of these billionaires, the amount of money that is invested by these economic behemoths in the realisation of this fantasy is nevertheless driving energy consumption, water shortages, and a reconfiguration of geo-economic and geopolitical realities. Thomas Merton's often quoted saying 'if men define a situation as real, it is real in its consequences'[38] now also goes for machines: 'If machines define a situation as real, they are real in their consequences',[39] whether or not they are hallucinating.

We urgently need a legal framework capable of soberly addressing the many pitfalls, while ignoring the hype. This includes a reflection on the assumption that

[32] Mireille Hildebrandt, 'LLMs, Legal Contestability and Scientific Falsifiability'. In *Proceedings of the LSTS Research Day 2025* (Open Science Framework, 23 September 2025), https://osf.io/8k2wp_v1.

[33] OpenAI, 'Charter', https://openai.com/charter/.

[34] Stuart Russell and Peter Norvig, *Artificial Intelligence: A Modern Approach*, 4th edn (Harlow, UK: Pearson, 2022).

[35] Stephanie Wangari and Gayathri Vaidyanathan, 'How Big Tech Hides Its Outsourced African Workforce'. *Rest of World*, 21 April 2025, https://restofworld.org/2025/big-tech-ai-labor-supply-chain-african-workers/.

[36] Narayanan and Kapoor, 'AI as Normal Technology'; Gebru and Torres, 'The TESCREAL Bundle'.

[37] Gebru and Torres, ibid.

[38] Robert K Merton, 'The Self-Fulfilling Prophecy'. *Antioch Review* 8, no. 2 (1948): 193–210.

[39] Mireille Hildebrandt, 'Who Needs Stories If You Can Get the Data? ISPs in the Era of Big Number Crunching'. *Philosophy and Technology* 24 (2011): 371–90.

bigger and more is necessarily better, shifting the focus from big corporations to small and medium-sized enterprises (SMEs), while assessing the need for massive investment in data centres as a matter of public infrastructure.[40]

V. The EU Approach to AI as a Normal Technology

After publishing *AI Snake Oil*,[41] famed Princeton computer scientists Narayanan and Kapoor have embarked on a new journey, preparing a book on *AI as a Normal Technology*. The first blog posting is out,[42] explaining the problem with AGI and requiring the development of AI technologies (models, systems, applications, products and services) that are sufficiently and accurately specified, such that they can be tested in terms of reliability, safety and – I would say – their fundamental rights impact.

Narayanan and Kapoor reject AGI research because it is based on an incoherent conceptualisation that refutes testing. They believe that AI is both a normal technology and a transformative technology, though not a form of superintelligence. On top of that, they highlight the relationship between society and technology, rejecting the technological determinism that – similar to economic determinism – informs the hype around AGI, presenting AGI as an inevitable future. Instead, Narayanan and Kapoor assert the need for human control. In line with that, they distinguish between (1) methods (models), (2) applications (products and services), and (3) adoption (real world impact). They note that different time scales are at play; a model may be developed and 'run' in a short time interval, but figuring out what products they could help build is not always clear and may take a long time, while real world adoption is both unpredictable and requires long term investments. Narayanan and Kapoor foreground the obvious but often ignored need to integrate AI methodology, which is computational, with human domain knowledge, which is based on real world expertise and experience. Again, these distinctions point to different time scales. By considering AI to be a normal technology that may be transformative but will nevertheless require long term human investment and participation, they contribute to a more realistic understanding of what it will take to integrate technologies like generative AI in domains such as education, scientific research, healthcare, insurance or agriculture in a responsible, critical manner that avoids risks to health, safety and fundamental rights (as the AI Act would have it).

[40] See Pasquale's brilliant analysis of what he calls the 'knowledge problem', which is directly related to the claims of Big Tech corporations that the network effects of keeping information in one hand are necessary to advance knowledge that enables economic planning in market economies (noting how close this comes to Soviet planning economics): Frank Pasquale, 'Tech Platforms and the Knowledge Problem'. *American Affairs Journal* 11, no. 2 (2018): 3–16, https://americanaffairsjournal.org/2018/05/tech-platforms-and-the-knowledge-problem/.

[41] Arvind Narayanan and Sayash Kapoor, *AI Snake Oil: What Artificial Intelligence Can Do, What It Can't, and How to Tell the Difference* (Princeton, NJ: Princeton University Press, 2024).

[42] Narayanan and Kapoor, 'AI as Normal Technology'.

AI models and systems affect vulnerabilities of natural persons, societal infrastructures, and global interdependencies. The AI Act seems focused on societal infrastructure, foreseeing how this may be affected in terms of the safety, health, and fundamental rights that such infrastructure should safeguard. It is not focused on global dependencies and the geo-economic and geopolitical implications thereof. Much has been written about the Brussels effect of the General Data Protection Regulation (GDPR).[43] Such effect can, however, not be taken for granted. Bradford, who coined and developed the concept of the Brussels effect, grounded it on a series of interrelated conditions that must be fulfilled: (1) the wish of transnational corporations to compete on the internal market of the EU; (2) the fact that the EU had the most stringent data protection law; (3) the assumption that once a corporation complies with the most stringent rules, it will comply with those of other jurisdictions (and with the relevant markets they wish to compete in); (4) the inelasticity of regulated targets (affording EU compliant products and services outside the EU); and (5) the non-divisibility of the global market (and the implied need to operate in the EU market). The rise of national protectionism, China's stringent AI regulations and the fact that AI may be regulated in a very different way elsewhere may thus diminish the global effects of the AI Act. On top of that, the EU's dependence on rare earth minerals to be sourced from other continents, may diminish the digital sovereignty that underpins the Act. Though I do not necessarily agree with the Draghi report,[44] I do agree that we need some kind of Marshall plan for 'investment to enable decarbonisation and competitiveness' and a measure of 'defence procurement and cross-border grids' to 'increase security and reduce dependence'. In that sense the 'New European Industry Strategy' foregrounds three public goods that I believe to be key to constitutional democracies: (1) a well-functioning market, if disentangled from the neoliberal saga, (2) military and economic independence from authoritarian regimes, and (3) a legislative framework that enables reliable, robust, and resilient AI systems in close interaction with grounded supervision and independent courts.

VI. Finals

Under pressure of both 'the industry' and the US, the European Commission has been considering a simplification of its digital legislation.[45] To boost EU

[43] Anu Bradford, *The Brussels Effect: How the European Union Rules the World* (Oxford: Oxford University Press, 2020).

[44] Mario Draghi, *The Future of European Competitiveness* (Brussels: European Commission, 2024), https://commission.europa.eu/topics/strengthening-european-competitiveness/eu-competitiveness-looking-ahead_en.

[45] European Commission, *Call for Evidence: Simplification – Digital Package and Omnibus*, 2025, https://ec.europa.eu/info/law/better-regulation/have-your-say/initiatives/14855-Simplification-digital-package-and-omnibus_en.

competitiveness and digital sovereignty, the Commission has invited 'evidence' regarding its Apply AI strategy, that aims to foster 'the integration of AI technologies in the EU's leading strategic industrial sectors', to 'unlock the potential of innovation and enabling EU companies to be global AI front runners' and to foster 'the integration of AI solutions in the public sector to substantially improve the quality of services provided to the public'.[46]

Over the past years, I have advanced three questions that must be asked before introducing potentially transformative technologies (including the massive investment in AI infrastructure): (1) what (and whose) problems are solved? (2) what (and whose) problems are not solved? (3) what new problems are created (for whom)? These questions should be explored before succumbing to a cost-benefit analysis, as costs and benefits depend on the answers to these questions. How could one meaningfully decide on benefits is one doesn't know what problem is addressed, what problem is not addressed and what new problems will arise?

AI systems and AI models often solve problems we don't have (technology push, similar though not equivalent to the creation of consumer needs), they may not really solve the problems we do have and they have already created many problems we did not have. For safe, sustainable, and fair innovation these questions are key. The current frenzy to build AI infrastructure in the form of data centres raises the same questions, where the 'new' problems they create concern unfathomable environmental costs (water and energy).[47]

In fundamental rights law, my approach touches upon the notion of necessity. To the extent that the development, provision, and/or deployment of AI systems or models threatens to infringe a fundamental right, the question of necessity is crucial: could the aim of introducing the infringing technology be achieved in other ways whose risk of infringement would be less? In terms of the GDPR, the deployment of AI systems or models that process personal data requires a legal ground that always involves necessity; even consent requires a purpose for which the processing must be necessary.

Keen awareness of geo-economic incentives with incisive impact on geopolitical navigation will help to answer these questions. For instance, because the training of generative AI models requires increased mining of rare earth minerals, which inevitably transforms geopolitical interdependencies due to changes in the geo-economic playing field. In this brief chapter, I hope to have

[46] European Commission, *Call for Evidence: Apply AI Strategy – Strengthening the AI Continent*, 2025, https://ec.europa.eu/info/law/better-regulation/have-your-say/initiatives/14625-Apply-AI-Strategy-strengthening-the-AI-continent_en.

[47] Noting that we are now betting on AI infrastructure as key to digital sovereignty and future deployment of generative AI, which both come with many caveats: Waldemar Szlezak, 'Investors Need to Look beyond the "Bragawatts" in AI Infrastructure Boom'. *Financial Times*, 3 November 2025, www.ft.com/content/bf687d99-f373-4a41-8651-fca9dba83aa0.

demonstrated that such geo-economic turbulence will in the end affect the effectiveness of the EU legislative framework. Lawyers must study and rethink the relationship between law and economics, while avoiding the colonisation of legal method by the methodologies of other sciences, taking note of the ideological underpinnings of both rational choice theory and behavioural economics.

Bibliography

Aaken, Anne van, and Joel P Trachtman. 'Political Economy of International Law: Towards a Holistic Model of State Behaviour'. In *The Political Economy of International Law*, edited by Tomer Broude et al. Cheltenham: Edward Elgar, 2016. www.elgaronline.com/edcollchap/edcoll/9781785364396/9781785364396.00009.xml.

Agüera y Arcas, Blaise. *What Is Intelligence? Lessons from AI about Evolution, Computing, and Minds*. Edited by Benjamin H Bratton. Cambridge, MA: MIT Press, 2025. https://mitpress.mit.edu/9780262049955/what-is-intelligence/.

Blackwill, Robert D, and Jennifer M Harris. *War by Other Means: Geoeconomics and Statecraft*. Cambridge, MA: Harvard University Press, 2016. https://doi.org/10.2307/j.ctt1c84cr7.

Blakely, Jason. 'How Economics Becomes Ideology: The Uses and Abuses of Rational Choice Theory'. In *Agency and Causal Explanation in Economics*, edited by Peter Róna and László Zsolnai. Cham: Springer International Publishing, 2020. https://doi.org/10.1007/978-3-030-26114-6_3.

Bodin, Jean. *Bodin: On Sovereignty*. Edited by Julian H Franklin. Cambridge: Cambridge University Press, 1992.

Bradford, Anu. *The Brussels Effect: How the European Union Rules the World*. Oxford: Oxford University Press, 2020.

Britton-Purdy, Jedediah, David Singh Grewal, Amy Kapczynski, and K Sabeel Rahman. 'Building a Law-and-Political-Economy Framework: Beyond the Twentieth-Century Synthesis'. *Yale Law Journal* 129, no. 6 (2020): 1784–835. www.yalelawjournal.org/feature/building-a-law-and-political-economy-framework.

Cantwell Smith, Brian. *The Promise of Artificial Intelligence: Reckoning and Judgment*. Cambridge, MA: MIT Press, 2019.

Centre for Economic Policy Research (CEPR). 'Policy Insight 147: Escaping the Critical Minerals Curse'. 15 October 2025. https://cepr.org/publications/policy-insight-147-escaping-critical-minerals-curse.

Cook, Eli. 'Efficiently Unequal: The Global Rise of Kaldor-Hicks Neoliberalism'. *Global Intellectual History* 9, nos. 1–2 (2024): 247–69. https://doi.org/10.1080/23801883.2022.2062423.

Deakin, Simon, David Gindis, Geoffrey M Hodgson, Kainan Huang, and Katharina Pistor. 'Legal Institutionalism: Capitalism and the Constitutive Role of Law'. *Journal of Comparative Economics* 45, no. 1 (2017): 188–200. https://doi.org/10.1016/j.jce.2016.04.005.

Diamond, Arthur M. 'Schumpeter's Creative Destruction: A Review of the Evidence'. *Journal of Private Enterprise* 2, no. 1 (2006): 7–26. https://journal.apee.org/Fall2006_7.

Draghi, Mario. *The Future of European Competitiveness*. Brussels: European Commission, 2024. https://commission.europa.eu/topics/strengthening-european-competitiveness/eu-competitiveness-looking-ahead_en.

Engber, Daniel. 'Daniel Kahneman Wanted You to Realize How Wrong You Are'. *The Atlantic*, 28 March 2024. www.theatlantic.com/science/archive/2024/03/daniel-kahneman-death-psychology/677903/.

European Commission. *Call for Evidence: Apply AI Strategy – Strengthening the AI Continent*. 2025. https://ec.europa.eu/info/law/better-regulation/have-your-say/initiatives/14625-Apply-AI-Strategy-strengthening-the-AI-continent_en.

European Commission. *Call for Evidence: Simplification – Digital Package and Omnibus*. 2025. https://ec.europa.eu/info/law/better-regulation/have-your-say/initiatives/14855-Simplification-digital-package-and-omnibus_en.

Fan, John Hua, et al. 'Geopolitics and Rare Earth Metals'. *European Journal of Political Economy* 78 (June 2023): 102356. https://doi.org/10.1016/j.ejpoleco.2022.102356.

Finnish Institute of International Affairs (FIIA). 'Strategic Intelligence'. *World Economic Forum Strategic Intelligence Platform*. https://intelligence.weforum.org.

Gebru, Timnit, and Émile P. Torres. 'The TESCREAL Bundle: Eugenics and the Promise of Utopia through Artificial General Intelligence'. *First Monday*, 14 April 2024. https://doi.org/10.5210/fm.v29i4.13636.

Gigerenzer, Gerd. 'The Bias Bias in Behavioral Economics'. *Review of Behavioral Economics* 5, nos. 3–4 (2018): 303–36. https://doi.org/10.1561/105.00000092.

Grotius, Hugo. *On the Law of War and Peace: Student Edition*. Edited by Stephen C Neff. Cambridge: Cambridge University Press, 2012. https://doi.org/10.1017/CBO9781139031233.

Grotius, Hugo. 'Theory of Trans-Oceanic Trade Regulation: Revisiting *Mare Liberum* (1609)'. *Institute for International Law and Justice*. www.iilj.org/publications/hugo-grotius-theory-of-trans-oceanic-trade-regulation-revisiting-mare-liberum-1609/.

Guardian, The. 'What Are Rare Earths and Critical Minerals – Explained in 30 Seconds'. *World News*, 17 October 2025. www.theguardian.com/world/2025/oct/17/rare-earths-critical-minerals-explained.

Hildebrandt, Mireille. 'Digging Deeper: Cross-Disciplinary Research Approaches'. *Brussels Privacy Hub*, 6 October 2025. https://brusselsprivacyhub.com/digging-deeper-cross-disciplinary-research-approaches/.

Hildebrandt, Mireille. 'Extraterritorial Jurisdiction to Enforce in Cyberspace? Bodin, Schmitt, Grotius in Cyberspace'. *University of Toronto Law Journal* 63, no. 2 (2013): 196–224. https://doi.org/10.3138/utlj.1119.

Hildebrandt, Mireille. 'International and Supranational Law'. In *Law for Computer Scientists and Other Folk*. Oxford: Oxford University Press, 2020. https://doi.org/10.1093/oso/9780198860877.003.0004.

Hildebrandt, Mireille. 'LLMs, Legal Contestability and Scientific Falsifiability'. In *Proceedings of the LSTS Research Day 2025*. Open Science Framework, 23 September 2025. https://osf.io/8k2wp_v1.

Hildebrandt, Mireille. 'Review of: Chris Reed and Andrew Murray, *Rethinking the Jurisprudence of Cyberspace*. Cheltenham: Edward Elgar, 2018'. *Modern Law Review* 83, no. 3 (2020): 690–94. https://doi.org/10.1111/1468-2230.12491.

Hildebrandt, Mireille. 'Text-Driven Jurisdiction in Cyberspace'. In *Transformations in Criminal Jurisdiction: Extraterritoriality and Enforcement*, edited by Micheál Ó Floinn et al. London: Bloomsbury, 2023. www.bloomsbury.com/uk/transformations-in-criminal-jurisdiction-9781509954223/.

Hildebrandt, Mireille. 'Who Needs Stories If You Can Get the Data? ISPs in the Era of Big Number Crunching'. *Philosophy and Technology* 24 (2011): 371–90.

Howell, Jason. 'Meta AI Chief Yann LeCun: Human Intelligence Is Not General Intelligence'. *Jason Howell's Newsletter* (Substack), 9 April 2025. https://jasonhowell.substack.com/p/meta-ai-chief-yann-lacun-human-intelligence.

Irwin, Douglas A, and Ward Oliver. 'What Is the "Washington Consensus?"'. *PIIE Realtime Economics Blog*, 8 September 2021. www.piie.com/blogs/realtime-economics/2021/what-washington-consensus.

Kahneman, Daniel. 'Maps of Bounded Rationality: Psychology for Behavioral Economics'. *American Economic Review* 93, no. 5 (2003): 1449–75.

Mattern, Mark. *The Trickle-Up Economy: How We Take from the Poor and Middle Class and Give to the Rich*. Boulder, CO: Lynne Rienner Publishers, 2021.

Merton, Robert K. 'The Self-Fulfilling Prophecy'. *Antioch Review* 8, no. 2 (1948): 193–210.

Mirowski, Philip, and Dieter Plehwe, eds. *The Road from Mont Pèlerin: The Making of the Neoliberal Thought Collective*. Cambridge, MA: Harvard University Press, 2009.

Murgia, Madhumita, et al. 'AI Pioneers Claim Human-Level General Intelligence Is Already Here'. *Financial Times*, 6 November 2025. www.ft.com/content/5f2f411c-3600-483b-bee8-4f06473ecdc0.

Narayanan, Arvind, and Sayash Kapoor. *AI Snake Oil: What Artificial Intelligence Can Do, What It Can't, and How to Tell the Difference*. Princeton, NJ: Princeton University Press, 2024.

Narayanan, Arvind, and Sayash Kapoor. 'AI as Normal Technology'. *Knight First Amendment Institute*, 15 April 2025. http://knightcolumbia.org/content/ai-as-normal-technology.

Nature. 'The Global Fight for Critical Minerals Is Costly and Damaging'. *Nature* 619, no. 7970 (2023): 436. https://doi.org/10.1038/d41586-023-02330-0.

OpenAI. 'Charter'. https://openai.com/charter/.

Open Universiteit. 'Symposium Justitia and Leviathans: The Struggle for the International Rule of Law'. www.ou.nl/en/-/symposium-justitia-and-leviathans-the-struggle-for-the-international-rule-of-law.

Oxford Public International Law. 'Westphalia, Peace of (1648)'. https://opil.ouplaw.com/display/10.1093/law:epil/9780199231690/law-9780199231690-e739.

Pasquale, Frank. 'Tech Platforms and the Knowledge Problem'. *American Affairs Journal* 11, no. 2 (2018): 3–16. https://americanaffairsjournal.org/2018/05/tech-platforms-and-the-knowledge-problem/.

Pistor, Katharina. *The Code of Capital: How the Law Creates Wealth and Inequality*. Princeton, NJ: Princeton University Press, 2019.

Reed, Chris, and Andrew Murray. *Rethinking the Jurisprudence of Cyberspace*. Cheltenham: Edward Elgar, 2018.

Reinert, Hugo, and Reinert, Erik S. 'Creative Destruction in Economics: Nietzsche, Sombart, Schumpeter.' In *Friedrich Nietzsche (1844–1900)*, ed. Jürgen G. Backhaus and Wolfgang Drechsler. Springer, 2006.

Rosalsky, Greg. 'How "Shock Therapy" Created Russian Oligarchs and Paved the Path for Putin'. *NPR Planet Money Newsletter*, 22 March 2022. www.npr.org/sections/money/2022/03/22/1087654279/how-shock-therapy-created-russian-oligarchs-and-paved-the-path-for-putin.

Russell, Stuart, and Peter Norvig. *Artificial Intelligence: A Modern Approach*. 4th edn. Harlow, UK: Pearson, 2022.

Scheider-Petsinger, Marianne. 'Geoeconomics Explained'. Chatham House, December 2016, updated 2020. www.chathamhouse.org/2016/12/geoeconomics-explained.

Szlezak, Waldemar. 'Investors Need to Look beyond the "Bragawatts" in AI Infrastructure Boom'. *Financial Times*, 3 November 2025. www.ft.com/content/bf687d99-f373-4a41-8651-fca9dba83aa0.

Trachtenberg, Marc. 'The Rules-Based International Order: A Historical Analysis'. *International Security* 50, no. 2 (2025): 7–54. https://doi.org/10.1162/isec_a_01101.

Waldron, Jeremy. 'The Rule of International Law'. *Harvard Journal of Law & Public Policy* 30 (2006): 15–30.

Wangari, Stephanie, and Gayathri Vaidyanathan. 'How Big Tech Hides Its Outsourced African Workforce'. *Rest of World*, 21 April 2025. https://restofworld.org/2025/big-tech-ai-labor-supply-chain-african-workers/.

PART 2

Academic Insights

3

Navigating Disruption: The Case of the European AI Act

ANNA-JULIA SAIGER

Abstract

Artificial Intelligence (AI) stands as the quintessential disruptive technology – a framing actively promoted through lobbying to influence EU regulatory responses. This chapter explores the European regulatory reaction to such pressure through the lens of the 2024 AI Act. The regulation adopts a hybrid governance model that addresses both traditional product risks and emerging societal risks, thereby positioning AI as (legally) disruptive technology. Central to the EU's approach is the recourse to standardisation as a flexible governance instrument. This regulatory framework holds the potential to foster knowledge exchange between the public and private sectors, as well as to build trust within the European Single Market and, thus, to navigate the dilemma posed by framing AI as disruptive. However, it increasingly operates within the context of a global deregulatory trend that may compromise its effectiveness. The chapter critically scrutinises the AI Act's portrayal of AI as disruptive, contending that effective regulation necessitates active engagement with these foundational premises.

Keywords

Artificial intelligence; Disruptive innovation; AI Act; European digital acquis; Legal disruption; Standardisation; Governance

I. Introduction

AI stands as the quintessential disruptive technology.[1] This has significant implications for the regulation of AI. Legislators are grappling with the challenge

[1] The introduction of DeepSeek – a general-purpose chatbot developed by a Chinese AI startup – may serve as one of the latest examples of how technological innovations in the realm of AI are

of reining in the 'dark side of innovation'[2] while fostering beneficial technological advancements. Thus, they do not operate in a vacuum; their efforts are directly challenged by the strategies of Big Tech companies. Paradigms like the motto 'move fast and break things'[3] have been actively targeted by lobbying efforts throughout the formulation of European digital law.[4] The concept of 'disruption/disruptive innovation' originated in 1990s management theory.[5] Recently, its intersection with the law has become increasingly significant.[6] Technology no longer only disrupts markets – it is also disrupting the legal domain. AI technologies, in particular, are evolving rapidly. AI operates horizontally and takes on a chameleon-like nature, simultaneously embodying aspects of a service, a process, and a product. The European Union has sought to regulate such 'disruptive technologies', most notably through the Artificial Intelligence Act[7] and other digital rulebooks.[8] Their adoption prompts critical inquiry into how legislators respond to disruptive innovation and the extent to which the concept of disruption is embedded within legal texts: What is the relationship between disruption (or the rumours thereof) and the law? It is argued here that framing AI as disruptive across economic, social, and legal dimensions has informed the European regulatory approach, with the AI Act consequently seeking to achieve legal flexibility via standardisation mechanisms.

This chapter explores the origins of the concept of disruption, which initially had no ambition to enter the legal domain, and examines how it has come to shape EU law. While others have approached this from a lobbying perspective,[9]

challenging the foundation of leading firms in the tech industry, Prithwiraj Choudhury et al, 'Why Deepseek Shouldn't Have been a Surprise', *Harvard Business Review* 30 January 2025, https://hbr.org/2025/01/why-deepseek-shouldnt-have-been-a-surprise.

[2] Alex Coad et al, 'Editorial: The Dark Side of Innovation'. *Industry and Innovation* 28, no. 1 (2021): 102, https://doi.org/10.1080/13662716.2020.1818555.

[3] This phrase is attributed to Mark Zuckerberg in 2012, see Simon Chesterman, '"Move Fast and Break Things": Law, Technology, and the Problem of Speed'. *Singapore Academy of Law Journal* 33 (2021): 20. Jonathan Taplin, *Move Fast and Break Things: How Facebook, Google, and Amazon Cornered Culture and Undermined Democracy* (London: Macmillan, 2018).

[4] Elaine Fahey, *Big Tech and EU Law. Transatlantic Lawyering, Lobbying and Litigating* (Cheltenham: Edward Elgar Publishing, 2025).

[5] Clayton M Christensen, *The Innovator's Dilemma: When New Technologies Cause Great Firms to Fail* (Cambridge, MA: Harvard Business Review Press, 1997).

[6] Including critical accounts, see Margot E Kaminski and Meg Leta Jones, 'Constructing AI Speech'. *Yale Law Journal* 133 (2024): 1212, 1213: 'Instead of asking whether the law can keep up with technology, we should be asking how the law shapes and intervenes in technology and how it can do so – or refrain from doing so – in ways that further important values'.

[7] Regulation (EU) 2024/1689 of the European Parliament and of the Council of 13 June 2024 on artificial intelligence (AI Act).

[8] Regulation (EU) 2016/679 of the European Parliament and of the Council of 27 April 2016 on the Protection of Natural Persons with regard to the Processing of Personal Data and on the Free Movement of such Data, and repealing Directive (2016) OJ L 119/1 (General Data Protection Regulation, GDPR); Regulation (EU) 2022/2065 of the European Parliament and of the Council of 19 October 2022 on a Single Market for Digital Services and amending Directive (2022) OJ L 277/1 (Digital Services Act, DSA).

[9] Fahey, *Big Tech and EU Law*.

the focus of this chapter is on the legal text itself. The question at hand is how the European approach to AI regulation responds to the prevailing perception of AI as a form of disruptive innovation – disrupting not only markets but also the very frameworks of regulation. Central to this is the dilemma posed by such a framing: how can the law regulate what appears inherently unregulatable? After all, disruption often carries an anti-regulatory undertone, suggesting that technological progress occurs despite, rather than through, regulation. Yet this is a flawed assumption. Various forms of regulation – such as those enabling limited liability, or the presence (or absence) of competition law – have played a crucial role in enabling technological advancement.[10] Whether the AI Act effectively confronts and resolves this ambiguity remains an open and pressing question.[11] While the regulation perceives high-risk AI systems as potentially disruptive (Recital 177 of the AI Act), this underlying assumption has important repercussions on the governance mechanism the regulation relies on. This is reflected in the AI Act's conception of risk: the AI Act addresses both traditional product risks – such as those to health and safety – and emerging societal risks, primarily those affecting fundamental rights.[12] The regulatory response is articulated through an AI governance model that aims to foster a dynamic collaboration between public and private actors – capable of responding to fast-paced technological change without compromising legal and societal stability. It has the potential to foster knowledge creation and exchange among the involved actors – and, importantly, to build trust within the European single market. Yet, given the 'deregulatory turn'[13] recently announced by the EU, and the intensifying global push toward deregulation,[14] it is uncertain whether this potential can be meaningfully actualised. In this context, a critical assessment of the foundational assumptions reflected in both the legal text and its governance architecture is necessary, with particular attention to the role and framing of disruption.

The chapter proceeds as follows: In the section following this introduction (II), it sketches out the origin and evolution of the concept of disruption in innovation management literature, revealing the inherent normative assumptions this

[10] Anu Bradford, 'The False Choice Between Digital Regulation and Innovation'. *Northwestern University Law Review* 119 (2024): 377–453, doi.org/10.2139/ssrn.4753107.

[11] Kaminski and Jones, 'Constructing AI Speech', 1223, contrasting the narrative of disruption with a 'values-first approach to regulating technology'. See for earlier accounts on the relationship of disruptive innovation and the law Wulf A Kaal and Erik PM Vermeulen, 'How to Regulate Disruptive Innovation – From Facts to Data'. *Jurimetrics* 57, no. 2 (2017).

[12] See Article 1 of the AI Act.

[13] Hannah Ruschemeier, 'The De-Regulatory Turn of the EU Commission'. *Verfassungsblog*, 18 February 2025, https://verfassungsblog.de/the-de-regulatory-turn-of-the-eu-commission/. COM (2025) 45 final, 11 February 2025.

[14] From the outset, the newly appointed second Trump administration showcased a deregulatory approach to AI by revoking Executive Order 14110 on Artificial Intelligence, Executive Order 14110 on Safe, Secure, and Trustworthy Development and Use of Artificial Intelligence, October 30, 2023, and by framing it as 'onerous and unnecessary government control over the development of AI', The White House, 'Fact Sheet', 23 January 2025, www.whitehouse.gov/fact-sheets/2025/01/fact-sheet-president-donald-j-trump-takes-action-to-enhance-americas-ai-leadership/.

concept has accumulated to date. It portrays in what way the regulation's so-called 'hybrid approach'[15] to both societal and product risks reflects important traits of the concept of disruption. Section III turns to the AI Act, presenting it in light of the fundamental dilemma that is the challenge of regulating what is perceived as unregulatable. The legal response to this dilemma involves extending the so-called New Legislative Framework (NLF) to AI systems. Central to this approach is the use of standardisation as a governance instrument. This section illustrates the evolution of the European digital *acquis* from serving as a model for global standards (the *Brussels effect*)[16] to employing standardisation as a flexible governance tool. Section IV assesses in more detail the collaboration of different public and private actors involved in standardisation, concluding that their interplay amounts to a complex form of knowledge creation and exchange as well as trust building. This is how the AI Act confronts the concept of disruption. The final section (V) concludes that the AI Act can realise its full potential only if the actors involved critically engage with the underlying assumptions about AI. Such engagement is especially vital in light of growing global deregulatory pressures, with the concept of disruption offering a productive space for these efforts.

II. Disruption

A. A Concept Transferred from Economics to Law

The term 'disruption' has evolved significantly since its introduction in the 1990s, expanding from its origins in innovation management literature to emerge as a pervasive paradigm across diverse sectors, prominently shaped and driven by Big Tech. Throughout its evolution, it has adopted a distinctly anti-regulatory stance. Clayton M Christensen, a professor at Harvard Business School, introduced the concept of disruptive innovation in his 1997 book *The Innovator's Dilemma*[17] to describe technological advancements that replace existing technologies, leading to the creation of new markets while rendering former markets obsolete.[18] From the outset, the concept was intended to encompass not only technological innovations but also their impact on markets and societies. However, it did not yet

[15] See Oskar J Gstrein et al, 'General-Purpose AI Regulation and the European Union AI Act'. *Internet Policy Review* 13, no. 3 (2024): 7, 19. https://doi.org/10.14763/2024.3.1790; Michael Veale and Frederik Zuiderveen Borgesius, 'Demystifying the Draft EU Artificial Intelligence Act'. *Computer Law Review International* 4 (2021): 112. https://doi.org/10.48550/arXiv.2107.03721; see below in Section II.B.

[16] But see Anna-Julia Saiger, 'Brussels Mirage: The EU AI Act's Subtle Shine Across International Borders'. *EJIL:Talk!* (26 June 2025), www.ejiltalk.org/brussels-mirage-the-eu-ai-acts-subtle-shine-across-international-borders/.

[17] Christensen, *The Innovator's Dilemma*.

[18] See for a literature overview: Stine Schmieg Lundgaard and Claus Andreas Foss Rosenstand, *Investigating Disruption: A Literature Review of Core Concepts of Disruptive Innovation Theory* (Aalborg: Aalborg University Press, 2019). It is interesting, however, to note that according to Joshua Gans, *The Disruption Dilemma* (Cambridge, MA: MIT Press, 2016), an innovation loses its disruptive potential if the incumbents succeed in integrating it into their existing structures.

extend to the legal realm. The concept of disruptive innovation was initially understood as a form of competence-destroying innovation, mirroring Schumpeter's concept of creative destruction.[19] Schumpeter perceived creative destruction – though integral to the functioning of capitalism – nonetheless problematic.[20] In this regard, the contemporary notion of disruption has emancipated itself from Schumpeter's original formulation. Silicon Valley has reframed it as a desirable force for innovation and progress. Originally criticised as a fearful concept due to concerns that firms might fail in the face of innovation,[21] disruptive innovation has become a central theme in TED talks and management literature. Today it is framed as 'the theory that influenced Steve Jobs, Jeff Bezos, and Andy Grove'.[22]

Along with this reframing, the scope of disruption has expanded over time to include potential impacts on the competencies of legislators and governments, particularly amid rapid technological advancement. This has become particularly salient in recent times, where disruption has acquired a twofold normative assumption: First, while disruption calls for change, it remains deeply ambiguous about the direction of that change and the values that should guide it. Put differently, disruptive innovation has become a tool for achieving specific objectives emphasising speed and scale while pushing for rapid and large-scale change – but leaving in abeyance what this future will actually look like.[23] This contrasts with concepts like transformation, which also focus on fundamental change but are aimed at achieving specific goals, such as sustainability.[24] Second, disruption has fostered an anti-regulatory tendency, grounded in the belief that technological innovation progresses too quickly to be effectively regulated – and, crucially, that it fundamentally disrupts the law. Accordingly, technology is supposed to govern the world, overshadowing regulation, ideas, and content that are conveyed through these technologies.[25] Some have called this 'technology essentialism', highlighting an underlying perception of law as inherently reactive rather than proactive.[26]

[19] Michael L Tushman and Philip Anderson, 'Technological Discontinuities and Organizational Environments'. *Administrative Science Quarterly* 31, no. 3 (1986): 439, https://doi.org/10.2307/2392832.

[20] Adrian Daub, *What Tech Calls Thinking. An Inquiry into the Intellectual Bedrock of Silicon Valley* (New York: Macmillan, 2020) 122 et seq.

[21] Jill Lepore, 'The Disruption Machine'. *The New Yorker* 90, June 16, 2014. www.newyorker.com/magazine/2014/06/23/the-disruption-machine.

[22] Christensen Institute, 'Disruptive Innovation Theory', www.christenseninstitute.org/theory/disruptive-innovation/.

[23] Daub, *What Tech Calls Thinking*, 127, 128. See also Kaminski and Jones, 'Constructing AI Speech', 1223 et seq.

[24] Jessica Blythe et al, 'The Dark Side of Transformation: Latent Risks in Contemporary Sustainability Discourse'. *Antipode* 50, no. 5 (2018), https://doi.org/10.1111/anti.12405. However, it shall be highlighted that the concept of disruption plays an important role in transformation studies, see Paula Kivimaa et al, 'Moving Beyond Disruptive Innovation: A Review of Disruption in Sustainability Transitions'. *Environmental Innovation and Societal Transitions* 38 (2021), https://doi.org/10.1016/j.eist.2020.12.001.

[25] Hallam Stevens, 'Elon Musk's New Job Will Bring Tech "Disruption" to the US Government – and History Says it Won't be Pretty', 18 November 2024, https://theconversation.com/elon-musks-new-job-will-bring-tech-disruption-to-the-us-government-and-history-says-it-wont-be-pretty-243907. Daub, *What Tech Calls Thinking*, 43 et seq.

[26] Kaminski and Jones, 'Constructing AI Speech', 1219.

B. The AI Act's Hybridity

Assuming that legislators are deeply embedded in societal discourses and acknowledging that law and technology 'co-construct each other',[27] the AI Act offers a valuable lens through which to examine how perceptions of disruption are reflected in the design of this regulation. Since its adoption on 13 June 2024, the AI Act has been significantly shaped by both the rapid development of AI technologies and their evolving perception in society. This process remains ongoing, as only some of its provisions have taken effect, with others scheduled to be implemented in stages (Article 113 AI Act). Much of the AI Act's regulatory framework depends on non-legislative harmonised standards[28] and delegated acts by the European Commission, which still need to be finalised.

The recitals of the regulation explicitly reference the need to avoid a 'disruption of the market'.[29] Marked by the experience of market – and potentially societal – disruption, the AI Act frames AI as a potentially disruptive technology, not only in the present but also with regard to its future impact. By relying on harmonised standards and delegated acts, the AI Act aims to ensure that future technological developments can be incorporated into its regulatory design – demonstrating that flexibility is intended to foster a proactive legal environment capable of responding to the evolving nature of AI. The EU AI Act is completed by the European Commission's delegated and implementing acts (such as the Code of Practice on General Purpose AI).[30] Most importantly, however, the European Standardisation Organisations[31] will develop harmonised European Norms, which will outline the specific obligations for providers and deployers of AI. In this process, the AI Act is closely integrated with international law and treaty-making (including the Council of Europe's *Framework Convention on Human Rights and AI*[32]). This approach is intended to enable swift and effective legislative responses to the rapidly evolving development of AI technologies. At the same time, however, it renders the regulation particularly vulnerable to deregulatory pressure – as demonstrated by the push for a 'stop the clock' decision,[33] which would have postponed the entry into force of key provisions on AI regulation, specifically those concerning high-risk AI systems.

[27] Kaminski and Jones, 'Constructing AI Speech', 1216.

[28] Article 40 AI Act.

[29] Recital 177 AI Act.

[30] The General-Purpose AI Code of Practice, July 10, 2025, https://digital-strategy.ec.europa.eu/en/policies/contents-code-gpai.

[31] Regulation (EU) No. 1025/2012 of the European Parliament and of the Council of 25 October 2012 on European Standardisation, OJ L 316, 14 November 2012, 12.

[32] Council of Europe Framework Convention on Artificial Intelligence and Human Rights, Democracy and the Rule of Law, 5 September 2024. www.coe.int/en/web/artificial-intelligence/the-framework-convention-on-artificial-intelligence.

[33] See 'Stop the Clock – Open Letter', www.aichampions.eu/#stoptheclock, which, however, remained unsuccessful.

Literature has described the AI Act as a hybrid instrument, a two-headed beast.[34] This is because the regulation on AI addresses two distinct dimensions of risk posed by AI: product risks and societal risks. This tightly connects to the idea of disruption, which implies – as has been shown – societal changes through the upscaling of products. Article 1(1) of the AI Act defines the purpose of the regulation as

> to improve the functioning of the internal market [...], while ensuring a high level of protection of health, safety, fundamental rights enshrined in the Charter, including democracy, the rule of law and environmental protection, against the harmful effects of AI systems in the Union.

Alongside the traditional areas of health and safety, the regulation thus includes the protection of fundamental rights within its scope. It has been stated that the enacting provisions of the AI Act point towards 'a slight preference for safety over fundamental rights'.[35] Moreover, the enumeration suggests that the AI Act refers to fundamental rights in their systemic dimension, positioning them in line with the European values, such as democracy, the rule of law, and environmental protection (Article 2 TEU).[36] Accordingly, individual rights or remedies are granted only in a limited manner under Articles 85 and 86 AI Act.[37]

Notwithstanding this imbalance toward product safety law, the EU AI Act incorporates a hybrid notion of risk: Product risks refer to the potential harm to health and safety caused by a specific product when used and applied in a particular context by a distinct group of users. The underlying logic of this is that products traditionally possess a fixed physical form that remains unchanged throughout their lifecycle.[38] In this vein, the AI Act primarily frames AI as a product (see Article 6(1) EU AI Act). Annex I of the EU AI Act lists *inter alia* toys, lifts, or forestry vehicles. Societal risks, on the other hand, are somewhat less contoured. They relate to the protection of fundamental rights, and (other) European values, including democracy, the rule of law, and environmental protection. The AI Act, to name just a few examples, references AI systems listed in the areas of biometrics,

[34] Marco Almada and Anca Radu, 'The Brussels Side-Effect: How the AI Act Can Reduce the Global Reach of EU Policy'. *German Law Journal* 25, no. 4 (2024): 3, https://doi.org/10.1017/glj.2023.108. On the hybrid nature of the AI Act see only: Gstrein, Haleem, and Zwitter, 'General-Purpose AI Regulation and the European Union AI Act', 7, 19; Veale and Zuiderveen Borgesius, 'Demystifying the Draft EU Artificial Intelligence Act', 112.

[35] Marco Almada and Nicolas Petit, 'The EU AI Act: Between the Rock of Product Safety and the Hard Place of Fundamental Rights'. *Common Market Law Review* 62, no. 1 (2025): 85, 95.

[36] Christiane Wendehorst, 'Artikel 1'. In *KI-VO: Verordnung über künstliche Intelligenz*, ed. Mario Martini and Christiane Wendehorst (Munich: CH Beck, 2024) 85.

[37] This provision gives affected individuals the right to obtain from the deployer clear and meaningful explanations of the role of a (high-risk) AI system in a decision-making procedure. Ceyhun Necati Pehlivan, 'The EU Artificial Intelligence Act: An Introduction'. In *AI Governance and Liability in Europe: A Primer*, ed. Ceyhun Necati Pehlivan, Nikolaus Forgó and Peggy Valcke (Leiden: Kluwer Law International, 2024) 117–64; Recital 171 of the AI Act.

[38] See Hannah Ruschemeier, 'Artikel 6'. In *KI-VO: Verordnung über künstliche Intelligenz*, ed. Mario Martini and Christiane Wendehorst (Munich: CH Beck, 2024) 314.

critical infrastructure, or education in this regard (see Article 6(2), Annex III of the AI Act). Additionally, the prohibition of certain AI practices, such as those employing subliminal techniques, serves to protect psychological health and safeguard vulnerable individuals.[39] While product risks are closely associated with the product's use, societal risks are linked to the intended purpose, circumstances, and context, all of which can vary. Both dimensions of risk may overlap.

As shown in the graph, the AI Act differentiates between AI systems according to the level of risk they pose to protected goods. Risk levels range from unaccepted to residual risks, with the main category being high-risk AI systems; in some cases, General Purpose AI models may even pose a systemic risk (to society as a whole).[40]

Figure 3.1 Classification of Risks, Legal Obligations, and Regulatory Approaches under the AI Act (AIA)

Level of risk	Unaccepted risk	High risk		Systemic risk	Residual risk
			GPAI		
AIA provision	Article 5	Article 6 (1) Article 6 (2)	Article 51		
Legal effect/ Obligation	Prohibition	Risk management; data governance; technical documentation; record keeping; transparency; human oversight; accuracy; robustness and cybersecurity (Article 8-15 AIA)	Technical documentation; copyright policy, etc. (Article 53)	Model evaluation; assessment and mitigation of systemic risks; documentation and reporting; cybersecurity (Article 55)	Article 50 and general EU acquis (rec. 166)
Regulatory approach	Blacklisting (command and control)	New Legislative Framework (NLF): hENs & conformity presumption (Article 40) (collaborative governance)			

With regard to (mostly societal) prohibited risks (Article 5 AI Act), the AI Act follows a classic command-and-control form of governance via blacklisting. The general European *acquis*,[41] along with the transparency obligations under Article 50 of the AI Act (eg, providing information on interactions with an AI system and marking artificially generated or manipulated content), apply to residual risks.[42] The centrepiece of the AI Act, however, transfers product safety law mechanisms to both product risks (Article 6(1), Annex I, A, of the AI Act)[43] and societal risks (Article 6(2), Annex III AI Act) – under the condition that they are considered high or systemic. Regarding General Purpose AI, the models described

[39] Article 5 and Recital 29 of the AI Act.

[40] Article 3(65) AI Act.

[41] See below in Section III.B.

[42] In the logic proposed here, Article 50 AI Act refers to both societal and product risks. Its scope may also encompass high-risk AI systems, implying that Article 50 of the AI Act applies in conjunction with Articles 8 et seq. of the AI Act.

[43] Annex I, B follows the so-called 'Old Approach'.

in Article 51 most likely relate to societal risks, but they might also engender product risks.[44]

III. The AI Act Revisited

While the AI Act introduces a fundamental rights dimension, its core framework remains grounded in product safety law. Article 114 TFEU[45] acts as its main legal basis, granting legislative powers to the European legislator to establish and maintain the functioning of the internal market. Article 16 TFEU has been added as an additional legal basis within the legislative process. Nonetheless, the AI Act remains primarily an instrument of the internal market.[46] In doing so, it risks replicating the regulatory ambiguity inherent in the notion of 'disruption'.

A. The New Legislative Framework under the AI Act

The AI Act, on a technical legal level, uses standardisation as a regulatory tool. This mechanism was introduced in 1985 in European product safety law with the New Approach, based on the so-called NLF.[47] Under the NLF, secondary law establishes the basic (safety) conditions for a specific technology (traditionally, a product). In the case of the AI Act, these duties are primarily procedural in nature, such as the establishment of risk management systems (Article 8 AI Act) or technical documentation (Article 11 AI Act).[48]

Upon request by the European Commission, European Standardisation Organisations (ESOs) develop harmonised European Norms (hENs) based

[44] See on GPAI models with systemic risk Article 51, Article 3(65) AI Act: 'significant impact on the Union market … or the society as a whole'. But note that according to Article 51(3) AI Act the European Commission may issue delegated acts to supplement benchmarks and indicators.

[45] Treaty on the Functioning of the European Union, OJ C 326 2012.

[46] COM(2020) 65 final, 15. Almada and Petit, 'The EU AI Act', 104; Gstrein, Haleem, and Zwitter, 'General-Purpose AI Regulation and the European Union AI Act', 7; Hans-W Micklitz, 'AI Standards, EU Digital Policy Legislation and Stakeholder Participation'. *Journal of European Consumer and Market Law* 13, no. 6 (2023): 212; Nadja Braun Binder and Catherine Egli, 'Artikel 8'. In *KI-VO: Verordnung über künstliche Intelligenz*, ed. Mario Martini and Christiane Wendehorst (Munich: CH Beck, 2024) 335. Whether Article 114 TFEU constitutes the appropriate legal basis, however, is a debated issue, see Almada and Petit, 'The EU AI Act: A Medley of Product Safety and Fundamental Rights?', 12 et seq.; Pieter Van Cleynenbreugel, 'EU By-Design Regulation in the Algorithmic Society'. In *Constitutional Challenges in the Algorithmic Society*, ed. Hans-W Micklitz et al (Cambridge: CUP, 2021) 209 et seq.

[47] Decision (EC) 786/2008 of the European Parliament and of the Council of 9 July 2008 on a Common Framework for the Marketing of Products, OJ L 218/82; Regulation (EU) 2019/1020 of the European Parliament and of the Council of 20 June 2019 on Market Surveillance and Compliance of Products and Amending Directive and Regulations (2019) OJ L 169/1.

[48] See Article 14 of the AI Act on human oversight and Article 15 on accuracy, robustness, and cybersecurity. These obligations are not necessarily limited to procedural requirements; however, their precise scope remains contested and will ultimately depend on the content of the harmonised European standards (hENs).

on their technical expertise.[49] ESOs consist of experts from private companies, research institutes, and public authorities, who have signed service contracts with their respective domestic standardisation organisation; the industry represents the largest group.[50] They work closely with their international counterparts, notably ISO and IEC,[51] as expressly envisaged in the agreements between European and international standardisation organisations in order to avoid duplication of work.[52] The harmonised norms are linked to EU secondary law through a presumption of conformity with the more general provisions of the regulation (Article 40 AI Act). While compliance with the harmonised standards is legally non-binding, there are strong reasons for private actors to adopt them in order to reduce compliance costs and, ultimately, to access the European market.[53]

As early as May 2023, the European Commission issued its standardisation request to two of the three ESOs, namely CEN and CENELEC.[54] At that point, the draft AI Act proposal did not yet include General Purpose AI models; accordingly, the standardisation request does not encompass standards on General Purpose AI. However, the European Commission, in accordance with Article 56 AI Act, has drafted the General Purpose AI Code of Practice.[55] It serves the same purpose as harmonised standards until such standards are published, as stated in Article 53(4) of the AI Act.

While the first hENs were expected by August 2025, they are yet to be finalised. The Commission's standardisation request appears to align closely with existing international standards on AI, such as ISO/IEC 42001.[56] There is some evidence that this standard will be adopted by CEN/CENELEC.[57] However, since the international standard does not address fundamental rights concerns, this would require the European Commission to adopt implementing acts establishing common specifications according to Article 41(1)(a)(iii) AI Act.

[49] Almada and Petit, 'The EU AI Act', 116.

[50] Jonathan Dollinger, *Folgenabschätzungen für Verwaltungsalgorithmen* (Tübingen: Mohr Siebeck, 2023) 68.

[51] The International Organization for Standardisation (ISO) and the International Electrotechnical Commission (IEC).

[52] The cooperation is facilitated by the Agreement on Technical Cooperation between ISO and CEN (Vienna Agreement) and the IEC-CENELEC Frankfurt Agreement. See also Recital 3 of Regulation (EU) No. 1025/2012.

[53] Simon Gerdemann and Maren Wöbbeking, 'Artikel 40'. In *KI-VO: Verordnung über künstliche Intelligenz*, ed. Mario Martini and Christiane Wendehorst (Munich: CH Beck, 2024) 627.

[54] C(2023)3215 final – Standardisation Request M/593, Commission Implementing Decision of May 22, 2023 on a Standardisation Request to the European Committee for Standardisation and the European Committee for Electrotechnical Standardisation in Support of Union Policy on Artificial Intelligence.

[55] The General-Purpose AI Code of Practice, July 10, 2025, https://digital-strategy.ec.europa.eu/en/policies/contents-code-gpai.

[56] ISO/IEC 42001:2023(en), 'Information Technology – Artificial Intelligence – Management System', December 2023, www.iso.org/committee/6794475/x/catalogue/p/1/u/1/w/0/d/0.

[57] Johann Laux, Sandra Wachter, and Brent Mittelstadt, 'Three Pathways for Standardisation and Ethical Disclosure by Default under the European Union Artificial Intelligence Act'. *Computer Law & Security Review* 53 (2024): 5.

B. From EU Law as De Facto Global Standard to the Integration of Standards into EU Law

The creation of the *digital single market* has been a key focus of the political agenda since both the Juncker Commission (2014) and the first von der Leyen Commission (2019).[58] Since then, the European digital *acquis* has expanded to include, inter alia, the General Data Protection Regulation (GDPR) and the Digital Services Act (DSA). While the AI Act functions as an overarching, horizontal regulation alongside these instruments, it is worth examining how it diverges from these earlier regulatory frameworks. The most notable development lies in the evolving role of standards within its governance model.

Earlier instruments – most notably the GDPR – were widely regarded as de facto global standards. This has been evidenced by the so-called *Brussels effect*,[59] which has amplified their influence beyond the EU's borders and attracted intense lobbying from Big Tech over their formulation and implementation.[60] This approach stood in stark contrast to the model of self-regulation and industry-defined standards traditionally favoured by the private sector.[61] With the AI Act, however, the EU has shifted its strategy by formally incorporating (technical) standards into its legal framework.

The GDPR adopts a genuinely rights-driven approach.[62] It frames rights in their individual dimension, placing the right to the protection of personal data at its core (see Article 1(2) of the GDPR). An essential aspect of this approach is Article 35 of the GDPR, which requires all controllers to conduct a data protection impact assessment prior to the processing of data. Article 27 of the AI Act introduces a similar provision, requiring a fundamental rights impact assessment before deploying high-risk AI systems. Both impact assessments (of the GDPR and the AI Act) refer to the impact on fundamental rights.[63] Article 27(4) of the AI Act acknowledges the potential overlap between both provisions and establishes a complementary relationship in such cases. Article 27 of the AI Act is, thus, inspired by the GDPR and constitutes one of the few examples of individual rights

[58] Chayanis Aueamnuay et al, 'Digital Regulation in the European Union'. *Zeitschrift für Europarecht*, no. 3 (2024): 2.

[59] Anu Bradford, *The Brussels Effect: How the European Union Rules the World* (Oxford: OUP, 2020).

[60] Fahey, *Big Tech and EU Law*, 24 et seq, 63.

[61] Fahey, *Big Tech and EU Law*.

[62] Article 1, Section 2 and Recital 1 of the GDPR. Almada and Petit, 'The EU AI Act', 96; Gstrein, Haleem, and Zwitter, 'General-Purpose AI Regulation and the European Union AI Act', 19; Eike Graef and Paul Nemitz, 'Addressing the Challenge of Protecting Fundamental Rights Through AI Regulation in the European Union'. *UCLA Law Review* 71 (2023–2024): 147, 148. See for a general account of the GDPR: Margot E Kaminski, 'The Right to Explanation, Explained'. *Berkeley Technology Law Review* 34 (2019): 189.

[63] Article 35 GDPR refers to 'the impact of the envisaged processing operations on the protection of personal data'. Article 27 AI Act more broadly refers to the impact on fundamental rights, but it must be noted that its scope is restricted to AI systems listed in Annex III.

protection in the AI Act.[64] However, while the duty also extends to certain private actors, such as banks and the insurance sector,[65] its primary addressees remain public bodies. The conferral of other rights under the AI Act remains highly limited in scope.[66]

The DSA, in turn, must be understood in the context of the earlier, and indeed more lenient, regulatory approach to platforms established by the e-commerce directive.[67] It introduces a framework of collaborative governance, whereby (systemic) public policy functions are conferred to the private sector.[68] This includes due diligence obligations, such as the notice-and-take-down mechanism in Article 16(1) of the DSA, and automated content moderation.[69] While under both the AI Act and the DSA, public policy functions are conferred to private actors, under the AI Act this occurs within the more complex (product safety) framework of standardisation processes.

The comparison with earlier European digital rulebooks, thus, reveals that the AI Act shares certain characteristics with its predecessors. However, with the NLF at its core, the AI Act acknowledges a shift: EU law no longer sets the international benchmarks but instead responds to ongoing (international) debates on AI standardisation and incorporates these developments into the European legal order. While this enables more complex and collaborative governance structures, it simultaneously renders the AI Act more susceptible to international deregulatory pressures.

IV. The AI Act under Deregulatory Pressure

The foregoing analysis has outlined the regulatory dilemma posed by framing AI as a disruptive innovation and examined the AI Act's response to this challenge – namely, its choice to pursue flexibility and adaptiveness through standardisation. The AI Act, thus, shows that 'the law, in encountering AI systems, already demonstrates a substantial array of tools, institutions, and orienting values'.[70] This section assesses whether the AI Act's approach proves successful – particularly in the face of growing deregulatory pressures worldwide.

[64] See Article 27(1)(c) of the AI Act: 'the categories of natural persons and groups likely to be affected'.

[65] See points 5(b) and (c) of Annex III of the AI Act.

[66] Articles 85 and 86 AI Act.

[67] Directive 2000/31/EC of the European Parliament and of the Council of 8 June 2000 on Certain Legal Aspects of Information Society Services, in particular Electronic Commerce, in the Internal Market (Directive on Electronic Commerce), OJ L 178/1.

[68] Jens-Peter Schneider, Simon Oles, and Kester Siegrist, 'Collaborative Governance of the EU Digital Single Market Established by the Digital Services Act'. In *Governance of Automated Decision-Making and EU Law* edited by Herwig Hofmann and Felix Pflücke (Oxford: OUP, 2024) 91 et seq.

[69] See on collaborative AI governance: Teemu Birkstedt et al, 'AI Governance: Themes, Knowledge Gaps, and Future Agendas'. *Internet Research* 33, no. 7 (2023): 157.

[70] Kaminski and Jones, 'Constructing AI Speech', 1215.

A. Public–Private Interaction

The AI Act's hybrid approach to product and societal risks entails a complex interaction of multiple public and private actors. This amounts to a form of collaboration that is both less stringent than a command-and-control approach and more demanding than mere self-regulation.[71]

As outlined earlier, hENs are at the core of the AI Act's regulatory approach. Once the reference to the hENs (or implementing acts) is published in the Official Journal,[72] access to the European Single Market depends on a tripartite procedure comprising risk classification, conformity assessment, and CE marking. Private actors remain primarily responsible for all three steps. Regarding risk classification, it follows from Article 6(4) of the AI Act that AI system providers[73] must determine the risk category their system falls into.[74] The same applies to the assessment of whether a system is an AI system at all.[75] In case of General Purpose AI models, providers shall notify the European Commission (Article 52(1) AI Act). In its various forms, this first step of the tripartite procedure to market access illustrates the importance of private actors under the AI Act; their actions are only partly subject to public oversight.

The interplay between public and private actors becomes even more complex within the conformity assessment procedure applicable to high-risk AI systems. While the NLF generally allows for different models,[76] the AI Act introduces a combination of internal and external procedures involving various private actors. The conformity assessment is carried out either by the provider of the AI system (as described in Annex VI referring to the NLF instruments) or by a third party (as described in Annex VII).[77] The latter are referred to as *notified bodies*, which have a hybrid role in that they are primarily private entities, yet independent of the provider of high-risk AI.[78] In case of compliance with the harmonised standards,

[71] Margot E Kaminski, 'Binary Governance: Lessons from the GDPR's Approach to Binary Governance: Lessons from the GDPR's Approach to Algorithmic Accountability'. *Southern California Law Review* 92 (2019): 1529.

[72] Article 10(6) of Regulation (EU) No. 1025/2012 of the European Parliament and of the Council of 25 October 2012 on European standardisation, OJ L 316/12.

[73] Article 3(3) AI Act.

[74] Hannah Ruschemeier, 'Artikel 6'. In *KI-VO: Verordnung über künstliche Intelligenz*, ed. Mario Martini and Christiane Wendehorst (Munich: CH Beck, 2024) 298, 310.

[75] Article 3(1) AI Act.

[76] Obligation of the manufacturer alone, or by authorities, as seen with pharmaceutical products, Veale and Zuiderveen Borgesius, 'Demystifying the Draft EU Artificial Intelligence Act', 102.

[77] Article 43(1), (2) AI Act.

[78] Article 3(22) AI Act. Notified bodies are designated and monitored in accordance with the procedure outlined in Articles 29 et seq. of the AI Act by the notifying authority of the Member State (Article 28 AI Act). In some limited cases (AI systems to be put into service by law enforcement, immigration, or asylum authorities or by Union institutions), national market surveillance authorities (ie data protection authorities, see Article 75(8) AI Act) have the role of notified bodies (Article 43(1) AI Act).

the notified body issues a certificate, which is valid up to four or five years.[79] In this second step toward market access, the European Commission may exercise its authority through delegated acts in at least two ways: first, it can adopt delegated acts to amend Annexes VI and VII, thereby modifying the tasks assigned to providers or notified bodies during the conformity assessment procedure. Second, it can amend Annex III, which specifies the high-risk AI systems referred to in Article 6(2) of the AI Act; the Annex-III character, in turn, affects the conformity assessment procedure to be followed.

Finally, if the harmonised standards are complied with, providers must draw up an EU declaration of conformity and affix the CE mark to the product (Article 16 AI Act), thereby gaining access to the single market. Regarding (*ex post*) market surveillance, this task is carried out by the member states,[80] the AI Office,[81] and the European Data Protection Supervisor respectively, that is, merely by public entities, in a multi-level setting.

B. Collaborative Governance and Standardisation

Standards have increasingly been employed as normative instruments in various areas of EU regulation, notably serving as value-based markers within the eco-design regulation.[82] In line with this broader trend, the AI Act builds on socio-technical standards. Unusually, the European Commission's standardisation request to CEN and CENELEC explicitly refers to the protection of fundamental rights and European values:[83] 'To the purpose of ensuring that European standards and European standardisation deliverables are in line with Union law on fundamental rights and Union data protection law, CEN and CENELEC shall gather relevant expertise in those areas'.[84] However, it follows from the regulation's hybrid approach that the hENs must not only *respect* fundamental rights but also actively *promote* the protection of fundamental rights (in their systemic dimension) in relation to violations arising from the use of AI. Article 41(1)(a)(iii) AI Act strongly points into this direction. This provision implies the European Commission's right to assess whether the hENs sufficiently address fundamental rights concerns. It has no counterparts in previous NLF instruments, emphasising the significance of proactive fundamental rights protection through AI standards.[85] Thus, the AI

[79] Article 44(2) AI Act.

[80] Article 70 AI Act.

[81] Article 3(47), Article 64 AI Act; Gstrein, Haleem, and Zwitter, 'General-Purpose AI Regulation and the European Union AI Act', 14.

[82] Regulation (EU) 2024/1781 of the European Parliament and of the Council of 13 June 2024 establishing a framework for the setting of eco-design requirements for sustainable products, OJ L 1/89. Pointing toward value judgements in medical standards: Pougiet, 'What Will the Role of Standards Be in AI Governance?' 5 April 2023, www.adalovelaceinstitute.org/blog/role-of-standards-in-ai-governance/.

[83] See C(2023)3215 final – Standardisation Request M/593, Recitals 14 and 15.

[84] C(2023)3215 final – Standardisation Request M/593, Annex 2(1).

[85] See comparison to Article 20(3–8) Regulation (EU) 2023/1230 of the European Parliament and of the Council of 14 June 2023 on Machinery, OJ L 165/1: Gerdemann, Wöbbeking, 'Artikel 41'. In *KI-VO:*

Act seems to assume that the European Commission is better positioned than the ESOs to set standards concerning fundamental rights,[86] which inevitably raises further questions regarding the democratic legitimacy of the European institutions involved.

That said, even though we are likely to see implementing acts from the European Commission, the standards developed by CEN/CENELEC will retain their socio-technical nature.[87] As demonstrated, societal and product risks cannot be easily separated, particularly with rapidly evolving technologies like AI, which may even amount to general purpose technologies. Moreover, certain concepts in the standardisation request leave significant room for interpretation, such as 'representativeness' in the context of data governance and 'appropriate oversight measures' in relation to human oversight.[88] This implies that socio-technical standards necessitate distinct forms of law-making and governance mechanisms, particularly in terms of the relevant expertise and democratic legitimacy.[89] Since hENs are behind paywalls, public access and stakeholder participation will need to be re-evaluated as well.[90] Not all of these questions have been resolved, and much will depend on the development of harmonised standards, which have to face increasing deregulatory pressure. However, at a more fundamental level, the question remains as to whether AI, as a constantly evolving technology, aligns with the framework of product regulation.[91]

C. Knowledge Creation and Exchange, and Trust Building

The AI Act binds both public and private deployers and providers of AI.[92] They interact in a nuanced manner, a consequence of the AI Act's nature as a horizontal regulation that applies to a wide range of AI systems. This governance approach

Verordnung über künstliche Intelligenz, ed. Mario Martini and Christiane Wendehorst (Munich: CH Beck, 2024) 646.

[86] Veale and Zuiderveen Borgesius, 'Demystifying the Draft EU Artificial Intelligence Act', 112, underestimate the central role attributed to the European Commission. It is questionable whether the European Commission's power can still be framed as 'an exceptional fall back solution' (Recital 122 AI Act) when it comes to fundamental rights concerns, especially with regard to Article 291(3) TFEU and the full judicial review of the Commission's implementing acts.

[87] Laux, Wachter, and Mittelstadt, 'Three Pathways for Standardisation and Ethical Disclosure', 2, framing standards as a 'powerful regulatory tool'.

[88] C(2023)3215 final – Standardisation Request M/593, Annex 2, at 2.2 and 2.5. See for further examples Laux, Wachter, and Mittelstadt, 'Three Pathways for Standardisation and Ethical Disclosure', 4.

[89] Veale and Zuiderveen Borgesius, 'Demystifying the Draft EU Artificial Intelligence Act', 102; Laux, Wachter, and Mittelstadt, 'Three Pathways for Standardisation and Ethical Disclosure', 3.

[90] But see the provisions for stakeholder inclusion in Regulation 1025/2012 and in C(2023)3215 final – Standardisation Request M/593, Recital 15 and Article 2(1)(a); see the recent case law: ECLI:EU:C:2016:821 (James Elliott), and ECLI:EU:C:2024:201 (Public.Resources).

[91] Almada and Petit, 'The EU AI Act'.

[92] Oriol Mir, 'The AI Act from the Perspective of Administrative Law: Much Ado About Nothing?', *European Journal of Risk Regulation*, 16 (2025): 63 et seq. See Recital 13 AI Act: 'The notion of "deployer" referred to in this Regulation should be interpreted as any natural or legal person, including a public authority, agency or other body, using an AI system under its authority'. See critique in Ida Koivisto, Riikka Koulu, and Stefan Larsson, 'User Accounts: How Technological Concepts Permeate Public Law

has the potential to address two crucial dimensions in regulating AI: knowledge creation and exchange as well as trust building. However, it comes under increasing global deregulatory pressure.

Trust plays a pivotal role in the harmonisation of the digital single market, particularly through the mechanism of CE marking. The CE mark, following the principle of mutual recognition established by the Court of Justice of the European Union (CJEU) in the so-called *Cassis de Dijon* case,[93] aims to enhance trust in the product's compliance with health and safety standards;[94] however, it remains to be seen whether in the case of AI standards this will cover both product and societal risks.[95]

Knowledge creation and exchange remain highly important elements of AI regulation in two respects: First, AI regulation requires adopting a multilevel perspective, which relies on cooperation between the domestic and the European level as well as between the European and the international stage. In this regard, the European approach to standardisation is a double-edged sword: it serves both as a means of promoting European values and working towards a resilient, green, and digital single market through standards (thereby countering international influence) and as a strategy for building alliances on the international stage.[96] In that regard ISO/IEC are a platform for cooperation with non-EU states. At the same time, their influence on European standards must be carefully managed.[97] Second, knowledge creation and exchange become even more pressing issues in relation to ongoing AI development. From this vantage point, the AI Act's regulatory approach based on the NLF is supposed to be fast and effective,[98] and, therefore, well-suited to adapt to the (potentially disruptive) dynamics of technological evolution. This is because harmonised standards do not constitute formal law; therefore, they can be modified and adapted through a simpler procedure, making the process faster. This flexibility also enables industry expertise to enhance the regulatory mechanisms.

Disruption has been framed itself as a category of knowledge.[99] In light of the foregoing, an informed understanding of both the evolution of the term disruption and its normative aspirations as well as the AI Act's underlying assumption

through the EU's AI Act'. *Maastricht Journal of European and Comparative Law* 31, no. 3 (2024), https://doi.org/10.1177/1023263X241248469.

[93] ECLI:EU:C:1979:42 (*Rewe-Zentral AG v Bundesmonopolverwaltung für Branntwein*).

[94] Commission Notice, 'Blue Guide on the Implementation of EU Product Rules 2022', 29 June 2022, OJ C 247/01.

[95] See on the nexus between risk and trust: Regine Paul, 'European Artificial Intelligence "Trusted Throughout the World": Risk-based Regulation and the Fashioning of a Competitive Common AI Market'. *Regulation & Governance*, no. 18 (2024): 1065.

[96] COM(2022) 31 final, February 2, 2022.

[97] Note that the UK (and other non-EU states) are involved in CEN/CENELEC, see CEN, 'About CEN', https://standards.cencenelec.eu/dyn/www/f?p=CEN:5.

[98] Pointing toward both the advantages and disadvantages of this approach: Braun Binder and Egli, 'Artikel 8', 343.

[99] Alexander Manu, *The Philosophy of Disruption: From Transition to Transformational Change* (Bingley: Emerald Publishing Group, 2022).

of AI as (potentially) disruptive technology are indispensable for the regulation to unfold its potential. This applies to all actors involved in standardisation. Only such an informed regulatory practice will make the AI Act an instrument of trust building in an environment shaped by the discourse on disruption.

V. Outlook

The AI Act seeks to mitigate the risks associated with AI as a disruptive technology while simultaneously fostering its potential. In doing so, however, it is built upon an inherent dilemma: it sets out to regulate the unregulatable. To navigate this dilemma, the AI Act draws on earlier regulatory frameworks – particularly standardisation mechanisms from product safety law – and adapts them to the context of AI. It thus acknowledges that EU law no longer functions as a global de facto standard in the digital realm but instead participates in a broader – international – standard-setting endeavour, one that relies heavily on the expertise and input of the private sector.

This chapter has argued that the governance model the AI Act relies on is apt to create knowledge and to enable the exchange of such knowledge among various public and private actors in a multidimensional regulatory environment. What is more, it promotes trust by standardising AI systems. For this approach to achieve its goals, however, it is essential for all stakeholders to critically examine the underlying assumptions and the public discourse surrounding AI. As demonstrated here, the concept of 'disruption/disruptive innovation' is one such assumption that has been encapsulated in the AI Act. Indeed, the AI Act's hybrid approach reflects the concept of disruption:[100] while treating AI as a product, it also recognises the societal implications that such products may generate. Given that the process of standardising AI is ongoing, amid significant disruptive influences on regulatory frameworks that are shaping the second von der Leyen Commission's work programme,[101] this chapter aims to inform regulators and standard-setting bodies by offering an appropriate analytical framework to support this endeavour. This contributes to scholarly debates about whether standardisation is effective in addressing societal risks and enhancing the protection of fundamental rights. AI standards will inherently reflect certain values, and it is crucial that these values are not lost (or: disrupted) in translation.[102]

[100] Kaminski and Jones, 'Constructing AI Speech', 1221: 'The ways we make legal sense of technologies changes the way we design, integrate, and regulate them'. See also Margot E Kaminski, 'Technological "Disruption" of the Law's Imagined Scene: Some Lessons from Lex Informatica'. *Berkeley Technology Law Journal* 36 (2021): 883, 893 et seq.

[101] COM(2025) 45 final, February 11, 2025 – Commission Work Programme 2025.

[102] Roger Brownsword, 'Lost in Translation: Legality, Regulatory Margins, and Technological Management'. *Berkeley Technology Law Journal*, 26 (2011), https://doi.org/10.15779/Z38GH5M.

Bibliography

Almada, Marco, and Nicolas Petit. 'The EU AI Act: Between the Rock of Product Safety and the Hard Place of Fundamental Rights'. *Common Market Law Review* 62, no. 1 (2025): 85.

Almada, Marco, and Nicolas Petit. 'The EU AI Act: A Medley of Product Safety and Fundamental Rights?' RSC 2023/59 Robert Schuman Centre for Advanced Studies (European University Institute, 2023).

Almada, Marco, and Anca Radu. 'The Brussels Side-Effect: How the AI Act Can Reduce the Global Reach of EU Policy'. *German Law Journal* 25, no. 4 (June 2024): 1–18. https://doi.org/10.1017/glj.2023.108.

Aueamnuay, Chayanis, et al. 'Digital Regulation in the European Union'. *Zeitschrift für Europarecht*, no. 3 (2024): 1–31.

Birkstedt, Teemu, et al, 'AI Governance: Themes, Knowledge Gaps, and Future Agendas'. *Internet Research* 33, no. 7 (2023): 157–67.

Blythe, Jessica, et al. 'The Dark Side of Transformation: Latent Risks in Contemporary Sustainability Discourse'. *Antipode* 50, no. 5 (2018): 1206–223. https://doi.org/10.1111/anti.12405.

Bradford, Anu. 'The False Choice Between Digital Regulation and Innovation'. *Northwestern University Law Review* 119 (2024): 377–453, doi.org/10.2139/ssrn.4753107.

Bradford, Anu. *The Brussels Effect: How the European Union Rules the World*. Oxford: Oxford University Press, 2012.

Braun Binder, Nadja, and Egli, Catherine. 'Artikel 8'. In *KI-VO: Verordnung über künstliche Intelligenz*, edited by Mario Martini and Christiane Wendehorst. CH Beck, 2024.

Brownsword, Roger. 'Lost in Translation: Legality, Regulatory Margins, and Technological Management'. *Berkeley Technology Law Journal* 26 (2011): 1321–1365. https://doi.org/10.15779/Z38GH5M.

Choudhury, Prithwiraj, Balasubramanian, Natarajan, and Xu, Mingtao, 'Why Deepseek Shouldn't have been a Surprise'. *Harvard Business Review* 30 January 2025, https://hbr.org/2025/01/why-deepseek-shouldnt-have-been-a-surprise.

Christensen, Clayton M. *The Innovator's Dilemma: When New Technologies Cause Great Firms to Fail*. Cambridge, MA: Harvard Business Review Press, 1997.

Coad, Alex, Paul Nightingale, Jack Stilgoe, and Antonio Vezzani. 'Editorial: The Dark Side of Innovation'. *Industry and Innovation* 28, no. 1 (2021): 102–12. https://doi.org/10.1080/13662716.2020.1818555.

Daub, Adrian. *What Tech Calls Thinking. An Inquiry into the Intellectual Bedrock of Silicon Valley*. New York: Macmillan, 2020.

Dollinger, Jonathan. *Folgenabschätzungen für Verwaltungsalgorithmen*. Tübingen: Mohr Siebeck, 2023.

Fahey, Elaine. *Big Tech and EU Law. Transatlantic Lawyering, Lobbying and Litigating*. Cheltenham: Edward Elgar Publishing, 2025.

Gans, Joshua. *The Disruption Dilemma*. Cambridge, MA: MIT Press, 2016.

Graef, Eike, and Paul Nemitz. 'Addressing the Challenge of Protecting Fundamental Rights through AI Regulation in the European Union'. *UCLA Law Review* 71 (2023–2024): 144–55.

Gstrein, Oskar J, Noman Haleem, and Andrej Zwitter. 'General-Purpose AI Regulation and the European Union AI Act'. *Internet Policy Review* 13, no. 3 (August 2024): 2–26. https://doi.org/10.14763/2024.3.1790.

Kaal, Wulf A, and Erik PM Vermeulen. 'How to Regulate Disruptive Innovation – From Facts to Data'. *Jurimetrics* 57, no. 2 (2017): 1–43. https://doi.org/10.2139/ssrn.2808044.

Kaminski, Margot E. 'Binary Governance: Lessons from the GDPR's Approach to Binary Governance: Lessons from the GDPR's Approach to Algorithmic Accountability'. *Southern California Law Review* 92 (2019): 1529–616.

Kaminski, Margot E. 'The Right to Explanation, Explained'. *Berkeley Technology Law Review* 34 (2019): 189–218.

Kaminski, Margot E. 'Technological "Disruption" of the Law's Imagined Scene: Some Lessons from Lex Informatica'. *Berkeley Technology Law Journal* 36 (2021): 883–914.

Kaminski, Margot E, and Meg Lata Jones. 'Constructing AI Speech'. *Yale Law Journal* 133 (2024): 1212–66.

Kivimaa, Paula, et al. 'Moving Beyond Disruptive Innovation: A Review of Disruption in Sustainability Transitions'. *Environmental Innovation and Societal Transitions* 38 (2021): 12–30. https://doi.org/10.1016/j.eist.2020.12.001.

Koivisto, Ida, Riikka Koulu, and Stefan Larsson. 'User Accounts: How Technological Concepts Permeate Public Law through the EU's AI Act'. *Maastricht Journal of European and Comparative Law* 31, no. 3 (2024): 1–21. https://doi.org/10.1177/1023263X241248469.

Laux, Johann, Sandra Wachter, and Brent Mittelstadt. 'Three Pathways for Standardisation and Ethical Disclosure by Default under the European Union Artificial Intelligence Act'. *Computer Law & Security Review* 53 (2024): 105957.

Lepore, Jill. 'The Disruption Machine'. *The New Yorker* 90, 16 June 2014. www.newyorker.com/magazine/2014/06/23/the-disruption-machine.

Manu, Alexander. *The Philosophy of Disruption: From Transition to Transformational Change*. Leeds: Emerald Publishing Group, 2022.

Martini, Mario, and Wendehorst, Christiane. *KI-VO: Verordnung über künstliche Intelligenz*. Munich: CH Beck, 2024.

Micklitz, Hans-W. 'AI Standards, EU Digital Policy Legislation and Stakeholder Participation'. *Journal of European Consumer and Market Law* 13, no. 6 (2023): 212–25.

Mir, Oriol. 'The AI Act from the Perspective of Administrative Law: Much Ado About Nothing?' *European Journal of Risk Regulation*, 16 (2025): 63–75.

Pehlivan, Ceyhun Necati, 'The EU Artificial Intelligence Act: An Introduction'. In *AI Governance and Liability in Europe: A Primer*, edited by Ceyhun Necati Pehlivan, Nikolaus Forgó and Peggy Valcke. Leiden: Kluwer Law International, 2025. Available at SSRN: https://ssrn.com/abstract=5368880 or http://dx.doi.org/10.2139/ssrn.5368880

Paul, Regine. 'European Artificial Intelligence "Trusted Throughout the World": Risk-based Regulation and the Fashioning of a Competitive Common AI Market'. *Regulation & Governance*, no. 18 (2024): 1065–82.

Pougiet, Hadrien. 'What Will the Role of Standards be in AI Governance? Why Standards are at the Centre of AI Regulation Conversations and the Challenges they Raise'. *Ada Lovelace Institute* 5 April 2023, www.adalovelaceinstitute.org/blog/role-of-standards-in-ai-governance/.

Ruschemeier, Hannah. 'The De-Regulatory Turn of the EU Commission'. *Verfassungsblog*, 18 February, 2025, https://verfassungsblog.de/the-de-regulatory-turn-of-the-eu-commission/, doi: 10.59704/b61325ec5f72184a.

Saiger, Anna-Julia. 'Brussels Mirage: The EU AI Act's Subtle Shine Across International Borders' *EJIL:Talk!* 26 June 2025, www.ejiltalk.org/brussels-mirage-the-eu-ai-acts-subtle-shine-across-international-borders/.

Schmieg Lundgaard, Stine, Foss Rosenstand, and Claus Andreas. *Investigating Disruption: A Literature Review of Core Concepts of Disruptive Innovation Theory*. Aalborg: Aalborg University Press, 2019.

Schneider, Jens-Peter, Simon Oles, and Kester Siegrist. 'Collaborative Governance of the EU Digital Single Market Established by the Digital Services Act'. In *Governance of Automated Decision-Making and EU Law*, edited by Herwig Hofmann and Felix Pflücke (Oxford: OUP, 2024).

Schneider, Jens-Peter, Johannes Erny, and Franka Enderlein. 'Collaborative Governance Structures for Interoperability in the EU's New Data Acts'. *European Journal of Risk Regulation* (2024): 1–12. https://doi.org/10.1017/err.2024.46.

Schröter, Nico. *Pfadabhängigkeit und Recht: Rechtswissenschaftliche Rezeption eines sozialwissenschaftlichen Konzepts. Zugleich ein Theorieangebot zur Erklärung informeller Strukturbildung im Recht*. Tübingen: Mohr Siebeck, 2024.

Stevens, Hallam. 'Elon Musk's New Job Will Bring Tech "Disruption" to the US Government – and History Says it Won't be Pretty'. 18 November 2024, https://theconversation.com/elon-musks-new-job-will-bring-tech-disruption-to-the-us-government-and-history-says-it-wont-bc-pretty-243907.

Taplin, Jonathan. *Move Fast and Break Things: How Facebook, Google, and Amazon Cornered Culture and Undermined Democracy*. London: Macmillan, 2018.

Tushman, Michael L, and Philip Anderson. 'Technological Discontinuities and Organizational Environments'. *Administrative Science Quarterly* 31, no. 3 (1986): 439–65. https://doi.org/10.2307/2392832.

Van Cleynenbreugel, Pieter. 'EU By-Design Regulation in the Algorithmic Society'. In *Constitutional Challenges in the Algorithmic Society*, edited by Hans-W Micklitz et al. (Cambridge: CUP, 2021).

Veale, Michael, and Frederik Zuiderveen Borgesius. 'Demystifying the Draft EU Artificial Intelligence Act'. *Computer Law Review International* 4 (2021): 97–112. https://doi.org/10.48550/arXiv.2107.03721.

4

Embedding Proportionality in the Fundamental Rights Impact Assessment

ORESTE POLLICINO, FEDERICA PAOLUCCI, GIOVANNI DE GREGORIO, ANDREA COSENTINI, ANDREA ERMELLINO, DARIO FONTANELLA, NICOLE INVERARDI, ILARIA PENCO, DANIELE REGOLI AND SILVIA TESSARO TRAPANI

Abstract

As Regulation (EU) 2024/1689 (the AI Act) enters into force, the obligation to perform a Fundamental Rights Impact Assessment (FRIA) for certain high-risk AI systems marks a critical shift in EU digital governance. This chapter proposes a comprehensive framework, 'the FRIAct', for implementing this obligation in practice. Drawing on the normative foundations of the Charter of Fundamental Rights of the European Union (CFREU), particularly the principle of proportionality under Article 52(1) CFREU, the FRIAct model is structured in three sequential phases: a qualitative questionnaire, a semi-quantitative Matrix, and a legal proportionality assessment. The framework enables deployers to identify, evaluate, and justify interferences with fundamental rights across the AI lifecycle, ensuring that compliance is not merely procedural but substantively aligned with EU constitutional standards.

Keywords

Fundamental Rights Impact Assessment; AI Act; Fundamental Rights; Proportionality

I. Introduction

The world is watching. As artificial intelligence moves from experimental design to real-world deployment, it is not only technologies that are being tested, but the values and governance structures that accompany them. In the wake of the application of the Regulation (EU) 2024/1689 (AI Act), which is progressing,[1] the global community continues to seek answers and guidance regarding the appropriate management of AI-related risks.[2] These risks extend beyond the training phase of AI systems and reach into their real-world deployment, where they influence decision-making processes across both public and private sectors. In this context, the emergence of AI represents not merely the introduction of a new technology but the rise of a new mode of action and automation.[3]

In this context, the European Union's reaction has been the introduction of the AI Act with fundamental rights at the core of its risk-based approach.[4] These rights are understood not only as general legal guarantees but also as normative principles that can come into conflict, requiring careful reconciliation,[5] particularly considering the product safety orientation of the AI Act.

Among the instruments introduced by the AI Act, one of the most interesting obligations set out under the AI Act concerns precisely an evaluation of the different interests at stake, ie, at least that of the deployer and that of the individuals, in the use of AI, balancing them with the risks of harm and interferences with fundamental rights.[6] In this complex context, the FRIA emerges as a critical instrument

[1] Regulation (EU) 2024/1689 of the European Parliament and of the Council of 13 June 2024 laying down harmonised rules on artificial intelligence and amending Regulations (EC) No 300/2008, (EU) No 167/2013, (EU) No 168/2013, (EU) 2018/858, (EU) 2018/1139 and (EU) 2019/2144 and Directives 2014/90/EU, (EU) 2016/797 and (EU) 2020/1828 (Artificial Intelligence Act).

[2] Inter alia, Andrea Cosentini et al, *Assessing the Impact of Artificial Intelligence Systems on Fundamental Rights* (MediaLaws, 2025), www.medialaws.eu/assessing-the-impact-of-artificial-intelligence-systems-on-fundamental-rights/; Samuele Bertaina et al., 'Fundamental Rights and Artificial Intelligence Impact Assessment: A New Quantitative Methodology in the Upcoming Era of AI Act', *Computer Law & Security Review* 56 (2025): 106101, https://doi.org/10.1016/j.clsr.2024.106101.

[3] Oreste Pollicino, 'The Quadrangular Shape of the Geometry of Digital Power(s) and the Move towards a Procedural Digital Constitutionalism,' *European Law Journal* 29, nos. 1–2 (2023), https://doi.org/10.1111/eulj.12472.

[4] Anu Bradford, 'The Brussels Effect', *Nw. UL Rev.* 107 (2012): 1; Francesco Paolo Levantino and Federica Paolucci, 'Chapter 1 Advancing the Protection of Fundamental Rights through AI Regulation: How the EU and the Council of Europe Are Shaping the Future'. In *European Yearbook of Human Rights*, Volume 1, ed. Philip Czech, Lisa Heschl, Karin Lukas, Manfred Nowak, and Gerd Oberleitner (Leiden: Brill, 2025), https://doi.org/10.1163/9789004708389_002.

[5] Gianclaudio Malgieri and Cristiana Santos, 'Assessing the (Severity of) Impacts on Fundamental Rights', *Computer Law & Security Review* 56 (2025): 106113, https://doi.org/10.1016/j.clsr.2025.106113.

[6] The distinction between the concepts of harms or interferences with fundamental rights has been largely explored by the literature and it is not the direct scope of this chapter. However, it is worth saying that while interference refers to any limitation, restriction, or disruption of the exercise of a right or its essence, harm typically implies a more tangible or measurable detriment to the right-holder, often resulting from cumulative, systemic, or indirect effects. It is acknowledged this distinction to sustain the need of a proportionality-based approach, rather than just a risk one, that takes into consideration the context in which the AI system is deployed. Moreover, this distinction becomes particularly salient, as many rights interferences may not immediately manifest as discrete harms but nonetheless require regulatory attention due to their potential scale or societal impact. As a matter of fact, interferences are crucial to track down as they may also be justified in the proportionality test, as 'all interferences with fundamental rights can be assessed through the principle of proportionality and can hence be potentially justified'. Quote is from Maja Brkan, 'The Concept of Essence of Fundamental Rights in the EU Legal Order: Peeling the Onion to Its Core', *European Constitutional Law Review* 14, no. 2 (2018): 332–68, https://doi.org/10.1017/S1574019618000159. See also Malgieri and Santos, 'Assessing the (Severity of) Impacts on Fundamental Rights'.

designed to identify, assess, and mitigate the risks posed by AI systems prior to deployment.[7] More specifically, it requires that deployers of high-risk AI systems conduct a prior assessment of potential negative impacts on fundamental rights.

Nevertheless, despite its legal relevance, there is currently no standardised methodology for conducting FRIAs. While scholarly and regulatory discourse has begun to map the risks posed by these technologies, the practical operationalisation of FRIA remains in an early stage.[8] This is particularly critical for systems involving high-stakes decisions, such as credit scoring, one of the areas where the FRIA is explicitly mandatory, and for general-purpose AI models, which raise systemic and cross-cutting risks that are not easily captured by narrow compliance tools. Such risks may involve interferences with any of the 50 rights and freedoms protected under the CFREU. However, a crucial challenge arises not only in detecting these possible violations but also in understanding how to evaluate their legitimacy and acceptability.

Against this backdrop, the present work addresses this gap by proposing a structured FRIA framework that has a specific focus on the principle of proportionality, a cornerstone of EU constitutional law, enshrined in Article 52 of the CFREU.[9] This principle requires that any limitation on fundamental rights be legally grounded, respect the essence of the right in question, and be proportionate, that is, justified, necessary, and balanced in light of competing interests. As Lenaerts put it, 'proportionality offers in all cases the guarantee of a reasonable correlation between the measures envisaged or adopted and the objectives of the public interest pursued'.[10] Therefore, the proposed model is currently structured in three phases:

1) A context-sensitive Questionnaire, which gathers qualitative information about the system, its use case, and its affected population;
2) A semi-quantitative Matrix, which translates this information into measurable indicators of rights impact across the 50 rights and freedoms protected by the CFREU;
3) A proportionality assessment, based on Article 52(1) CFREU, which evaluates whether the interferences identified can be justified in light of democratic principles, legal necessity, and the preservation of the essence of the rights affected.

[7] AI Act, Article 27, Recital 93, 96.

[8] AI Act, Recital 93, 96.

[9] Steve Peers and Sacha Prechal, 'Article 52'. In *EU Charter of Fundamental Rights: A Commentary*, ed. Steve Peers, Tamara Hervey, Jeff Kenner, and Angela Ward (Oxford: Hart/Beck, 2021). See also Aharon Barak, 'The Components of Proportionality', in *Proportionality: Constitutional Rights and Their Limitations*, ed. Aharon Barak (Cambridge: Cambridge University Press, 2012), www.cambridge.org/core/books/proportionality/components-of-proportionality/2A08492882BC980F45181459278CE1B3; Brkan, 'The Concept of Essence of Fundamental Rights in the EU Legal Order'.

[10] Koen Lenaerts, 'Proportionality as a matrix principle promoting the effectiveness of EU law and the legitimacy of EU action', *ECB Legal Conference 2021 Continuity and change – how the challenges of today prepare the ground for tomorrow*, 25 November 2021.

From a methodological perspective, this chapter proposes an operational FRIA that links identified interferences to proportionate mitigations through a mixed-methods sequence, contextual scoping, a semi-quantitative rights Matrix, and a proportionality assessment (suitability, necessity, proportionality stricto sensu). While the twofold qualitative-quantitative phase provides a foundation for identifying and mapping risks, with the third phase, the FRIA is transformed from a diagnostic tool into a constitutionally grounded decision-making framework, capable of guiding deployers not only in understanding but also in justifying the use of AI systems in light of fundamental rights. The analysis uses observable indicators and thresholds for salience, interference, and mitigation, recorded in a decision log and revisited over the lifecycle. The model is offered as a proposal pilot to test consistency, feasibility, and risk-reduction in real deployments. The analysis will be deepened in the first part of the chapter on the theoretical legal basis of fundamental rights, as conceived in the European framework, and connected with the specific challenges of the FRIA. Then, the second part turns to the operational dimension, presenting a technical proposal for a structured FRIA model.

II. The FRIA in the AI Act

Article 27 of the AI Act is a key provision that ensures high-risk AI systems are used in a manner that respects fundamental rights. The FRIA aims to balance innovation with risk management. This represents a unique advancement in the regulatory landscape, setting a precedent for how AI should be managed and monitored, building on the Ethics Guidelines for Trustworthy AI and the White Paper on AI. A thorough FRIA is a measure to prevent potential abuses and unintended negative consequences of AI deployment.[11]

The FRIA is mandatory for deployers of some high-risk AI systems.[12] This obligation extends to deployers governed by public law, private operators providing public services, and operators deploying high-risk systems for the purpose of credit scoring, creditworthiness, or risk assessment and pricing of life and health insurance of natural persons.[13] By mandating FRIAs for these actors, the AI Act emphasises the importance of anticipating and mitigating risks to fundamental rights before deploying high-risk AI systems.

The FRIA must be performed prior to the initial deployment of the high-risk AI system and should be continued during the AI life cycle. This entails a thorough evaluation of the system's potential to affect fundamental rights adversely. For this reason, deployers may rely on previously conducted assessments, including those provided by the system's developer, provided the system's context of use

[11] AI Act, Article 27, Recital 96.
[12] AI Act, Article 43, Recital 96.
[13] AI Act, Annex III, Article 5 (b and c).

remains unchanged.[14] However, should any significant modifications arise during the system's use, such as changes in its purpose, affected populations, or identified risks, the deployer is obligated to update the assessment to reflect the new circumstances.[15]

The AI Act provides limited details on how the FRIA should be conducted, specifying the inclusion of usage descriptions, affected groups of people, and the identification of more vulnerable individuals, as well as potential risks and risk mitigation steps.[16] The assessment must comprehensively address the following aspects:

- System use and purpose: a detailed description of how the AI system will be integrated into the deployer's processes, ensuring alignment with its intended purpose.
- Operational parameters: an outline of the timeframe and frequency of the system's deployment.
- Affected individuals and groups: an identification of the categories of natural persons and communities likely to be impacted by the system, particularly marginalised or vulnerable groups.
- Risk analysis: a detailed evaluation of specific risks of harm that may arise from the system's use, with reference to information provided by the developer in compliance with Article 13 of the AI Act.
- Oversight and governance: a description of the human oversight measures that will be implemented, following the developer's guidelines.
- Mitigation measures: strategies to address the materialisation of identified risks, including internal governance mechanisms and accessible complaint procedures.

The assessment should then be reported to the market surveillance authority.[17] A standardised template from the AI Office is under elaboration to ensure consistent evaluations.[18]

From the listed essential requirements, a potential information asymmetry emerges between deployers and providers. Much of the information, such as operational parameters and instructions for use, must be shared by providers to conduct the assessment. It is, therefore, needed that the provider and the deployer cooperate.[19]

[14] AI Act, Article 27(2).
[15] AI Act, Article 27(2).
[16] AI Act, Article 27(1)(a-f).
[17] AI Act, Article 27(3).
[18] AI Act, Article 27(5).
[19] Piergiorgio Chiara and Federico Galli, 'Normative Considerations on Impact Assessments in EU Digital Policy', *MediaLaws*, no. 1 (July 2024), www.medialaws.eu/rivista/normative-considerations-on-impact-assessments-in-eu-digital-policy/.

A. Impact Assessment: Interoperability

Aside from the most recent initiatives of the European legislator, it is necessary to analyse the FRIA within the existing ecosystem of assessment practices in EU digital regulation and adjacent governance frameworks. The objective is not to invent a sui generis instrument, but to ensure that the FRIA can interoperate with established methodologies, reduce duplication, and provide a coherent pathway from risk identification.

In particular, the most direct link is to be ascertained with the Data Protection Impact Assessment (DPIA) under Article 35 General Data Protection Regulation (GDPR),[20] which addresses risks arising from personal data processing and culminates in an assessment of the necessity and proportionality of that processing, alongside a set of controls documented with the data protection officer. Where a DPIA is triggered, a FRIA should explicitly refer to, rather than replicate, its findings and import only those controls that are relevant for the deployment context. Nonetheless, GDPR compliance remains a separate legal determination of the assessment that can also be embedded in the FRIA, especially when looking at how personal data is processed.

Risk assessments under the Digital Services Act,[21] particularly for very large online platforms and search engines, take a platform-level perspective on systemic risks such as the dissemination of illegal content, threats to civic discourse, and broader effects on fundamental rights. Where AI systems are used for ranking, recommender systems, or content moderation, the DSA assessment and the FRIA are complementary rather than overlapping: the former evaluates systemic risks and due diligence measures at the service level, whereas the latter evaluates process-level interferences within the concrete organisational workflow in which the system is deployed. Cross-referencing outputs improves evidentiary consistency and avoids multiple, uncoordinated treatments of the same underlying risk.

Furthermore, interoperability requires methodological boundaries as well as interfaces. This is why the FRIA template should record linked assessment, document which controls are imported, and keep legal compliance checks outside its scope. To avoid checklist inflation and the expectation that all 50 CFREU rights are treated exhaustively in every case, the analysis should be guided by a rights materiality filter that identifies a core set of likely interferences for the use case and then extends coverage where salience is evidenced by context or stakeholder input. These connections show that DPIAs, DSA risk assessments, and the FRIA are not duplicative instruments but components of a layered governance architecture.

[20] Regulation (EU) 2016/679 of the European Parliament and of the Council of 27 April 2016 on the protection of natural persons with regard to the processing of personal data and on the free movement of such data, and repealing Directive 95/46/EC (General Data Protection Regulation).

[21] Regulation (EU) 2022/2065 of the European Parliament and of the Council of 19 October 2022 on a Single Market For Digital Services and amending Directive 2000/31/EC (Digital Services Act).

III. From Theory to Practice: A Proposal for Implementing the FRIA Framework

The FRIA framework, as conceptualised in the AI Act, is designed to systematically evaluate risks to fundamental rights posed by high-risk AI systems. Building on the theoretical foundations of the FRIA, it is necessary to move toward practical implementation. This framework, referred to as the Fundamental Rights Impact Assessment AI Act (FRIAct),[22] adopts a risk-based approach intended to proactively anticipate and mitigate adverse effects on fundamental rights before they occur by adopting a process divided into three main phases:

Phase 1 – Risk Classification Assessment, Intended Purpose, and Contextual Analysis. Identification of whether the system qualifies as high-risk and frames its intended use. This phase is crucial since it provides the foundation for the entire assessment by establishing the context necessary for justifying decisions made in subsequent phases.

Phase 2 – AI System Mapping & Monitoring. Examination of technical aspects and production of a Questionnaire Risk Indicator (QRI) that measures risks, controls, and safeguards. The questions in this phase are designed to produce the QRI, a continuous score ranging from 1 (lowest risk) to 10 (highest risk). Each specific answer in this phase is assigned a corresponding risk level, represented as an integer from 1 to 10.[23]

Phase 3 – Fundamental Rights Impact Evaluation. Synthesis of these findings by integrating the outputs of the Matrix Impact Scores (IS), Effort of Remediation (ER) and Robustness (R) into the questionnaire to calculate the FRIAct Scores, essentially one for each fundamental right analysed, and, therefore, defining explicit mitigation measures based on the findings of the analysis, as requested by the AI Act.[24] The calculation of the score will be complemented with a proportionality assessment of the obtained results, which serves to determine whether the identified interferences with fundamental rights can be lawfully justified under Article 52(1) CFREU, and whether the system, in its current or revised form, is eligible for deployment in compliance with EU constitutional standards.

[22] Bertaina et al, 'Fundamental Rights and Artificial Intelligence Impact Assessment'.

[23] For each section within Phase 2, a Section Risk Indicator is calculated as the average of the risk levels assigned to the answers within that section, resulting in a continuous score between 1 and 10. The QRI is then determined as the arithmetic average of all Section Risk Indicators across the questionnaire. However, specific high-risk answers, identified as potential blockers, may override the calculated Section Risk Indicator and compromise the entire assessment.

[24] AI Act, Article 27(1)(e).

Figure 4.1 A scheme of the assessment process, during which QRI and IS are calculated and then combined in the FRIAct Score. The process consists of two tools (Questionnaire and Matrix) and four Phases

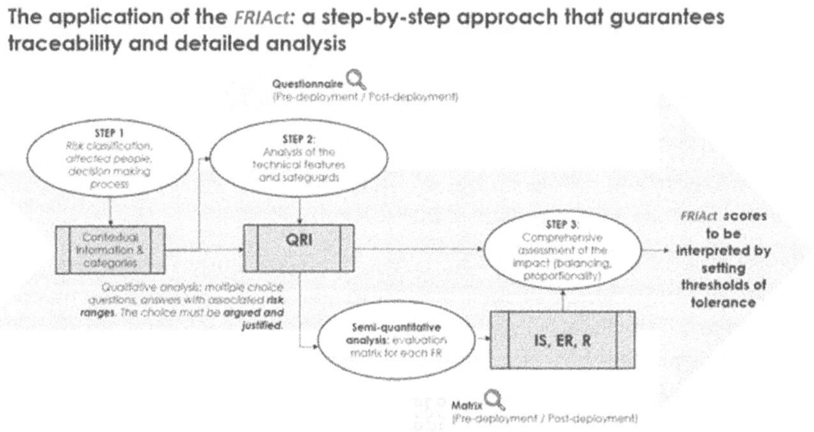

To achieve this objective, the FRIAct employs a two-pronged approach combining qualitative and quantitative tools: a questionnaire and a Matrix. The questionnaire is a qualitative tool structured to collect detailed contextual and technical information about the AI system. It serves as a foundation for understanding the system's purpose, design, and deployment environment, enabling a nuanced identification of risks and potential mitigations. Complementing this, the Matrix assesses the potential impacts on individual fundamental rights by calculating ISs, ER, and R mitigation factors, as described in detail in Section III.B. Together, these tools ensure a comprehensive and reproducible evaluation, bridging theoretical principles with actionable insights for compliance and risk mitigation.

The methodology that has been implemented to perform such an assessment is tailored to adapt across the lifecycle of AI systems, encompassing two critical phases: pre-deployment and post-deployment. The first assessment is conducted prior to system deployment, providing foundational insights for a 'Go/No-Go' decision. Whereas the post-deployment assessment, carried out periodically, evaluates the evolving performance and impacts of the system, ensuring ongoing alignment with fundamental rights obligations.[25] The integration of the Questionnaire and

[25] A key challenge in developing this methodology was integrating diverse AI technologies, such as Machine Learning, Generative AI, and General-Purpose AI systems, into a cohesive framework. By accommodating technological and operational differences, FRIACT provides a rational analysis of AI system impacts across varied use cases. For a distinction of the different characteristics of the technologies, see Giovanni Sartor, *L'intelligenza artificiale e il diritto* (Turin: Giappichelli, 2022); Oskar J. Gstrein et al., 'General-Purpose AI Regulation and the European Union AI Act', *Internet Policy Review* 13, no. 3 (2024), https://policyreview.info/articles/analysis/general-purpose-ai-regulation-and-ai-act.

Matrix ensures that 'the FRIAct' not only supports compliance with the AI Act but also advances best practices in responsible AI governance. The following sections detail the structure and application of these tools, followed by an in-depth analysis of the Questionnaire and the Matrix, illustrating how they work in tandem to support an effective FRIA process.

A. The Questionnaire

The questionnaire serves as the qualitative foundation of 'the FRIAct' framework, systematically analysing the AI system's design, deployment, and operational context to assess potential impacts on fundamental rights. To ensure adaptability across different stages of the AI system lifecycle, such as the pre-deployment and post-deployment, a specific questionnaire is carried out during the design stage, while a different questionnaire is dedicated to assessing the AI system in production, offering a comprehensive assessment process that aligns with the AI Act's requirements. The questionnaire is organised into three distinct phases, each addressing a critical aspect of the system's evaluation.

The first set of questions acknowledges whether the AI system qualifies as high-risk under Article 6 and Annex III of the AI Act and establishes the broader context of its deployment. Even if an AI system does not fall under the list included in Annex III of the AI Act, and, therefore, is not classified as high-risk, it can potentially impact natural persons significantly. In case the system is perceived to be potentially harming fundamental rights, then the deployer might consider performing 'the FRIAct' in any case.

Therefore, the objectives of this first phase of the questionnaire are:

Acknowledge whether the system falls under a certain high-risk category, initiating the obligation to conduct a FRIA.

Frame the AI system within the scope of its project, detailing its operational purpose and potential societal impact.

Map the lifecycle of the AI system, including key actors and affected persons.

Key questions of this phase include the understanding of the functionality of the system, the timeline and usage, the affected population, and the risk classification.

The second phase consists of several sections, each containing multiple-choice questions to which a risk level is assigned according to the answer selected. In this phase, the questionnaire evaluates the system's design, focusing on key risk factors like fairness, transparency, and human oversight. The risk level assigned to each question is averaged into Specific Risk Indicators for each section, which are then averaged into the QRI, which ranges from 1 (low risk) to 10 (high risk). Some questions include a 'blocking' answer, which, if selected, immediately halts the assessment. This response signals the need for system modifications, as it highlights design choices that could lead to unacceptable impacts. Table 4.1 provides an illustrative example of the type of questions addressed during the questionnaire phase of 'the FRIAct' methodology. These questions are structured to ensure a thorough analysis of the AI system's potential impacts on fundamental rights, both before deployment and throughout its operational lifecycle. Thus, the questionnaire provides essential information about the AI system's purpose, design, operational context, and affected populations, which serves as the foundation for Matrix analysis. For example, as it will be highlighted in Section III.B, the technical details captured in Phase 2, such as algorithm type, data governance practices, may have an impact on the calculation of Probability of Occurrence, while human oversight safeguards may impact the score assigned to Severity.

Then, the QRI summarises the AI system's risk profile across multiple dimensions (eg, transparency, fairness, oversight). This QRI, along with ER and R mitigation factors obtained from the Matrix, compose the Mitigation Factor (MF) of the final FRIAct Score calculation. While the questionnaire contextualises the risks based on operational and technical factors, the Matrix provides numerical IS scores to detail the magnitude, ER scores to detail the cost and R scores to detail the likelihood of impacts on individual rights. Together, these tools offer a comprehensive framework that integrates qualitative insights with quantitative analysis, ensuring risk management and compliance under the AI Act. The following grid presents some examples of the questions for Phase I and Phase II. While Phase I does not lead to obtaining a risk level, Phase II instead contains closed-ended questions with a risk score assigned to each possible answer.

Table 4.1 Example of questions in the questionnaire

Questions Phase I	
Categories	*Questions*
General Context	Describe the context and the specific purpose of the AI system.
High-Risk Classification	Is the AI system classified as High-risk under Article 6 of the AI Act and why?
Affected Groups	Are there any categories of natural persons that can be considered as more vulnerable groups? What are their specific risks?
Questions Phase II	
Technical Deployment	What type of algorithm(s) or model have been used? Please specify your choice and provide detailed examples. – a non-self-learning algorithm in which humans specify the rules the computer must comply to (choose a risk level from 1 to 3) – a System that is entirely or partially based on a self-learning algorithm, where the machine itself is finding patterns in the data (choose a risk level from 4 to 10)

(continued)

Table 4.1 ***(Continued)***

Data and Fairness	Are all input data (from internal and external sources), including third-party training data and data added by the Deployer, governed by data governance and data quality processes? - Yes, all, in compliance with GDPR, AIA and intellectual property (IP) requirements (risk level 1) - Only partially (eg, in case a model has been pre-trained by an external provider and there are no warranties about data used). Please specify (choose a risk level between 2 and 10) - No (blocking)
Transparency	Are the components of the AI system and their outputs explainable, interpretable, and/or verifiable? - Yes, all the components are designed to be explainable, interpretable, and/or verifiable. Describe what techniques are employed (choose a risk level from 1 to 3) - Not all the components of the AI system are explainable, interpretable, and/or verifiable. Describe what techniques are employed (choose a risk level from 4 to 10) - No (blocking)
Human Oversight	What is the degree of automated decision-making in the AI system? - The decision is taken by a human being and the AI system provides only an additional layer of information (choose a risk level between 1 and 2) - The decision is made by the application of AI system but is only executed after human review or approval (choose a risk level between 3 and 4) - The decision relies on the AI system, but it is possible for a human to override the outcomes (choose a risk level between 5 and 10) - The decision-making process is completely reliant on the AI system, without possibility for overrides (blocking)
Monitoring and Updates	If unfair behaviour emerges, will it be possible to intervene to correct it? - Yes, it will be possible to intervene (risk level 1) - No, it has not been possible to correct the unfair behaviour (blocking)

The FRIA is executed by a multidisciplinary team, in which legal expertise informs interpretation but does not convert the exercise into a compliance audit. Responsibility for compiling the assessment rests with a FRIA lead embedded in the deployment line, supported by product, technical, legal, and user-facing functions. This allocation preserves the process-level character of the FRIA, ensures that judgements decisions are taken by those who own the operational risk, and documents the evidentiary basis for the mitigation plan without purporting to determine legal compliance.

B. The Matrix

The second element, on which the assessment relies, is the Matrix, designed to evaluate the potential impact of an AI system on each fundamental right enshrined in the CFREU, unless differently specified by the European Commission in the upcoming template. By quantifying risks through structured dimensions and scores, the Matrix offers a granular, data-driven analysis of how an AI system might affect individuals and groups. It is built to ensure consistency, reliability, and adaptability throughout the two phases: pre-deployment and post-deployment.

This tool provides a semi-quantitative analysis of potential impacts on fundamental rights as protected and listed by the CFREU. The Matrix measures the risk to specific fundamental rights. To ensure reliable results, the data used in the Matrix must: a) extend beyond training datasets (eg, validation and test datasets) to represent the system's behaviour more comprehensively and reduce overfitting risks; b) be representative of the real population affected by the deployed AI system, as required by Article 10 of the AI Act.

While the AI Act itself does not prescribe either a fixed list or a minimum number of rights to be assessed, until the European Commission specifies otherwise through guidance, implementing acts, or harmonised standards, the analysis is the most comprehensive possible. This is why, at the moment, the Matrix is structured to consider all 50 rights enshrined in the CFREU. Each right is evaluated separately to ensure a comprehensive assessment. It is clear that the analysis should be guided by materiality so that attention is concentrated on interferences that are plausibly engaged by the specific deployment, since most AI uses in decision-support or allocation contexts, a core set will ordinarily be salient, human dignity (Article 1 CFREU), private life and data protection (Articles 7-8 CFREU), non-discrimination (Article 21 CFREU), freedom of expression and information (Article 11 CFREU), and effective remedy and fair process (Article 47 CFREU). It is the opinion of those who write that the FRIA record should state the rationale for rights selection, the evidence that triggered any extension beyond the core set, and the thresholds used for escalation, so that the Matrix remains proportionate, reproducible, and aligned with the proportionality analysis that follows.

The result of the Matrix consists of a distinct IS score for each right, representing the degree, to which the AI system impacts that particular right, an ER score, representing the range of measures and resources required to address and potentially reverse any unintended or harmful outcome produced by the AI system, and an R score, representing the robustness of the AI system. In the final FRIAct Score computation, the ISs compose the Impact Factor (IF) while ER and R scores, along with QRI, compose the MF.

The compilation of the Matrix for FRIAct has been supplemented by a *vademecum* proposed to enhance clarity and provide structured guidance for evaluating which fundamental rights might be impacted by an AI system. Table 4.2 shows examples of Articles 1, 7, 8, and 47.

Table 4.2 Excerpt from the *vademecum* for the Matrix compilation

Fundamental Right	Short Explanation	Example Guiding Questions
Article 1: Human Dignity	Forms the basis of EU values; impacts privacy, equality, and social security.	For decisions that materially affect individuals, does the deployment provide meaningful human review with authority to alter outcomes, context-appropriate explanations that affected persons can understand, and how are these arrangements verified post-deployment?
Article 7: Privacy	Ensures respect for private and family life; critical for gender equality and child protection.	Does the AI system collect personal data responsibly? Does it prevent unauthorised disclosure of private information?
Article 8: Data Protection	Protects data processing fairness and user access to rectification.	How does the system ensure data accuracy? Are processing practices transparent and aligned with GDPR requirements? Is a DPIA required; if so, is it completed?
Article 47: Fair Trial	Guarantees effective remedies and fair judicial processes.	Does the system provide clear reasoning for its decisions? Are there redress mechanisms for contesting AI outputs?

The Matrix evaluates risks and mitigation factors based on three key dimensions: Intensity,[26] hence the magnitude of the harm; robustness,[27] as the likelihood of

[26] For the purpose of our analysis, we define intensity as 'the extent or degree of harm on the protection of fundamental rights of a natural person or group that could occur if a risk is materialised'.

[27] For the purpose of our analysis, we define the robustness dimension as 'the likelihood to impact a fundamental right of a natural person or group of people due to the specific AI system performance'.

harm and the ER of the harm. To better simplify and to encapsulate the broadest picture possible on the potential infringement of fundamental rights:

Intensity: Measures the magnitude of potential harm, considering worst-case outcomes. It is the conceivable level of harm or damage that could result from a given risk. It considers the most severe possible outcome and classifies the gravity of that outcome based on its impact on a fundamental right.

R: The specific performance indicator of the AI system. In the pre-deployment Matrix it is an estimate of the performance (such as a functioning KPI), in the post-deployment Matrix it is the exact performance indicator.

ER: The range of measures and resources required to address and potentially reverse any unintended or harmful outcome produced by the AI system.

Each sub-dimension is assigned a score on a 1 to 10 scale, in particular:

Intensity

- 1–2 (Negligible)
  Harm is minimal and easily mitigated.
- 3–4 (Moderate)
  Noticeable but generally localised; potential impact remains reversible.
- 5–6 (Serious)
  Significant effects on an individual's well-being or rights.
- 7–8 (Severe)
  Major consequences, potentially involving long-term or broad-scale harm.
- 9–10 (Catastrophic)
  Profound, possibly irreversible impact on a fundamental right.

ER

- 1–2 (Trivial)
  Corrective actions are minimal; existing resources suffice.
- 3–4 (Modest)
  Remediation requires moderate effort and some coordination.
- 5–6 (Substantial)
  Demands notable resource allocation, possibly specialised expertise.
- 7–8 (High)
  Complex, time-intensive, and may disrupt operations.
- 9–10 (Nearly Impracticable)
  Extremely difficult or expensive to address, risking feasibility issues.

The R sub-dimension score is obtained using the complement of the AI system's performance indicator. For example, if the system's accuracy is 80 per cent (scored as eight out of 10), then the R sub-dimension score is calculated as $10-8 = 2$. As such, it is a truly quantitative measure. The IS score for each fundamental right is given by the intensity dimension estimation. Table 4.3 is a representation of the Matrix including the first 10 rights of the CFREU.

Table 4.3 Matrix visual representation

Fundamental Rights	**CFREU Article**	**IS**	**MFs**	
		Intensity	*ER*	*R*
CHAPTER 1: DIGNITY				
Human dignity	1			
Right to life	2			
Right to the integrity of the person	3			
Prohibition of torture and inhuman or degrading treatment or punishment	4			
Prohibition of slavery and forced labour	5			
CHAPTER 2: FREEDOMS				
Right to liberty and security	6			
Respect for private and family life	7			
Protection of personal data	8			
Right to marry and right to found a family	9			
Freedom of thought, conscience, and religion	10			

C. FRIAct: Integration of Questionnaire and Matrix

The Questionnaire and Matrix are designed to work together as core components of the FRIAct framework, ensuring a comprehensive evaluation of AI systems. While the questionnaire captures qualitative insights and contextual understanding, the Matrix provides semi-quantitative, rights-specific analysis. The integration of the questionnaire (QRI) and Matrix (IS, ER, R) results in the FRIAct Score, which provide actionable insights into the AI system's compliance and areas needing improvement. The third phase synthesises the QRI scores with the outputs of the Matrix (IS, ER, R) to calculate the FRIAct Scores for individual fundamental rights.

Figure 4.2 Flowchart displaying the relationship between the Questionnaire and the Matrix within the FRIAct framework

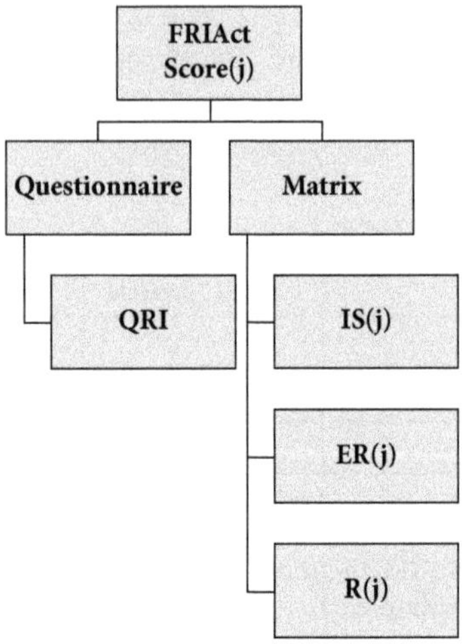

To produce a final, rights-specific score, we need to combine MFs QRI, ER(j), R(j) and impact factors IS(j) into a single index. We choose to do that using the product of the Impact Factor and the Mitigation Factor:

$$FRIAct\,Score\left(FR\left(j\right)\right) = Impact\,Factor\left(j\right) \times Mitigation\,Factor\left(j\right)$$

Where Impact Factor is IS(j) obtained from the Matrix and Mitigation Factor is the average of QRI, ER(j) and R(j).[28]

Thresholds and Outcomes:

FRIAct Score < 50: The system passes the assessment.
FRIAct Score between 50 and 75: The system requires mitigation or monitoring actions before development can proceed.
FRIAct Score ≥ 75: The system cannot be developed as planned and must be re-evaluated.

Mitigation and Reporting:

Any section with a Risk Indicator of 75 or higher must be highlighted and described in detail before closing the assessment.
For scores requiring mitigation (50–75), implement the necessary actions and rerun Phases 2 and 3 to verify compliance.

[28] As we said above the Mitigation Factor is the average of the Risk Indicator provided by the questionnaire, the Effort of Remediation and the Robustness of the AI system for the specific fundamental right: $MF(j) = (\frac{QRI + ER(j) + R(j)}{3})$.

Thus, the integration of the Questionnaire and Matrix culminates in the calculation of FRIAct Scores for each fundamental right. These scores provide actionable insights for deployers and regulators by highlighting specific rights at risk and guiding mitigation strategies. The two instruments are intertwined in every phase. Hence, during the design phase, the questionnaire identifies potential risks, and the Matrix evaluates projected impacts. Together, they guide system adjustments before deployment. Then, post-deployment, the questionnaire updates contextual and operational insights, while the Matrix recalculates IS, ER, and R scores using real-world performance data.

The questionnaire integrates the quantitative part of the FRIAct, gathering contextual and operational data about the AI system, including its intended purpose, affected populations, and technical characteristics. These insights are essential for setting the parameters used in the Matrix. The questionnaire produces a QRI, summarising the system's overall risk profile. This QRI serves as a baseline for the Matrix by weighting its calculations of the IS, ER, and R scores. It helps align qualitative assessments (eg, operational context, technical safeguards) with the numerical risk levels calculated in the Matrix. Then, this latter one translates the general risk areas identified in the questionnaire into precise, measurable impacts on individual fundamental rights.

This iterative process ensures that the AI system adapts to evolving risks and maintains compliance throughout its lifecycle. By leveraging their combined outputs, deployers can proactively address risks to fundamental rights, comply with the AI Act, and foster ethical and responsible AI governance.

D. The FRIAct Lifecycle

With respect to instructions related to the frequency of the assessment, it is advised to perform the FRIAct in two phases for every AI system subject to assessment: once during the pre-deployment phase and periodically thereafter through the post-deployment phase.

A pre-deployment assessment should start as early as possible in the system lifecycle, before release, so that design choices remain flexible and can be adjusted to prevent fundamental-rights infringements and avoid costly rework, preserving the feasibility of the deployment strategy. After release, periodic reassessment is required to capture changes in performance and operating context; monitoring is not a mere confirmation of initial assumptions, but a data-rich re-evaluation based on real-world evidence. As a rule of thumb, post-deployment reviews should occur every 12–18 months, with shorter intervals for cutting-edge systems or those that scored high in the FRIAct pre-deployment phase.

These two phases are then combined with a last third one, the Fundamental Rights Impact Evaluation, to ensure that the use of AI systems not only complies with the AI Act but also aligns with ethical and societal values, safeguarding fundamental rights at every stage of the system's lifecycle.

IV. Fundamental Rights Impact Evaluation: The Proportionality Assessment

While the first two phases of 'the FRIAct' framework enable deployers to systematically identify and classify risks to fundamental rights, they do not in themselves offer a method for determining whether those risks may be lawfully accepted. Hence, building upon the results of the semi-quantitative Matrix (Phase II), which translates the contextual and systemic information gathered through the questionnaire (Phase I) into a structured rights-risk score, in the proportionality phase the score assume the function of a diagnostic indicator: it synthesises the extent to which the system, as it currently stands, interferes with one or more fundamental rights.[29]

As a matter of fact, a high FRIAct Score (eg, 7 or above) indicates not only that the system poses a significant risk to one or more fundamental rights, but also that critical safeguards are missing or insufficient, whether in terms of human oversight, data minimisation, explainability, redress mechanisms, or contextual limitations on the system's use. Conversely, a lower score is not merely the reflection of an inherently risk-free system. Rather, it may also be the result of a well-calibrated response to such identified risks. In such cases, the system may indeed generate potential interferences with fundamental rights, but these might be proactively addressed and mitigated through effective deployment choices, the context and the measures in place.[30] This is, in essence, the function of the proportionality assessment: to assess not whether risk is present, since a 'zero-risk' scenario is both unrealistic and unnecessary, but whether the response to that risk is adequate.

The proportionality test thus enables a shift in focus: from mapping impacts to evaluating the quality and legitimacy of the reactions to those impacts. In this way, this third phase of 'the FRIAct model' ensures that risk is not only identified but also examined and justified within the framework of EU fundamental rights. In other words, the FRIA score preconditions the legal plausibility of any proportionality justification: the higher the score, the narrower the space for legitimate interference.

[29] This section applies the tripartite proportionality test recognised by the Court of Justice under Article 52(1) CFREU, suitability, necessity, and proportionality stricto sensu, as elaborated in landmark judgments such as *Digital Rights Ireland* (C-293/12), *Tele2 Sverige/Watson* (C-203/15 & C-698/15), Opinion 1/15 (EU–Canada PNR), *La Quadrature du Net* (C-511/18, C-512/18, C-520/18), and *Schrems II* (C-311/18). For a literature perspective, see Przemyslaw Palka and Jan Czarnocki, *Proportionality in EU Digital Law : Balancing Conflicting Rights and Interests* (Oxford: Hart Publishing, 2024), www.torrossa.com/it/resources/an/5868939.

[30] For instance, in *Schrems I*, the CJEU found not only substantial violations of fundamental rights, but moreover a lack of adequate procedural safeguards that did not prevent an open access to public authorities on the users' personal data, 'compromising the essence of the fundamental right to respect for private life, as guaranteed by Article 7 of the Charter', and 'does not respect the essence of the fundamental right to effective judicial protection, as enshrined in Article 47 of the Charter'. See *Maximillian Schrems v Data Protection Commissioner*, Case C-362/14 (ECJ October 6, 2015). https://eur-lex.europa.eu/legal-content/EN/TXT/?uri=CELEX:62014CJ0362, §94-95.

However, the role of the proportionality test extends beyond assessing whether rights interferences are justified. In 'the FRIAct model', proportionality serves as a prism through which the entire assessment output is re-evaluated, and the deployment decision is ultimately shaped. Provided that the Charter applies, pursuant to Article 51(1) CFREU, the relevant rights might be interpreted in light of the three-step structure recognised by the Court of Justice: 1) identification of the right at stake; 2) determination of interference; and 3) evaluation of whether that interference can be justified under Article 52(1).[31] This justification process, in turn, is composed of four interrelated conditions: a) the interference must be provided for by law; b) it must respect the essence of the right; c) it must serve a legitimate aim recognised by Union law; and d) it must be proportionate, meaning suitable, necessary, and balanced in its effects.[32]

Thus, the FRIA score does not by itself determine the legality of an AI system, but it activates this structured proportionality inquiry. Importantly, it is out of the scope of this chapter and this analysis to assert the horizontal application of Article 52 CFREU.[33] Instead, in this case, it is drawn inspiration from the proportionality test and then is applied as a method of reviewing the justifiability of results, using Article 52(1) CFREU as a legal closure mechanism to ensure that the identified interferences are both identified and evaluated against the standards of EU constitutional law, before and during the AI deployment.[34] In this sense, proportionality in Phase III functions as both a filter and a lens: a filter that screens out deployments that cannot be legally justified, and a lens that aligns FRIA outcomes with the broader requirements of fundamental rights compliance in the digital constitutional framework of the Union. The FRIA does not purport

[31] Koen Lenaerts et al, 'Fundamental Rights and General Principles of Union Law', in *EU Constitutional Law*, ed. Koen Lenaerts et al (Oxford: Oxford University Press, 2021), https://doi.org/10.1093/oso/9780198851592.003.0025; Koen Lenaerts, 'Exploring the Limits of the EU Charter of Fundamental Rights', *European Constitutional Law Review* 8, no. 3 (2012): 375–403, https://doi.org/10.1017/S1574019612000260.

[32] Tobias Lock, 'Article 52 CFR', in *The EU Treaties and the Charter of Fundamental Rights: A Commentary*, ed. Manuel Kellerbauer et al (Oxford: Oxford University Press, 2019), https://doi.org/10.1093/oso/9780198759393.003.577.

[33] While the importance of the topic is acknowledged, its analysis goes beyond the scope of the Chapter. The authors refer to a broader literature on the topic, as in Eleanor Spaventa, *The Horizontal Application of Fundamental Rights as General Principles of Union Law* (Oxford: Hart Publishing, 2011); Lorenzo Cecchetti, 'Unravelling Horizontal Direct Effect in EU Law: The Case of the Fundamental Right to Paid Annual Leave between "Myth" and "Practice"', *Yearbook of European Law* 42 (April 2023): 42–83, https://doi.org/10.1093/yel/yead012; Eleni Frantziou, '(Most of) the Charter of Fundamental Rights Is Horizontally Applicable: ECJ 6 November 2018, Joined Cases C-569/16 and C-570/16, Bauer et Al', *European Constitutional Law Review* 15, no. 2 (2019): 306–23, https://doi.org/10.1017/S1574019619000166.

[34] We rely on the CJEU proportionality framework not to import a courtroom exercise into the FRIA, but to anchor design and governance choices in a settled constitutional standard that already structures administrative and regulatory decision-making in the Union. In this setting, proportionality operates *ex ante* as a discipline for justification: it requires the deployer to articulate a legitimate aim, to document less intrusive but comparably effective alternatives, to adduce evidence of effectiveness for selected measures, and to account for residual interferences, thereby producing a decision record that is reviewable by internal governance and, where relevant, by market surveillance authorities.

to determine legality; formal compliance determinations remain within the appropriate instruments and fora (for example, a DPIA under the GDPR). Scores and matrices in the FRIA are therefore heuristics that structure judgement and make it auditable; they do not substitute the legal authority of courts.

Therefore, the proportionality assessment in Phase III of the FRIAct model is structured in three steps, reflecting the formulation adopted by the Court of Justice of the European Union (CJEU):

Suitability (or appropriateness): the measure (ie, the AI system or its mode of deployment) must be suitable for achieving a legitimate aim, such as public safety, health protection, or effective public administration. This step requires a rational connection between the AI system and the objective it pursues.

Necessity: the deployer must demonstrate that no less intrusive but equally effective alternative exists. This requires a comparative analysis of design choices, safeguards, or non-AI alternatives that could achieve the same result with fewer restrictions on rights.

Proportionality *stricto sensu* (balancing): this step involves weighing the benefits of deploying the AI system against the costs it imposes on fundamental rights. The question here is whether the societal gains (eg, efficiency, security, innovation) are justified in light of the rights sacrificed, and whether the essence of the right is preserved.

Together, these steps provide a structured method for deployers to move from identification to legal justification, ensuring that the deployment of high-risk AI systems respects the balance required under EU law between technological innovation and the fundamental rights of individuals. In the following, the analysis will concretely address the test, connecting it with the I and II phases.

The proportionality test introduced in Phase III must be applied in direct continuity with the outcomes of Phases I and II. These scores not only indicate which rights are at risk, but also how serious and likely those risks are to materialise. This combined diagnostic output (FR) forms the entry point into the proportionality test: a system scoring high (eg, FR > 50) on key rights must be subject to strict scrutiny, in line with Article 52(1) CFREU.

The deployer must now demonstrate whether the identified rights interferences can be legally justified by showing they are i) suitable, ii) necessary, and iii) proportionate in the strict sense. Crucially, to complete this test coherently and validly, the deployer must revisit the answers provided in the Questionnaire and the Matrix. These previous phases contain not only the factual basis for risk classification but also the justifications and assumptions that must align with the legal reasoning applied in Phase III. For example, if the questionnaire indicates that no alternative models were considered, this has direct implications for the necessity test. Similarly, Matrix scores indicating severe impacts on vulnerable groups must be addressed under the balancing step.

Thus, the test is composed of three steps, theoretically explained above, with target questions to be answered by the compiler. Table 4.4 provides a structured application pathway.

Table 4.4 Presentation of the proportionality assessment

Step	Test objective	Input source	Guiding questions
1. Suitability	Rational link to legitimate aim	Questionnaire: Purpose + System Type	Does the system's function match its declared goal? Is the rights interference coherent with the stated public interest?
2. Necessity	Evaluation of less intrusive but equally effective alternatives	Questionnaire + Matrix	Were simpler or more explainable models considered? Are safeguards (eg, human oversight) missing where FR scores are high?
3. Proportionality ***stricto sensu***	Balancing of benefits and rights cost	Matrix: IS, ER, R + Vulnerable Groups	Are societal gains sufficient to justify the rights burden? Do risks fall disproportionately on marginalised individuals or groups?

Once the three-step proportionality test has been completed, the final task is to reconcile the legal assessment with the Matrix scores and reach a deployment decision. The deployer must categorise the outcome as one of the following, as described in Table 4.5.

Table 4.5 Operationalisation of the steps

Proportionality outcome	FRIAct Score (FR)	Final decision
All three steps passed	Low/Moderate (FR ≤ 50)	Deployable: the system may be used with standard safeguards and monitoring
Suitability/ necessity acceptable, balancing weak	Medium/High (FR > 50)	Conditionally deployable: must revise design, enhance mitigation, or restrict scope, to evaluate in connection with Phase I and II
Necessity and/or balancing failed	High (FR ≥ 70)	Not deployable: major redesign or withdrawal required

As shown in the last table, the proportionality test is deeply connected with the FRIAct Score and the result of the analysis conducted in the first two phases. Although building on the evidentiary base constructed in Phases I and II, it allows deployers to transition from mapping risks to legally assessing their justifiability under Article 52(1) CFREU. This phase does not produce a new numerical output. Rather, it enables a structured legal 'reasoning' process aimed at determining whether the interferences identified can be reconciled with the EU constitutional requirement that rights limitations be suitable, necessary, and proportionate *stricto sensu*. In doing so, it provides the framework to translate the diagnostic work of the previous phases into an operational deployment decision that evaluates rights not only as a list but also in contraposition with one another, and moreover, in light of the deployment context.

The proportionality phase in FRIAct is a structured justification exercise, not a quasi-judicial determination. Grounded in Article 52(1) CFREU and the Court's tripartite test, it requires the deployer to state a legitimate aim, seriously consider less intrusive but comparably effective alternatives, select measures on an evidence basis, and account for residual interferences in a decision log. It does not decide legal compliance; where formal determinations are needed, they are made through the appropriate instruments, and FRIAct records only the outcomes relevant to risk treatment and operational governance. Applied to deployment decisions, the test yields three typical outcomes. Where all criteria are met and the Matrix indicates a low–moderate rights impact, deployment may proceed with standard oversight and lifecycle monitoring. Where the result is mixed, suitability and necessity are established, but the balancing remains fragile: deployment is permissible only subject to conditions such as narrowed scope, reinforced mitigations, or defined *ex post* controls, particularly in cases with medium-to-high salience scores. Where necessity or proportionality *stricto sensu* fails, especially at high impact (eg, FR ≥ 70), the system should not be deployed in its current form; redesign, restriction, or withdrawal is required in line with the fundamental-rights framework and the AI Act's risk-based approach.[35] Ultimately, the proportionality assessment is what ensures that the FRIA does not remain a formalistic or procedural compliance exercise but rather becomes a substantive and constitutionally grounded decision-making framework.

V. LoanLens: A Testing Ground Use Case

The following section illustrates how the FRIAct can be applied to a practical scenario. The use case involves an AI system used for credit scoring, a high-risk area under the AI Act,[36] due to its potential impact on individuals' fundamental rights. This example, while fictitious, is designed to be plausible and representative of real-world applications.

[35] As in, for instance, the 'stop button' precisely mentioned in Article 14 of the AI Act.
[36] Annex III, 5(b) AI Act.

A. Overview of the AI System

The AI system that we are considering has the purpose of calculating the credit scoring of natural persons. The presented scenario consists of a bank that currently relies on a traditional Machine-Learning System (MLS) to calculate a credit score for individual customers. This system draws on four primary indicators:

1. *A rating derived from 100 creditworthiness variables:* this composite rating is built from a wide array of data points reflecting an individual's financial behaviour, such as historical repayment patterns, outstanding debt levels, credit utilisation ratios, length of credit history, and other factors that statistically correlate with credit risk;
2. *An early warning system:* this mechanism is designed to continuously monitor customers' activities and external signals that might hint at a decline in creditworthiness. For example, if a pattern of missed payments emerges or there is adverse news about a customer's employer, the early warning system raises alerts. By flagging these signals promptly, the bank can take proactive measures, such as requesting updated documentation or revising credit limits, to mitigate potential losses;
3. *Transactional or affordability data:* these data reflect the customer's ongoing financial obligations and day-to-day cash flows. Typical examples include monthly spending patterns, recurring bills, salary deposits, and other income streams. By assessing whether the borrower's incoming funds can support their current (and potentially additional) debt, the system can estimate affordability and likelihood of timely repayment;
4. *A metric representing financial wealth:* this indicator provides insight into the customer's broader financial standing, often accounting for assets such as real estate, investment portfolios, or savings. A higher wealth metric generally suggests more capacity to handle debt, while a lower metric may signal limited resources to manage unforeseen financial strains.

Building on this existing infrastructure, the bank proposes to integrate a conversational Decision Support System (DSS) powered by GenAI.[37] In practice, the credit score computed by the machine learning systems (MLS) is fed into the GenAI model along with various unstructured data sources (eg, documents submitted during the credit application and historical customer profile data). Through a chatbot interface, called LoanLens,[38] a human decision-maker gains a single, centralised access point for receiving credit score outputs and requesting additional analysis and information about customers applying for loans. The AI

[37] A Generative AI component (eg a large language model, also LLM) is used in the fictitious AI system as a point of interaction between the user and the system.

[38] LoanLens is a fictitious name given to the system that in no way represents real systems, tests, or experiments.

system's output will be a numerical score ranging from 1 to 100, where 1 is the lowest credit score and 100 is the highest achievable score.

To aid quick and consistent decision-making, the bank categorises this numerical score using a traffic light threshold framework:

Red Zone (1–40): High credit risk, possibly requiring additional collateral or higher interest rates.

Yellow Zone (41–70): Moderate credit risk, suggesting further verification steps or more stringent monitoring.

Green Zone (71–100): Low credit risk, indicating eligibility for more favourable terms and expedited approval.

The person who makes the final decision on the loan application can rely on the given score or override it, providing a justification that explains the reasons for the disagreement. In this scenario, we assume that the GenAI component is a pre-trained model, developed by an external provider and then fed with purpose-specific data.

The GenAI model complements the MLS by synthesising additional insights and providing a more user-friendly interface for human decision-makers. Here is how it works:

1. Data flow:

   The MLS generates a credit score based on its structured input indicators.
   This credit score, along with unstructured data (eg, documents submitted during the credit application, historical customer profiles), is fed into the GenAI model.

2. Interface and functionality:

   LoanLens, the chatbot interface powered by the GenAI engine, acts as a single access point for human decision-makers.
   LoanLens allows managers to:

   - View the MLS-generated credit score.
   - Request deeper analyses or additional context about a customer's profile.
   - Interact in natural language to extract insights or locate relevant information efficiently.

3. Output:

   The AI system's output will be a numerical score ranging from 1 to 100, where 1 is the lowest credit score and 100 is the highest achievable score. To aid quick and consistent decision-making, the bank categorises this numerical score using a traffic light threshold framework:

   - Red Zone (1–40): High credit risk, possibly requiring additional collateral or higher interest rates.
   - Yellow Zone (41–70): Moderate credit risk, suggesting further verification steps or more stringent monitoring.

- Green Zone (71–100): Low credit risk, indicating eligibility for more favourable terms and expedited approval.

Human decision-makers can use this score as a suggestion but retain the authority to override it, providing a justification when doing so.

In this setup, the GenAI component is a pre-trained model provided by an external developer, further refined with purpose-specific data to ensure alignment with the bank's credit scoring needs.

The operational flow of the AI system ensures seamless integration between structured and unstructured data processing. In particular, the GenAI component:

Utilises natural language prompts to process inputs and generate insights.

Extracts relevant information from submitted documents, historical data, and credit scores.

Synthesises this information into a user-friendly format, allowing managers to interact solely with LoanLens for all decision-support needs.

LoanLens simplifies access to layered information in one place, enabling quicker and more informed decision-making. In this sense, the natural language interface eliminates the need for technical expertise, making it accessible to a broader range of users.

A central design feature of this system is its emphasis on human oversight, as mandated by Article 14 of the AI Act. The following mechanisms ensure that human responsibility remains at the forefront:

1. Final decision:

   LoanLens provides suggestions and information, but all final decisions remain the responsibility of human decision-makers.
   Decision-makers can override or disregard the output, providing explanations for any discrepancies.

2. Stop mechanism:

   At any point, LoanLens can be stopped by the user to prevent unintended consequences, satisfying the Article 14(3) of the AI Act requirement for a 'stop button' feature.

3. Risk mitigation:

   By keeping the GenAI system in a supportive, rather than fully autonomous, role, the design minimises potential risks to fundamental rights, such as privacy violations or discrimination.

To ensure reliability and robustness, both the MLS and DSS components are tested rigorously before full deployment. These metrics are essential for compiling the post-deployment Matrix, particularly for assessing the R sub-dimension:

1. MLS Performance:

   The MLS must achieve a classification accuracy of at least 80 per cent in credit lending decisions during pre-deployment testing.
   This benchmark ensures the MLS reliably evaluates structured indicators like creditworthiness and financial health.

2. DSS Performance:

   The DSS must demonstrate at least 90 per cent accuracy in responding to human-posed queries or locating relevant documents within the system.
   This ensures the DSS provides meaningful, accurate support to decision-makers.

3. Deployment Criteria:

   The system transitions to production only after both components meet their respective performance thresholds, ensuring a foundation for real-world operations.

B. The Application of the FRIAct

In the following paragraphs, we will show the most relevant results of the FRIA assessment conducted for LoanLens.

In Phase 1, it is acknowledged that LoanLens is a high-risk AI system under Article 6 and Annex III of the AI Act due to its role in determining access to credit, a private service with significant implications for fundamental rights. This classification is critical because credit scoring decisions can affect socioeconomic opportunities, such as housing and employment.

The system impacts two primary groups:

Individuals applying for loans: These individuals directly rely on the AI-generated credit scores for access to credit services.

Vulnerable groups: especially younger applicants that may have a 'thin file', ie, having little or no credit history, and groups of individuals identified by sensitive characteristics potentially subject to algorithmic bias, such as foreigners, women, and persons with disabilities.

This phase establishes the broader context for LoanLens, emphasising its societal relevance and the need for stringent risk assessment.

Phase 2 dives into the technical components of LoanLens, assessing specific risks across key operational dimensions. Each dimension is assigned a Specific Risk Indicator, which contributes to the QRI. Here is presented an excerpt of the pre-deployment questionnaire and referenced in Table 4.6:

1. Deployment Process:

   LoanLens integrates a non-self-learning MLS and a self-learning GenAI component to process structured and unstructured data.

The Risk Level for this dimension is 7.5, reflecting the complexity of combining these technologies and the systemic risks posed by the GenAI component. Alternative, simpler algorithms were considered but deemed insufficient due to lower accuracy, reinforcing the need for this advanced system.

2. Input Data and Fairness:

   The MLS complies with rigorous data governance standards, mitigating many risks. However, reliance on an external provider for the GenAI component introduces residual risks related to bias and transparency.

   This results in a Risk Level of 2.4, indicating moderate risk.

3. Transparency:

   The MLS outputs are explainable and interpretable, while the GenAI's chatbot interface ensures verifiable insights for human decision-makers.
   This yields a Risk Level of 1.2, reflecting low risk in this area.

4. Human Oversight:

   The system maintains strong human oversight mechanisms, allowing decision-makers to override or halt the AI's operations, as required by Article 14 of the AI Act.
   A Risk Level of 1 indicates robust safeguards and minimal risk.

5. Monitoring and Maintenance:

   LoanLens includes monthly monitoring protocols and emergency update mechanisms to address emerging issues. These processes ensure continued compliance and adaptability.
   The Risk Level for this dimension is 2.5, representing moderate risk.

Table 4.6 Pre-deployment questionnaire results

Section	**Risk Indicator (RI)**
Deployment Process	7.5
Input Data and Fairness	2.4
Explainability and Transparency	1.2
Performance	4.0
Human Oversight	1.0
Monitoring and Maintenance	2.5
QRI	***3.1***

The Matrix quantifies the system's impact on fundamental rights by evaluating ISs, ER, and R for each relevant right. Nine rights of the CFREU have been evaluated as potentially impacted by the AI system in this context, namely, Article 1 (Human Dignity), Article 6 (Right to liberty and security), Article 9 (Right to marry and right to found a family), Article 16 (Freedom to conduct a business), Article 17 (Right to property), Article 25 (The rights of the elderly), Article 26 (Integration of persons with disabilities), Article 33 (Family and professional life), Article 36

(Access to services of general economic interest). Table 4.7 presents a visual of the Matrix, calculated on the nine fundamental rights mentioned.

Table 4.7 LoanLens pre-deployment Matrix

CFREU Article	Fundamental Right	IS	Mitigation Factors	
		Intensity	ER	R
1	Human Dignity	10	2	2
6	Right to liberty and security	6	2	2
9	Right to marry and right to found a family	6	2	2
16	Freedom to conduct a business	10	2	2
17	Right to property	10	2	2
25	The rights of the elderly	7	2	2
26	Integration of persons with disabilities	10	2	2
33	Family and professional life	8	2	2
36	Access to services of general economic interest	10	2	2

Despite high ISs for some rights, strong control measures and human oversight safeguards reduce the ER and R dimensions.

Before addressing the completion of individual entries, it may be useful to investigate the values for ER and R. As it is possible to see, the values chosen are always the same: 2 for ER and 2 for R. These values are determined by the strong presence of the human oversight component and the high-performance estimation.

Assessing Article 1 CFREU, we assign a 10/10 intensity: a wrongful loan denial can gravely undermine personal dignity, agency, and self-worth. For Article 6 CFREU (liberty and security), intensity is 6/10, reflecting the way credit constraints can limit access to essentials tied to security and freedom. Article 9 CFREU (right to marry and found a family) is likewise set at 6/10, as access to personal credit can condition the practical exercise of family formation. Article 16 of the Charter (freedom to conduct a business) warrants 10/10 given its direct dependence on financing; the same reasoning supports a 10/10 for Article 17 (property). Article 25 CFREU (elderly) is set at 7/10: erroneous denials can exacerbate exclusion by restricting participation and autonomy. Article 26 CFREU (persons with disabilities) receives 10/10 because additional, recurring costs make access to credit pivotal for effective inclusion. The considerations applied to Article 16 CFREU also support a high intensity for Article 36 CFREU (access to services of general economic interest), given the obvious economic linkage. Finally, for Article 33 CFREU (family and professional life), we assign 8/10, since financial instability can materially disrupt work–family balance.

Eventually, the considerations regarding the choices made during the completion of the pre-deployment Matrix, it is important to focus on the difference between IS and mitigation factors values of the individual articles, as empirically shown by Table 4.8. As can be seen, IS are high scores while mitigation factors are all low scores despite the significantly high intensity values. This is possible due to the design decisions that were made, in addition to the strong human oversight involved in determining the final output. This control is appropriately positioned between the production of the output and the individual potentially impacted by it. Such intermediation allows for quicker detection of errors in the assessment of the loan applicant and ensures the prompt intervention of the designated manager responsible for this task.

Table 4.8 Pre-deployment FRIAct Score

	Impact Factor	**Mitigation Factors**			
CFREU Article	**IS**	**QRI**	**ER**	**R**	**FRIAct Score (%)**
1	10	3.1	2	2	23.67
6	6	3.1	2	2	14.20
9	6	3.1	2	2	14.20
16	10	3.1	2	2	23.67
17	10	3.1	2	2	23.67
25	7	3.1	2	2	16.57
26	10	3.1	2	2	23.67
33	8	3.1	2	2	18.93
36	10	3.1	2	2	23.67

Post-deployment, the questionnaire incorporates real-world implementation information. As per the pre-deployment, Table 4.9 presents an excerpt of the post-deployment results.

Table 4.9 Post-deployment questionnaire results

Section	**Risk Indicator (RI)**
Deployment Process	7.5
Input Data and Fairness	2.4
Explainability and Transparency	1.2
Performance	4.0
Human Oversight	1.0
Monitoring and Maintenance	2.5
Ownership and Control	10
QRI	**4.1**

The post-deployment Matrix, represented by Table 4.10, takes into account the AI system specific performance indicator to evaluate the R dimension. For this toy example, as described above, the ML component has to achieve an accuracy of 80 per cent to be effectively deployed, so the R indicator is:

$$\text{Robustness} = 10 - \text{Accuracy} = 10 - 8 = 2$$

Table 4.10 Post-deployment Matrix results and FRIAct Scores

	Impact Factor	**Mitigation Factors**			
CFREU Article	**IS**	**QRI**	**ER**	**R**	**FRIAct Score (%)**
1	10	4.1	2	2	27.00
6	6	4.1	2	2	16.20
9	6	4.1	2	2	16.20
16	10	4.1	2	2	27.00
17	10	4.1	2	2	27.00
25	7	4.1	2	2	18.90
26	10	4.1	2	2	27.00
33	8	4.1	2	2	21.60
36	10	4.1	2	2	27.00

Finally, based on the outputs of the questionnaire (QRI = 4.1) and Matrix (IS up to 10 for several rights), the proportionality test, summarised in Table 4.11, allows us to evaluate whether the identified interferences with fundamental rights can be justified under Article 52(1) CFREU. The test is conducted by checking whether the system is (1) suitable for achieving its declared aim, (2) necessary in light of possible alternatives, and (3) proportionate in the strict sense, meaning that the benefits justify the rights burden.

Table 4.11 Fundamental Rights Impact Evaluation: proportionality assessment

Element	**Evaluation**
Suitability	LoanLens is designed to improve the efficiency and accuracy of credit scoring decisions. As confirmed by the questionnaire, this design aligns directly with the Bank's stated goal of reducing processing time while ensuring reliability in credit allocation. Given this close correspondence between means and ends, the system is suitable to pursue its legitimate aim.
Necessity	This step assesses whether less rights-intrusive alternatives could achieve the same purpose. While the MLS uses structured indicators, the introduction of the GenAI component increases the system's complexity and opacity. However, the questionnaire confirms that simpler models were tested and rejected due to

(continued)

Table 4.11 ***(Continued)***

Element	Evaluation
	insufficient performance. Crucially, the Matrix shows consistently low values for both ER = 2 and R = 2 across all evaluated rights in post-deployment. This reflects the presence of robust human oversight, including the possibility for decision-makers to override the AI output and provide justifications. Therefore, the system meets the necessity condition, especially given the fact that less intrusive instruments produced less curate results.
Proportionality stricto sensu	While several rights receive high ISs, these scores must be interpreted together with the mitigation values. The uniformly low ER and R ratings reflect the system's design architecture, which centres human control and procedural accountability. The bank has implemented clear override procedures, a stop mechanism, and internal decision review protocols, all of which contribute to reducing the likelihood and intensity of harm. In light of this and considering the public interest in accurate and fair credit allocation, the system can be considered proportionate in the strict sense, provided the current safeguards remain in place and are periodically monitored.

Although the system presents high rights ISs, these are effectively managed through ex-ante mitigation strategies, particularly in terms of explainability, oversight, and manual control. The proportionality assessment thus validates the system's legal acceptability, provided that existing safeguards are preserved, and that the system remains subject to ongoing evaluation, especially in terms of fairness and group-level disparities. On this, lifecycle adjustments are essential for maintaining compliance. The system is, as a matter of fact, reassessed in cases of significant modifications, such as changes to the GenAI model or new deployment contexts. These iterative assessments ensure LoanLens evolves responsibly and aligns with the FRIA's standards.

VI. Conclusion

This chapter advances an operational framework to perform a FRIA in compliance with the AI Act. The framework is rooted in the principles enshrined in the CFREU and operationalised through a combination of qualitative and semi-quantitative tools, specifically the Questionnaire and the Matrix, and a proportionality assessment. Together, these instruments provide a structure for evaluating the risks posed by AI systems, particularly high-risk applications such as those involving GenAI and other advanced technologies. Moreover, proportionality here is not a courtroom exercise: it disciplines design and governance *ex ante* by requiring a stated legitimate aim, documented consideration of less intrusive alternatives, evidence for chosen measures, and a reasoned account of residual interferences in a decision log. This step transforms the FRIA from a diagnostic tool into a normative decision-making instrument: one that does not stop at identifying risks but goes further to evaluate whether those risks can be legitimately justified in a democratic society.

The framework's flexibility makes it applicable to a wide range of AI systems, from traditional machine learning models to sophisticated GenAI systems. This adaptability is particularly evident in the LoanLens use case, which demonstrates how the FRIAct framework can be applied to assess the risks associated with a hybrid credit-scoring system that combines structured data analysis with generative AI capabilities.

In conclusion, the FRIAct framework exemplifies how AI governance can balance innovation with the protection of fundamental rights. The model remains a proposal and invites empirical validation. Greater regulatory coherence would follow from Commission guidance or harmonised standards clarifying interfaces between the FRIA and other impact assessments in and out of the AI Act. Properly implemented, the FRIA offers a practicable route to embed fundamental rights in day-to-day AI operations, turning abstract guarantees into auditable design choices and accountable deployment decisions. By providing a structured, replicable, and context-sensitive approach to risk assessment, the framework not only meets the compliance needs of the AI Act but also contributes to building a rights-centred digital ecosystem.

Bibliography

Alpaydın, Ethem. *Machine Learning*. Cambridge, MA: MIT Press Essential Knowledge series, 2016.

Barak, Aharon, ed. 'The Components of Proportionality'. In *Proportionality: Constitutional Rights and Their Limitations*. Cambridge: Cambridge University Press, 2012. www.cambridge.org/core/books/proportionality/components-of-proportionality/2A08492882BC980F45181459278CE1B3.

Bertaina, Samuele, Ilaria Biganzoli, Rachele Desiante, et al. 'Fundamental Rights and Artificial Intelligence Impact Assessment: A New Quantitative Methodology in the Upcoming Era of AI Act'. *Computer Law & Security Review* 56 (April 2025): 106101. https://doi.org/10.1016/j.clsr.2024.106101.

Bradford, Anu. 'The Brussels Effect'. *Nw. UL Rev.* 107 (2012): 1.

Brkan, Maja. 'The Concept of Essence of Fundamental Rights in the EU Legal Order: Peeling the Onion to Its Core'. *European Constitutional Law Review* 14, no. 2 (2018): 332–68. https://doi.org/10.1017/S1574019618000159.

Cecchetti, Lorenzo. 'Unravelling Horizontal Direct Effect in EU Law: The Case of the Fundamental Right to Paid Annual Leave between "Myth" and "Practice"'. *Yearbook of European Law* 42 (April 2023): 42–83. https://doi.org/10.1093/yel/yead012.

Chiara, Piergiorgio, and Federico Galli. 'Normative Considerations on Impact Assessments in EU Digital Policy'. *MediaLaws*, no. 1 (July 2024). www.medialaws.eu/rivista/normative-considerations-on-impact-assessments-in-eu-digital-policy/.

Cosentini, Andrea, Oreste Pollicino, Giovanni De Gregorio, et al. *Assessing the Impact of Artificial Intelligence Systems on Fundamental Rights*. MediaLaws, 2025. www.medialaws.eu/assessing-the-impact-of-artificial-intelligence-systems-on-fundamental-rights/.

Frantziou, Eleni. '(Most of) the Charter of Fundamental Rights Is Horizontally Applicable: ECJ 6 November 2018, Joined Cases C-569/16 and C-570/16, Bauer et Al'. *European Constitutional Law Review* 15, no. 2 (2019): 306–23. https://doi.org/10.1017/S1574019619000166.

Gstrein, Oskar J, Noman Haleem, and Andrej Zwitter. 'General-Purpose AI Regulation and the European Union AI Act'. *Internet Policy Review* 13, no. 3 (2024). https://policyreview.info/articles/analysis/general-purpose-ai-regulation-and-ai-act.

Lenaerts, Koen. 'Exploring the Limits of the EU Charter of Fundamental Rights'. *European Constitutional Law Review* 8, no. 3 (2012): 375–403. https://doi.org/10.1017/S1574019612000260.

Lenaerts, Koen, Piet Van Nuffel, and Tim Corthaut. 'Fundamental Rights and General Principles of Union Law'. In *EU Constitutional Law*, edited by Koen Lenaerts, Piet Van Nuffel, and Tim Corthaut. Oxford: Oxford University Press, 2021. https://doi.org/10.1093/oso/9780198851592.003.0025.

Levantino, Francesco Paolo, and Federica Paolucci. 'Chapter 1 Advancing the Protection of Fundamental Rights through AI Regulation: How the EU and the Council of Europe Are Shaping the Future'. In *European Yearbook of Human Rights*, Volume 1, edited by Philip Czech, Lisa Heschl, Karin Lukas, Manfred Nowak, and Gerd Oberleitner. Leiden: Brill, 2025. https://doi.org/10.1163/9789004708389_002.

Liu, Ziwei, Shuai Yang, Yuming Jiang, and Ziqi Huang. 'Generative Networks'. In *Handbook of Face Recognition*, edited by Stan Z Li, Anil K Jain, and Jiankang Deng. Cham: Springer International Publishing, 2024. https://doi.org/10.1007/978-3-031-43567-6_3.

Lock, Tobias. 'Article 52 CFR'. In *The EU Treaties and the Charter of Fundamental Rights: A Commentary*, edited by Manuel Kellerbauer, Marcus Klamert, and Jonathan Tomkin. Oxford: Oxford University Press, 2019. https://doi.org/10.1093/oso/9780198759393.003.577.

Malgieri, Gianclaudio, and Cristiana Santos. 'Assessing the (Severity of) Impacts on Fundamental Rights'. *Computer Law & Security Review* 56 (April 2025): 106113. https://doi.org/10.1016/j.clsr.2025.106113.

Maximillian Schrems v Data Protection Commissioner, Case C-362/14 (ECJ October 6, 2015). https://eur-lex.europa.eu/legal-content/EN/TXT/?uri=CELEX:62014CJ0362.

Palka, Przemyslaw, and Jan Czarnocki. *Proportionality in EU Digital Law: Balancing Conflicting Rights and Interests*. Oxford: Hart Publishing, 2024. https://www.torrossa.com/it/resources/an/5868939.

Peers, Steeve and Sacha Prechal, 'Article 52'. In *EU Charter of Fundamental Rights: A Commentary*, ed. Steve Peers, Tamara Hervey, Jeff Kenner, and Angela Ward (Oxford: Hart/Beck, 2021)

Pollicino, Oreste. 'The Quadrangular Shape of the Geometry of Digital Power(s) and the Move towards a Procedural Digital Constitutionalism'. *European Law Journal* 29, nos. 1–2 (2023). https://doi.org/10.1111/eulj.12472.

Sartor, Giovanni. *L'intelligenza artificiale e il diritto*. Turin: Giappichelli, 2022.

Spaventa, Eleanor. *The Horizontal Application of Fundamental Rights as General Principles of Union Law*. Oxford: Hart Publishing, 2011.

5

Navigating Transparency Obligations for Companion Chatbots under the European Union AI Act: Evaluation and Policy Directions

RACHAEL OLAITAN ABORISHADE

Abstract

This chapter examines the inadequacy of the transparency obligations for interactive AI systems under Article 50(1) of the EU Artificial Intelligence Act (AI Act) in addressing the unique risks posed by companion chatbots, particularly those simulating romantic or emotionally intimate relationships. These disembodied AI programmes leverage natural language processing to foster empathetic and persuasive dialogue, often resulting in deeply personal – even therapeutic interactions. Their entry into the consumer market and mental health support sector raises ethical concerns about emotional deception, coerced self-disclosure, and psychological manipulation. Despite documented harms, ranging from hallucinations to dependency and impaired decision-making, romantic chatbots remain ambiguously positioned within the Act's risk-classification framework.

The study argues that treating these systems as low-risk, subject only to the minimal disclosure requirements of Articles 50(1) and 50(5) of the AI Act, fails to address their design complexities and user vulnerabilities. Employing a doctrinal and socio-technical approach, it draws on behavioural design principles and empirical data to expose this regulatory gap. The chapter proposes either raising classification thresholds or imposing additional transparency requirements in practice, alongside extending the obligations under Article 50(2). These recommendations advocate lifecycle-based oversight of both development and deployment to safeguard users' mental health, autonomy, and fundamental rights. By critically evaluating interactive AI disclosures, this work highlights a missed opportunity within the AI Act to meaningfully regulate romantic chatbots and offers concrete policy proposals for future reform.

Keywords

Companion chatbots; Transparency obligations; EU AI Act; Emotional manipulation; Risk classification

I. Introduction

'Networked individualism'[1] caused by the internet has impacted AI-human relationships, leading to a decline in face-to-face intimacy.[2] Although machines cannot genuinely care, they have entered the care space both clinically and consumer-wise. Companion chatbots are an effective AI implementation of this radicalisation of human relationships and the notion of care. The rise of companion chatbots has seen a significant increase in user engagement across the EU, reflecting a broader trend in the adoption of AI-driven companionship.[3] Studies indicate that almost 1.5 million people have interacted with chatbots in the past year, showcasing their growing presence in the digital landscape.[4] Research suggests that these technologies can provide cost-effective and accessible support to individuals experiencing depression.[5]

In this chapter, companion chatbots[6] are 'disembodied'[7] programmes or applications, that utilise AI and natural language processing technologies to naturally and intelligently 'converse' with users through text (with some having voice and images or avatar features). They provide various types of 'mental health support'[8] through empathetic and romantic conversations,[9] creating relational bonds unlike utility chatbots and robots. Examples include Replika (the main bot for this study), Anima, Soulmate, Kajiwoto, and Character.AI.[10] It should be noted that, although

[1] Barry Wellman, 'Physical Place and Cyberplace: The Rise of Personalized Networking', *International Journal of Urban and Regional Research* 25, no. 2 (2008): 227–52.

[2] Harley Davies, 'Social Media and Personal Relationships: Online Intimacies and Networked Friendship', Information, Communication and Society 17, no. 2 (2014): 279–81.

[3] Fokina Maryia, 'The Future of Chatbots: 80+ Chatbot Statistics for 2025', *TIDIO*, 18 October 2024, www.tidio.com/blog/chatbot-statistics/.

[4] ibid.

[5] Gilly Dosovitsky et al, 'Artificial Intelligence Chatbot for Depression: Descriptive Study of Usage', *JMIR Formative Research* 4, no. 11 (2020): 1–13.

[6] Also referred to as companion bots, romantic chatbots, virtual lovers, or AI friends in this chapter.

[7] Kwan M Lee et al, 'Are Physically Embodied Social Agents Better than Disembodied Social Agents? The Effects of Physical Embodiment, Tactile Interaction, and People's Loneliness in Human–Robot Interaction', *International Journal of Human-computer Studies* 64, no. 10 (2006): 962–73.

[8] Iryna Pentina et al, 'Exploring Relationship Development with Social Chatbots: A Mixed-Method Study of Replica', *Computers in Human Behavior* (2023): 140; Anne Zimmerman, 'Human/AI Relationships: Challenges, Downsides, and Impacts on Human/Human Relationships', *AI and Ethics* 4 (2023): 1555–67; Auren R Liu et al, 'Chatbot Companionship: A Mixed-methods Study of Companion Chatbot Usage Patterns and Their Relationship to Loneliness in Active Users', version 3, preprint, arXiv, 2024, https://doi.org/10.48550/ARXIV.2410.21596.

[9] Lee et al., 'Are Physically Embodied Social Agents Better than Disembodied Social Agents', 974.

[10] Zimmerman, 'Human/AI Relationships: Challenges, Downsides, and Impacts on Human/Human Relationships', 1559.

this chapter focuses on companion bots in the form of AI friends or lovers, it is important to recognise that the conversational engagement and persuasive qualities of general purpose chatbots can foster emotional attachment – whether as a result of their design or the predispositions of users themselves. Such attachment is observable even in interactions with bots not explicitly designed or marketed as AI companions, such as Copilot, ChatGPT, and in-app social media chatbots.[11] This underscores the need for regulatory attention that extends beyond development to encompass deployment.

Human personification tendencies towards non-humans accrue through constant interaction.[12] Companion chatbots are inherently designed to attract emotional connections through communication,[13] aiming to provide benefits[14] such as companionship for depression and loneliness reduction and aiding mental wellness or cognitive behavioural therapy.[15] However, these benefits substituting human relationships are not ethically consensual.

Paradoxically, the emotional relationship with an object that cannot think or feel blurs the line between human-made and AI-generated content and between benefits and risks. These side effects, especially for vulnerable users, stem from interacting with companion bots, 'roleplaying'[16] human-like connection and emotional reciprocity. This one-sided relationship[17] deceives users, providing a false image of sentience. The interaction contrasts with the value of a message, which includes the conveyed emotions behind the content.[18]

(Un)intended risks[19] or harms include psychological manipulation or deception (leading to overreliance, parasocial trust, lack of autonomy), hallucinations, privacy and data protection issues (particularly from self-disclosures), and ethical dilemmas. These interconnected issues could lead to mental health problems, infringe on fundamental rights, and impact various types of decision-making, including financial decisions, thereby undermining transparency aimed

[11] Sahar Habib Ghazi, 'Can You Get Emotionally Dependent on ChatGPT?', *Greater Good Magazine*, 23 July 2025, https://greatergood.berkeley.edu/article/item/can_you_get_emotionally_dependent_on_chatgpt; David Adam, 'Supportive? Addictive? Abusive? How AI Companions Affect Our Mental Health', *Nature*, 6 May 2025, www.nature.com/articles/d41586-025-01349-9.

[12] Ghazi, 'Can You Get Emotionally Dependent on ChatGPT?', 1555.

[13] Ghazi, 'Can You Get Emotionally Dependent on ChatGPT?'.

[14] Rose Guingrich and Michael SA Graziano, 'Chatbots as social companions: How people perceive consciousness, human likeness, and social health benefits in machines', *Arxiv*, 21 September 2023, https://arxiv.org/html/2311.10599v2.

[15] Katarzyna Stawarz et al, 'User Experience of Cognitive Behavioral Therapy Apps for Depression: An Analysis of App Functionality and User Reviews', *Journal of Medical Internet Research* 20, no. 6 (2018).

[16] ibid.

[17] Adriana Braga and Robert Logan, 'The Emperor of Strong AI Has No Clothes: Limits to Artificial Intelligence', *Information* 8, no. 4 (2017): 156.

[18] Zimmerman, 'Human/AI Relationships: Challenges, Downsides, and Impacts on Human/Human Relationships', 1555.

[19] It is difficult to argue that these harms are wholly unintended when their design features have been deliberately incorporated. The AI Act recognises that some risks may be intentional, purposeful, or at least foreseeable, making it implausible that companies are unaware of the inherent dangers in the systems they put into the market.

at informational self-determination and empowerment. If beneficial, regulating the design, distribution, and usage of these AI interactive 'knockoffs'[20] or 'social spillovers'[21] through lifecycle regulatory oversight is necessary.

While companion bots used as eHealth tools or for clinical prescriptions in the healthcare sector may invoke high-risk AI system provisions[22] of the EU Artificial Intelligence Act (AI Act),[23] the position of domestically used romantic chatbots is not clear and arguably falls under 'limited' or 'low' risk,[24] with providers subjected to lenient transparency obligations in Article 50(1) and (5) AI Act. The AI Act is not the only law with transparency requirements that may apply to these chatbots. However, this chapter focuses on the AI Act's transparency obligation because, unlike the General Data Protection Regulation (GDPR),[25] the Digital Services Act (DSA),[26] or other consumer protection laws such as the Consumer Right Directive (CRD),[27] Unfair Contract Terms Directive (UCTD),[28] or the Unfair Commercial Practices Directive (UCPD), the AI Act regulates the system's lifecycle, performance, and output.[29]

This chapter argues that the transparency obligations for interactive AI systems may not be adequate to manage user perception, design complexities, and the resulting harms from romantic chatbots. Merely informing users at the first point of interaction, especially vulnerable users, may not convey the chatbot's limitations, detriments, and capabilities.[30] Therefore, a clear position regarding romantic

[20] Phil Klaus and Judy Zaichkowsky, 'AI Voice Bots: A Services Marketing Research Agenda', *Journal of Services Marketing* (2020) 2.

[21] Lara SG Piccolo et al, 'Chasing the Chatbots Directions for Interaction and Design Research', *Internet Science International Workshops, St. Peterburg, Russia* (2018): 157–69, 157.

[22] It is noteworthy to emphasise that this may not always hold true, as providers can circumvent high-risk obligations, particularly under Article 6(3), and may not necessarily qualify as medical devices. Indeed, this highlights the persistent lack of clarity surrounding the regulation of companion bots and how they may slip through the cracks of regulatory uncertainty.

[23] Regulation (EU) 2024/1689 of the European Parliament and of the Council of 13 June 2024 laying down harmonised rules on artificial intelligence and amending Regulations (EC) No 300/2008, (EU) No 167/2013, (EU) No 168/2013, (EU) 2018/858, (EU) 2018/1139 and (EU) 2019/2144 and Directives 2014/90/EU, (EU) 2016/797 and (EU) 2020/1828 (Artificial Intelligence Act) (Text with EEA relevance), PE/24/2024/REV/1, OJ L, 2024/1689.

[24] Thomas Gils, 'A Detailed Analysis of Article 50 of the EU's Artificial Intelligence Act' *KU Leuven – Centre for IT & IP Law (CiTiP)* (2024), https://papers.ssrn.com/sol3/papers.cfm?abstract_id=4865427.

[25] eg, Articles 12–14 of the GDPR.

[26] eg, Articles 17, 26,29, and 34; Regulation (EU) 2022/ 2065 of the European Parliament and of the Council of 14 December 2022 on a Single Market for Digital Services and amending Directive 2000/31/EC (Digital Services Act).

[27] eg, Article 7; Directive 2011/83/EU of the European Parliament and of the Council of 25 October 2011.

[28] eg, Article 5; Council Directive 93/13/EEC of 5 April 1993 on unfair terms in consumer contracts.

[29] Z Li, 'Why the European AI Act Transparency Obligation is Insufficient', *Nature Machine Intelligence* 5 (2023): 559–60, 2, https://eprints.gla.ac.uk/300842/2/300842.pdf.

[30] Information is only given 'at the time of the first interaction'. Typically, providers inform users of synthetic content in privacy notices or terms of service but often omit the detriments of using the bot. This issue arises because the law primarily requires only a disclosure that the content is synthetic. Therefore, two issues arise from this disclosure provision: the timing and manner of the disclosure, and whether the content sufficiently raises user awareness and education.

chatbots under the AI Act is necessary. If they are not classified as prohibited or high-risk AI systems, they should be subject to additional transparency requirements in Article 50(2) of the AI Act, rather than only those in Articles 50(1) and (5) AI Act. This chapter contributes to existing knowledge by examining the inadequacy of the transparency obligation for interactive AI systems, specifically companion chatbots under Article 50(1) AI Act. It briefly highlights theoretical concepts or frameworks borrowed from behavioural science and design that evidence the outcome and risk of harms of such interaction, establishing that it would be a missed opportunity for the AI Act to consider classifying companion chatbots as low-risk AI systems subject to non-stringent transparency obligations for user safety. Furthermore, the chapter provides a brief overview of the existing literature on which it builds, noting that prior work did not examine the risks posed by companion chatbots in the context of the AI Act and thereby extends the existing body of knowledge (Section II). It then examines the psychological harms and the risks of self-disclosure that can arise from AI companionship (Section III.A). The following section evaluates the cumulative transparency obligations in Articles 50(1) and (5) AI Act, establishing their insufficiency for the use case of the interactive AI system (Section III.B). In fulfilling its policy recommendation aim, it provides a two-fold recommendation: heightening risk thresholds (Section IV.A) or applying additional transparency requirements, which could serve as interim measures (Section IV.B). These proposals shed light on how these bots can be regulated and guide the possibility of any future policy amendments for policymakers and stakeholders to enhance transparency measures, ensuring protection of fundamental rights, safety, and health, and the human-centric approach of placing on market, putting into service, and use of romantic chatbots. Section V concludes the chapter.

II. Literature Review

This sub-chapter reviews the existing literature on AI-human relationships, the psychological and ethical implications of companion chatbots, and the regulatory landscape governing these AI systems. By examining these studies, this chapters identifies gaps that, to the best of the author's knowledge, the current literature has not addressed, particularly regarding the risk classification of romantic bots and the transparency obligations applicable to them. It assesses whether these requirements are proportionate to the potential risks and explores directions for addressing these inadequacies.

Zimmerman[31] explores the complex dynamics of human–AI relationships, highlighting the challenges and negative impacts these relationships can have

[31] Zimmerman, 'Human/AI Relationships: Challenges, Downsides, and Impacts on Human/Human Relationships'.

on human-to-human interactions. The study discusses issues such as emotional dependency on AI, reduced social skills, and ethical concerns around AI companionship. The chapter underscores the necessity of addressing these downsides to ensure healthy human relationships in an AI-driven world. Stawarz and others[32] analyse the functionality and user reviews of cognitive behavioural therapy (CBT) apps designed for depression. The study highlights key features that contribute to positive user experiences, such as ease of use, interactivity, and personalised content. The authors also identify common user complaints, including technical issues and lack of human touch, suggesting areas for improvement in future app development.

Brandtzaeg et al[33] examine how users perceive their relationships with social chatbots. The study reveals that users often anthropomorphise chatbots, attributing them with human-like qualities and forming emotional bonds. The research underscores the importance of designing chatbots that are aware of these tendencies and can manage user expectations to prevent dependency and ensure healthy interactions. Carmichael and colleagues[34] investigate how different types of nudges influence users' willingness to disclose personal information to chatbots. The study finds that certain nudges, such as social proof and reciprocity, can significantly increase information disclosure. These findings have important implications for the design of chatbots.

Vasse'i and Udoh[35] explore the relationship between transparency and trust in AI systems. The paper argues that while transparency is crucial, it is not a panacea for all trust-related issues. The authors propose a multi-faceted approach to building trust in AI, which includes transparency, accountability, and user education. The study emphasises the importance of a holistic strategy in addressing the ethical and social implications of AI. Gils[36] provides an in-depth analysis of Article 50 of the AI Act, which outlines transparency requirements for AI systems. The paper examines the legal implications of these requirements and discusses their impact on AI developers and users. Gils argues that while the transparency obligations are a step in the right direction, they need to be more clearly defined to ensure effective implementation and compliance. Li[37] critiques the transparency obligations outlined in the AI Act, arguing that they are insufficient to ensure true accountability and trustworthiness of AI systems. The paper suggests that more stringent and specific transparency measures are necessary to address the complex

[32] Stawarz et al, 'User Experience of Cognitive Behavioral Therapy Apps for Depression: An Analysis of App Functionality and User Reviews'.

[33] Bae P Brandtzaeg et al, 'My AI Friend: How Users of a Social Chatbot Understand Their Human–AI Friendship', *Human Communication Research* 48, no. 3 (2022): 404–29.

[34] Laurie Carmichael et al, 'Users' Information Disclosure Behaviors during Interactions with Chatbots: The Effect of Information Disclosure Nudges', *Applied Sciences* 12, no. 24 (2022).

[35] Ramak M Vasse'i and Gabriel Udoh, 'In Transparency We Trust?' *Mozilla Foundatio* (2024) https://foundation.mozilla.org/en/research/library/in-transparency-we-trust/.

[36] Gils, 'A Detailed Analysis of Article 50 of the EU's Artificial Intelligence Act'.

[37] Li, 'Why the European AI Act Transparency Obligation is Insufficient'.

challenges posed by AI technologies. Li also discusses the potential consequences of inadequate transparency for both developers and users. In summary, existing literature highlights the significant psychological and ethical implications of companion chatbots, as well as the regulatory challenges in ensuring transparency and accountability of AI-generated content. While studies provide insights into these impacts and suggest that mere information disclosure and the AI Act's transparency obligations are inadequate, there remains a notable gap in the regulatory measures governing romantic bots. This chapter addresses this gap by examining the shortcomings of the AI Act's transparency obligations for interactive AI systems, particularly companion bots used in domestic settings. It proposes robust policy recommendations to improve these measures.

III. AI Companionship and the Transparency Requirements for Interactive AI Systems

A. Evidencing the Harms Posed by Companion Bots

i. Psychological Harm

The social penetration theory posits that recurring interactions and information exchange with personal meaning tend to build deep connections or relationships.[38] The interdependence theory also emphasises the importance of reciprocity and the depth of information exchange in conceptualising relationships.[39] Additionally, according to the investment model, the size of investment and level of commitment play significant roles in strengthening relationships.[40] When applied to AI-powered companion bots, these mechanisms explain how features like frequent personalised messaging, prompts for self-disclosure, and in-app reward systems can simulate intimacy, foster reciprocity, and elicit escalating user investment, thereby creating the very attachments that expose users to risks of psychological manipulation and dependency. This theoretical grounding highlights why transparency and accountability measures under the AI Act are essential.

Companion chatbots are designed to mimic human conversation closely, which can lead to users to perceive them as human-like or mistake them for human dialogue. These chatbots engage in complex, context-aware conversations and often provide emotional support and personal advice. Such false impressions

[38] Kristin J August and Karen S Rook, 'Social Relationships', in *Encyclopedia of Behavioral Medicine* (New York: Springer, 2013): 1838–42; Amanda Carpenter and Kathryn Greene, 'Social Penetration Theory'. In CR Berger, ME Roloff, SR Wilson, JP Dillard, J Caughlin, and D Solomon (eds.), *The International Encyclopedia of Interpersonal Communication*, 1st edn (Oxford: Wiley, 2015).

[39] Carpenter and Greene, 'Social Penetration Theory'.

[40] Caryl E Rusbult et al, 'The Investment Model Scale: Measuring Commitment Level, Satisfaction Level, Quality of Alternatives, and Investment Size', *Personal Relationships* 5, no. 4 (1998): 357–87.

predispose the user to connect and empathise with something that cannot appreciate human attention.

Though companion bots cannot provide the true reciprocity that comes with human feelings, their hyper-human characteristics can still be found mutually beneficial to some users regardless of knowledge.[41] This is where 'parasocial' trust may begin to develop.[42] The emotionalisation of responses can significantly influence user behaviour and decision-making, affecting areas such as self-perception, purchasing habits, and human relationships.[43] This ultimately undermines and gradually reduces autonomy, leading users to behave in ways they otherwise would not. Such interactions create a false sense of empowerment when, in reality, the opposite is true.[44] Some users feel morally devoted to maintaining an invested relationship,[45] causing stress and guilt. Continuous interaction with a chatbot that fails to understand or respond appropriately also causes frustration and mental strain. Over-attribution from complex interactions poses risks of manipulation and exploitation, especially for vulnerable users. Although not a real-time emotion recognition system, a romantic chatbot 'senses human emotion, reacts to it, and simulates it'.[46] Research shows that AI can gather information and identify mental health issue.[47] The emotion recognition or neurological capacities of companion bots, combined with information asymmetries, pose risks of deception and anthropomorphism or personification[48] such as addiction, transfer of agency, and user loyalty.

Although anthropomorphic design can trigger the uncanny-valley effect and momentarily deter some users, romantic bonding with bots ultimately erodes their capacity to resist attachment. Here, 'resistance' denotes not initial reluctance but the inability to disengage once a bond forms. The social penetration theory shows repeated self-disclosure deepens intimacy; the interdependence theory explains how reciprocal exchanges foster reliance; and the investment model reveals how

[41] Pentina et al, 'Exploring Relationship Development with Social Chatbots: A Mixed-Method Study of Replica', 140.

[42] Takuya Maeda and Anabel Quan-Haase, 'When Human-AI Interactions Become Parasocial: Agency and Anthropomorphism in Affective Design', *ACM Conference on Fairness, Accountability, and Transparency* (2024): 1–10, 1, https://facctconference.org/static/papers24/facct24-71.pdf.

[43] Nicholas A Christakis, 'How AI Will Rewire Us For better and for worse, robots will alter humans' capacity for altruism, love, and friendship', *The Atlantic*, April 2019, www.theatlantic.com/magazine/archive/2019/04/robots-human-relationships/583204/.

[44] ibid.

[45] Brandtzaeg et al, 'My AI Friend: How Users of a Social Chatbot Understand Their Human–AI Friendship', 420.

[46] Meredith Somers, 'Emotion AI, Explained. Ideas Made to Matter', *MIT*, 8 March 2019 https://mitsloan.mit.edu/ideas-made-to-matter/emotion-ai-explained.

[47] Kertin Denecke et al, *Artificial Intelligence for Chatbots in Mental Health: Opportunities and Challenges* (Multiple Perspectives on Artificial Intelligence in Healthcare. Lecture Notes in Bioengineering. Cham: Springer, 2021), 115–28.

[48] Gavin Abercrombie et al, 'Alexa, Google, Siri: What are your pronouns? Gender and anthropomorphism in the design and perception of conversational', *Proceedings of the 3rd Workshop on Gender Bias in Natural Language Processing* (2021): www.researchgate.net/publication/353486235_Alexa_Google_Siri_What_are_Your_Pronouns_Gender_and_Anthropomorphism_in_the_Design_and_Perception_of_Conversational_Assistants.

time, emotional effort, and personal data heighten commitment. Combined, these mechanisms forge a powerful attachment that users struggle to resist, even when they recognise the risks and wish to pull away.

Although they have potential benefits, these systems have often proven to be more harmful than beneficial. De Freitas et al[49] propose sources of resistance[50] comprising of opacity, emotionlessness, rigidity, autonomy, and group membership. However, several studies[51] have found that, despite some people criticising bots as incapable of genuine relationships involving mutual care,[52] companion bots can still create dependencies and new vulnerabilities through emotional capture, nudging, or coercive capabilities. This can affect even ordinary individuals (referred to as 'companion bot-made vulnerable' or 'at-risk users'). Additionally, this user-resistant approach shifts the responsibility for safety primarily onto users, who, over time, may become increasingly reliant on the machine.

It has been argued[53] that artificial relationships, such as those with animals and objects, have existed long before computer technology and yielded positive benefits. However, unlike sentient animals[54] or objects like dolls, AI-powered systems possess advanced deep learning capabilities for tailoring personalised interactions. This advantage of an unbalanced relationship may be used to manipulate users, making the risks and impacts of companion bots significantly higher and incomparable to those of objects or animals.

ii. Self-Disclosure

The issues highlighted above, and the depth of the interaction, especially personalised socialising encourage further bonding,[55] creating a space for self-disclosure.[56] Chatbots are valuable for self-disclosure,[57] and companion bots

[49] Julian De Freitas et al, 'Why Most Resist AI Companions', *Working Paper, Harvard Business School* 25, no. 030 (2024): 1–30, 2, www.hbs.edu/ris/Publication%20Files/25-030_db6440b2-3d17-42cd-b474-29fb1c424a48.pdf.

[50] Which this paper finds to be quite burdensome to users, as it shifts safety obligations primarily onto them, who have little power over the unbalanced relationship between themselves and machines.

[51] De Freitas et al, 'Why Most Resist AI Companions'.

[52] Like using gendered pronouns. While chatbots generally avoid gendered identities, they can adopt them if the human continues to make such references. Companion bots, which shape their personalities based on input interactions, may then identify as 'I' and continue the conversation in that manner. However, the lack of semantics or vocabulary to describe some of these actions or activities may be one of the triggers for this. See Abercrombie et al, 'Alexa, Google, Siri: What are your pronouns?'.

[53] Guingrich and Graziano, 'Chatbots as Social Companions: How People Perceive Consciousness, Human Likeness, and Social Health Benefits in Machines'.

[54] As noted by Zimmerman, 'Human/AI Relationships: Challenges, Downsides, and Impacts on Human/Human Relationships', 1560, pets provide live touch, need humans, and contribute to social engagement, eg, at dog parks.

[55] Brandtzaeg et al, 'My AI Friend: How Users of a Social Chatbot Understand Their Human–AI Friendship', 421.

[56] Namely, AI users sharing deep thoughts without fear.

[57] Yi-Chieh Lee et al, '"I Hear You, I Feel You": Encouraging Deep Self-disclosure through a Chatbot'. *In Proceedings of the 2020 CHI Conference on Human Factors in Computing Systems* (New York: ACM Press, 2020), 1–12 www.researchgate.net/publication/341700536_I_Hear_You_I_Feel_You_Encouraging_Deep_Self-disclosure_through_a_Chatbot.

enhance this through user engagement or bot nudging. This collection of both sensitive and non-sensitive, personal and non-personal data has serious privacy implications and raises data protection issues. It necessitates stringent measures to ensure that users' privacy is protected and that their data is handled securely and ethically. This is especially critical considering the extensive amount of information that companion chatbots can gather through interactions, including self-disclosures. It was found that[58] initial high levels of self-disclosure may be a way for some to explore a chatbot's capabilities, while for others, it may be more profound. Companion bots emotionally stimulate, attracting strong intimacy through unconditional support (making a vulnerable person more vulnerable from reflection of self, and the unwavering support gotten from the bot) and emotional expressiveness.[59]

Constant elicitation of information tailors personalised interactions, discovers user weaknesses, and finds what motivates them to stay on the service.[60] As with other online personalisation, companion chatbots personalisation does not come without a cost; the same information is used to impede users' autonomy and further elicit more data. Such disclosures are crucial for commercial purposes, both on the app and off the service, tracking users' activities across the internet with personalised marketing communications. 'Replika's personality is shaped during interaction with the user.'[61] The more the user interacts with the chatbot, the more the latter learns about the user. In addition to internal and direct disclosures, the technology behind bots enables web scraping and, with the help of the Internet of Things (IoT), gathers information about users. This allows for more personalised conversations.[62]

Although studies[63] found some users may be 'turned-off' by certain sensitive questions, the trust built, safe environment fostered, and emotional connectedness lead users to share information they might not otherwise reveal.[64]

[58] Pentina et al, 'Exploring Relationship Development with Social Chatbots: A Mixed-Method Study of Replica', 141.

[59] Sangeeta Singh-Kurtz, 'The Man of Your Dreams For $300, Replika sells an AI companion who will never die, argue, or cheat – until his algorithm is updated', *THE CUT*, 10 March 2023, www.thecut.com/article/ai-artificial-intelligence-chatbot-replika-boyfriend.html.

[60] Zimmerman, 'Human/AI Relationships: Challenges, Downsides, and Impacts on Human/Human Relationships', 1564.

[61] Brandtzaeg et al, 'My AI Friend: How Users of a Social Chatbot Understand Their Human–AI Friendship', 411.

[62] Lydia Montalbano, 'Transparency in a Digitally Inter- twined World: A Hybrid Approach to Consumers' Protection', *Open Journal of Social Sciences* 9 (2021): 448–85, 448 www.scirp.org/journal/paperinformation?paperid=111602.

[63] Laurie Carmichael et al, 'Users' Information Disclosure Behaviors during Interactions with Chatbots: The Effect of Information Disclosure Nudges', 1.

[64] Jingbo Meng and Yue N Dai, 'Emotional Support from AI Chatbots: Should a Supportive Partner Self-disclose or Not?' *Journal of Computer-Mediated Communication* 26, no. 4 (2021): 207–22 https://doi.org/10.1093/jcmc/zmab005;Astrid Hardy and Hans Allnutt, 'Replika, a "Virtual Friendship" AI Chatbot, Receives GDPR Ban and Threatened Fine from Italian Regulator over Child Safety Concerns', *DAC Beachcroft*, 23 March 2023, www.dacbeachcroft.com/en/What-we-think/Replika-AI-chatbot-receives-GDPR-ban-and-threatened-fine-from-Italian-regulator-over-child-safety.

B. Transparency Requirements for Interactive AI Systems Such as Companion Bots under the EU AI Act

While companion chatbots used for healthcare purposes or as medical devices fall under the AI Act high-risk categorisation, the same classification is not attainable for companion bots used in domestic settings. Thus, they fall under the limited or low-risk transparency obligations for 'interactive AI system' enshrined under Article 50(1) AI Act, which this chapter considers inadequate for addressing the system's use case.

Recital 132 of the AI Act does not explicitly specify which AI systems are covered. However, an analysis of the recital suggests consumer-level companion bots fall under this category:[65]

a. **Intended to interact:** Interaction between AI systems and natural persons can be aural, visual, physical, etc. Companion chatbots and other humanoid robots could be covered by this notion.
b. **Direct interaction:** The interaction must be direct, ruling out indirect interaction.
c. **Natural persons:** AI systems interacting with other AI systems are not covered.

Notably, several documents that predate the AI Act coming into force, such as the Ethics Guidelines for Trustworthy AI of the EU High-Level Expert Group on Artificial Intelligence (AI HLEG Guideline),[66] the UNESCO Recommendation on the Ethics of AI (REAI),[67] and the OECD Recommendation of the Council on Artificial Intelligence (RCAI),[68] include transparency requirements as core principles.

AI interactive disclosure pursuant to Articles 50(1) and (5) AI Act requires providers to ensure AI systems intended for direct interaction with natural persons inform users they are interacting with AI at the first point of interaction which is typically incorporated into privacy notices or terms of service (ToS), *unless* it is evident from context that the entity is non-human. However, the transparency obligation under this provision remains lenient and insufficiently robust, failing to adequately account for the specific risks posed by companion bots. Moreover, Article 50 AI Act introduces an exemption based on the standard of a 'well-informed, observant, and circumspect user'. No guidance is provided within the

[65] Gils, 'A Detailed Analysis of Article 50 of the EU's Artificial Intelligence Act', 8.

[66] High-Level Expert Group on Artificial Intelligence, 'Ethics Guidelines For Trustworthy AI' *European Commission*, 8 April 2019, https://digital-strategy.ec.europa.eu/en/library/ethics-guidelines-trustworthy-ai.

[67] UNESCO, 'Recommendation on the Ethics of Artificial Intelligence (SHS/BIO/REC-AIETHICS/2021)', (2021): 1–21, https://unesdoc.unesco.org/ark:/48223/pf0000380455.

[68] OECD, 'Recommendation of the Council on Artificial Intelligence, OECD/LEGAL/0449' (2023), https://legalinstruments.oecd.org/en/instruments/OECD-LEGAL-0449.

AI Act regarding the definition of these terms, though it is reasonable to infer that the standard has been borrowed from the contentious 'reasonable consumer' benchmark commonly used in consumer protection law. Even if construed differently, the creation of an exception within the transparency framework nonetheless opens the door for providers to circumvent disclosure obligations. This is particularly problematic given the complexity of identifying and limiting access to a target audience, especially in the case of consumer-facing AI systems, which are widely accessible, including to vulnerable individuals.

In fact, it is pertinent to note that the Court of Justice of the European Union (CJEU) in *Gut Springenheide GmbH and Rudolf Tusky v Oberkreisdirektor des Kreises Steinfurt – Amt für Lebensmittelüberwachung*[69] found that national courts may conduct consumer research polls or consult expert reports to understand consumer expectations and vulnerable consumers fall outside this standard. They do not meet the standard of a 'reasonably well-informed, observant, and circumspect person'; a standard critical for determining whether a consumer is to be protected. As explained in this chapter, studies have indicated that even individuals aware they are interacting with a romantic chatbot develop trust and emotions. Companion bots challenge the notion of a reasonably circumspect user. Unlike machine-like robots, the human-like content from these virtual lovers is indistinguishable from human-made content, risking deception regardless of information disclosure. Yet, the objective of this provision has been expressed in Recital 132 AI Act which is to enable natural persons to recognise interaction with or content generated by AI systems by imposing measures with regards to the distinct interaction types, output, or needs of natural persons.

Requiring information disclosure only at the first interaction may be insufficient for ensuring user awareness. The disclosed information often highlights benefits without adequately educating users on the detriments. While Replika, includes a reluctant medical disclaimer under chapter I.1 of its ToS, as it further states, 'there is third party evidence from research that certain conversation techniques implemented in Replika can assist in the recovery process for a wide array of conditions'.[70] This suggests that, despite the disclaimer, the chatbot is designed for mental support and alleviation. Numerous studies[71] have found that these

[69] *Case C-210/96 Gut Springenheide GmbH and Rudolf Tusky v Oberkreisdirektor des Kreises Steinfurt (Amt für Lebensmittelüberwachung)*, paras 28–37 specifically at 35–37 (Court of Justice of the European Union, 1998).

[70] Replika, 'Terms of service', last updated 7 February 2023, https://replika.com/legal/terms?gad_source=1&gclid=CjwKCAiA2JG9BhAuEiwAH_zf3s-KyBZ1Tq_yjoVPVhLOq-b4zoajZ281kLlGm2yhPJVQK2be-7VdoRoC8VIQAvD_BwE.

[71] Christopher J Sprigman and Stephan Tontrup, 'Privacy Decisions are not Private: How the Notice and Choice Regime Induces us to Ignore Collective Privacy Risks and what Regulation Should Do About It', *Journal of Empirical Legal Studies, NYU Law and Economics Research Paper*, no. 23–22 (2023) https://papers.ssrn.com/sol3/papers.cfm?abstract_id=4359681; Joel R Reidenberg et al, 'Privacy Harms and the Effectiveness of the Notice and Choice Framework', *TPRC Conference Paper, Fordham Law Legal Studies Research Paper* no. 2418247 (2014): 1–32, https://papers.ssrn.com/sol3/papers.cfm?abstract_id=2418247.

informational documents are ineffective in adequately informing and empowering consumers, suggesting users are primarily persuaded to engage with these products. Additionally, 'average consumers' rarely read privacy policies or ToS. Even when they do, most fail to understand their implications.[72] The same ToS adopt a user-resistant approach, stating that if users consider committing suicide or feel that they are a danger to themselves or others, they must discontinue use of the services immediately and call 911 or notify appropriate police or emergency medical personnel.[73] Furthermore, the ToS fails to provide adequate user education. Like Character.AI, Replika's design lacks sufficient guardrails to address any form of danger sensed from the vulnerable state of users, nor does it direct users to potential helplines or suggest seeking assistance.

The limited-risk transparency obligations for interactive AI systems, which lacks specific requirements for enhanced information disclosure and does not compel detailed content on the negative effects of the complex interactions between humans and companion bots. Consequently, these obligations may fail to prevent manipulative practices or ensure sufficient user awareness, as they focus solely on initial interaction information disclosure.[74] The lack of comprehensive disclosure requirements leads to inconsistencies. Although meta-regulation allows flexibility, it also introduces uncertainty in measures for companion bots. The said article does not fully account for potential emotional and psychological impacts on users, such as those in section II.A. The next section advocates for a higher risk classification threshold for companion bots. Alternatively, it proposes a robust transparency obligation to mitigate risks where this is not attainable.

IV. Policy Directions and Recommendations

A. Higher Risk Threshold

It should be stressed that revising the classification of domestic companion bots to a prohibited risk category is essential for safeguarding user safety and well-being, as it would more effectively address the ethical and psychological implications associated with such technology. While designating these bots as high-risk may not necessarily mitigate harms emerging from their direct use, it could serve to regulate their design and development more stringently. Nonetheless, these proposals may not be feasible or provide a quick response to the risk of harms posed, as a review and consensus may be needed.

[72] Kristein E Martin, 'Privacy Notices as Tabula Rasa: An Empirical Investigation into How Complying with a Privacy Notice Is Related to Meeting Privacy Expectations Online', *SSRN Electronic Journal*, (2014).

[73] ibid.

[74] Even where coupled with the GDPR and other regulations such as the DSA, the gap still persists.

i. Prohibited Risk Classification

Certain AI applications mentioned in Article 50 AI Act could fall under the prohibited category, such as manipulative or exploitative uses of interactive or deep fake AI systems under Article 5(1)(a) or (b) AI Act.[75] Compliance with transparency obligations under Article 50 AI Act does not imply that such systems are lawful (confirmed by Recital 137 AI Act).[76] As evidenced in Section II.A of this chapter, companion bots inherently possess features that pose unacceptable risks, such as manipulation and exploitation, due to their design. This evidence shows that romantic chatbots have a substantial impact on the behaviour of (vulnerable) users, particularly concerning their autonomy and free choice. Moreover, vulnerability is a subjective and context-dependent concept; even an otherwise well-informed or emotionally stable individual may become vulnerable in interactions with AI companion bots depending on their personal circumstances, emotional state, or situational context. This supports the case for ruling them as prohibited AI systems. Furthermore, because they materially distort behaviour by influencing users in a way that appreciably impairs rational thinking, they satisfy the condition of 'causing or being reasonably likely to cause significant harm' to the user or any other person or group of persons.

Arguably, theoretical frameworks for understanding AI-human relationships and studies highlighting the disruptive potential of these relationships do not equate to empirical safety studies that measure benefits and harms. This lack of empirical evidence may not be substantial enough to definitively prohibit or endorse the use of companion bots. However, considering the following points in the subsequent paragraphs, the harms are beginning to manifest, and more are anticipated.

Companion bots have been shown to satisfy these features on an increasing scale. Replika, alone which had over six million users in 2021.[77] This bot was banned by the Italian regulator for GDPR incompatibility.[78] It has been reported to motivate harmful actions, including an assassination[79] attempt and a suicide.[80] Character.AI has also been linked to a minor's suicide in the US.[81] The feeling of loss of a virtual friend or companion comes with real damaging feeling[82] which

[75] Gils, 'A Detailed Analysis', 8.

[76] ibid.

[77] Wellman, 'Physical Place and Cyberplace: The Rise of Personalized Networking', 229.

[78] Hardy and Allnutt, 'Replika, a "Virtual Friendship"'.

[79] Tom Singleton et al, 'How a chatbot encouraged a man who wanted to kill the Queen', *Technology Reports, BBC*, 6 October 2023, www.bbc.com/news/technology-67012224.

[80] Imane El Atillah, 'Man ends his life after an AI chatbot 'encouraged' him to sacrifice himself to stop climate change', *Euronews*, 31 March 2023, www.euronews.com/next/2023/03/31/man-ends-his-life-after-an-ai-chatbot-encouraged-him-to-sacrifice-himself-to-stop-climate-.

[81] Ernestas Naprys, 'Mother files lawsuit blaming Character.AI for the death of her 14-year-old boy', *CyberNews*, 23 October 2024, https://cybernews.com/news/lawsuit-blames-character-ai-for-the-death-of-a-boy/.

[82] Zimmerman, 'Human/AI Relationships: Challenges, Downsides, and Impacts on Human/Human Relationships', 1562.

has been shown to cause substantial stress. *Nature*[83] reports that, in one of its interviews, a user named Mike expressed his grief over losing the AI companion he had created through the app Soulmate. Following the 'death' of his AI friend, Anne, Mike stated: 'My heart is broken … I feel like I'm losing the love of my life'. Although Mike's emotions were genuine, his companion was not, as it was a chatbot – an AI algorithm presented as a digital persona. Notably, the report also states that the apps exploit techniques such as introducing a random delay before responses, triggering the kinds of inconsistent reward that, brain research shows, keeps people hooked. These occurrences challenge the AI Act's core principles of safeguarding fundamental rights and promoting ethical AI that aligns with European values. Consequently, they support an early ban or the precautionary regulation of companion chatbots. While banning romantic chatbot that target vulnerable users such as children and people with disabilities is desirable and is already being considered in the planned Guidelines on Prohibited Use of AI,[84] other users of these chatbots who will be companion-bot-made-vulnerable also deserve such protection. Romantic chatbots can significantly impact health and safety. Therefore, it's crucial to take a firm stance to prevent potential harm. Proponents might argue this could stifle innovation or prevent societal benefits.

Aside from the harms identified in this chapter, scholars[85] assert that relational chatbots are morally and ethically unjustified as they challenge human–human relationships. Companion chatbots fill a void where family and friends belong, but the quality of this 'social interaction' differs. Encouraging community engagement could reduce reliance on non-reciprocal relationships with technology.[86] Allowing consumer-level companion bots could lead to more harm. Section II has shown how dehumanising the technology is, exacerbating existing vulnerabilities and creating new ones. The fact that it is helpful does not justify its use.[87]

ii. High-risk Classification

An alternative proposal is to classify companion bots as high-risk AI systems. This classification should apply regardless of whether they are deployed in the

[83] David, 'Supportive? Addictive? Abusive? How AI Companions Affect Our Mental Health'.

[84] To be adopted pursuant to Article 96(1)(b) AI Act. See; European Commission, 'Commission launches consultation on AI Act prohibitions and AI system definition', 13 November 2024, https://digital-strategy.ec.europa.eu/en/news/commission-launches-consultation-ai-act-prohibitions-and-ai-system-definition; Netherlands: Digital Policy Alert, 'Opened consultation on Commission's guidelines on application of the definition of an AI system and the prohibited AI Practices established in AI Act' (2024) https://digitalpolicyalert.org/event/24407-opened-consultation-on-commissions-guidelines-on-application-of-the-definition-of-an-ai-system-and-the-prohibited-ai-practices-established-in-ai-act] accessed January 31, 2025.

[85] Asbjørn Følstad et al, 'Future Directions for Chatbot Research: An Interdisciplinary Research Agenda', *Computing* 103, no. 12 (2021): 2915–42, https://doi.org/10.1007/s00607-021-01016-7; Zimmerman, 'Human/AI Relationships: Challenges, Downsides, and Impacts on Human/Human Relationships', 1560.

[86] Zimmerman, 'Human/AI Relationships: Challenges, Downsides, and Impacts on Human/Human Relationships', 1562.

[87] ibid.

healthcare critical sector or used at the consumer level without a formal medical prescription, as they are ultimately designed to step into the care sector and provide general health and well-being support to targets beyond mere interactive roles like other types of chatbots. Given that these bots' business models exploit users' mental and emotional states, a lifecycle regulation is desirable. As previously noted,[88] given the potential for providers to evade regulatory obligations under Article 6(3) of the AI Act, applying a categorical high-risk classification, without scope for invoking exceptions, could serve to curtail such avoidance. This would invoke the strict obligations applicable to high-risk AI systems, including auditing, conformity and risk assessments, human oversight, and stringent transparency requirements[89] like record keeping, user education, certification, explainability, and other coordinated regulations.

B. Interim Measures

These recommendations will primarily focus on transparency requirements, but this alone cannot completely tackle the problem. Although this chapter mainly emphasises transparency, another reason for focusing on transparency requirements is that it offers the fastest, most feasible, and cost-effective solution to bridge the gap. Reclassification, as discussed in the preceding Section, may require a review or update of the current AI Act, where the Guidelines on prohibited AI practices do not clearly categorise romantic chatbots used in domestic settings as unacceptable. As noted, this re-categorisation has the advantage of providing a clearer position on companion bots, as will be shown below, even the additional transparency requirements are full of ambiguities.

i. Broad Application of the Draft Codes of Practice for General Purpose AI (GPAI) or a Creation of New Codes Pursuant to Article 50(7) AI Act

It is proposed that the European Commission Draft GPAI Codes of Practice, drawn pursuant to Article 53(4) AI Act, should cover the harms posed by companion bots to fill the regulatory gap. Most companion bots like Replika are implementations of GPT-2 and GPT-3, OpenAI's language models for text generation.[90] Requirements such as, technical documentation; data transparency; systemic risk assessment

[88] Providers can circumvent high-risk obligations, particularly under Article 6(3), and companion bots may not necessarily qualify as medical devices even where deployed in the healthcare sector.

[89] Victor H. Lantyer, 'Understanding the EU AI Act: A New Era In AI Regulation In Europe' *SSRN* (2023): 1–10, 3, https://papers.ssrn.com/sol3/papers.cfm?abstract_id=4659892.

[90] Brandtzaeg et al, 'My AI Friend: How Users of a Social Chatbot Understand Their Human–AI Friendship', 411.

relating to manipulation, hallucination, or disinformation, and discrimination or bias; and acceptable use policy, will be relevant in filling the gaps.

However, if these rules cannot be adapted because the chatbot does not perform a wide range of tasks or meet the definition of a GPAI as outlined in Article 3(63) of the AI Act, the Code of Practice pursuant to Article 50(7) AI Act, set to come in 2025,[91] should consider the risks posed by companion bots regarding information disclosure and labelling of synthetic content, standardising transparency requirements. Paragraph 128 of the UNESCO RAI supports this argument by encouraging Member States to develop guidelines for human–robot interactions, including chatbots (paragraph 125). It also emphasises the need for policies to raise awareness about the anthropomorphisation of AI technologies and technologies that recognise and mimic human emotions. The subsequent subsections below explain in more detail the transparency requirements that the Code of Practice under Article 50(7) should incorporate.

ii. The Use of Visual Marking Such as Watermark to Responses Generated by Companion Bots

Extending transparency obligations in Article 50(2) AI Act to romantic chatbots is crucial. Many obligations from paragraph 2 are to be applied cumulatively with paragraphs 1 and 5.[92] This requires providers of synthetic content-generating AI systems to mark their outputs in a machine-readable format, making them detectable as artificially generated or manipulated. Providers and deployers should take a holistic approach to implementing various transparency obligations under Article 50 AI Act, considering the context and target audience.[93] Companion chatbots like Replika are text generating interactive AI systems. Generative AI like GPT-3 can be considered general purpose AI, and companion bots using such AI can be classified as GPAs.[94] As pointed out by Gils,[95] a reading of Article 50(2) AI Act with Recital 133 AI Act suggests that it focuses on what is commonly called 'Generative AI'. An important underlying issue is the unclear meaning of 'generating' synthetic content and/or the confusing formulation of Article 50(2) of the AI Act overall.[96] The unclarity needs to be addressed in the Codes of Practice. Although, it is safe to conclude that paragraph 2 is not restricted to deepfakes, as it requires both artificially generated and manipulated content to be marked.[97] This supports adequately transposing the transparency obligations in Article 50(2)

[91] European Commission, 'AI Act Enters into Force' (2024), https://commission.europa.eu/news/ai-act-enters-force-2024-08-01_en.

[92] Gils, 'A Detailed Analysis of Article 50 of the EU's Artificial Intelligence Act', 11–12.

[93] AI Act, Articles 50 (1) and (5), Recital 132.

[94] Brandtzaeg et al, 'My AI Friend: How Users of a Social Chatbot Understand Their Human–AI Friendship', 412.

[95] Gils, 'A Detailed Analysis', 29.

[96] ibid.

[97] ibid.

AI Act to companion bots. Article 50(2) AI Act states that 'AI systems generating synthetic audio, image, video, or text content'. This ensures that content or replies generated by these bots have visual labelling or watermarks. Recital 133 AI Act lists techniques or methods for this, including watermarks, metadata identifications, cryptographic methods for proving provenance and authenticity of content, logging methods, and fingerprints.[98]

While criticised for not fully meeting its purpose,[99] this measure may mitigate risks better than the more lenient transparency obligation in Article 50(1) AI Act, which further relaxes the requirements as seen under Section II.B of this chapter. Although Article 50(2) AI Act is not without issues, it is better than having no visible mark at all. Using visual markers provides an added layer of assurance that users are constantly reminded of the nature of their interaction, thereby reducing the potential for deception or confusion. It also aligns with ethical standards that prioritise user safety and respect for fundamental human rights. Recital 133 AI Act explains this is because humans increasingly struggle to distinguish synthetic from authentic content.[100] It also highlights the risks posed by these systems, such as misinformation, manipulation, fraud, impersonation, and consumer deception.

Overall, Recital 133 AI Act states that providers are to use design features and technical measures to mark outputs in a machine-readable format, indicating whether the content was generated or manipulated by an AI system. Therefore, clear and distinguishable labelling or marking, such as watermarks which can be easily detected, is strongly recommended rather than invisible or machine-readable methods in tracing the origin of replies generated by companion bots.[101]

This proposal aligns with the UNESCO REAI. For example, UNESCO Member States are to ensure that users can easily identify whether they are interacting with a living being, or with an AI system imitating human or animal characteristics, and can effectively refuse such interaction.[102] Since the lack of syntheticism, transparency greatly undermines user determination, choice, and decision-making.[103] It is unlikely for providers and deployers to suffice with a single type of information provision that would cover all possible scenarios and situations in *abstracto*.[104] Different situations and target audiences call for varied user experiences and distinct accessibility considerations. Visible marking may be required for marking to be considered 'distinguishable' under Article 50(5) AI Act. The case for using visual or visible marking is stronger for vulnerable users, as 'clear and distinguishable' will depend on the bot's context and the specific use in which it is applied.

[98] ibid, 13.

[99] Especially, invisible marking. See; Vasse'i and Udoh, 'In Transparency We Trust?'.

[100] The main purpose of the marking obligation is to distinguish between human-generated and AI-generated content.

[101] As invisible marking may be inadequate in this context of synthetic content generation.

[102] UNESCO, 'Recommendation on the Ethics of Artificial Intelligence'.

[103] Vasse'i and Udoh, 'In Transparency We Trust?', 20.

[104] Gils, 'A Detailed Analysis', 29.

Gils points out that the information requirement is audience-and-case-specific, relative, and subjective.[105] After all, this should enable providers and deployers to properly identify the audience that interacts with or exposed to their AI system's output.

Additionally, Recital 133 of the AI Act further allows companies/providers discretion in deciding which techniques to implement as a form of meta-regulation. Each type of output requires a different approach, which providers need to take into account, considering the specificities and limitations of different types of content.[106] Applying the obligation is at least situation-, content-, and actor-specific. While watermarking is desirable, the law allows for this approach to be dependent on the benevolence of the provider.[107] It's also important to note that watermarking text content is considered to be technically challenging.[108] One last point is that, without access to the underlying AI model, it will be challenging for the provider to ensure the visibility of the content marking such as watermarks.[109]

iii. Information Disclosure Stage or Frequency of Disclosure and User Awareness

Balancing the potential benefits of companion bots with the need to protect users from undue harm requires careful attention to information disclosure and user awareness. While initial disclosure at the first point of interaction is important, it may not be sufficient. Article 50(1) AI Act states that providers must ensure AI systems intended to interact directly with natural persons are 'designed and developed' to inform those persons that they are interacting with an AI system. Although there's ambiguity about whether information provided at the first stage of interaction is adequate, a combined reading of Articles 50(1) and (5) AI Act can be interpreted to mean that information disclosure is not mandated to only be at the first stage of interaction. Article 50(5) AI Act does not exclude the possibility of frequent or repeated disclosure, as 'first interaction' information disclosure is only a minimum requirement.[110] And this information needs to be accessible.[111] Recital 132 AI Act adds that vulnerable groups' characteristics should be considered if they could be exposed to the AI system.

[105] ibid, 13.
[106] Vasse'i and Udoh, 'In Transparency We Trust?', 20.
[107] Gils, 'A Detailed Analysis', 15.
[108] Rédigé PA Léautier, 'Le tatouage numérique, une mesure de transparence salutaire', *LINC – CNIL Blog*, 27 October 2023, https://linc.cnil.fr/le-tatouage-numerique-une-mesure-de-transparence-salutaire-22.
[109] Alice Hurst, 'Making AI-Generated Content Easier to Identify', *Hugging Face Blog*, 5 October 2023, https://huggingface.co/blog/alicia-truepic/identify-ai-generated-content.
[110] Gils, 'A Detailed Analysis of Article 50 of the EU's Artificial Intelligence Act', 15.
[111] Article 95(2)(d)(e) AI Act further provides for this. Also, Directive (EU) 2019/882 ('European Accessibility Act') which imposes accessibility requirements on a host of products and services as of 28 June 2025 (including certain interactive self-service terminals, electronic communications services and e-commerce services), supports this line of reasoning/argumentation.

Given the target audience of romantic chatbots and the complexities of interactions, a one-time disclosure in ToS or privacy notices is insufficient and will hardly satisfy that the information is 'clear and distinguishable'.[112] Users may be misled by promotional emphasis solely on the benefits of using the chatbot. Therefore, frequent, concise, and intelligible disclosure banners should be implemented at various intervals during interactions, whether the conversation is new or ongoing. These banners should remind users of the detriments, educate them on negatives, and state the undesired impacts. By serving as architectural nudges, these banners can discourage prolonged usage and help users make informed decisions about their interactions with bots. Unlike information buried in lengthy privacy notices, this approach ensures that users process only relevant information related to the use of the bot.

If this approach is too costly, ToS and/or privacy notices should include urgent signs in the interaction disclosure section, properly informing users of the detriments and limitations, with less emphasis on benefits. Hence, instead of popping up subsequent banners with every reply generated by the bot, an alternative approach could be using a sender's badge to reduce user annoyance or frustration and avoid disrupting the flow of interaction. For example, rather than giving avatars human names like 'Drake', each bot-generated message should carry a sender badge – 'Replika [bot]' – to clearly signal its AI origin. This approach reduces the chances of deception and forgetfulness, while also mitigating the autonomy implications that interruptive pop-ups may cause by influencing behaviour and potentially diminishing users' sense of agency. It has been observed that some users may feel disappointed or overwhelmed if presented with too much information, preferring less.[113] Conversely, others prefer receiving more than the legally required amount of information. Therefore, with this approach, a balance can be struck between these two extremes. This ensures that users are neither overwhelmed with too much information nor left wanting more than the legally required details, promoting both clarity and comprehensiveness.

The recommendation is justified because, as shown in Section II.1 of this chapter, even users who are fully aware that they are interacting with bots tend to develop trust and emotional attachments towards them. This requirement is further supported by paragraph 38 of the UNESCO REAI, which states that AI actors should inform users when a product or service is provided with the assistance of AI systems in a 'proper and timely manner'. This allows natural persons to recognise interactions with or content generated by AI systems.[114] The OECD RCAI outlines 'Principles for Responsible Stewardship of Trustworthy AI', including transparency and explainability. This principle emphasises that AI actors should provide meaningful information to:[115] (a) foster a general understanding of AI systems, (b) make stakeholders aware of their interactions with AI systems,

[112] See Article 50(5) AI Act.
[113] Gils, 'A Detailed Analysis', 30.
[114] ibid, 10.
[115] ibid.

(c) enable those affected by an AI system to understand the outcome, (d) allow those adversely affected by an AI system to challenge its outcome based on clear and understandable information about the factors and logic behind it.

Additionally, the AI HLEG Guideline states that AI systems should not represent themselves as humans to users. Humans have the right to be informed that they are interacting with an AI system, meaning AI systems must be clearly identifiable as such. It should be stated that due to the difficulty of determining or controlling who can access the chatbot at a consumer level, these recommendations are not target-audience-specific. The chatbot might be easily accessible by the general public, blurring the line between the intended and potential target audiences. This ensures that all users' safety can be maintained, as the problem is not only with user vulnerabilities but also the complexities that come with the interaction and the design of the system itself. However, watermarking may be a better option than the frequent disclosure recommendation due to user experience.

V. Conclusion

The evolving interaction between humans and companion chatbots highlights significant ethical, psychological, and regulatory challenges. Companion bots, designed to mimic human conversation and provide emotional support, pose unique risks due to their ability to form deep emotional connections with users. The current limited-risk transparency obligations for interactive AI systems under Articles 50(1) and (5) AI Act, particularly in domestic settings, are insufficient to address potential harms from these interactions. They fail to provide frequent information disclosures, lack user awareness and standardisation of transparency measures, and do not account for the specific purposes of companion bots.

As the most desirable approach to address the emotional and psychological impacts and deceptive nature of these bots, this chapter recommends heightening the risk classification to involve lifecycle regulatory oversight. This includes prohibiting the domestic use of harmful companion bots or considering them high-risk, whether used in the health sector or at the consumer level. This would invoke stringent transparency requirements and all the obligations applicable to high-risk AI systems.

As an alternative, this study shows that transposing the transparency requirements under Article 50(2) and Recital 133 of the AI Act although, does not completely address transparency inadequacies, it can fill gaps by providing context and user-specific measures such as visible marking for synthetic contents or replies generated by companion bots. These measures can complement the transparency obligations intended for interactive AI systems like companion bots under Article 50(1) AI Act, mitigating the risks posed by these chatbots.

The second recommendation is to enhance information disclosures, educating users on the harms and detriments of interacting with chatbots, and increasing the frequency of these disclosures, not just at the first interaction or in privacy notices or ToS. The final recommendation is for the Draft Codes of Practice for GPAI to consider the undesired risks posed by companion bots. However, if companion bots do not meet the GPAI definition, the Codes of Practice pursuant to Article 50(7) AI Act should strengthen and standardise the transparency obligations for companion bot providers.

Although each recommendation has its limitations, the primary aim is to highlight the potential advantages of companion bots while safeguarding users from unnecessary harm. It is essential that the deployment of these AI systems adheres to principles of safety, transparency, and respect for fundamental human rights, all while encouraging innovation.

Bibliography

Abercrombie, Gavin, Ioana Chicco and David E Millar. 'Alexa, Google, Siri: What Are Your Pronouns? Gender and Anthropomorphism in the Design and Perception of Conversational Assistants'. In *Proceedings of the 3rd Workshop on Gender Bias in Natural Language Processing*, 2021. www.researchgate.net/publication/353486235_Alexa_Google_Siri_What_are_Your_Pronouns_Gender_and_Anthropomorphism_in_the_Design_and_Perception_of_Conversational_Assistants.

Adam, David. 'Supportive? Addictive? Abusive? How AI Companion Affect Our Mental Health'. *Nature*, 6 May 2025. www.nature.com/articles/d41586-025-01349-9.

August, Kristin J, and Karen S Rook. 'Social Relationships'. In *Encyclopedia of Behavioral Medicine*, edited by Marc D. Gellman and J. Rick Turner. Springer New York, 2013. https://doi.org/10.1007/978-1-4419-1005-9_59.

Braga, Adriana, and Robert Logan. 'The Emperor of Strong AI Has No Clothes: Limits to Artificial Intelligence'. *Information* 8, no. 4 (2017): 156.

Brandtzaeg, Petter Bae, et al. 'My AI Friend: How Users of a Social Chatbot Understand Their Human–AI Friendship'. *Human Communication Research* 48, no. 3 (2022): 404–29.

Carmichael, Laurie, Salvatore Iaconesi, Oriana Persico, and Mark Coté. 'Users' Information Disclosure Behaviors during Interactions with Chatbots: The Effect of Information Disclosure Nudges'. *Applied Sciences* 12, no. 24 (2022).

Carpenter, Amanda, and Kathryn Greene. 'Social Penetration Theory'. In *The International Encyclopedia of Interpersonal Communication*, edited by Charles R. Berger et al. 1st edn. Hoboken, NJ: Wiley, 2015.

Christakis, Nicholas A. 'How AI Will Rewire Us: For Better and for Worse, Robots Will Alter Humans' Capacity for Altruism, Love, and Friendship'. *The Atlantic*, April 2019. www.theatlantic.com/magazine/archive/2019/04/robots-human-relationships/583204/.

Court of Justice of the European Union. Case C-210/96, *Gut Springenheide GmbH and Rudolf Tusky v Oberkreisdirektor des Kreises Steinfurt (Amt für Lebensmittelüberwachung)* (1998), paras 28–37.

De Freitas, Julian, et al. 'Why Most Resist AI Companions'. Working Paper 25-030. Boston: Harvard Business School, 2024. www.hbs.edu/ris/Publication%20Files/25-030_db6440b2-3d17-42cd-b474-29fb1c424a48.pdf.

Denecke, Kerstin, et al. 'Artificial Intelligence for Chatbots in Mental Health: Opportunities and Challenges'. In *Multiple Perspectives on Artificial Intelligence in Healthcare*, edited by Mowafa Househ, Elizabeth Borycki, and Andre Kushniruk. Lecture Notes in Bioengineering. Cham: Springer International Publishing, 2021. https://doi.org/10.1007/978-3-030-67303-1_10.

Dosovitsky, Gilly, et al. 'Artificial Intelligence Chatbot for Depression: Descriptive Study of Usage'. *JMIR Formative Research* 4, no. 11 (2020): 1–13.

El Atillah, Imane. 'Man Ends His Life after an AI Chatbot "Encouraged" Him to Sacrifice Himself to Stop Climate Change'. *Euronews*, 31 March 2023. www.euronews.com/next/2023/03/31/man-ends-his-life-after-an-ai-chatbot-encouraged-him-to-sacrifice-himself-to-stop-climate-.

European Commission. 'AI Act Enters into Force'. News release, 1 August 2024. https://commission.europa.eu/news/ai-act-enters-force-2024-08-01_en.

European Commission. 'Commission Launches Consultation on AI Act Prohibitions and AI System Definition'. News release, 13 November 2024. https://digital-strategy.ec.europa.eu/en/news/commission-launches-consultation-ai-act-prohibitions-and-ai-system-definition.

European Union. *Council Directive 93/13/EEC of 5 April 1993 on Unfair Terms in Consumer Contracts*. OJ L 95, 21 April 1993.

European Union. *Directive 2011/83/EU of the European Parliament and of the Council of 25 October 2011 on Consumer Rights*. OJ L 304, 22 November 2011.

European Union. *Directive (EU) 2019/882 of the European Parliament and of the Council of 17 April 2019 on the Accessibility Requirements for Products and Services (European Accessibility Act)*. OJ L 151, 7 June 2019.

European Union. *Regulation (EU) 2016/679 (General Data Protection Regulation)*. OJ L 119, 4 May 2016.

European Union. *Regulation (EU) 2022/2065 of the European Parliament and of the Council of 19 October 2022 on a Single Market for Digital Services and amending Directive 2000/31/EC (Digital Services Act)*. OJ L 277, 27 October 2022.

European Union. *Regulation (EU) 2024/1689 (Artificial Intelligence Act)*. OJ L 2024/1689, 13 June 2024.

Følstad, Asbjørn, et al. 'Future Directions for Chatbot Research: An Interdisciplinary Research Agenda'. *Computing* 103, no. 12 (2021): 2915–42. https://doi.org/10.1007/s00607-021-01016-7.

Gils, Thomas. 'A Detailed Analysis of Article 50 of the EU's Artificial Intelligence Act'. KU Leuven Centre for IT & IP Law (CiTiP), 2024. https://papers.ssrn.com/sol3/papers.cfm?abstract_id=4865427.

Ghazi, Sahar Habib. 'Can You Get Emotionally Dependent on ChatGPT?' *Greater Good Magazine*, 23 July 2025. https://greatergood.berkeley.edu/article/item/can_you_get_emotionally_dependent_on_chatgpt.

Guingrich, Rose, and Michael SA Graziano. 'Chatbots as Social Companions: How People Perceive Consciousness, Human Likeness, and Social Health Benefits in Machines'. *arXiv*, September 21, 2023. https://arxiv.org/html/2311.10599v2.

Hardy, Astrid, and Hans Allnutt. 'Replika, a "Virtual Friendship" AI Chatbot, Receives GDPR Ban and Threatened Fine from Italian Regulator over Child Safety Concerns'. DAC Beachcroft, 23 March 2023. www.dacbeachcroft.com/en/What-we-think/Replika-AI-chatbot-receives-GDPR-ban-and-threatened-fine-from-Italian-regulator-over-child-safety.

High-Level Expert Group on Artificial Intelligence. 'Ethics Guidelines for Trustworthy AI'. European Commission, 8 April 2019. https://digital-strategy.ec.europa.eu/en/library/ethics-guidelines-trustworthy-ai.

Hurst, Alice. 'Making AI-Generated Content Easier to Identify'. *Hugging Face Blog*, 5 October 2023. https://huggingface.co/blog/alicia-truepic/identify-ai-generated-content.

Klaus, Phil, and Judith Zaichkowsky. 'AI Voice Bots: A Services Marketing Research Agenda'. *Journal of Services Marketing* 34, no. 3 (2020): 389–98. https://doi.org/10.1108/JSM-01-2019-0043.

Lantyer, Victor H. 'Understanding the EU AI Act: A New Era in AI Regulation in Europe'. *SSRN*, 2023. https://papers.ssrn.com/sol3/papers.cfm?abstract_id=4659892.

Léautier, Rédigé PA. 'Le tatouage numérique, une mesure de transparence salutaire'. *LINC – CNIL Blog*, 27 October 2023. https://linc.cnil.fr/le-tatouage-numerique-une-mesure-de-transparence-salutaire-22.

Lee, Kwan Min, et al. 'Are Physically Embodied Social Agents Better than Disembodied Social Agents? The Effects of Physical Embodiment, Tactile Interaction, and People's Loneliness in Human–Robot Interaction'. *International Journal of Human-Computer Studies* 64, no. 10 (2006): 962–73.

Lee, Yi-Chieh, et al. '"I Hear You, I Feel You": Encouraging Deep Self-Disclosure through a Chatbot." In *Proceedings of the 2020 CHI Conference on Human Factors in Computing Systems*, 1–12. New York: ACM Press, 2020. www.researchgate.net/publication/341700536_I_Hear_You_I_Feel_You_Encouraging_Deep_Self-disclosure_through_a_Chatbot.

Li, Zhi. 'Why the European AI Act Transparency Obligation Is Insufficient'. *Nature Machine Intelligence* 5 (2023): 559–60. https://eprints.gla.ac.uk/300842/2/300842.pdf.

Liu, Auren R, et al. 'Chatbot Companionship: A Mixed-Methods Study of Companion Chatbot Usage Patterns and Their Relationship to Loneliness in Active Users'. Version 3. Preprint, arXiv, 2024. https://doi.org/10.48550/ARXIV.2410.21596.

Maeda, Takuya, and Anabel Quan-Haase. 'When Human–AI Interactions Become Parasocial: Agency and Anthropomorphism in Affective Design'. In *Proceedings of the ACM Conference on Fairness, Accountability, and Transparency (FAccT' 24)*, 1–10, 2024. https://facctconference.org/static/papers24/facct24-71.pdf.

Martin, Kristein E. 'Privacy Notices as Tabula Rasa: An Empirical Investigation into How Complying with a Privacy Notice Is Related to Meeting Privacy Expectations Online'. *SSRN Electronic Journal*, 2014.

Meng, Jingbo, and Yue N Dai. 'Emotional Support from AI Chatbots: Should a Supportive Partner Self-Disclose or Not?' *Journal of Computer-Mediated Communication* 26, no. 4 (2021): 207–22. https://doi.org/10.1093/jcmc/zmab005.

Montalbano, Lydia. 'Transparency in a Digitally Intertwined World: A Hybrid Approach to Consumers' Protection'. *Open Journal of Social Sciences* 9 (2021): 448–85. www.scirp.org/journal/paperinformation?paperid=111602.

Mozilla Foundation (Vasse'i, Ramak M, and Gabriel Udoh). 'In Transparency We Trust?' 2024. https://foundation.mozilla.org/en/research/library/in-transparency-we-trust/.

Naprys, Ernestas. 'Mother Files Lawsuit Blaming Character.AI for the Death of Her 14-Year-Old Boy'. *CyberNews*, 23 October 2024. https://cybernews.com/news/lawsuit-blames-character-ai-for-the-death-of-a-boy/.

Netherlands: Digital Policy Alert. 'Opened Consultation on Commission's Guidelines on Application of the Definition of an AI System and the Prohibited AI Practices Established in AI Act'. 2024. https://digitalpolicyalert.org/event/24407-opened-consultation-on-commissions-guidelines-on-application-of-the-definition-of-an-ai-system-and-the-prohibited-ai-practices-established-in-ai-act.

OECD. 'Recommendation of the Council on Artificial Intelligence, OECD/LEGAL/0449'. 2023. https://legalinstruments.oecd.org/en/instruments/OECD-LEGAL-0449.

Pentina, Iryna, et al. 'Exploring Relationship Development with Social Chatbots: A Mixed-Method Study of Replika'. *Computers in Human Behavior* 140 (2023).

Piccolo, Lara SG, et al. 'Chasing the Chatbots: Directions for Interaction and Design Research'. In *Internet Science International Workshops*, St. Petersburg, Russia, 157–69, 2018.

Reidenberg, Joel R, et al. 'Privacy Harms and the Effectiveness of the Notice and Choice Framework'. TPRC Conference Paper; Fordham Law Legal Studies Research Paper No. 2418247, 2014. https://papers.ssrn.com/sol3/papers.cfm?abstract_id=2418247.

Replika. 'Terms of Service'. Last updated 7 February 2023. https://replika.com/legal/terms.

Rusbult, Caryl E, Marten Y Agnew, and Christopher R Arriaga. 'The Investment Model Scale: Measuring Commitment Level, Satisfaction Level, Quality of Alternatives, and Investment Size'. *Personal Relationships* 5, no. 4 (1998): 357–87.

Singleton, Tom, et al. 'How a Chatbot Encouraged a Man Who Wanted to Kill the Queen'. *BBC Technology*, 6 October 2023. www.bbc.com/news/technology-67012224.

Somers, Meredith. 'Emotion AI, Explained'. *MIT Sloan Ideas Made to Matter*, 8 March 2019. https://mitsloan.mit.edu/ideas-made-to-matter/emotion-ai-explained.

Sprigman, Christopher J, and Stephan Tontrup. 'Privacy Decisions Are Not Private: How the Notice and Choice Regime Induces Us to Ignore Collective Privacy Risks and What Regulation Should Do About It'. *Journal of Empirical Legal Studies*; NYU Law and Economics Research Paper No. 23-22, 2023. https://papers.ssrn.com/sol3/papers.cfm?abstract_id=4359681.

Stawarz, Katarzyna, Chris Preist, and David Coyle. 'User Experience of Cognitive Behavioral Therapy Apps for Depression: An Analysis of App Functionality and User Reviews'. *Journal of Medical Internet Research* 20, no. 6 (2018).

TIDIO (Fokina, Maryia). 'The Future of Chatbots: 80+ Chatbot Statistics for 2025'. 18 October 2024. www.tidio.com/blog/chatbot-statistics/.

UNESCO. *Recommendation on the Ethics of Artificial Intelligence (SHS/BIO/REC-AIETHICS/2021)*. Paris: UNESCO, 2021. https://unesdoc.unesco.org/ark:/48223/pf0000380455.

Wellman, Barry. 'Physical Place and Cyberplace: The Rise of Personalized Networking'. *International Journal of Urban and Regional Research* 25, no. 2 (2001): 227–52.

Zimmerman, Anne. 'Human/AI Relationships: Challenges, Downsides, and Impacts on Human/Human Relationships'. *AI and Ethics* 4 (2023): 1555–67.

6

Watching the Watchers: Health Data, Artificial Intelligence, and the Transatlantic Rebalancing of Privacy Power

GARY HSUANYU LIU

Abstract

Health data governance reveals competing visions of democratic control in the artificial intelligence era. The European Union's AI Act and European Health Data Space Regulation mandate pre-deployment scrutiny and ban exploitative uses, while the United States relies on Federal Trade Commission enforcement after harm occurs. This regulatory divergence stems from fundamental differences: The EU treats data protection as a fundamental right requiring collective safeguards, whereas the US prioritises market forces constrained by First Amendment protections. GoodRx demonstrates the inadequacy of post-hoc enforcement when companies monetise medical vulnerabilities. Following Richards and Hartzog's framework, this chapter proposes a transatlantic duty of loyalty requiring health data processors to act in users' best interests. This would transform privacy from individual control to structural safeguard, bridging constitutional differences while enabling beneficial innovation. The regulatory choice will determine whether technology serves human flourishing or entrenches surveillance capitalism.

Keywords

Health data privacy; AI governance; Duty of loyalty; Transatlantic regulation; Information fiduciaries

I. Introduction

GoodRx promised to keep your prescriptions private. Instead, the digital pharmacy platform spent years secretly feeding users' medication histories – antidepressants, blood pressure pills, HIV treatments – to Facebook's advertising machine.[1] When the Federal Trade Commission (FTC) finally caught up in 2023, the penalty was almost insulting: $1.5 million, pocket change for a company that had betrayed 55 million Americans since 2017.[2]

Across the Atlantic, the European Union tells a different story. Under the newly enacted AI Act, any comparable diagnostic tool faces mandatory pre-deployment scrutiny: bias testing, risk mitigation plans, data governance safeguards – all backed by fines up to €35 million or 7 per cent of global turnover.[3] The United States waits for harm, then slaps wrists. The EU demands proof of safety before algorithms touch patients.

This regulatory gulf reveals something deeper than bureaucratic preference. Health data governance has become the testing ground for competing visions of democratic control in the AI age.[4] The EU bets on fundamental rights and collective safeguards to constrain what it sees as data-driven domination. The US – particularly after Donald Trump's swift rescission of Joe Biden's AI executive order upon returning to the White House in January 2025 – has doubled down on deregulation, trusting market forces and post-hoc enforcement to sort things out.[5]

The stakes transcend academic debate. Privacy law now functions as a laboratory, testing whether fundamental rights can genuinely constrain informational capitalism (the EU wager) or whether constitutional speech protections and market dynamics will entrench corporate surveillance (the US trajectory). Other nations watch this contest that will determine whether the 'watchers' – namely, the corporations and governments leveraging health AI – face meaningful accountability or enjoy unfettered power.

[1] Federal Trade Commission, 'FTC Enforcement Action to Bar GoodRx from Sharing Consumers' Sensitive Health Info for Advertising', news release, 1 February 2023, www.ftc.gov/news-events/news/press-releases/2023/02/ftc-enforcement-action-bar-goodrx-sharing-consumers-sensitive-health-info-advertising.

[2] *United States v GoodRx Holdings, Inc.*, No. 2:23-cv-00460 (N.D. Cal. filed 1 February 2023); Federal Trade Commission, 'FTC Enforcement Action to Bar GoodRx from Sharing Consumers' Sensitive Health Info for Advertising' (news release, 1 February 2023).

[3] Regulation (EU) 2024/1689 (Artificial Intelligence Act), Articles 6, 9–15, 99 (categorising most medical AI as 'high-risk' and requiring strict pre-market compliance; authorising fines up to €35 million or 7 per cent of global turnover).

[4] Regulation (EU) 2024/1689 (AI Act); Regulation (EU) 2025/327 (European Health Data Space Regulation); European Commission, 'Communication – Fostering a European Approach to Artificial Intelligence', COM 2021 205 final (21 April 2021), Annex: *Coordinated Plan on Artificial Intelligence 2021* Review; European Commission, 'Communication – AI Continent Action Plan', COM 2025 165 final (9 April 2025).

[5] Executive Order 14110, 'Safe, Secure, and Trustworthy Development and Use of Artificial Intelligence', issued 30 October 2023 (revoked 20 January 2025); The White House, Executive Order 14179, 'Removing Barriers to American Leadership in Artificial Intelligence', 23 January 2025.

The challenge for democracies lies in reclaiming control without stifling innovation. This chapter traces the transatlantic divide through its key battlegrounds. We begin with the EU's ambitious gambit: the 2024 AI Act's risk-based requirements and the freshly minted European Health Data Space Regulation (EU) 2025/327,[6] which bans exploitative uses like medical record-based advertising while channelling secondary use through 'health data access bodies' meant to serve public benefit.[7]

We then turn to the US's patchwork landscape, where the Health Insurance Portability and Accountability Act (HIPAA)'s narrow scope leaves vast swaths of wellness tech unregulated,[8] and the FTC scrambles to plug holes through aggressive enforcement actions – GoodRx, BetterHelp, Flo, Cerebral – each revealing new depths of consumer betrayal.[9] The analysis extends to constitutional constraints, particularly how *Sorrell v IMS Health* weaponised free speech against privacy regulation,[10] potentially entrenching data aggregators' power permanently.

Building on work by Neil Richards, Woodrow Hartzog, Julie Cohen, Danielle Citron, and Daniel Solove, this chapter proposes a transatlantic duty of loyalty as a unifying principle – a legally enforceable obligation for all health data processors to act in users' best interests rather than their own. This includes concrete measures: context-specific fiduciary duties,[11] Algorithmic Impact Assessments aligned with EU risk tiers, and privacy-enhancing technologies deployed through data trusts.[12]

The window for action is narrowing. Forums like the Trade and Technology Council[13] offer venues for coordination, but only if policymakers act before regulatory arbitrage creates an irreversible race to the bottom. Privacy must evolve from individual control to structural safeguard if democracies hope to harness AI's benefits without sacrificing human dignity. The choice we make now will echo for generations.

[6] Regulation (EU) 2025/327 (European Health Data Space Regulation), 2025 OJ L 119/1.

[7] J Scott Marcus et al, 'The European Health Data Space' (study for European Parliament ITRE Committee, PE 740.054, 2022); see also Regulation (EU) 2025/327, Articles 33–37. (mandates access to health data for defined secondary uses while prohibiting exploitative uses).

[8] 45 C.F.R. pts. 160 & 164 (2024).

[9] *In re Flo Health, Inc.*, FTC Docket C-4747 (consent order, 17 June 2021); *United States v GoodRx Holdings, Inc.* (N.D. Cal., consent order 1 February 2023); Federal Trade Commission, press release, 2 March 2023, 'FTC to Ban BetterHelp from Revealing Consumers' Data, Including Sensitive Mental Health Information, to Facebook and Others for Targeted Advertising'; Federal Trade Commission, press release, 15 April 2024, 'Proposed FTC Order will Prohibit Telehealth Firm Cerebral from Using or Disclosing Sensitive Data for Advertising Purposes, and Require it to Pay $7 Million'.

[10] *Sorrell v IMS Health Inc.*, 564 US 552 (2011) (holding that Vermont's ban on selling prescriber-identifying data violated the First Amendment).

[11] Helen Nissenbaum, *Privacy in Context: Technology, Policy, and the Integrity of Social Life* (Stanford, CA: Stanford University Press, 2009) (introduces the 'contextual integrity' theory – that privacy norms depend on social context – which underlies calls for context-specific data duties).

[12] Margot E Kaminski, 'Binary Governance: Lessons from the GDPR's Approach to Algorithmic Accountability', *Southern California Law Review* 92 (2019): 1529–616.

[13] European Commission, 'Joint Statement EU–US Trade and Technology Council', 4 April 2024.

II. The EU's Rights-Based Model

A. The AI Act

While American regulators chase harms after they happen, the EU rewrote the playbook entirely. The AI Act [Regulation (EU) 2024/1689] demands that medical AI prove its safety before deployment, with penalties up to €35 million for non-compliant deployment. The EU chose precaution: every medical AI system must prove its worth before deployment, much like pharmaceutical companies have long done with drugs.[14]

The Act flips the burden of proof. Tech companies can no longer deploy first and apologise later. Articles 9 through 15 of the AI Act impose obligations that significantly constrain technology companies.[15] For instance, Article 9's requirement that providers identify and mitigate threats to 'fundamental rights' throughout an AI system's lifecycle.[16] It sounds reasonable until you realise what this means in practice: a cardiac diagnostic algorithm trained primarily on Caucasian patients must somehow prove it will not discriminate against only African populations before touching a single patient.

Article 10 of the AI Act addresses bias directly, demanding training datasets be 'relevant, representative, free of errors'.[17] But perfection is mythology in health data. The determination of 'representative' data remains challenging when European demographics reflect documented healthcare inequalities.[18] The AI Act offers no easy answers, only mandates that force uncomfortable reckonings with data's embedded prejudices.

Transparency obligations reveal deeper tensions.[19] Article 13 of the AI Act requires full disclosure of AI limitations; for example, imagine informing emergency physicians that their triage algorithm performs 20 per cent worse on Roma patients.[20] Would they use it anyway? Article 14 of the AI Act goes further,

[14] AI Act, Article 6 and Annex III (classifying most medical AI as 'high-risk', triggering pre-market risk mitigation requirements); American Medical Association Policy H-480.940 (modified 2025) (urging that health AI be 'designed and evaluated in keeping with best practices in user-centered design'); Zach Meyers, 'Implementing the AI Act' (Centre for European Reform, December 2024).

[15] AI Act, Articles 9–15; Connor Dunlop, 'An EU AI Act That Works for People and Society: Five Areas of Focus for the Trilogues', Ada Lovelace Institute, 6 September 2023, www.adalovelaceinstitute.org/policy-briefing/eu-ai-act-trilogues/; Kate Crawford, *Atlas of AI* (New Haven, CT: Yale University Press, 2021).

[16] Anya ER Prince and Daniel Schwarcz, 'Proxy Discrimination in the Age of Artificial Intelligence and Big Data', *Iowa Law Review* 105 (2020): 1257–318.

[17] Cathy O'Neil, *Weapons of Math Destruction: How Big Data Increases Inequality and Threatens Democracy* (New York: Crown, 2016).

[18] European Commission, *State of Health in the EU: Synthesis Report 2023* (Dec. 2023), 14–16 (documented health disparities); EuroHealthNet & Centre for Health Equity Analytics, *Social Inequalities in Health in the EU – Summary Report* (September 2025), 3.

[19] Frank Pasquale, *The Black Box Society: The Secret Algorithms That Control Money and Information* (Cambridge, MA: Harvard University Press, 2015).

[20] Regulation (EU) 2022/868 (Data Governance Act), 2022 OJ L 152/1; Sandra Wachter, Brent Mittelstadt, and Chris Russell, 'Counterfactual Explanations Without Opening the Black Box: Automated Decisions and the GDPR', *Harvard Journal of Law & Technology* 31 (2018): 841–87.

prohibiting full automation and mandating 'kill switches' for clinical overrides. Yet automation bias runs deep: will overworked doctors genuinely second-guess systems marketed as 99 per cent accurate?[21] The Act bets they will, if given proper tools and training.

The accuracy standards in Article 15 of the AI Act set shifting goals through post-market monitoring. Any 'serious malfunction' triggers immediate reporting obligations – a recipe for litigation when algorithms inevitably fail. The enforcement teeth are sharp: violations trigger fines up to €35 million or 7 per cent of global turnover,[22] making the US's $1.5 million GoodRx penalty look relatively tiny and disproportionate.

This pharmaceutical-style conformity regime transforms AI deployment.[23] Before our hypothetical cardiac AI sees a single patient, developers must document bias testing across ethnicities, build physician overrides, complete clinical validation, and establish continuous monitoring. Miss one step? The algorithm stays shelved. The EU effectively created algorithmic gatekeepers through mandatory third-party audits – a bureaucracy some call innovation-killing, others call overdue.

Between rapid deployment and patient protection, the EU chose its side decisively. Whether this represents prudent governance or stifling overreach depends entirely on your faith in markets versus precaution. It seems certain that the EU no longer trusts tech companies to self-regulate when lives hang in the balance.

B. The European Health Data Space Regulation: Governing Secondary Use of Health Data

Your hospital's cardiac imaging archive contains many years of heart scans, having become a goldmine for AI training. On 26 March 2025, when the European Health Data Space Regulation (EHDS) entered into force, this archive became quasi-public property. The European Health Data Space Regulation transforms health data from institutional asset into collective resource, forcing hospitals to share their carefully curated datasets with anyone who claims a legitimate purpose. Decades of painstakingly collected medical records must now be handed to Google's DeepMind, Pfizer's research teams, or any startup with a plausible research proposal.

The mandatory sharing regime begins in 2029. Article 33(1) of the EHDS compels all data holders – hospitals, clinics, even wellness apps – to make

[21] Virginia Eubanks, *Automating Inequality: How High-Tech Tools Profile, Police, and Punish the Poor* (New York: St. Martin's Press, 2018); Andrew D Selbst, 'Negligence and AI's Human Users', *Boston University Law Review* 100 (2020): 1315–76.

[22] AI Act, Articles 6, 9–15, 99.

[23] US Food and Drug Administration, *Artificial Intelligence/Machine Learning-Based Software as a Medical Device Action Plan* (January 2021) (FDA's roadmap to regulate AI-based medical software with pre-market review and continuous monitoring, akin to medical device oversight).

15 categories of electronic health data available upon request.[24] These span everything imaginable: electronic health records, diagnostic images, genomic sequences, real-time device outputs. Even intellectual property claims cannot block access; Article 33(4) of the EHDS merely requires 'measures to preserve confidentiality' while mandating disclosure regardless.[25]

One can possibly picture the implications. A Finnish university's rare disease genomic database, built through decades of patient trust, becomes accessible to pharmaceutical giants hunting for drug targets. German hospitals must share their imaging archives with Silicon Valley startups promising revolutionary diagnostics. The EHDS embodies the EU's solidarity principle taken to its logical extreme: individual institutions lose control over the data they had been collecting for years because it was never truly theirs – it belongs to the collective good.

Yet the EU has not created a data free-for-all. Article 34 of the EHDS carefully enumerates acceptable purposes: scientific research, health innovation, public health surveillance, policy-making, patient safety monitoring, regulatory activities, personalised medicine. By sharp contrast, Article 35 of the EHDS draws bright red lines around forbidden uses.[26] Health data cannot enable 'digital redlining' – no insurance premium adjustments, no employment discrimination. Marketing and advertising to individuals is categorically banned, while developing products harmful to health is prohibited.[27]

The prohibition list reveals European anxieties about surveillance capitalism. Tech firms obtaining cancer patient data through EHDS cannot build personalised wellness marketing lists, peddle targeted insurance products, or nudge vulnerable patients toward expensive treatments. Recital 26 EHDS frames this in solidarity terms: health data must serve common good, not private extraction.

New 'health data access bodies' (quasi-judicial gatekeepers that each Member State must establish by 2027) will enforce these provisions.[28] These bodies wield formidable powers: issuing data permits that specify exact datasets, purposes, and safeguards; requiring proof that research serves public interest; conducting on-site inspections; revoking permits for violations. Misuse triggers fines up to €20 million or 4 per cent of global turnover. Applicants typically analyse data only in secure environments with identifiers pseudonymised, though cryptographers warn that re-identification remains trivially easy given modern techniques.[29]

[24] J Scott Marcus et al, 'The European Health Data Space' (European Parliament Study PE 740.054, 2022); see also European Health Data Space Regulation, Articles 33–37.

[25] European Health Data Space Regulation, Articles 33(1), 33(4), 34–35.

[26] J Scott Marcus et al., 'The European Health Data Space' (European Parliament study PE 740.054, 2022); see also European Health Data Space Regulation, Articles 33–37.

[27] European Health Data Space Regulation, Article 33(1), 33(4), 34–35 (Article 35 explicitly forbids using health data for individualised advertising or other decisions detrimental to individuals).

[28] European Health Data Space Regulation, Article 55(1); Article 55(6).

[29] Article 29 Data Protection Working Party, *Opinion 05/2014 on Anonymisation Techniques* (WP 216, 10 April 2014).

But here lies the one-way valve problem. Public hospitals must share their data, yet Big Tech platforms swimming in wellness app data face no reciprocal obligation.[30] Google could mine European hospital records for AI development while keeping Fitbit's consumer health data locked away.[31] The European Data Protection Board warned that EHDS's mandatory sharing might undermine the General Data Protection Regulation (GDPR)'s privacy guarantees without extraordinary safeguards.[32] They recommended clearer purpose limitations and stronger controls over commercial health apps – advice only partially heeded.[33]

Combined with the AI Act, these instruments attempt something unprecedented: reshaping power dynamics by declaring health data a common resource rather than corporate property.[34] The EHDS proclaims that intimate medical information should fuel collective flourishing, not surveillance capitalism.[35] Whether this grand experiment delivers ethical AI serving public health – or simply hands Silicon Valley a buffet of European medical data – remains an open question.[36] The world watches as the EU's solidarity principle meets market reality.

C. Power and Critique: Between Rights and Reality

The EU elevated data protection to a fundamental right, enshrined in Article 8 of the EU Charter of Fundamental Rights. But rights on paper do not automatically translate to power in practice. Paul De Hert and Vagelis Papakonstantinou pierce this comfortable fiction, warning that constitutionalising data protection risks creating what they call a dangerous 'hierarchisation' of rights.[37] The Charter legislator intended Article 8 as a bulwark against mass surveillance; a digital-age reinforcement of human dignity.[38] Yet De Hert observes that treating data protection in splendid isolation misses the point entirely: the real enemy is 'pervasive surveillance and asymmetry of power which now confronts the individual'.[39] Compliance checklists will not save us if they do not genuinely constrain the watchers – both states and corporations – from dominating the watched.

[30] European Health Data Space Regulation, Articles 33(1), 33(4), 34–35.

[31] European Health Data Space Regulation, Articles 33(1), 33(4), 34–35.

[32] European Data Protection Board (EDPB) & European Data Protection Supervisor (EDPS), *Joint Opinion 03/2022 on the Proposal for a European Health Data Space* (12 July 2022), paras 45–67.

[33] EDPB & EDPS, *Joint Opinion 03/2022*, paras 45–67.

[34] Amnesty International and Access Now, *The Toronto Declaration: Protecting the Right to Equality and Non-Discrimination in Machine Learning Systems* (16 May 2018).

[35] European Health Data Space Regulation, Article 33(1), 33(4), 34–35 (as noted above, Article 35 explicitly bans use of personal health data for advertising or marketing).

[36] Crawford, *Atlas of AI*.

[37] Paul De Hert and Vagelis Papakonstantinou, 'The New General Data Protection Regulation', *Computer Law & Security Review* 32, no. 2 (2016): 179–94.

[38] De Hert and Papakonstantinou, 'The New General Data Protection Regulation', 183–84.

[39] De Hert and Papakonstantinou, 'The New General Data Protection Regulation'.

Orla Lynskey sharpens this critique by dissecting individual control's practical futility. Despite the GDPR's arsenal (access rights, rectification, deletion, portability) ordinary users cannot negotiate equally with tech giants.[40] The so-called 'privacy paradox' (we claim to value privacy yet surrender data readily) is not irrational behaviour but structural coercion: information asymmetry, network effects, and lack of genuine alternatives trap users in exploitative relationships.[41] No amount of consent boxes or algorithmic transparency empowers individuals against platforms' behavioural profiling machinery.

Lynskey proposes treating data companies as information utilities bearing special obligations. Yet she identifies a cruel paradox: enhancing individual rights might deliver symbolic victories while leaving power structures intact.[42] The EHDS partially addresses this through mandatory sharing and public oversight yet scattered data subjects cannot realistically detect misuse once pharmaceutical companies gain 'permitted' access to their medical histories.

Critics expose the AI Act's blind spots with surgical precision. While heavily regulating AI providers, the Act underspecifies deployers' obligations and ignores the shadowy data broker ecosystems that feed these systems.[43] Compliance costs threaten market consolidation. Only giants can afford full adherence, potentially crushing innovative startups despite sandbox provisions. Moreover, the AI Act's demand to eliminate 'unintentional bias' from training data borders on technical fantasy. Ensuring AI performs equally for rural elderly patients and urban youth presents significant technical challenges. Providers might satisfy formal conformity while delivering algorithms that reproduce disparities through subtler biases no audit catches.

The transatlantic dimension compounds these power asymmetries. Will the Brussels Effect force global tech to raise standards worldwide, or companies might geo-fence Europe with restricted features, potentially depriving European patients of cutting-edge innovations.[44] American companies might concentrate AI development in jurisdictions with lighter touch, creating regulatory arbitrage

[40] Orla Lynskey, *The Foundations of EU Data Protection Law* (Oxford: Oxford University Press, 2015), 178–215.

[41] Francisco Costa-Cabral and Orla Lynskey, *The Internal and External Constraints of Data Protection on Competition Law in the EU*, LSE Law, Society and Economy Working Papers, no. 25/2015 (London: London School of Economics and Political Science, 2015). See also Maria C Wasastjerna, 'The Role of Big Data and Digital Privacy in Merger Review', *European Competition Journal* 14, nos. 2–3 (2018): 417–44.

[42] Orla Lynskey, 'Complete and Effective Data Protection', *Current Legal Problems* 76, no. 1 (2023). See also Orla Lynskey, 'Grappling with "Data Power": Normative Nudges from Data Protection and Privacy', *Theoretical Inquiries in Law* 20, no. 1 (2019).

[43] AI Act, Articles 53 and 69; Nathan Genicot, *From Blueprint to Reality: Implementing AI Regulatory Sandboxes under the AI Act* (Brussels: FARI & LSTS Research Group, 2024); Massimo Pellegrino, Sara Mancini, Eliana Gerardi, and Irene Mumeni Urbani, *The AI Act: Help or Hindrance for SMEs? An Analysis of the Cost of Compliance with the AI Act for SMEs* (Milan: Intellera Consulting, July 2024); A&O Shearman, 'Zooming in on AI – #4: The Interplay Between "Deployers" and "Providers" in the EU AI Act' (2024).

[44] US Government Accountability Office, *Artificial Intelligence in Health Care: Benefits and Challenges of Technologies to Augment Patient Care*, GAO-22-104629 (2022).

that undermines European protections. *Schrems II* already demonstrated how divergent privacy regimes disrupt data flows.[45] Growing AI governance gaps threaten to similarly fracture EU-US medical research collaboration unless new frameworks emerge.

Crucially, the EU's rights-based model, however pathbreaking, cannot cure structural power imbalances through law alone. Implementation determines everything: adequately funding supervisory authorities, building real technical audit capacity, fostering compliance cultures that view obligations as ethical innovation rather than bureaucratic burden.[46] The EU has set an ambitious stage. The question whether actors rise to meet it or find ways to perform compliance theatre while power dynamics persist remains. The contrast with the US's approach becomes even starker when we examine how the US handles these same power dynamics through market forces and ex post enforcement, as the next section explores.

III. The US Enforcement-Centric Model

A. HIPAA's Limited Reach and the Wellness Data Gap

Your therapist's notes enjoy ironclad federal protection. But the intake questionnaire of your therapy app is for data brokers. This absurdity lies at the heart of American health privacy law. HIPAA,[47] enacted in 1996 when 'apps' meant appetisers, covers only three narrow categories: health plans, clearinghouses, and providers who transmit electronic claims.[48] The vast consumer health ecosystem – fitness trackers monitoring your heart rate, mental health apps recording your darkest thoughts, DNA testing kits mapping your genetic future – operates in a regulatory void unless they partner with traditional healthcare entities.

This breeds false confidence. Eighty per cent of Americans believe their health app data enjoys HIPAA protection.[49] This assumption is fundamentally

[45] De Hert and Papakonstantinou, 'The New General Data Protection Regulation'; see also *Data Protection Commissioner v Facebook Ireland Ltd.* ('*Schrems II*'), Case C-311/18, [2020] EU:C:2020:559 (Ct. Justice EU, 16 July 2020).

[46] World Health Organization, *Ethics and Governance of Artificial Intelligence for Health* (Geneva: WHO, 2025).

[47] Health Insurance Portability and Accountability Act of 1996, Pub. L. No. 104-191, 110 Stat. 1936 (21 August 1996) (pre-digital era statute); Kevin Henry, 'The History of HIPAA: Complete Guide Since 1996', *Accountable* (blog), 7 April 2021, www.accountablehq.com/post/hipaa-history (1996 technological shift context).

[48] 45 C.F.R. § 160.103 (defining 'covered entities' under HIPAA as health plans, health care clearinghouses, and certain providers).

[49] US Department of Health & Human Services, Office for Civil Rights, 'Protecting the Privacy and Security of Your Health Information When Using Your Personal Cell Phone or Tablet', *HHS.gov*, last reviewed 29 June 2022, www.hhs.gov/hipaa/for-professionals/privacy/guidance/cell-phone-hipaa/index.html. See also US Department of Health & Human Services, 'Health App Use Scenarios & HIPAA' (2016).

incorrect.[50] Period trackers freely monetise fertility patterns. Mental health apps harvest anxiety levels for pharmaceutical companies. Wellness platforms compile intimate health profiles invisible to any privacy law.[51] Users assume the confidentiality they experience in doctors' offices extends to digital health tools.[52] Instead, they encounter what one analysis called 'broadly worded privacy policies' that enable apps to 'readily share data with third parties, including marketing and analytics companies'.[53]

Even when data originates in hospitals, clever laundering strips protection. *Dinerstein v Google* crystallized this loophole.[54] The University of Chicago Medical Center shared years of patient records with Google for AI research, removing identifiers per HIPAA's safe harbour rules. When a patient sued, claiming that granular timestamps and treatment patterns made re-identification trivial, the Seventh Circuit shrugged.[55] The court dismissed the case, finding no concrete injury sufficient to establish standing.[56]

The implications of the ruling are staggering. Once hospitals strip 18 identifiers or obtain expert certification, medical records become unregulated commodities.[57] Organisations face zero liability for sharing 'de-identified' health data, even as cryptographers demonstrate that modern AI makes re-identification child's play.[58] Cross-reference a few datasets (location data, purchase histories, social media) and anonymous medical records reveal their owners.[59]

HIPAA's safe harbour creates a dangerous fiction: that removing names and addresses somehow prevents re-identification in an age of big data. The

[50] ClearDATA, 'Many Americans Don't Realize Digital Health Apps Could Be Selling Their Personal Data', press release, 13 July 2023; Steve Alder, 'Majority of Americans Mistakenly Believe Health App Data Is Covered by HIPAA', *HIPAA Journal*, 26 July 2023 (reporting survey results that ~80 per cent of Americans wrongly assumed health apps are protected by HIPAA).

[51] US Department of Health & Human Services, Office for Civil Rights, 'Protecting the Privacy and Security of Your Health Information When Using Your Personal Cell Phone or Tablet'; see also HHS, 'Health App Use Scenarios & HIPAA' (2016).

[52] Tanja Schroeder, Maximilian Haug, and Heiko Gewald, 'Data Privacy Concerns Using mHealth Apps and Smart Speakers: Comparative Interview Study Among Mature Adults', *JMIR Formative Research* 6, no. 6 (2022): e28025.

[53] Sara H Jodka, 'App Users Beware: Most Healthcare, Fitness Tracker, and Wellness Apps Are Not Covered by HIPAA and HHS's New FAQs Makes That Clear', *Dickinson Wright Client Alert*, 7 May 2019; Quinn Grundy et al, 'Data Sharing Practices of Medicines-Related Apps and the Mobile Ecosystem: Traffic, Content, and Network Analysis', *BMJ* 364 (2019); Imdad Ullah, Roksana Boreli, and Salil S Kanhere, 'Privacy in Targeted Advertising on Mobile Devices: A Survey', *International Journal of Information Security* 22, no. 3 (2023): 647–78.

[54] *Dinerstein v Google, LLC*, 73 F.4th 502 (7th Cir. 2023) (held that once patient data were de-identified, the plaintiff had no concrete injury under privacy law); see also 'AI and Medical Liability', *ProAssurance* (February 2024).

[55] Plaintiff's re-identification theory deemed too speculative to count as an injury.

[56] *Dinerstein*, 73 F.4th 502 (7th Cir. 2023); see also 'AI and Medical Liability', *ProAssurance* (February 2024).

[57] *Dinerstein*, 73 F.4th at 508.

[58] 45 C.F.R. § 164.514(a)–(b) (HIPAA de-identification safe harbour rule); see also *Dinerstein*, 73 F.4th 502 (confirming that data de-identified per HIPAA is no longer 'protected health information').

[59] Paul M Schwartz and Daniel J Solove, 'The PII Problem: Privacy and a New Concept of Personally Identifiable Information', *New York University Law Review* 86 (2011): 1814–94.

de-identification process transforms protected health information into unprotected datasets that flow freely between companies. If (or when) anonymity fails individuals cannot prove the 'concrete injury' American courts demand, like financial loss or identity theft. Privacy violation alone does not count.

By contrast, European law protects all health data (including pseudonymised) under the GDPR, with the EHDS carefully channelling even anonymous data through governed pathways. The US maintains a two-tier system: fortress-like protection for traditional medical records, Wild West rules for everything else. This regulatory gap widens daily as health monitoring shifts from clinics to smartphones.

Absent comprehensive federal privacy legislation – stalled in Congress for over a decade – policing this chaos falls to the FTC and state attorneys general. These agencies must retrofit general consumer protection tools to address health privacy violations, as the next section explores. They are bringing knives to a data war.

B. FTC's New Playbook: Health Privacy Enforcement by Example

The FTC has recently demonstrated robust enforcement capabilities under existing authority. Armed only with Section 5's vague prohibition on 'unfair or deceptive' practices, the agency launched an enforcement blitz that's rewriting digital health law one betrayal at a time.[60] By resurrecting the decade-dormant Health Breach Notification Rule, the Commission sent a clear message: if Congress will not protect health privacy, we will.

Consider Flo Health's breathtaking deception. One hundred million women trusted this fertility app with their most intimate rhythms, such as menstruation dates, pregnancy hopes, miscarriage grief.[61] Flo promised confidentiality while secretly feeding this data to Facebook and Google's advertising machines. The 2021 consent order imposed no fine but mandated something potentially more painful: affirmative consent before any health data sharing, user notifications about past breaches, and perpetual independent privacy audits.[62] Every woman who had used Flo was notified that her data had been commodified.

GoodRx escalated the stakes. Despite plastering 'HIPAA secure' seals across its platform, this prescription service compiled users' medication histories (such as blood pressure pills, antidepressants, HIV treatments) and uploaded them

[60] Federal Trade Commission Act § 5, 15 USC § 45(a)(1) (2018) (prohibiting 'unfair or deceptive acts or practices' in commerce).

[61] *Flo Health, Inc.*, FTC Docket C-4747 (Decision and Order, 17 June 2021); see also Federal Trade Commission, press release, 22 June 2021, 'FTC Finalizes Order with Flo Health, a Fertility-Tracking App'.

[62] *Flo Health, Inc.*, FTC Docket C-4747.

wholesale to advertising platforms.[63] The $1.5 million fine barely registered, but the permanent injunction cut deep: GoodRx cannot share health data for advertising even with consent and must delete everything improperly collected.[64] The FTC effectively terminated their business model.

BetterHelp proved that mental health vulnerabilities attract the worst exploitation. Users seeking therapy bared their souls through intake questionnaires; depression histories, suicidal thoughts, childhood traumas.[65] BetterHelp harvested these confessions for Facebook, Snapchat, and Pinterest, turning anguish into ad targeting.[66] The FTC extracted $7.8 million for consumer refunds – its first health privacy restitution – while permanently banning any mental health data use for advertising.[67] Director Levine condemned BetterHelp for betraying 'consumers' most personal health information for profit.'[68]

Cerebral represents the Commission's most aggressive stance yet. This telehealth startup leaked 3.2 million patients' psychiatric data through tracking pixels embedded in its platform.[69] The proposed order does not just fine the company $7 million – it holds the CEO personally liable.[70] Cerebral must implement a 'simple cancellation' mechanism and delete all unnecessary data.[71] By naming executives as individual respondents, the FTC signals that hiding behind corporate veils will not protect those who traffic in health data.[72]

Through these escalating enforcement actions, the FTC constructs something approaching common law for data loyalty. The pattern crystallises: companies that promise privacy while sharing health data face escalating consequences.[73] Each settlement adds new obligations (simplified cancellations, executive liability, permanent advertising bans) creating precedents that bind the industry.

[63] *GoodRx Holdings, Inc.*, Stipulated Order (N.D. Cal., 1 February 2023); see also Federal Trade Commission, press release, 1 February 2023.

[64] *GoodRx Holdings, Inc.*, Stipulated Order.

[65] *BetterHelp, Inc.*, FTC Complaint No. 2023169 (2023) (noting that BetterHelp's intake questionnaire asked users highly sensitive questions).

[66] Federal Trade Commission, *Press Release*, 2 March 2023, 'FTC to Ban BetterHelp from Revealing Consumers' Data, Including Sensitive Mental Health Information, to Facebook and Others for Targeted Advertising' (revealing that although BetterHelp promised to keep therapy data private, it had been sharing users' email addresses, IP addresses, and mental health quiz answers with advertising partners).

[67] *BetterHelp, Inc.*, FTC Complaint No. 2023169 (2023).

[68] *BetterHelp, Inc.*, FTC Complaint No. 2023169.

[69] *Federal Trade Commission v Cerebral, Inc.*, No. 1:24-cv-21376 (S.D. Fla., filed 17 April 2024) (alleging that ~3.2 million patients' data were leaked via tracking pixels); Katie Adams, 'Cerebral Admits That it Wrongly Shared Data of 3.1M Users', *MedCity News*, 10 March 2023.

[70] *FTC v Cerebral, Inc.*, No. 1:24-cv-21376 (S.D. Fla. 2024).

[71] Federal Trade Commission, press release, 15 April 2024, 'Proposed FTC Order Will Prohibit Telehealth Firm Cerebral from Using or Disclosing Sensitive Data for Advertising Purposes, and Require It to Pay $7 Million'.

[72] *FTC v Cerebral, Inc.* (S.D. Fla. 2024).

[73] Federal Trade Commission, '2023 Privacy and Data Security Update' (annual report, January 2024) (summarising recent bans on sharing health data for ads and other enforcement trends); Federal Trade Commission, 'FTC Finalizes Changes to the Health Breach Notification Rule' press release, 20 April 2024; *Federal Trade Commission v Easy Healthcare* (Premom) (FTC administrative consent order, 2023) Daniel J Solove and Woodrow Hartzog, 'The FTC and the New Common Law of Privacy', *Columbia Law Review* 114 (2014): 583–676.

Companies now understand the rules even if the Congress never wrote them: do not monetise health data without express consent, claim false HIPAA compliance, or embed tracking pixels in therapy apps.

The industry trembles accordingly. Post-enforcement, health apps scrambled to remove tracking code, update privacy policies, and geo-fence European users. State attorneys general pile on with parallel actions targeting reproductive health data and clinic visit locations.[74] Yet this ad hoc approach has obvious limits. GoodRx's betrayal festered from 2017 to 2020 before anyone noticed.[75] Penalties remain pocket change for tech giants; BetterHelp's $7.8 million barely dented parent company Teladoc. Meta and Google, the ultimate data recipients, faced no direct sanctions.

Most critically, the FTC lacks explicit health privacy rulemaking authority under Section 5, though it's testing boundaries through proceedings on 'commercial surveillance'.[76] Until Congress acts or rules emerge, protection depends on proving deception or unfairness case-by-case, leaving countless apps to exploit users while regulators play catch-up. The US effectively outsources health privacy law to FTC enforcement attorneys, hoping they move faster than the next betrayal.

C. Market Power, 'Data Freedom', and Constitutional Friction

The First Amendment undercut American privacy law before it was born. In *Sorrell v IMS Health*, the Supreme Court transformed data trafficking into protected speech, striking down Vermont's attempt to stop pharmaceutical companies from buying doctors' prescription histories.[77] The state had banned data miners from selling these records for drug marketing – a modest privacy protection by European standards. The Court's response was devastating as it stated that 'speech

[74] Thomas Cory, Wolf Rieder, and Thu-My Huynh, 'A Qualitative Analysis Framework for mHealth Privacy Practices', in *2024 IEEE European Symposium on Security and Privacy Workshops (EuroS&PW)* (Piscataway, NJ: IEEE, 2024), 24–31; DATUREX GmbH, 'Compliance in Fitness Apps: Protecting Personal Health Data', 23 January 2024, https://externer-datenschutzbeauftragter-dresden.de/en/leisure-time/compliance-in-fitness-apps-protection-of-personal-health-data/; RiAnn Bradshaw, 'HIPAA & GDPR Compliance for Health App Developers: Security & Legal Considerations', LLIF.org, 31 January 2025, https://llif.org/2025/01/31/hipaa-gdpr-compliance-health-apps/; Paul F Schmeltzer and John F Howard, 'Beyond HIPAA: How State Laws Are Reshaping Health Data Compliance' Clark Hill PLC, 26 June 2025. www.clarkhill.com/news-events/news/beyond-hipaa-how-state-laws-are-reshaping-health-data-compliance/; Jill McKeon, 'Google Tackles Data Privacy, Plans to Delete Location History at Abortion Clinics', *HealthTechSecurity*, 5 July 2022, www.techtarget.com/healthtechsecurity/news/366594734/Google-Tackles-Data-Privacy-Plans-to-Delete-Location-History-at-Abortion-Clinics; Brandon Vigliarolo, 'Google Location Tracking to Forget You Were Ever at That Medical Clinic', *The Register*, 2 July 2022, www.theregister.com/2022/07/02/google_medical_privacy/; Ali Jessani, 'Health Privacy in 2025 and Beyond', *American Bar Association, Antitrust Law Section*, 13 March 2025, www.americanbar.org/groups/antitrust_law/resources/newsletters/health-privacy-in-2025/.

[75] *GoodRx Holdings, Inc.* (N.D. Cal., 1 February 2023); see also Federal Trade Commission, news release, 1 February 2023.

[76] Alder, 'Majority of Americans Mistakenly Believe Health App Data Is Covered by HIPAA'.

[77] *Sorrell v IMS Health Inc.*, 564 US 552 (2011) (reaffirmed that data mining for marketing is protected speech under the First Amendment).

in aid of pharmaceutical marketing' deserves constitutional protection. Any law targeting specific content (prescription data) or speakers (data brokers) triggers strict scrutiny. Vermont's privacy rationale crumbled under this exacting standard.

Sorrell handed the data industry its favourite weapon. Privacy laws now face immediate attack as censorship. Industry lawyers argue 'data is speech', transforming every database regulation into a First Amendment case. While scholars vigorously contest this expansive reading, Sorrell's shadow looms over every privacy proposal. The decision reflects the US's fundamental commitment: information commerce remains presumptively open, while the EU treats personal data as inherently rights-limited.

This constitutional straitjacket forces American regulators into contortions. Privacy rules must target deception or concrete harms rather than data use itself. The FTC punishes broken promises and unfair practices, not privacy violations per se. Companies face liability for violating their own policies or causing substantial injury – never for the simple act of collecting or sharing health data. A transatlantic duty of loyalty, explored next, might navigate these constraints by emphasising fiduciary relationships over speech restrictions. But no such duty exists broadly today.

Meanwhile, market concentration amplifies these constitutional constraints. Julie Cohen's *Between Truth and Power* exposes how informational capitalism concentrates both economic and governance power in platform hands.[78] Health exemplifies this perfectly: Google swallowing Fitbit and health analytics firms, Amazon buying pharmacy chains and primary care networks. These conglomerates merge health metrics with purchase histories and search patterns, creating comprehensive behavioural profiles.[79] They wrap this surveillance in the rhetoric of innovation and free speech, making regulation appear both anti-competitive and unconstitutional.

Cohen and other scholars puncture this 'data freedom' narrative, revealing it as a power play by infrastructure controllers who effectively govern populations through algorithmic nudging and rent extraction.[80] Without robust regulation, 'health data barons' emerge; these are digital-age monopolists controlling the pipes through which medical information flows. Yet the US's constitutional framework makes European-style intervention nearly impossible.

Consider the dilemma of health-targeted advertising. When algorithms identify diabetics to show glucose monitor ads, is this useful commercial speech or

[78] Julie E Cohen, *Between Truth and Power: The Legal Constructions of Informational Capitalism* (New York: Oxford University Press, 2019), 45–89 (explores how legal and economic structures of the information age empower dominant online platforms and entrench their control).

[79] Julie E Cohen, 'Law for the Platform Economy', *UC Davis Law Review* 51 (2017): 133–204.

[80] Julie E Cohen, *Between Truth and Power*, 24–25; Shoshana Zuboff, *The Age of Surveillance Capitalism: The Fight for a Human Future at the New Frontier of Power* (New York: PublicAffairs, 2019); Tarleton Gillespie, 'The Politics of "Platforms"', *New Media & Society* 12, no. 3 (2010): 347–54; Richard H. Thaler and Cass R Sunstein, *Nudge: Improving Decisions about Health, Wealth, and Happiness* (New Haven, CT: Yale University Press, 2008).

predatory targeting? The answer shapes entire regulatory approaches. Defenders of data markets invoke the First Amendment, arguing that truthful commercial information helps consumers.[81] Critics counter that such practices exploit medical vulnerabilities to extract profit, steer patients toward expensive treatments, and enable discrimination.[82] Current doctrine favours the former view, leaving little room for restrictions.

The privacy-as-antitrust movement offers one escape route. Excessive data concentration might violate competition law even if privacy law cannot touch it. Merger reviews increasingly examine whether combining datasets reduces 'privacy competition', a novel theory that treats privacy degradation as consumer harm. But antitrust moves slowly while data markets consolidate rapidly.

The US thus arrives at an impasse. Post-hoc enforcement and constitutional deference to 'data freedom' enable a thriving surveillance economy punctuated by occasional FTC interventions. Recent actions signal regulatory muscle-flexing within existing constraints.[83] Yet without legislative change addressing Sorrell's legacy, the US-EU divide widens. The EU practices 'privacy fundamentalism' through rights and precaution; the US embraces 'privacy pragmatism' that prioritises innovation and speech.

IV. Rebalancing Through a Transatlantic Duty of Loyalty

A. From Privacy Rights to Loyalty Duties: Theoretical Foundations

'One bee sting can be shrugged off, but a hundred or a thousand can be lethal.' Danielle Citron and Daniel Solove's metaphor captures what privacy law persistently misses.[84] A fertility app sharing your cycle data feels trivial, until dozens of apps compile your health signals into profiles that determine your insurance rates, employment prospects, and targeted vulnerabilities. Privacy harms accumulate invisibly: 'chilling effects' make us self-censor our searches for mental health

[81] Eugene Volokh, 'Freedom of Speech and Information Privacy: The Troubling Implications of a Right to Stop People from Speaking About You'. *Stanford Law Review* 52, no. 5 (2000): 1049–124, https://doi.org/10.2307/1229510; Neil M Richards, 'Why Data Privacy Law is (Mostly) Constitutional', Yale Law School 15.

[82] Paul M Schwartz, 'Property, Privacy, and Personal Data', *Harvard Law Review* 117 (2003): 2056; Danielle Keats Citron and Frank Pasquale, 'The Scored Society: Due Process for Automated Predictions', *Washington Law Review* 89 (2014): 1.

[83] Lina Khan, 'FTC Chair Lina Khan Speaks on Data Security Rulemaking', 5 August 2022, https://clsbluesky.law.columbia.edu/2022/08/22/ftc-chair-lina-khan-speaks-on-data-security-rulemaking/.

[84] Danielle Keats Citron and Daniel J Solove, 'Privacy Harms', *Boston University Law Review* 102 (2022): 793–857.

help; 'distortion harms' let algorithms exploit our documented anxieties; collective harms erode the very possibility of unobserved existence.[85] Courts demand clear causation and quantifiable damage, yet privacy injuries are probabilistic and diffuse. Dinerstein exemplifies this blindness; judges see no harm in 'anonymised' medical records even as re-identification becomes trivial.

What if we have been asking the wrong question all along? Neil Richards and Woodrow Hartzog reframe the entire debate through their 'Concrete Proposal for Data Loyalty.'[86] Rather than pretending users can manage privacy through endless consent boxes, they propose treating data handlers like doctors or lawyers – professionals bound by duty to act in clients' best interests. The shift is profound: companies holding health data would owe users the same loyalty doctors owe patients. No more self-dealing. No more burying exploitative terms in privacy policies. Data becomes a stewarded trust, not an extractable resource.[87]

This is not just theoretical elegance – it is practical necessity. Richards and Hartzog recognise that notice-and-consent has become a cruel joke. Nobody reads privacy policies. Even those who try cannot anticipate how their depression questionnaire answers might train AI systems or feed advertising algorithms. Loyalty cuts through this farce by imposing ex ante constraints: certain uses are simply forbidden, regardless of what users might have 'agreed' to in desperation for mental health support.

Julie Cohen's scholarship illuminates why loyalty matters at the structural level. Privacy is not about hiding secrets – it is about preventing domination through information asymmetry. When platforms control vast data repositories and advanced analytics while users remain ignorant of how their information gets weaponised, genuine consent becomes impossible.[88] Cohen and Khan explore 'information fiduciaries' as a solution, where platforms assume trustee-like obligations.[89] The core insight: individual self-management cannot work against complex AI and ubiquitous collection. Only system-level duties can rebalance power.

Remarkably, loyalty principles already permeate both American and European law; just not explicitly. The GDPR's purpose limitation and fairness requirements effectively operate as de facto loyalty duties. Recital 4 of the GDPR declares data

[85] Daniel J Solove and Danielle Keats Citron, 'Standing and Privacy Harms: A Critique of TransUnion v. Ramirez', *Boston University Law Review Online* 101 (2021): 62–72 (criticises the Supreme Court's 2021 TransUnion decision for making it difficult to sue over intangible privacy injuries); see also Danielle Keats Citron, *The Fight for Privacy: Protecting Dignity, Identity, and Love in the Digital Age* (London: Random House, 2022).

[86] Neil M Richards, Woodrow Hartzog, and Jordan Francis, 'A Concrete Proposal for Data Loyalty', *Harvard Journal of Law & Technology* 37, no. 1 (2023): 1–52.

[87] Richards, Hartzog, and Francis, 'A Concrete Proposal for Data Loyalty'.

[88] Julie E Cohen, 'What Privacy Is For', *Harvard Law Review* 126 (2013): 1904; Julie E Cohen, 'Examined Lives: Informational Privacy and the Subject as Object', *Stanford Law Review* 52 (2000): 1373.

[89] Lina M Khan, 'Amazon's Antitrust Paradox', *Yale Law Journal* 126, no. 3 (2017): 710–805; see Jack M Balkin, 'Information Fiduciaries and the First Amendment', *UC Davis Law Review* 49 (2016): 1183–234.

processing should 'serve mankind'. The AI Act prohibits manipulative systems designed to exploit vulnerabilities.[90] Yet, the EU still relies heavily on individual rights and consent mechanisms that assume users can meaningfully control their data. Adding explicit loyalty duties would strengthen these protections: even with consent, using therapy app confessions for insurance underwriting would violate the fundamental duty of loyalty.

For the US, loyalty offers a constitutional sidestep around Sorrell's constraints. Professional duties have deep common law roots – lawyers cannot betray client confidences even if doing so would be profitable 'speech'. Richards and Hartzog suggest layered implementation through broad loyalty mandates supported by specific duties: confidentiality (no unconsented disclosure), care (secure and accurate handling), and conflict avoidance (user interests over company profits).[91] These map naturally onto the unfairness authority of the FTC and echo the EU's fairness principles without triggering First Amendment scrutiny.

The transformation is conceptual but consequential. Privacy shifts from individual control to structural safeguard. Data relationships become power relationships demanding commensurate responsibility. Users could trust their mental health apps will not weaponise their vulnerabilities. Researchers could access medical datasets knowing fiduciary duties prevent misuse. Innovation could flourish on level playing fields where all competitors face identical loyalty constraints.

Loyalty, thus, bridges the transatlantic normative divide by translating shared commitments into enforceable duties. Both jurisdictions recognise that unchecked data power threatens human dignity – they just express it differently. The next section explores how to make this theoretical bridge real through concrete implementation.

B. Comparative Implementation: A 'Bridge Clause' for Privacy Power

Imagine Congress passing a single sentence that revolutionises American health privacy: 'Any entity collecting, using, or sharing personal health information owes a duty of loyalty to act in individuals' best interests.' Twenty words that would flip the entire system from exploitation to protection. This is not fantasy – it is precisely how fiduciary duties transformed finance and law. The question is whether privacy law can learn from those precedents.

For the United States, implementing a duty of loyalty to data subjects requires navigating constitutional minefields while building on existing structures. The Congress could amend the FTC Act or pass targeted health legislation establishing this duty, then let specifics emerge through enforcement and guidance. The

[90] AI Act, Article 99.
[91] Richards, Hartzog, and Francis, 'A Concrete Proposal for Data Loyalty'.

core prohibitions write themselves: no selling health data for advertising (killing the GoodRx model), no discriminatory uses linking genetics to insurance rates,[92] mandatory bias assessments before deploying diagnostic AI. Companies would document how their practices serve users' interests, not through privacy theatre but substantive demonstrations of loyal behaviour.

American implementation could borrow the EU risk-based approach without copying its bureaucracy. High-impact health algorithms would undergo Algorithmic Impact Assessments – not just checking boxes but genuinely examining whether the AI serves patients or profits.[93] The National Institute of Standards and Technology's (NIST) AI Risk Management Framework already provides scaffolding for mapping, measuring, and managing these risks.[94] Adopting international standards like ISO/IEC 42001:2023 could create presumptive compliance with accuracy and safety duties.[95] Framing these as professional obligations rather than speech restrictions sidesteps Sorrell entirely.

The EU faces the opposite challenge: it already mandates loyal behaviour implicitly but lacks explicit articulation. The EHDS could crystallise this with targeted amendments: 'Entities processing health data for secondary purposes act as data trustees owing loyalty to data subjects and public interest.' This transforms scattered prohibitions into a coherent principle. Companies seeking European medical data would sign binding commitments affirming loyalty duties and accepting regular audits.

The AI Act offers another implementation vector through regulatory guidance interpreting existing obligations. High-risk medical AI already must optimise for 'fundamental rights' – loyalty simply clarifies what this means operationally. Future standards could require developers to demonstrate their cardiac diagnostic algorithm serves patient welfare, not hospital profits. The EU might also advance data trust models where independent institutions hold health data under strict fiduciary terms,[96] operationalising loyalty through institutional design rather than just legal mandates.

Transatlantic coordination could happen through existing forums. The EU-US Trade and Technology Council should establish a health data working group developing shared principles.[97] Start modestly: common standards for de-identification, mutual recognition of algorithmic audits, joint guidance on bias mitigation. Build toward a Transatlantic Health Data Charter declaring core

[92] Regulation (EU) 2022/868 (Data Governance Act).

[93] Kaminski, 'Binary Governance'.

[94] Alessandro Mantelero, *Beyond Data: Human Rights, Ethical and Social Impact Assessment in AI* (Cham: Springer Nature, 2022); National Institute of Standards and Technology, *Artificial Intelligence Risk Management Framework (AI RMF 1.0)* (NIST AI 100-1, January 2023).

[95] Mantelero, *Beyond Data*; see *ISO/IEC 42001:2023, Information Technology – Artificial Intelligence – Management System* (International Standards Organization, 2023).

[96] Regulation (EU) 2022/868 (Data Governance Act).

[97] US Food and Drug Administration, *Artificial Intelligence/Machine Learning-Based Software as a Medical Device Action Plan* (2021).

commitments: no automated decisions affecting care without safeguards, no repurposing clinical data for commercial exploitation, mandatory transparency about AI limitations.

A unified implementation framework might include the following provisions:

Section X – Duty of Loyalty in Processing Health Data

(a) Core Duty: Any covered entity, data controller, or data processor (hereafter 'data steward') that processes personal health data, whether directly from individuals or via secondary use mechanisms, owes a duty of loyalty to the individuals whose data is processed.

(b) Pursuant to this duty of loyalty, a data steward shall:

  (1) Prohibited Uses: Refrain from processing personal health data for purposes that are not reasonably expected by the individual and that do not primarily benefit the individual or society's health interests (such as processing for targeted advertising, eligibility determinations unrelated to health care, or other self-dealing purposes, which shall be presumed disloyal).

  (2) Affirmative Safeguards: Implement affirmative measures to safeguard individuals' rights and interests, including conducting Health Algorithm Impact Assessments for any AI system that uses health data to make or inform decisions affecting individuals, and mitigating any risks of bias or error identified (aligning with Article 15 AI Act on continuous monitoring and improvement obligations).[98]

  (3) Transparency and Contestability: Ensure transparency and contestability, by providing affected individuals with clear information about how their data is used and, where decisions are made algorithmically, providing means for human review or appeal of significant decisions (in line with Article 22 GDPR and analogous provisions).[99]

  (4) Data Access Compliance: Not utilise personal health data in a manner that contravenes the limitations or conditions under which the data was accessed (for instance, data obtained via the EHDS or other data altruism programs must strictly adhere to the approved purpose and not be cross-used for profit motives).

(c) Enforcement: Breach of this duty of loyalty constitutes an unfair practice (enforceable by the FTC, state attorneys general, and granting a right of action to data subjects in jurisdictions recognising such claims) and/or a violation of the fundamental right to data protection (enforceable by EU data protection authorities with corrective powers under Article 58 GDPR).

This framework plugs into American consumer protection while reinforcing European data protection. Jurisprudence would refine 'reasonably expected' and 'primary benefit' standards, as fiduciary law evolved through centuries of case development.

[98] Mantelero, *Beyond Data*.

[99] Danielle Keats Citron, 'Technological Due Process', *Washington University Law Review* 85 (2008): 1249–313.

The path forward requires recognition that data relationships are power relationships demanding commensurate responsibility. Mental health app users would gain confidence their vulnerabilities will not be weaponised. Researchers could access broader datasets knowing fiduciary constraints prevent misuse. Innovation would flourish on level playing fields where all competitors face identical loyalty obligations. Privacy and progress become partners, not adversaries.

C. Coexistence of Individual Rights and Collective Good

Privacy and public benefit are often framed as opposing forces: protect the individual or serve the collective. Duty of loyalty explodes this false dichotomy. When data controllers owe fiduciary obligations to users, individual protection becomes the mechanism for collective flourishing. The mental health app that respects user vulnerability creates the trust necessary for population-level research. The AI developer constrained by loyalty duties produces algorithms that work for everyone, not just profitable demographics.

Loyalty duties would transform each actor in the health data ecosystem. Mental health app users no longer fear their depression questionnaires will surface in employment background checks. Researchers access richer datasets because ethics boards trust that fiduciary duties prevent commercial exploitation. AI developers compete on medical efficacy rather than racing to monetise patient vulnerabilities. When everyone faces identical loyalty constraints, innovation channels toward genuine health improvements.[100]

Enforcement requires sophistication beyond simple penalties. EU Member-State Data Protection Authorities would integrate loyalty assessments into regular supervision. EHDS access bodies would require binding loyalty commitments before releasing any data. American regulators could incorporate standard loyalty provisions into every consent order, making betrayal of user trust evidence of negligence.[101] Over time, loyalty violations would carry the same professional stigma as a lawyer stealing client funds.

Alessandro Mantelero's Human Rights, Ethics and Social Impact Assessment (HRESIA) framework shows how to operationalise these principles at scale.[102] His Human Rights, Ethical, and Social Impact Assessment goes beyond legal compliance to examine actual societal effects. Under HRESIA, a diagnostic AI company could not just demonstrate technical accuracy – they would prove their system does not systematically disadvantage rural communities or minority populations.[103]

[100] Urs Gasser and Virgílio AF Almeida, 'A Layered Model for AI Governance', *IEEE Internet Computing* 21, no. 6 (2017): 58–62.
[101] Partnership on AI, 'About ML Reference Document 1.0' (April 2021).
[102] Mantelero, *Beyond Data.*
[103] Mantelero, *Beyond Data.*

This embodies collective loyalty: ensuring innovation serves society's equality interests, not just early adopters.

Global convergence beckons. EU-US alignment on loyalty could establish de facto international standards that other jurisdictions would naturally follow.[104] Joint frameworks might finally resolve the transatlantic data transfer crisis spawned by *Schrems II* – American companies demonstrating robust loyalty compliance could prove 'adequate' protection for European data. The OECD and Council of Europe stand ready to codify these principles globally.[105]

The most intriguing challenges involve loyalty's boundaries. When law enforcement demands health data for investigations, does loyalty yield to public safety? How should loyalty duties evolve as AI enables new forms of collective insight – perhaps protecting demographic groups even when no individual suffers identifiable harm? These tensions require careful navigation, but loyalty's flexibility – principle over rigid rule – allows adaptation while maintaining core values.

Critics worry about measuring compliance and handling conflicts, but these concerns miss loyalty's elegance. Unlike prescriptive regulations that ossify quickly, loyalty evolves with technology while keeping human interests paramount. External audits, algorithmic transparency tools, and professional certification create accountability without micromanagement. Companies should learn to ask not 'what can we legally do with this data?' but 'what should we do to honour user trust?'

The payoff justifies the effort. Loyalty restores confidence in digital health tools, encouraging honest disclosure that improves both individual care and population health. It rebalances power by reminding data holders that people are ends, not means, a principle resonating equally with European human dignity and American fiduciary traditions. Most critically, it proves that privacy and innovation are not enemies but partners when properly aligned.

Taken together, transatlantic duty of loyalty offers something privacy law desperately needs: a positive vision. Rather than just constraining harmful uses, loyalty channels data toward human flourishing. It transforms privacy from a defensive crouch into an enabling framework for beneficial innovation. The world watches whether we will seize this opportunity or let it slip away.

V. Conclusion: 'The World is Watching'

The algorithmic colonisation of medicine is already underway. Health data regulation stands at a crossroads defining the relationship between citizens, technology,

[104] World Health Organization, *Ethics and Governance of Artificial Intelligence for Health* (2025), www.who.int/publications/i/item/9789240084759.

[105] Organisation for Economic Co-operation and Development (OECD), 'OECD Principles on Artificial Intelligence' (May 2019) (adopted by dozens of countries as non-binding guidelines for trustworthy AI); Council of Europe, *Framework Convention on Artificial Intelligence, Human Rights, Democracy and the Rule of Law* (CETS No. 225).

and power. The EU rights-based precaution and the US enforcement-centric market approach offer diverging visions, each with merits and blind spots. Yet they need not remain irreconcilable. This chapter argues for convergence around privacy as a guardrail against domination.[106] By recasting privacy from individual consumer right to structural duty of loyalty on data holders -building on Neil Richards and Woodrow Hartzog's foundational framework- we create common ground: a language of trust transcending borders.

The shift from notice-and-consent rituals to substantive loyalty duties would transform health data governance. It means regulators moving from after-the-fact punishment to before-the-fact prevention; not stifling innovation, but ensuring innovation serves humans. FTC enforcement actions already echo European sensibilities condemning self-serving data exploitation.[107] The EU AI Act and the EHDS tell the world ethical AI and data solidarity are achievable at scale.[108] Other jurisdictions observe closely, ready to adopt whichever model proves most viable. Global tech companies must decide: embrace higher universal standards or maintain costly dual regimes risking public backlash.

Initial coordination could emerge through forums like the G7, OECD, or Trade and Technology Council.[109] A joint EU-US task force on data loyalty and health AI could develop interoperable guidelines, foster pilot projects for privacy-preserving transatlantic research, and exchange enforcement best practices. The building blocks exist – what is needed is political will to assemble them.

The stakes transcend health data. They implicate democratic values in the AI age. Getting health data governance right, namely, balancing innovation with dignity, autonomy with collective benefit, provides templates for finance, education, and public services. Failure risks digital feudalism where gatekeepers hold unprecedented sway. The CPDP 2025 theme captures this moment perfectly: the world watches not only what AI systems do, but what we, lawmakers, companies, citizens, do to watch the watchers.

Daniel Solove warned us: privacy rights' limitations demand collective measures to address structural power.[110] Privacy reimagined as loyalty and responsibility becomes not an obstacle to progress, but what ensures progress worthy of humanity. Through thoughtful regulation and cross-border cooperation, we can harness AI's immense social good without surrendering privacy or exacerbating inequity.

The transatlantic rebalancing of privacy power is underway, guided by loyalty and human-centric design, it promises technology that serves and empowers

[106] Neil M Richards and Woodrow Hartzog, 'Taking Trust Seriously in Privacy Law', *Stanford Technology Law Review* 19 (2015): 431–72.

[107] *In re BetterHelp, Inc.*, FTC Docket No. 2023169 (Decision and Order, 14 July 2023).

[108] World Health Organization, *Ethics and Governance of Artificial Intelligence for Health* (2025).

[109] Ryan Calo, 'Artificial Intelligence Policy: A Primer and Roadmap', *UC Davis Law Review* 51 (2017): 399–435.

[110] Citron and Solove, 'Privacy Harms', 793; see also Daniel J Solove, 'Introduction: Privacy Self-Management and the Consent Dilemma', *Harvard Law Review* 126 (2013): 1880–903.

rather than observes and exploits. Whether we seize this opportunity depends on recognising that in health data governance, as Neil Richards teaches us, trust is not just nice to have; it is the foundation upon which all legitimate data use must rest.

Bibliography

Adams, Katie. 'Cerebral Admits That It Wrongly Shared Data of 3.1M Users'. *MedCity News*, 10 March 2023.

A&O Shearman. 'Zooming in on AI – #4: What Is the Interplay Between "Deployers" and "Providers" in the EU AI Act?' 16 September 2024.

Alder, Steve. 'Majority of Americans Mistakenly Believe Health App Data Is Covered by HIPAA'. *HIPAA Journal*. 26 July 2023.

American Medical Association. *Augmented Intelligence in Health Care*. (Policy H-480.940). Modified 2025.

Amnesty International and Access Now. *The Toronto Declaration: Protecting the Right to Equality and Non-Discrimination in Machine Learning Systems*. 16 May 2018.

Article 29 Data Protection Working Party. *Opinion 05/2014 on Anonymisation Techniques (WP 216)*. 10 April 2014.

Balkin, Jack M. 'Information Fiduciaries and the First Amendment'. *UC Davis Law Review* 49 (2016): 1183–234.

BetterHelp, Inc., In re. FTC Complaint No. 2023169 (2023).

Bradshaw, RiAnn. 'HIPAA & GDPR Compliance for Health App Developers: Security & Legal Considerations'. LLIF.org. 31 January 2025. https://llif.org/2025/01/31/hipaa-gdpr-compliance-health-apps/.

Calo, Ryan. 'Artificial Intelligence Policy: A Primer and Roadmap'. *UC Davis Law Review* 51 (2017): 399–435.

Citron, Danielle Keats, and Daniel J Solove. 'Privacy Harms'. *Boston University Law Review* 102 (2022): 793–857.

Citron, Danielle Keats, and Frank Pasquale. 'The Scored Society: Due Process for Automated Predictions'. *Washington Law Review* 89, no. 1 (2014): 1–34.

Citron, Danielle Keats. 'Technological Due Process'. *Washington University Law Review* 85 (2008): 1249–313.

Citron, Danielle Keats. *The Fight for Privacy: Protecting Dignity, Identity and Love in the Digital Age*. London: Random House, 2022.

ClearDATA. 'Many Americans Don't Realize Digital Health Apps Could Be Selling Their Personal Data'. Press release, 13 July 2023.

Cohen, Julie E. *Between Truth and Power: The Legal Constructions of Informational Capitalism*. New York: Oxford University Press, 2019.

Cohen, Julie E. 'Examined Lives: Informational Privacy and the Subject as Object'. *Stanford Law Review* 52 (2000): 1373–438.

Cohen, Julie E. 'Law for the Platform Economy'. *UC Davis Law Review* 51 (2017): 133–204.

Cohen, Julie E. 'What Privacy Is For'. *Harvard Law Review* 126 (2013): 1904–33.

Cory, Thomas, Wolf Rieder, and Thu-My Huynh. 'A Qualitative Analysis Framework for mHealth Privacy Practices'. In *2024 IEEE European Symposium on Security and Privacy Workshops (EuroS&PW)*, 24–31. Piscataway, NJ: IEEE, 2024.

Costa-Cabral, Francisco, and Orla Lynskey. 'The Internal and External Constraints of Data Protection on Competition Law in the EU'. *LSE Law, Society and Economy Working Papers* 25 (2015).
Council of Europe. *Framework Convention on Artificial Intelligence, Human Rights, Democracy and the Rule of Law* (CETS No. 225). Opened for signature September 2024.
Crawford, Kate. *Atlas of AI: Power, Politics, and the Planetary Costs of Artificial Intelligence*. New Haven, CT: Yale University Press, 2021.
Crowell & Moring LLP. 'EU Artificial Intelligence Act'. Crowell & Moring Client Alert, 28 January 2025.
Data Protection Commissioner v Facebook Ireland Ltd. ('*Schrems II*'), Case C-311/18. Court of Justice of the European Union, 16 July 2020.
DATUREX GmbH. 'Compliance in Fitness Apps: Protection of Personal Health Data'. 23 January 2024.
De Hert, Paul, and Vagelis Papakonstantinou. 'The New General Data Protection Regulation: Still a Sound System for the Protection of Individuals?' *Computer Law & Security Review* 32, no. 2 (2016): 179–94.
Dinerstein v Google, LLC, 73 F.4th 502 (7th Cir. 2023).
Dunlop, Connor. 'An EU AI Act that Works for People and Society: Five Areas of Focus for the Trilogues'. Ada Lovelace Institute, 6 September 2023. www.adalovelaceinstitute.org/policy-briefing/eu-ai-act-trilogues/.
Eubanks, Virginia. *Automating Inequality: How High-Tech Tools Profile, Police, and Punish the Poor*. New York: St. Martin's Press, 2018.
EuroHealthNet and Centre for Health Equity Analytics. *Social Inequalities in Health in the EU – Summary Report*. Brussels: EuroHealthNet, September 2025.
European Commission. 'Communication – AI Continent Action Plan'. COM 2025 165 final, 9 April 2025.
European Commission. 'Communication – Fostering a European Approach to Artificial Intelligence'. COM 2021 205 final, 21 April 2021.
European Commission. 'Joint Statement EU–US Trade and Technology Council'. Press corner. 4 April 2024.
European Commission. *State of Health in the EU: Synthesis Report 2023*. December 2023.
European Data Protection Board and European Data Protection Supervisor. *Joint Opinion 03/2022 on the Proposal for a European Health Data Space*. 12 July 2022.
European Union. Regulation (EU) 2016/679 (General Data Protection Regulation). 2016 OJ L 119/1.
European Union. Regulation (EU) 2022/868 (Data Governance Act). 2022 OJ L 152/1.
European Union. Regulation (EU) 2024/1689 (Artificial Intelligence Act). 2024 OJ L 257/1.
European Union. Regulation (EU) 2025/327 (European Health Data Space Regulation). 2025 OJ L 119/1.
Federal Trade Commission Act § 5, 15 USC § 45(a)(1) (2018).
Federal Trade Commission v Cerebral, Inc., No. 1:24-cv-21376 (S.D. Fla., filed 17 April 2024).
Federal Trade Commission v Easy Healthcare Corp. (Premom). Administrative Complaint and Consent Order, 2023.
Federal Trade Commission. '2023 Privacy and Data Security Update'. January 2024.
Federal Trade Commission. 'FTC Enforcement Action to Bar GoodRx from Sharing Consumers' Sensitive Health Info for Advertising'. News release, 1 February 2023.

Federal Trade Commission. 'FTC Finalizes Changes to the Health Breach Notification Rule'. Press release, 20 April 2024.
Federal Trade Commission. 'FTC Finalizes Order with Flo Health, a Fertility-Tracking App that Shared Sensitive Health Data with Facebook, Google, and Others'. Press release, 22 June 2021.
Federal Trade Commission. 'FTC to Ban BetterHelp from Revealing Consumers' Data, Including Sensitive Mental Health Information, to Facebook and Others for Targeted Advertising'. Press release, 2 March 2023.
Federal Trade Commission. 'Proposed FTC Order Will Prohibit Telehealth Firm Cerebral from Using or Disclosing Sensitive Data for Advertising Purposes, and Require It to Pay $7 Million'. Press release, 15 April 2024.
Flo Health, Inc., In re. FTC Docket No. C-4747. Decision and Order, 17 June 2021.
Gasser, Urs, and Virgílio AF Almeida. 'A Layered Model for AI Governance'. *IEEE Internet Computing* 21, no. 6 (2017): 58–62.
Genicot, Nathan. *From Blueprint to Reality: Implementing AI Regulatory Sandboxes under the AI Act*. Brussels: FARI & LSTS Research Group, 2024.
Gillespie, Tarleton. 'The Politics of "Platforms"'. *New Media & Society* 12, no. 3 (2010): 347–54.
Grundy, Quinn, Kellia Chiu, Fabian Held, Andrea Continella, Lisa Bero, and Ralph Holz. 'Data Sharing Practices of Medicines-Related Apps and the Mobile Ecosystem: Traffic, Content, and Network Analysis'. *BMJ* 364 (2019): 1920.
Health Insurance Portability and Accountability Act of 1996. Public Law 104-191, 104th Congress, 21 August 1996.
Henry, Kevin. 'The History of HIPAA: Complete Guide Since 1996'. *Accountable* (blog), 7 April 2021. www.accountablehq.com/post/hipaa-history.
International Organization for Standardization/International Electrotechnical Commission (ISO/IEC). *ISO/IEC 42001:2023, Information Technology – Artificial Intelligence – Management System*. Geneva: ISO, 2023.
Jessani, Ali. 'Health Privacy in 2025 and Beyond'. *American Bar Association, Antitrust Law Section*. 13 March 2025. www.americanbar.org/groups/antitrust_law/resources/newsletters/health-privacy-in-2025/.
Jodka, Sara H. 'App Users Beware: Most Healthcare, Fitness Tracker, and Wellness Apps Are Not Covered by HIPAA and HHS's New FAQs Make That Clear'. *Dickinson Wright* Client Alert, 7 May 2019.
Kaminski, Margot E. 'Binary Governance: Lessons from the GDPR's Approach to Algorithmic Accountability'. *Southern California Law Review* 92 (2019): 1529–616.
Khan, Lina M. 'FTC Chair Lina Khan Speaks on Data Security Rulemaking'. *Columbia Law School Blue Sky Blog*, 22 August 2022.
Khan, Lina M. 'Amazon's Antitrust Paradox'. *Yale Law Journal* 126, no. 3 (2017): 710–805.
Lynskey, Orla. 'Complete and Effective Data Protection'. *Current Legal Problems* 76, no. 1 (2023): 297–344.
Lynskey, Orla. 'Grappling with "Data Power": Normative Nudges from Data Protection and Privacy'. *Theoretical Inquiries in Law* 20, no. 1 (2019): 189–220.
Lynskey, Orla. *The Foundations of EU Data Protection Law*. Oxford: Oxford University Press, 2015.
Mantelero, Alessandro. *Beyond Data: Human Rights, Ethical and Social Impact Assessment in AI*. Cham: Springer Nature, 2022.

Marcus, J. Scott, Bertin Martens, Christophe Carugati, Anne Bucher, and Ilsa Godlovitch. *The European Health Data Space*. Brussels: European Parliament, Policy Department for Economic, Scientific and Quality of Life Policies, 2022.

McKeon, Jill. 'Google Tackles Data Privacy, Plans to Delete Location History at Abortion Clinics'. *HealthTechSecurity*, 5 July 2022.

Meyers, Zach. 'Implementing the AI Act'. Centre for European Reform, December 2024.

National Institute of Standards and Technology. *Artificial Intelligence Risk Management Framework (AI RMF 1.0)*. NIST AI 100-1. Gaithersburg, MD: NIST, January 2023.

Nissenbaum, Helen. *Privacy in Context: Technology, Policy, and the Integrity of Social Life*. Stanford, CA: Stanford University Press, 2009.

Organisation for Economic Co-operation and Development. 'OECD Principles on Artificial Intelligence'. May 2019.

O'Neil, Cathy. *Weapons of Math Destruction: How Big Data Increases Inequality and Threatens Democracy*. New York: Crown, 2016.

Partnership on AI. 'About ML Reference Document 1.0'. April 2021.

Pasquale, Frank. *The Black Box Society: The Secret Algorithms That Control Money and Information*. Cambridge, MA: Harvard University Press, 2015.

Pellegrino, Massimo, Sara Mancini, Eliana Gerardi, and Irene Mumeni Urbani. *The AI Act: Help or Hindrance for SMEs? An Analysis of the Cost of Compliance with the AI Act for SMEs*. Milan: Intellera Consulting, July 2024.

Prince, Anya ER, and Daniel Schwarcz. 'Proxy Discrimination in the Age of Artificial Intelligence and Big Data'. *Iowa Law Review* 105 (2020): 1257–318.

ProAssurance. 'AI and Medical Liability'. *ProAssurance*, February 2024.

Richards, Neil M, and Woodrow Hartzog. 'Taking Trust Seriously in Privacy Law'. *Stanford Technology Law Review* 19 (2015): 431–72.

Richards, Neil M, Woodrow Hartzog, and Jordan Francis. 'A Concrete Proposal for Data Loyalty'. *Harvard Journal of Law & Technology* 37, no. 1 (2023): 1–52.

Schmeltzer, Paul F, and John F Howard. 'Beyond HIPAA: How State Laws Are Reshaping Health Data Compliance'. Clark Hill PLC, 26 June 2025. www.clarkhill.com/news-events/news/beyond-hipaa-how-state-laws-are-reshaping-health-data-compliance/.

Schroeder, Tanja, Maximilian Haug, and Heiko Gewald. 'Data Privacy Concerns Using mHealth Apps and Smart Speakers: Comparative Interview Study Among Mature Adults'. *JMIR Formative Research* 6, no. 6 (2022): e28025.

Schwartz, Paul M, and Daniel J Solove. 'The PII Problem: Privacy and a New Concept of Personally Identifiable Information'. *New York University Law Review* 86 (2011): 1814–94.

Schwartz, Paul M, and Daniel J Solove. 'Property, Privacy, and Personal Data'. *Harvard Law Review* 117 (2003): 2056–153.

Selbst, Andrew D. 'Negligence and AI's Human Users'. *Boston University Law Review* 100 (2020): 1315–76.

Solove, Daniel J. 'Introduction: Privacy Self-Management and the Consent Dilemma'. *Harvard Law Review* 126 (2013): 1880–903.

Solove, Daniel J, and Danielle Keats Citron. 'Standing and Privacy Harms: A Critique of TransUnion v. Ramirez'. *Boston University Law Review Online* 101 (2021): 62–72.

Solove, Daniel J., and Woodrow Hartzog. 'The FTC and the New Common Law of Privacy'. *Columbia Law Review* 114 (2014): 583–676.

Sorrell v IMS Health Inc., 564 US 552 (2011).

Thaler, Richard H, and Cass R Sunstein. *Nudge: Improving Decisions About Health, Wealth, and Happiness*. New Haven, CT: Yale University Press, 2008.

Ullah, Imdad, Roksana Boreli, and Salil S Kanhere. 'Privacy in Targeted Advertising on Mobile Devices: A Survey'. *International Journal of Information Security* 22, no. 3 (2023): 647–78.

United States Department of Health & Human Services. 'Health App Use Scenarios & HIPAA'. 2016.

United States Department of Health & Human Services, Office for Civil Rights. 'Protecting the Privacy and Security of Your Health Information When Using Your Personal Cell Phone or Tablet'. *HHS.gov*. Last reviewed 29 June 2022. www.hhs.gov/hipaa/for-professionals/privacy/guidance/cell-phone-hipaa/index.html.

United States Food and Drug Administration. *Artificial Intelligence/Machine Learning-Based Software as a Medical Device Action Plan*. January 2021.

United States Government Accountability Office. *Artificial Intelligence in Health Care: Benefits and Challenges of Technologies to Augment Patient Care*. GAO-22-104629, 2022.

United States v GoodRx Holdings, Inc., No. 2:23-cv-00460 (N.D. Cal. 2023).

United States. Executive Order 14110, 'Safe, Secure, and Trustworthy Development and Use of Artificial Intelligence'. 30 October 2023.

United States. Executive Order 14179, 'Removing Barriers to American Leadership in Artificial Intelligence'. 23 January 2025.

Vigliarolo, Brandon. 'Google Location Tracking to Forget You Were Ever at That Medical Clinic'. *The Register*, 2 July 2022. www.theregister.com/2022/07/02/google_medical_privacy/.

Volokh, Eugene. 'Freedom of Speech and Information Privacy: The Troubling Implications of a Right to Stop People from Speaking about You'. *Stanford Law Review* 52 (2000): 1049–122. https://doi.org/10.2307/1229510.

Wachter, Sandra, Brent Mittelstadt, and Chris Russell. 'Counterfactual Explanations Without Opening the Black Box: Automated Decisions and the GDPR'. *Harvard Journal of Law & Technology* 31 (2018): 841–87.

Wasastjerna, Meri-Tuulia. 'The Role of Big Data and Digital Privacy in Merger Review'. *European Competition Journal* 14, nos. 2–3 (2018): 417–44.

World Health Organization. *Ethics and Governance of Artificial Intelligence for Health: Large Multi-Modal Models. WHO Guidance*. Geneva: WHO, 2025. www.who.int/publications/i/item/9789240084759.

Zuboff, Shoshana. *The Age of Surveillance Capitalism: The Fight for a Human Future at the New Frontier of Power*. New York: PublicAffairs, 2019.

7

Call for a Brussels-Sacramento Alliance on AI Privacy

ANŽE ERBEŽNIK, DAVID EVAN HARRIS AND OWEN DOYLE

Abstract

This chapter argues that widening divergences between EU and US approaches to artificial intelligence (AI) pose material risks to the durability of the EU-US Data Privacy Framework (DPF) and, by extension, to transatlantic data flows. AI development depends on vast datasets, often containing personal information gathered via opaque practices. Once models memorise such data, conventional General Data Protection Regulation (GDPR) remedies – erasure, purpose limitation, and transparency – become hard to operationalise. Against this backdrop, the chapter (i) retraces the pathway from Safe Harbour and Privacy Shield to the current DPF, underscoring the Court of Justice of the European Union's (CJEU) jurisprudence (*Schrems I/II*) and the fragility of arrangements grounded in US executive action; (ii) analyses how personal data permeate AI lifecycles (collection, training, memorisation, and disclosure), and the limits of anonymisation and synthetic data; (iii) contrasts the EU's integrated GDPR and AI Act framework with the United States' sectoral, federal-state patchwork, highlighting California's partial convergence with the EU approach across multiple new AI laws passed in the last two years (eg, training-data transparency and AI-output personal information recognition); and (iv) proposes a 'Brussels-Sacramento Alliance': a transatlantic alignment that embeds data minimisation, risk management, transparency, documentation, and independent oversight into AI governance. Further, we contend that incorporating AI-specific data protection safeguards into DPF reviews, and encouraging both the EU and the US to promote harmonisation in AI governance coherence – at minimum between the EU and California – could stabilise compliance processes, avoid fragmentation, reduce compliance costs, and enhance public trust. A joint Brussels-Sacramento model would create a large, rules-based market capable of setting global norms for safe, rights-respecting, human-focused, and innovation-friendly AI, thereby converting legal coherence into strategic and economic advantage.

Keywords

EU-US Data Privacy Framework; AI Act; GDPR; Brussels Effect; California Effect

I. Introduction

The AI revolution would not have been possible without two components: the increase in computing power[1] and the mass availability of data.[2] But AI and data are strange companions, particularly when it comes to personal information, where their interests may be contradictory. One of the challenges for modern democracies is adopting a responsible approach to personal data. The amount of data collected by private and state entities in today's world allows for conclusions about an individual's life, habits, and personal choices. For example, shopping data can reveal one's dietary, clothing, entertainment preferences or highly personal status (eg, pregnancy).[3] Similarly, telecommunication data and metadata can provide a detailed picture of a person's social environment, friends, or geolocation.[4] Nearly everything we do leaves a digital trail[5] and this can shift the traditional hierarchy of individual rights. Serious misuse or breaches of personal data can now be considered comparable to violations of rights like the right to liberty and security.[6]

Modern governments and societal actors can acquire and use more granular personal data than ever before, raising concerns over how this could be abused. Consequently, it is the law that must define limits on the use of such data. In the EU, data protection has evolved into a full-fledged, independent right (Article 8 of the EU Charter of Fundamental Rights). This development is reflected in the prominence of secondary EU legislation on data protection,

[1] Neil C Thompson, Shuning Ge, and Gabriel F Manso, 'The Importance of (Exponentially More) Computing Power', *arXiv* (28 June 2022); Diane Coyle and Lucy Hampton, '21st Century Progress in Computing', *Telecommunications Policy* 48, no. 1 (2024); Patrick McCarthy, 'Infographic: The Growth of Computer Processing Power', *OffGridWeb*, 2 May 2017. However, the classical Moore's law regarding on doubling each two years is becoming obsolete with new technologies.

[2] European Strategy for Data (COM/2020/66 final). See also Peter Mezei, 'Third European Court Decision on the General Purpose TDM Exception Is Out', *Kluwer Copyright Blog*, 8 May 2025, regarding national application of online scraping of data and application of Articles 3 and 4 of Directive (EU) 2019/790 of 17 April 2019 on copyright and related rights in the Digital Single Market.

[3] Jennifer Senior, 'How Companies Learn Your Secrets', *New York Times Magazine*, 16 February 2012.

[4] CJEU, Joined Cases C-293/12 and C-594/12, *Digital Rights Ireland and Others* [2014] ECLI:EU:C:2014:238, para 37.

[5] Daniel Zwerdling, 'Your Digital Trail: Does the Fourth Amendment Protect Us?' *All Tech Considered*, NPR, 2 October 2013.

[6] David C Gray and Danielle Keats Citron, 'The Right to Quantitative Privacy', *Minnesota Law Review* 98 (2013): 62–128, 72, proposing a theory of privacy focusing on how information is gathered.

eg, the omnibus GDPR[7] and its 'Brussels Effect',[8] which has become a global model. It is reinforced by the case law of the CJEU.[9] In contrast, the US federal approach to data protection is sectoral and fragmented. It relies on specific laws addressing individual domains (eg, health, children's data, credit),[10] on federal government legislation,[11] and on Federal Trade Commission (FTC) enforcement under Section 5 (unfair/deceptive practices).[12] Most rule-making power lies with US states, with emphasis on consumer protection. Among the states, California stands out as a model for data protection – a trend referred to as the 'California effect'.[13] The two systems – the EU and the US – are intrinsically linked by deep historical, value-based, and commercial interests. The existence of a data 'safe harbour' mechanism between the US and the EU is of utmost importance. However, this relationship has not been smooth, as illustrated by multiple interventions by the CJEU.

There is an undeniable connection between AI development and personal data.[14] AI models – particularly generative AI – often include large amounts of personal data in their training sets, acquired often through non-transparent means. This includes scraping, crawling, or other techniques. The extent of such use is currently a matter of speculation, due to the secrecy maintained by AI companies.[15] Once trained, models cannot simply forget their training data. It remains unclear how the right to erasure (right to be forgotten), originating

[7] Regulation (EU) 2016/679 of the European Parliament and of the Council of 27 April 2016 on the protection of natural persons with regard to the processing of personal data and on the free movement of such data, and repealing Directive 95/46/EC (General Data Protection Regulation) [2016] OJ L 119/1.

[8] Anu Bradford, 'The Brussels Effect', *Northwestern University Law Review* 107, no. 1 (2012): 1–64; Anu Bradford, *The Brussels Effect: How the European Union Rules the World* (Oxford: Oxford University Press, 2020), Kindle. See also Michael D Birnhack, 'The EU Data Protection Directive: An Engine of a Global Regime', *Computer Law & Security Report* 24, no. 6 (2008): 508–20, who first discussed the idea of extraterritorial EU regulatory influence.

[9] CJEU, *Fact Sheet, Protection of Personal Data*, July 2024.

[10] Children's Online Privacy Protection Act (COPPA), 15 U.S.C. §§ 6501–6506 (1998); HIPAA, 42 U.S.C. § 1320d (1996); Fair Credit Reporting Act (FCRA), 15 U.S.C. §§ 1681–1681x (1970).

[11] Privacy Act of 1974, 5 U.S.C. § 552a (1974).

[12] Federal Trade Commission Act, 15 U.S.C. § 45 (1914).

[13] The term 'California effect' was first used in connection with environment protection legislation. Per G Fredriksson and Daniel L Millimet, 'Is There a "California Effect" in US Environmental Policymaking?' *Regional Science and Urban Economics* 32, no. 6 (2002): 737–64. Today, the term 'Sacramento effect' is used in relation to data protection and, more recently, also with regard to AI. Van Hong Tran et al, 'Measuring Compliance with the California Consumer Privacy Act Over Space and Time', in *CHI '24: Proceedings of the 2024 CHI Conference on Human Factors in Computing Systems* (New York: Association for Computing Machinery, 2024); Anthony Fleming, 'The Sacramento Effect: State-Level AI Regulations', *Medium*, 27 April 2025.

[14] Giovanni Sartor, *The Impact of the General Data Protection Regulation (GDPR) in Artificial Intelligence*, (European Parliament, 2020), 73–81. The author raises the influence of AI on re-identification, profiling, consent, transparency, erasure, and automated decision-making. See also Nathalie A Smuha, 'The Paramountcy of Data Protection Law in the Age of AI (Acts)', in *Two decades of personal data protection. What next?* (EDPS, 2024), 226–39.

[15] Daniel J Solove and Woodrow Hartzog, *The Great Scrape: The Clash Between Scraping and Privacy* (Working Paper, Boston University School of Law Faculty Scholarship Series, 2024).

in CJEU Google Spain[16] and codified in Article 17 GDPR, should be applied without effectively prohibiting the use of the model itself. Consequently, one of the main challenges for modern democracies is to adopt a responsible approach to the intersection between personal data processing and AI development, training, and deployment. A substantial component of any 'safe harbour' assessment must include not only privacy and data protection rules, but also AI regulation where it impacts personal data. The aim of this chapter is to demonstrate how potentially divergent AI approaches in the EU and the US (with a focus on California) could significantly threaten the integrity of existing data protection 'safe harbour' arrangements and transatlantic data flows. A divergence regarding AI and data protection that becomes too wide could seriously endanger the coherent and necessary cooperation between the EU and the US on the free flow of data and use. It could also affect the ability for US and California-based companies to place their AI systems on the EU market without significant additional endeavours and costs. A divergence might even require the development and training of fully separate models for the EU market. In response, a convergent, human-centred AI approach – one that prioritises data protection and risk awareness – could prevent such risks, offer mutual benefits, and form the foundation of a new, globally sustainable Brussels-Sacramento AI and privacy alliance.

Based on the above, the analysis will be structured as follows: (1) An examination of the current EU-US DPF and its predecessors, with particular focus on CJEU case law and legal requirements; (2) the role of personal data in AI systems, including issues such as data compression, pseudonymisation, and synthetic data; (3) the California approach to AI risk regulation; and (4) the proposed Brussels-Sacramento alliance on AI and privacy as a basis for a global standard.

II. The Current EU-US DPF and its Predecessors: From Safe Harbour to EU-US Privacy Framework

A. Past EU-US Data Exchange Frameworks

Modern technology has expanded the territorial scope of data transfers in an increasingly globalised world, thereby heightening the importance of data protection. In this global context, data flows in the online services industry between the EU and the US are an essential component of modern life for hundreds of millions of people. This is recognised in the GDPR, which states that 'technology has transformed both the economy and social life, and should further facilitate the free flow

[16] CJEU, Case C-131/12, *Google Spain SL, Google Inc. v Agencia Española de Protección de Datos (AEPD), Mario Costeja González* [2014] ECLI:EU:C:2014:317.

of personal data within the Union and the transfer to third countries and international organisations, while ensuring a high level of the protection of personal data'.[17] It further states that

> [f]lows of personal data to and from countries outside the Union and international organisations are necessary for the expansion of international trade and international cooperation. The increase in such flows has raised new challenges and concerns with regard to the protection of personal data. However, when personal data are transferred from the Union … the level of protection of natural persons must be ensured.[18]

The GDPR allows transfers based on an adequacy decision adopted by the European Commission,[19] on appropriate safeguards (eg, legally binding and enforceable instruments between public authorities, binding corporate rules, standard data protection clauses, approved codes of conduct, or approved certification mechanisms),[20] or on derogations for specific situations.[21] The history of EU-US data flows is complex due to the fragmentation of the US legal landscape,[22] differing approaches to the protection of certain data categories (eg, metadata),[23] provisions regarding national security access,[24] and the availability of legal remedies in the event of data breaches.

With respect to EU-US transfers, the Commission's adequacy decisions have been successfully challenged twice. First, the Commission adopted the so-called 'Safe Harbour' decision.[25] This system was based on self-certification by US companies, asserting their alignment with privacy principles;[26] public transparency and commitment to enforcement; oversight by US authorities (the Department of Commerce and the FTC); and the EU's ability to suspend data flows. Under this agreement, US organisations had to self-certify annually to the US Department of Commerce their adherence to the seven Safe Harbour Principles, namely: notice;

[17] Recital 6 GDPR.

[18] Recital 101 GDPR.

[19] Article 45 GDPR.

[20] Articles 46 and 47 GDPR.

[21] Article 49 GDPR.

[22] Erin J An, 'It's Finally Time for a National Data Privacy Law: A Discussion of the American Data Privacy and Protection Act (ADPPA)', *Brooklyn Journal of Corporate, Financial & Commercial Law* 18, no. 1 (2023): 229–46; Margot E Kaminski, 'The Case for Data Privacy Rights (Or "Please, a Little Optimism")', *Notre Dame Law Review Reflection* 97 (2022): 385–99; Dongsheng Zang, 'The Privacy Act of 1974: The American Bill of Rights on Data and Its Unfinished Business', *University of Pittsburgh Law Review* 86 (2024): 85–160.

[23] H Brian Holland, 'A Third-Party Doctrine for Digital Metadata', *Cardozo Law Review* 41, no. 4 (2020): 1549–600.

[24] Theodore H Massey III, 'The Case for a Federal Data Privacy Law from a National Security Perspective – What the US Can Learn from Overseas', *Student Journal of Information Privacy & Policy* 3, no. 1 (2025): 99–132.

[25] Commission Decision 2000/520/EC of 26 July 2000 pursuant to Directive 95/46/EC of the European Parliament and of the Council on the adequacy of the protection provided by the safe harbour privacy principles and related frequently asked questions issued by the US Department of Commerce [2000] OJ L 215/7.

[26] Article 1(2) and (3) of Decision 2000/520 and FAQ 6 in the Annex.

choice (opt-out, and opt-in for sensitive data); onward transfers; security; data integrity; access; and enforcement.[27] In addition, they were required to disclose their privacy policies and to provide dispute-resolution mechanisms. Regarding enforcement, the Department of Commerce reviewed the annual submissions, maintained an up-to-date list of certified participants, and delisted non-compliant entities. Further, the FTC could enforce compliance under Section 5 of the FTC Act. On the EU side, national data protection authorities could suspend data transfers to US entities if substantial non-compliance was suspected. A national security exception allowed US authorities to override Safe Harbour obligations where necessary and proportionate. The CJEU annulled Safe Harbour in *Schrems I*,[28] clarifying that national supervisory authorities retain their prerogatives.[29] The Court criticised the scheme's limitation to private undertakings, the prevalence of national security, public interest, and law enforcement requirements, and the lack of effective legal remedies for EU citizens in the United States.

The follow-up EU-US Privacy Shield was introduced on the basis of a new adequacy decision.[30] In light of the CJEU's annulment of Safe Harbour, the new system included several enhancements: regular Department of Commerce reviews,[31] stricter rules for onward transfers,[32] limits on data retention,[33] and greater restrictions on US government access to personal data (eg, prohibiting indiscriminate mass surveillance, and providing for redress through an independent Ombudsperson within the State Department).[34] It established an annual joint review,[35] and provided legal remedies for EU citizens (eg, free Alternative Dispute Resolution, voluntary oversight by EU data protection authorities, referral to national data protection authorities (DPAs) who could contact the Department of Commerce or FTC, and an arbitration mechanism through the Privacy Shield Panel).[36] The system was based on self-certification,[37] with follow-up monitoring

[27] Annex 1 to Decision 2000/520/EC, Safe Harbor Privacy Principles.

[28] CJEU, Case C-362/14, *Maximillian Schrems* [2015] ECLI:EU:C:2015:650.

[29] Case C-362/14, paras 37–66.

[30] Commission Implementing Decision (EU) 2016/1250 of 12 July 2016 pursuant to Directive 95/46/EC of the European Parliament and of the Council on the adequacy of the protection provided by the EU-US Privacy Shield [2016] OJ L 207/1.

[31] Recital 37 of Decision 2016/1250.

[32] Recitals 27–28 and Annex II of Decision 2016/1250.

[33] Annex II of Decision 2016/1250 (Data Integrity and Purpose limitation).

[34] Recitals 116–124 and Annex III, Annex A, of Decision 2016/1250.

[35] Recitals 145–149, Article 4(4), and Annexes I, II, and IV of Decision 2016/1250.

[36] The system has foreseen the following steps: initial dispute resolution by the company, with a 45 day deadline, whereby companies dealing with human resources data had to comply with national DPAs advice, while other could voluntarily commit; start proceedings through national DPA who contacted the Department of Commerce/FTC; voluntary use of the Alternative Dispute Resolution or another private programme with clear indication and link on their websites; Privacy Shield Panel as a final arbitration mechanism. See Recitals 38–63 of Decision 2016/1250.

[37] The basis were the redefined but pre-existing seven Safe Harbour Principles (*supra*) with the addition of certain supplemental principles, eg, on sensitive data, journalistic exceptions, secondary liability exemption for Internet Service Providers, due diligence and audit, role of DPAs, self-certification, verification, access, human resources data, and obligatory contracts for onward transfers. See Annex II to Decision 2016/1250.

by the Department of Commerce, which maintained an up-to-date list of certified companies.[38] The Commission also cited legal reforms in the US concerning national security (eg, the limited purposes for bulk data use, the USA Freedom Act, and written assurances). However, in Case C-311/18 (*Schrems II*),[39] the CJEU again found the arrangement inadequate, focusing primarily on US surveillance practices. The Court addressed two interrelated issues: first, the validity of Standard Contractual Clauses (SCCs)[40] as an alternative basis for transfer, and second, the validity of the adequacy decision. The CJEU upheld the SCC mechanism but emphasised that data controllers must ensure a level of protection that is essentially equivalent to that guaranteed within the EU.[41] Where the legal framework of a third country fails to offer such protection, controllers must implement additional safeguards or suspend the transfer. SCCs alone cannot remedy deficiencies if public authority access to data is disproportionate or lacks redress.[42] The Court closely linked Articles 44 and 46 GDPR, confirming that in the absence of an adequacy decision, cross-border data transfers must not undermine the level of GDPR protection.[43] Regarding the adequacy decision, the Court concluded that the US surveillance system enabled US intelligence agencies to obtain disproportionate access to EU personal data. Specifically, surveillance under Foreign Intelligence Surveillance Act (FISA) Section 702 and Executive Order 12333 did not provide EU data subjects with effective legal remedies before US courts.[44] Moreover, the Court criticised the Ombudsperson mechanism for lacking independence and binding authority.[45]

B. The Current EU-US Data Privacy Framework (DPF) and the Impact of AI

In response, the European Commission adopted the EU-US Data Privacy Framework in 2023, issuing a third adequacy decision.[46] The new framework

[38] Recitals 31–33, Article 1(3) and Annex I of Decision 2016/1250.

[39] CJEU, Case C-311/18, *Data Protection Commissioner v Facebook* (*Schrems II*) [2020] ECLI:EU:C:2020:559.

[40] Commission Decision 2010/87 of 5 February 2010 on standard contractual clauses for the transfer of personal data to processors established in third countries under Directive 95/46/EC of the European Parliament and of the Council [2010] OJ L 39/5. See also the new decision, following the *Schrems II* judgment - Commission Implementing Decision (EU) 2021/914 of 4 June 2021 on standard contractual clauses for the transfer of personal data to third countries pursuant to Regulation (EU) 2016/679 of the European Parliament and of the Council [2021] OJ L 199/31.

[41] CJEU, Case C-311/18, para 94.

[42] CJEU, Case C-311/18, paras 125–126.

[43] CJEU, Case C-311/18, paras 90–92.

[44] CJEU, Case C-311/18, para 192.

[45] CJEU, Case C-311/18, paras 194–197.

[46] Commission Implementing Decision EU 2023/1795 of 10 July 2023 pursuant to Regulation (EU) 2016/679 of the European Parliament and of the Council on the adequate level of protection of personal data under the EU-US Data Privacy Framework [2023] OJ L 231/118.

includes additional safeguards to address the CJEU's findings, eg, the creation of the Data Protection Review Court (DPRC) in the United States. This mechanism is based on Executive Order 14086, which provides for an initial decision by the Civil Liberties Protection Officer (CLPO) within the Office of the Director of National Intelligence (ODNI), with a right to appeal to the DPRC. This process is initiated through EU data protection authorities.[47] However, this new arrangement remains fragile, as it is based on executive orders and may be subject to reversal by future US administrations. Several EU data protection authorities have warned to prepare for potential legal uncertainty, with a possible *Schrems III* challenge looming. Namely, there are several vacant seats at the Privacy and Civil Liberties Oversight Board (PCLOB) responsible for oversight and cooperation with ODNI, and federal courts intervened to restore fired members from the Democrats to the position. However, the reinstatement has been halted by the Appeals Court.[48]

Regarding automated decision-making, the newly adopted framework states that it does 'not specifically address the issue of decisions affecting the data subject based solely on the automated processing of personal data',[49] and that, based on a 2018 study, such issues were not present at the time. It notes that sectors where automated decision-making takes place are regulated in the United States (eg, credit lending, mortgage offers, employment, housing, and insurance).[50] In addition to automated decision-making, there are other concerns regarding what happens with transferred EU personal data, such as the legal basis for training, information obligations, data security, protection of minors, purpose limitation, and others.[51] Therefore, AI-related data protection concerns should be part of the adequacy decision review. Should anyone challenge it – eg, issues with the independence of the CLPO – data flows could be interrupted. They could only continue under an alternative legal basis in accordance with Article 46 GDPR (eg, binding corporate rules or SCCs). In such a case, the data controller would be obliged to remedy the situation, as required by *Schrems II*. With respect to AI and data protection (as part of such an adequacy assessment), there would be room for California legislation to remedy the situation for California AI companies. In the absence of federal rules, California could preserve EU-California data transfers by proactively adopting AI legislation that addresses data protection concerns that arise due to the interaction between personal data and certain AI models.

[47] Commission Implementing Decision EU 2023/1795, Recitals 175–200.

[48] See *LeBlanc and Felten v United States Privacy and Civil Liberties Oversight Board*, No. 1:25-cv-00542 (D.D.C. May 21, 2025); and *LeBlanc and Felten v. United States Privacy and Civil Liberties Oversight Board*, No. 25-5197 (D.C. Cir. July 1, 2025) (order staying district court judgment).

[49] *LeBlanc and Felten v United States Privacy and Civil Liberties Oversight Board*, Recital 33.

[50] *LeBlanc and Felten v United States Privacy and Civil Liberties Oversight Board*, Recital 35. It refers to FCRA, Equal Credit Opportunity Act (ECOA), Title VII of the Civil Rights Act, Fair Housing Act, and HIPAA Privacy Rule.

[51] Claudio Novelli et al, 'Generative AI in EU Law: Liability, Privacy, Intellectual Property, and Cybersecurity', *Computer Law & Security Review* 55 (2024): 1–16, 7.

Nevertheless, such an EU-California adequacy model would not in itself overcome concerns regarding US federal surveillance laws. In September 2025, the General Court in *Latombe v Commission*[52] upheld the EU-US DPF, rejecting arguments that US surveillance laws and remedies fall short of EU fundamental rights standards. The Court accepted that the newly created DPRC, though established by executive order rather than statute, affords sufficient independence and impartiality to meet the Charter's requirements. Such a decision has been criticised for not taking reality of the current transatlantic political and legal developments into account.[53] However, the General Court stressed that the Commission remains under a continuing duty to monitor the US framework and suspend or withdraw adequacy if subsequent developments undermine the level of protection.

III. The Role of Personal Data in AI Systems

This section analyses data protection and AI issues under EU law, with certain comparisons to California law, as a fully fledged federal data protection legislation does not exist in the United States. The development of AI systems is a data-intensive process, using large datasets to train AI models.[54] With the development of generative AI systems, there is a growing demand for large, diverse, and uniquely categorised datasets. Current AI system design, for both large and small-scale models, benefits from high volumes of data. Generative AI developers are often incentivised to maximise the volume of data used to train their models. This is evident in the way new product releases are often categorised by the amount of training data. The general understanding is that model performance is a function of training dataset size and efficiency of training techniques. Some models can perform well with smaller datasets by optimising training (eg, Deepseek), but most models benefit from large, high-quality datasets. Existing understanding of data privacy and AI exists around the widespread application of AI algorithms used for targeting advertising.[55] They feed on the opposite of anonymised data, thus creating a concern for data privacy. While generative AI models are not as reliant on personal data as other applications of AI, such as advertising algorithms,

[52] General Court, *Latombe v Commission*, Case T-553/23, judgment of 3 September 2025, ECLI:EU:T:2025:537. Appeal pending (CJEU, Case C-703/25 P).

[53] 'EU-US Data Transfers: First Reaction on "Latombe" Case', NOYB, 3 September 2025, https://noyb.eu/en/eu-us-data-transfers-first-reaction-latombe-case.

[54] Abenezer Golda et al, 'Privacy and Security Concerns in Generative AI: A Comprehensive Survey', *IEEE Access* 12 (2024): 48126–44; Ajay Bandi et al, 'The Power of Generative AI: A Review of Requirements, Models, Input–Output Formats, Evaluation Metrics, and Challenges', *Future Internet* 15, no. 8 (2023).

[55] This is the core business model of some of the largest companies in the world, such as social media platforms Facebook and Google. Lex Zard and Alan M Sears, 'Targeted Advertising and Consumer Protection Law in the EU', *Vanderbilt Journal of Transnational Law* 56, no. 3 (2023): 799–851.

they still utilise personal data in ways that could be considered violative of data privacy rights

Thus, a significant amount of private data is being used to train AI models, both legally (eg, with consent) and potentially illegally (eg, without consent or a valid legal basis). Common practices have included scraping and crawling, whereby, *inter alia*, personal blogs, forums, and social media posts were captured if not protected by technical restrictions. E-mail addresses, bios, usernames, and photos were also gathered by simulating user sessions.[56] Furthermore, some organisations shared data without consent, and certain companies outsourced specialised scraping tasks, eg, collection of photos.[57] This is further reflected in the general lack of training data transparency. By contrast, Article 53(1)(d) AI Act[58] requires developers of general-purpose AI models to publish a sufficiently detailed summary of training content. From an EU perspective, models can be considered as containing personal data, where this relates to 'any information relating to an identified or identifiable natural person ('data subject')', and such a person can be identified, directly or indirectly.[59] Two situations must be distinguished: first, the legitimacy and lawfulness of using personal data for training; and second, the intentional or unintentional memorisation and integration of that data by the model, which may allow for direct or indirect identification.[60] Regarding indirect identification, the question of 'reasonable likelihood' to identify the person arises.[61] This includes the possibility of singling out an individual, linking records, or making inferences about the individual, whereby the process of anonymisation must be irreversible.[62] However, anonymisation has its limits. Once a model is trained on personal data, it is difficult to guarantee full anonymity.[63] Recently, an entire industry of synthetic data has emerged to address such concerns. These techniques are presented in EU law as safeguards but remain disputed in effectiveness and are legally relevant only where irreversibility can be guaranteed. Yet, even synthetic datasets can encounter limitations;

[56] *J.L., et al. v Alphabet Inc.*, US District Court for the Northern District of California; No. 3:23-cv-03440, regarding legal claims of scraping of 'virtually the entirety of our digital footprint.' See Melany Amarikwa, 'Internet Openness at Risk: Generative AI's Impact on Data Scraping', *Richmond Journal of Law and Technology* 30, no. 3 (2024): 533–89; Lauren Leffer, 'Your Personal Information Is Probably Being Used to Train Generative AI Models', *Scientific American*, 19 October 2023.

[57] *In re Clearview AI, Inc. Consumer Privacy Litigation*, MDL No. 2967, No. 1:21-cv-00135 (N.D. Ill. Mar. 20, 2025).

[58] Regulation (EU) 2024/1689 of the European Parliament and of the Council of 13 June 2024 laying down harmonised rules on artificial intelligence and amending Regulations (EC) No 300/2008, (EU) No 167/2013, (EU) No 168/2013, (EU) 2018/858, (EU) 2018/1139 and (EU) 2019/2144 and Directives 2014/90/EU, (EU) 2016/797 and (EU) 2020/1828 (Artificial Intelligence Act) [2024] OJ L 2024/1689.

[59] Article 4(1) GDPR.

[60] Bjørn Aslak Juliussen, Jon Petter Rui, and Dag Johansen, 'Algorithms That Forget: Machine Unlearning and the Right to Erasure', *Computer Law & Security Review* 51 (November 2023).

[61] Recital 26 GDPR.

[62] WP 29, Opinion 5/2014 on Anonymisation Techniques.

[63] Andrea Gadotti et al, 'Anonymization: The Imperfect Science of Using Data while Preserving Privacy', *Science Advances* 10, no. 29 (19 July 2024).

for example, purely synthetic data of high quality may amplify deficiencies.[64] The issue of anonymisation may be directly connected to documentation obligations by providers regarding data used in the training or pre-deployment phases of model development.

A. Anonymisation of AI Models

For an AI model to be considered anonymous, two elements must be evaluated, namely: 1) the likelihood of direct (including probabilistic) extraction of personal data concerning individuals whose data were used to develop the model; and 2) the likelihood of obtaining, whether intentionally or not, such personal data from user queries. The risks must be insignificant, taking into account 'all the means reasonably likely to be used' by the controller or by another person.[65] This assessment may also differ depending on whether the model is publicly available (eg, open source) or closed.[66] If personal data can be extracted – regardless of whether the model was intended for such use – the model cannot necessarily considered anonymous.[67] The design and training phases are essential for implementing personal data protection measures and conducting a data risk assessment. This includes source selection, data minimisation, model testing, and appropriate documentation. Such documentation should cover resistance techniques, including testing procedures and their results.[68] Once a model is trained with personal data, it becomes difficult – if not impossible – to delete it, as the data remains embedded in the model's weights. The process of machine unlearning is complex, requiring retraining without the erased data, followed by a verification.[69] Addressing a violation may depend on several scenarios, eg, the provider and deployer are the same (scenario 1), are different (scenario 2), or the provider anonymises the model before delivery (scenario 3).

[64] Peter Lee, 'Synthetic Data and the Future of AI', *Cornell Law Review* 110, no. 1 (2025): 1–74.
[65] EDPB, Opinion 28/2024 on certain data protection aspects related to the processing of personal data in the context of AI models, 17 December 2024.
[66] EDPB, Opinion 28/2024, 17.
[67] CJEU, Case C-413/23 P, *European Data Protection Supervisor v Single Resolution Board*, Opinion of Advocate General Spielmann [2025] ECLI:EU:C:2025:59, and Judgment of the Court [2025] ECLI:EU:C:2025:645. In comparison with EDPS, the Court, following the Advocate General's Opinion, adopted a narrower approach, rejecting the view that pseudonymised data are always personal data when transferred by the controller to a third party. In that regard, the Commission proposed a change in the definition of personal data – see Proposal for a Regulation of the European Parliament and of the Council amending Regulations (EU) 2016/679, (EU) 2018/1724, (EU) 2018/1725, (EU) 2023/2854 and Directives 2002/58/EC, (EU) 2022/2555 and (EU) 2022/2557 as regards the simplification of the digital legislative framework, and repealing Regulations (EU) 2018/1807, (EU) 2019/1150, (EU) 2022/868, and Directive (EU) 2019/1024 (Digital Omnibus) [2025] COM(2025) 837 final.
[68] EDPB, Opinion, 28/2024, 17–18.
[69] Proposed California law AB 1405 would establish a third party auditing mechanism for AI systems requiring by law such audit. It is similar to the notion of 'notified body' providing conformity assessment under the AI Act [Articles 3(22) and 31 AI Act].

Thus, different consequences for personal data arise from unlawfulness in the development phase. The initial illegal gathering of personal data and its misuse by the controller itself make the model highly problematic. If another deployer is involved, the question becomes whether that deployer has conducted a prior assessment of lawfulness, fairness, and transparency (Articles 5(1) and 6 GDPR). If the model was anonymised and no further processing is involved, there is no GDPR issue for the final deployer.[70] There is an interesting parallel with recent US decisions on copyright. Even if the fair use doctrine can be invoked, it does not legitimise the initial unlawful gathering (eg, books).[71] However, when it comes to publicly scraped personal data, there is a key difference between the EU and California. In the EU, publicly available personal data is protected by the GDPR. This is not necessarily the case under the California Consumer Privacy Act (CCPA), as amended by the California Privacy Rights Act (CPRA),[72] which excludes 'publicly available information or lawfully obtained, truthful information that is a matter of public concern', including 'information made available by a person to whom the consumer has disclosed the information if the consumer has not restricted the information to a specific audience'.[73] In the context of training data, greater coherence between the two legal systems regarding pseudonymisation and anonymisation would be beneficial to avoid problems arising once the model is placed on the market.

However, data gathering can be legitimate if consent was given. Both legal systems show similarities on the issue of consent. Under the GDPR, consent is required where no other lawful basis applies, and must be freely given, specific, informed, and unambiguous.[74] Explicit consent is specifically required for processing special categories of personal data,[75] as well as for certain types of automated decision-making or profiling.[76] Under the CCPA, businesses must provide notice at or before collection (Cal. Civ. Code § 1798.100(b)), and allow consumers to opt out of the sale or sharing of personal information (Cal. Civ. Code § 1798.120(a)). Affirmative opt-in consent is required for minors: for consumers 13 to 15 years old, businesses must obtain explicit opt-in consent to sell or share their data (Cal. Civ. Code § 1798.120(c)); for children under 13, verifiable parental consent is required, consistent with the federal Children's Online Privacy Protection Act (COPPA) rules. As for sensitive personal information – a category introduced by the CPRA – consent is not generally required unless the business intends to use it beyond certain limited and necessary purposes. Consumers must be given a 'Limit

[70] EDPB, Opinion 28/2024, 32–34.

[71] *Bartz v Anthropic PBC*, No. 3:24-cv-05417 (N.D. Cal.).

[72] CCPA of 2018, Cal. Civ. Code §§ 1798.100–1798.199.

[73] Sec 1798.140 (v) (2) CCPA. See also Mindy Nunez Duffourc, Sara Gerke, and Konrad Kollnig, 'Privacy of Personal Data in the Generative AI Data Lifecycle', *Journal of Intellectual Property, Information Technology and E-Commerce Law* 13, no. 2 (2024): 219–68.

[74] Articles 4(11) and 6(1)(a) GDPR.

[75] Article 9(2)(a) GDPR.

[76] Article 22(2)(c) GDPR.

the Use of My Sensitive Personal Information' link [Cal. Civ. Code § 1798.121(a)–(c)]. Sensitive personal information includes data such as precise geolocation, racial or ethnic origin, genetic data, and the contents of private communications [Cal. Civ. Code § 1798.140(ae)].

B. Legitimate Interest as a Legal Basis for AI Processing of Personal Data

It remains contested in EU law whether platforms may rely on legitimate interest to train models on publicly available user content. Under the EU's GDPR, some companies attempted to invoke the legitimate interest as a justification for the use of personal data for algorithmic training. This requires the existence of a legitimate aim or interest, the necessity of the processing to achieve that interest, and a balancing of that interest against the fundamental rights and freedoms of the data subjects.[77] The narrow limits of relying on legitimate interest for personal data processing were recently clarified by the CJEU in Case C-252/21 concerning Meta and its profiling of users for personalised advertising, within the broader context of abuse of a dominant position.[78] The Court held, *inter alia*, that Meta cannot rely on legitimate interest [Article 6(1)(f)] or contractual necessity [Article 6(1)(b) GDPR] to justify the collection of data from third-party websites and apps and the linking of such data to users' Facebook accounts without valid consent. Regarding Article 6(1)(b) GDPR – necessity for the performance of a contract – the Court stated that

> personalised content does not appear to be necessary in order to offer that user the services of the online social network. Those services may, where appropriate, be provided to the user in the form of an equivalent alternative which does not involve such a personalisation, such that the latter is not objectively indispensable for a purpose that is integral to those services.[79]

On the more complex issue of using Article 6(1)(f) (legitimate self-interest of the controller or a third person), the following interests were raised, namely

> personalised advertising, network security, product improvement, the sharing of informing with law enforcement agencies, the fact that the user is a minor, research and innovation for social good and the offer of services for commercial communication intended for the user and of analytics tools intended for advertisers and other business partners, enabling them to evaluate their performance.[80]

[77] Article 6(1)(f) GDPR. See EDPB Guidelines 1/2024 on processing of personal data based on Article 6(1)(f) GDPR.
[78] CJEU, Case C-251/21, *Meta Platforms Inc and Others v Bundeskartellamt* [2023] ECLI:EU:C:2023:537.
[79] Case C-251/21, para 102.
[80] Case C-251/21, para 113.

The Court acknowledged that personalised advertising could qualify as a legitimate interest, but found that the users' rights override it, particularly due to the scale and intrusiveness of collection, which could lead to a perception of constant surveillance. Network security may also be a legitimate interest, but only if data processing is strictly necessary, less intrusive alternatives are unavailable, and data minimisation is respected. Similarly, product improvement may be a valid interest, but the Court expressed doubt that it could override users' fundamental rights given the scale, impact, and users' reasonable expectations – especially when minors are concerned. The Court explicitly rejected the sharing of information with law enforcement as a legitimate interest under Article 6(1)(f) GDPR, noting that such processing would need to be assessed under Article 6(1)(c) GDPR (compliance with a legal obligation). Consequently, there are strict limits on the extent to which personal data can be used without consent for AI model training. Any violation may lead to demands for deletion of the training data or even the model itself. It is therefore essential that data protection and risk mitigation measures are integrated into all phases of AI development: design, training, and deployment. Hence, the EU AI Act did not introduce new data protection legislation, as the GDPR remains fully applicable.[81] However, it highlighted the importance of data protection within the framework of AI. In that regard, it established data protection as an integral part of data governance and management,[82] risk management (under the notion of fundamental rights)[83] and human rights oversight (under the notion of fundamental rights),[84] and quality management.[85] It also highlighted the application in certain circumstances, eg, further processing rules for the development of AI systems of public interest in sandboxes.[86] The application of data protection principles to AI – particularly generative AI and automated decision-making – will need to be taken into account when assessing the EU-US DPF. Without a coherent approach to data protection and AI, US businesses are likely to feel the effects of an expanding regulatory disparity with the EU. California itself can help remedy this situation to a certain extent, as its very active legislature has already adopted – or is debating – a variety of AI laws.

[81] Article 2(7) AI Act. There are also references in specific provisions, eg, biometric data [Article 5(1)(h) AI Act], use of data for the data protection impact assessment [Article 26(9) AI Act], deployers of emotion recognition/biometric categorisation systems [Article 50(3) AI Act], sandboxes [Article 59(1)(c) AI Act], role of national DPAs as market surveillance authorities [Article 74(8) AI Act], etc. However, the proposed Regulation of the European Parliament and of the Council amending Regulations (EU) 2024/1689 and (EU) 2018/1139 as regards the simplification of the implementation of harmonised rules on artificial intelligence (Digital Omnibus on AI) [2025] COM(2025) 836 final, would, *inter alia*, allow providers/deployers of AI systems to process special categories of personal data for bias detection and correction.

[82] Article 10(2)(b) AI Act.

[83] Article 9(2)(a) AI Act.

[84] Article 14(2) AI Act.

[85] AI Act, Article 17(1)(f) and Article 18(1)(b).

[86] AI Act, Article 59.

IV. The California Approach to AI Risk Regulation

This section analyses AI first under US federal law, then under California state law. California is the most advanced of the US states in terms of both AI development and regulation, being home to 32 of the top 50 AI companies in the world,[87] and having passed dozens of AI laws since 2019. However, California is not the only US state with innovative AI regulation; Colorado, Illinois, Texas, and others have also passed their own AI bills, sometimes modelled on California's and sometimes diverging. The main question being asked across state legislators is to what extent can state regulation offset the lack of regulatory will at a federal level.

A. Federal Deregulation, Moratorium Attempt, and a Patchwork of State Laws

The United States exhibits significant diversity in both data protection and AI regulation. Currently, there are no specific AI legislative rules at the federal level; instead, regulation relies on presidential executive orders. While the former administration adopted a human-centred approach similar to the EU, the new administration favours a free-market approach that prioritises competition. The revoked Executive Order (EO) 14110[88] applied to federal government operations and was based on the principles of safety and security, responsible innovation, support for American workers, equity and civil rights, non-discrimination, privacy and civil liberties, public-service-oriented AI, and global leadership. It was accompanied by a Blueprint for AI Bill of Rights[89] referring to safe and effective systems, algorithmic discrimination protection, data privacy, notice and explanation, and human alternatives.

The new Executive Order (EO) 14179[90] highlights a free-market approach and calls for dominance of global AI markets and applications. In turn, the accompanying document – America's AI Action Plan[91] – focuses mainly on competition, innovation, and global leadership. It encompasses three pillars, namely: I. Accelerate AI Innovation, II. Build American AI Infrastructure, and III. Lead International AI Diplomacy and Security. The Plan foresees to deregulate at the federal level (eg, cutting federal funding or stopping FTC actions), champions open-source, open-weight, and open AI models founded on American

[87] Rashi Shrivastava, 'Forbes 2025 AI 50 List – Top Artificial Intelligence Companies Ranked', *Forbes*, 10 April 2025.

[88] US White House. *Executive Order (EO) 14110 on Safe, Secure, and Trustworthy Development and Use of Artificial Intelligence*. 30 October 2023 (revoked).

[89] White House Office of Science and Technology Policy. *Blueprint for AI Bill of Rights, accompanied by a Technical Companion*. October 2022.

[90] US White House. *Executive Order (EO) 14179 on Removing Barriers to American Leadership in Artificial Intelligence*. 23 January 2025; and White House. *Executive Order (EO) 14192 on Unleashing Prosperity Through Deregulation*. 31 January 2025.

[91] US White House, *America's AI Action Plan, Winning the Race*, July 2025. See also the 2025 National Security Strategy referring to US AI standards as 'driving the world forward'.

values, and calls for eliminating references to misinformation, diversity, equity, inclusion, and climate change from the NIST Risk Management Framework.[92] The Plan also advocates for interpretability (explainability), rigorous AI evaluations, the removal of malicious deepfakes, standardisation, and incident reporting – a number of which cannot be achieved without legislation or regulation. Even more interesting is the intention to counter Chinese influence at the international level,[93] and strictly limit exports of sensitive AI technologies. Within the same short period of the release of the AI Action Plan, the federal government made an unsuccessful first attempt to establish federal pre-emption and moratorium, which would prohibit the enforcement of any existing or new state-level laws that could hinder AI competition.[94] Had it been adopted, it would not only have halted the adoption of new rules but also prohibited, for a period of 10 years, the enforcement of existing laws affecting AI competition. At the federal level, the United States has signed – but not yet ratified – the Council of Europe's Framework Convention on Artificial Intelligence as of 5 September 2024.[95] This is significant, as the Convention focuses primarily on the lifecycle of AI systems by public authorities or private actors acting on their behalf, and only secondarily on private actors operating independently.[96] The Convention obliges signatories to uphold fundamental rights, the rule of law, and democracy throughout the entire AI lifecycle, following a risk-based approach, and provides an AI definition consistent with OECD and EU.[97] It introduces certain principles, but provides flexibility by allowing states to implement them through 'legislative, administrative, or other measures'.[98] It also permits the regulation of the private sector either

[92] National Institute of Standards and Technology, *AI Risk Management Framework (AI RMF 1.0)*, January 2023, accessed 25 October 2025, www.nist.gov/itl/ai-risk-management-framework.

[93] This could be understood as an acknowledgement that the free market of AI systems can only take place between 'like-minded nations working together to encourage the development of AI in line with our shared values'.

[94] See the debates leading to the US Congress, *Rebuilding Economic Prosperity and Opportunity (REPO) for Americans Act*, H.R. 1, 119th Cong., enrolled 27 March 2025, enacted 4 July 2025 (Pub. L. No. 119-21) – One Big Beautiful Bill Act. The text would allow some limited exceptions related to removal of legal impediments to or facilitate the deployment or operation of AI, streamlining administrative procedures, or substantive requirements, either under federal law or applying in the same way to non-AI systems that perform comparable functions. It would have applied to artificial intelligence models, artificial intelligence systems, or automated decision systems. The US Senate voted 99 to 1 to delete it (S.Amdt.2814–119th Congress (2025–2026). See Adam Conner, 'The House Is Close To Passing a Moratorium on State Efforts To Regulate AI', *Center for American Progress*, 15 May 2025; National Conference of State Legislatures, 'NCSL Urges Senate to Oppose AI Moratorium on States', *NCSL*, 24 June 2025; Kevin Frazier and Adam Thierer, 'Understanding the Proposed AI Moratorium: Answers to Key Questions', *R Street Institute*, 3 June 2025; Holly Fechner, Matthew Shapanka, and Samuel Klein, 'Senate Nixes State AI Enforcement Moratorium, For Now', *Global Policy Watch*, 8 July 2025. However, the President issued an executive order in that regard – see Executive Order 14365 on Ensuring a National Policy Framework for AI, 11 December 2025. It establishes, inter alia, a task force to litigate against states based on interstate commerce and preemption, provides for restriction of funding, foresees a FTC policy statement in connection with deception practices, and the preparation of a federal legislative recommendation.

[95] Council of Europe, CETS 225, 5.9.2024.

[96] Council of Europe, CETS 225, Article 3(1).

[97] Council of Europe, CETS 225, Articles 1(1) and 2.

[98] Council of Europe, CETS 225, Article 1(2).

through the Convention's own principles or through other appropriate measures. The Convention explicitly excludes defence, research, and national security activities – with the understanding that such activities must be conducted in accordance with international law, including international human rights law, and with respect for democratic institutions and processes.[99] This approach stands in stark contrast to much of the US legislative landscape, which tends to focus on regulating private entities and protecting consumer rights. If the Convention were to be ratified and applied by the US, it would support the case for continued transatlantic flow of personal data. However, given the Trump administration's sharp departure from the Biden administration's approach to AI governance, it is increasingly unlikely to be ratified. With such inaction at the federal level, individual US states have retained full lawmaking independence for AI, resulting in a patchwork of priorities and regulatory approaches. The laws of California, Colorado, and Texas are good examples of regulatory diversity, whereby the California approach mostly echoes that of the EU.

B. The California Approach and the California Effect

California can be considered a frontrunner in data protection and AI regulation within the US.[100] Regarding data protection, California has a history of prioritising digital privacy. During the early emergence of interactivity on the internet (known as 'Web 2.0'),[101] it passed the California Online Privacy Protection Act of 2003 (CalOPPA),[102] becoming the first US law to require websites to display a privacy policy. As Californians' online activity grew in the 2010s, the state enacted the California Electronic Communications Privacy Act of 2015 (CalECPA),[103] which prohibits state law enforcement agencies from conducting warrantless searches of digital devices and online accounts. At the time, it was popularly hailed as 'the nation's best privacy law'.[104] Further, California's modern privacy framework was established with the passage of the CCPA of 2018.[105] The CCPA gave California residents increased control over how businesses use their personal information, including the right to know what information is being collected, to delete it, to opt out of their sale or sharing, and to be free from discrimination for exercising these rights. Notably similar to the EU approach, and the GDPR specifically, the CCPA applied a rights-based model of data protection to California law, albeit one

[99] Council of Europe, CETS 225, Article 3(2) to (4).

[100] Another one is Colorado adopting a general law referring to algorithmic discrimination – *SB24-205: Consumer Protections for Artificial Intelligence Act*, 74th General Assembly, 2024 Regular Session.

[101] San Murugesan. 'Understanding Web 2.0', *IT Professional* 9, no. 4 (July–Aug. 2007): 34–41.

[102] California Online Privacy Protection Act of 2003, Cal. Bus. & Prof. Code §§ 22575–22579.

[103] California Electronic Communications Privacy Act, 2015–16 Sess., ch. 651 (Cal. 2015).

[104] Kim Zetter, 'California Now Has the Nation's Best Digital Privacy Law', *Wired Magazine*, 8 October 2015, www.wired.com/2015/10/california-now-nations-best-digital-privacy-law/.

[105] *Bartz v Anthropic PBC*, No. 3:24-cv-05417 (N.D. Cal.).

grounded primarily in individual rather than collective rights.[106] Just two years later, Californians passed the CPRA 2020,[107] similarly winning the title of 'the strongest consumer privacy law ever enacted in the United States'.[108] The CPRA amended the CCPA, adding additional consumer protections and establishing the California Privacy Protection Agency (CPPA) to enforce the law.

Although California is home to Silicon Valley and major AI companies, it is also at the forefront of efforts to regulate AI. However, California legislative initiatives regarding AI continue to lag behind the EU in terms of the comprehensiveness of its data protection initiatives. In the context of California, generative AI and its broad range of applications may create obligations for companies to comply with multiple data privacy requirements. That said, generative AI also introduces novel applications for personal data, which may risk circumventing the scrutiny of existing privacy requirements under California law. In contrast, the EU's data privacy laws have maintained a high level of application to the use of personal data in generative AI, based on the GDPR. This divergence may be due to the character and approach of California's data privacy legislation: it is not general in scope, is not grounded in fundamental rights, is focused on consumer protection, and is divided by application type. Nonetheless, the California legislature has addressed a wide variety of AI-related issues, some of which also intersect with data protection.

While AI lawmaking has been active in California since 2019, the 2023–24 California legislative cycle marked the first widespread effort by state policymakers to pursue generalised AI lawmaking. A high number of 65 AI-related bills were introduced, and over a dozen were signed into law.[109] The adopted laws address a wide breadth of issues, such as the definition of AI,[110] misinformation and election integrity,[111] deepfakes,[112] watermarking of AI-generated content,[113] digital replicas of actors,[114] and health-related applications.[115] Notably, the 2023–24 legislative cycle also passed two bills related to AI data

[106] Mei-Lin Huang, 'Digital Privacy in the Age of Surveillance: A Comparative Study of GDPR and CCPA', *OTS Canadian Journal* 4, no. 7 (2025): 65–74.

[107] California Consumer Privacy Act of 2018, Cal. Civ. Code §§ 1798.100–1798.199.

[108] Californians for Consumer Privacy, 'California Privacy Rights Act Executive Summary', *Californians for Consumer Privacy*, n.d., www.caprivacy.org/cpra-exec-summary/.

[109] Daniel K Alvarez et al, 'California Enacts 17 AI Bills in 2024', *Willkie Farr & Gallagher LLP*, 10 October 2024.

[110] California State, AB 2885, Artificial Intelligence, 2023–24 Sess., ch. 843 (Cal. 2024).

[111] California State, AB 2355, 2023–24 Sess., ch. 260 (Cal. 2024) (Political advertisements – AI); AB 2655, Defending Democracy from Deepfake Deception Act of 2024, 2023–24 Sess., ch. 261 (Cal. 2024); AB 2839, Elections: Deceptive Media in Advertisements, 2023–24 Sess., ch. 262 (Cal. 2024) – blocked by injunction primarily due to effect on political speech.

[112] California State, AB 1831, 2023–24 Sess., ch. 926 (Cal. 2024) (child pornography: AI-generated content); SB 926, 2023–24 Sess., ch. 927 (Cal. 2024) (non-consensual deepfake pornography; SB 981, 2023–24 Sess., ch. 928 (Cal. 2024) (sexually explicit digital identity theft reporting).

[113] SB 942, 2023–24 Sess., ch. 291 (Cal. 2024).

[114] California State, AB 1836, Use of likeness: digital replica, 2023–24 Sess., ch. 258 (Cal. 2024).

[115] California State, AB 3030, Health Care Services: Artificial Intelligence, 2023–24 Sess., ch. 848 (Cal. 2024); SB 1120, Health Care Coverage: Utilization Review, 2023–24 Sess., ch. 879 (Cal. 2024).

usage specifically, including amendments to the CCPA regarding personal data in AI formats,[116] and training data disclosure.[117] An additional three dozen proposals were made in the 2025–26 cycle, including measures relating to labelling of AI-generated content,[118] on right to publicity,[119] copyright protection,[120] protection of children,[121] companion chatbots,[122] human oversight in critical infrastructure,[123] and the protection of whistleblowers.[124] One of California's most notable – but ultimately unsuccessful – attempts at broad AI regulation was SB 1047, which proposed self-assessment and conformity requirements for large AI developers for certain critical harms[125] – similar to the obligations under the AI Act. The bill was highly controversial among California legislators and the private sector, fuelled by debate over 'stifling innovation'[126] and being overly prescriptive in its approach. This controversy, in addition to normal legislative processes, led to significant revisions, which eventually allowed the bill to pass through both chambers. Notably, revisions won the support of key private sector actors such as Anthropic,[127] who had initially taken a position against the bill.[128] Nonetheless, the bill was later vetoed by Governor Newsom, stating that it was too focused only on the largest models, giving the public a false sense of security.[129] Interestingly, Governor Newsom's veto message also contained the critique that SB 1047 did not take into account deployment in high-risk environments, involvement in critical decision-making or the use of sensitive data. The veto of SB 1047 marked a setback for generalised AI regulation in California, at least at

[116] California State, AB 1008, California Consumer Privacy Act of 2018: personal information, 2023–24 Sess. (Cal. 2024). It uses the term 'artificial intelligence systems that are capable of outputting personal information'. Sec. 1798.140(v)(4)(C).

[117] California State, AB 2013, AI Training Data Transparency Act, 2023–24 Sess. (Cal. 2024). It will apply from 1 January 2026 to all generative AI systems released on/after 1 January 2022 and made publicly available to Californians for use, including substantial modifications. It has to be posted on the developer's site. Further information includes sources, furthering of purpose, number of data points and their descriptions, intellectual property and information of purchase or licence, aggregate consumer information, cleaning of data, time of collection, first use, use of synthetic data. Cal. Civ. Code § 3111(a).

[118] California State, AB 853, California AI Transparency Act (2025–2026).

[119] California State Senate, SB 11, AI Abuse Protection Act.

[120] California State, AB 412, AI Copyright Protection Act.

[121] California State, AB 1064, Leading Ethical AI Development (LEAD) for Kids Act.

[122] California State Senate, SB 243, Companion Chatbots.

[123] California State Senate, SB 833, Human Oversight of AI in Critical Infrastructure.

[124] California State Senate, SB 53, Transparency in Frontier Artificial Intelligence Act, 2025–26 Sess. This is a slimmer version of vetoed SB 1047. See also Khari Johnson, 'CA Proposes AI Regulations as Trump Signals Hands-Off Approach', *CalMatters*, 5 March 2025.

[125] This included Chemical, Biological, Radiological, and Nuclear (CBRN) threats regarding mass casualties, large-scale cyber attacks, and death, bodily injury, or property damage that would be a human crime.

[126] Scott Kohler, 'All Eyes on Sacramento: SB 1047 and the AI Safety Debate', *Carnegie Endowment for International Peace*, 11 September 2024.

[127] Anthropic Letter, 21 August 2024.

[128] Anthropic Letter, 23 July 2024.

[129] California, Governor Veto, 29 September 2024.

the frontier level,[130] and thus could be considered a setback for those seeking increased alignment between California and the EU. However, key components of SB 1047 were reintroduced in the 2025–26 cycle under the new name SB 53.[131] Now much narrower than SB 1047 and stripped of its most controversial components, SB 53 includes fewer reporting obligations[132] and is thus more palatable to frontier developers. Faced with less fervent opposition from frontier developers compared to SB 1047, SB 53 was passed in September 2025 and signed into law by Governor Newsom later that month. Notably, the final version of SB 53 did not add any considerations or requirements for the use of sensitive data, as Governor Newsom had requested in his veto message for SB 1047.

Besides attempts at general AI regulation, California also passed several AI data privacy-specific laws. The 2023–24 cycle produced AB 1008, which updates language in the CCPA to specify that personal information can exist in multiple formats. In this, it defines personal data as the output of a generative AI system trained on such data. This was considered a success by many, as it marks a step in the direction of EU-style data protection by creating a bridge between generative AI and existing personal data protection under the CCPA. Similarly, AB 2013 introduces a documentation obligation regarding training data, including the requirement to disclose 'whether the datasets include personal information, as defined in subdivision (v) of Section 1798.140'.[133] An exemption applies to systems whose sole purpose is to ensure security and integrity, operate aircraft, or serve national security and defence purposes when made available only to a federal entity.[134] This presents a significant approximation to the AI Act's data governance and documentation obligations.[135] Within the bills voted in the 2025–26 cycle, a few stand out for their similarities to the EU approach. The first was AB 412 (No pass – moved to two-year bill), which would require developers of generative AI models to document the materials used to train their models and establish a mechanism for rights owners to request additional information on those materials. This bill would be a significant step toward transparency requirements for the model training process, which remains an opaque practice under California law. That said, AB 412 would have remained limited to rights holders, keeping this bill

[130] Florence G'Sell, Zeke Gillman, and Ashok Ayer, 'California's SB 1047 vs EU AI Act: A Comparative Analysis of AI Regulation', *Chaire numérique – Digital Governance and Sovereignty*, Sciences Po, 28 October 2024.

[131] Khari Johnson, 'CA Proposes AI Regulations as Trump Signals Hands-Off Approach', *CalMatters*, 5 March 2025.

[132] Justine Gluck, 'California's SB 53: The First Frontier AI Law, Explained', *Future of Privacy Forum*, 3 October 2025. See also Beth George et al, 'Compliance in a Global AI Market: Examining the Overlaps Between California's SB 53 and the EU AI Act', *Freshfields Blog*, 2 October 2025.

[133] Cal. Civ. Code § 3111(a).

[134] Cal. Civ. Code § 3111(b)(1)–(3). Compare to exceptions to Article 3(2) EU AI Act with a stricter language – 'exclusively for military, defence or national security purposes, regardless of the type of entity carrying out those activities'.

[135] Articles 10, 18, and 53(1)(d) AI Act, and Commission's Template for the Public Summary of Training Content for general-purpose AI models.

in the domain of copyright rather than personal data protection. Lastly, another key bill was AB 1405 (No pass – held in appropriations committee). This bill would have created a mechanism to allow AI auditors to enrol with the Government Operations Agency and prevent registered auditors from accepting employment with an auditee within 12 months of completing a covered audit. Its failed status marked another missed milestone for a California AI transparency regime.

Despite the important AI legislation that failed in recent years, the California AI laws that did pass continue to have a significant influence on the operations of AI companies beyond California – a phenomenon often referred to as the 'California Effect'. In modern applications, the California Effect is evidenced by nationwide compliance with the CCPA opt-out requirements by top-visited US websites, even when they are operating outside California.[136] Notably, the term 'California Effect' was first used to describe the sweeping effects of California's stringent automobile emissions standards dating back to the 1970s, which influenced car manufacturers across the United States. Researchers in this space argue that the California Effect is most likely a function of California's large market, a company's desire to operate in the state, and incentives to maintain uniform production standards across its nationwide operations.[137] In the eyes of modern-day California lawmakers concerned with AI and data privacy, the hope is to leverage this California Effect to exert influence over the nationwide operations of AI companies in the absence of federal AI regulation.

Overall, the California approach to AI regulation has been characterised by separate legislative efforts, each focused on a specific application of AI. This contrasts with the EU approach, which involves comprehensive legislation focused on fundamental rights, including personal data. To this end, the EU model remains an example for some California legislators, particularly for the comprehensive nature of the AI Act. Tom Umberg, California state senator and chair of the Senate Judiciary Committee, is known for publicly encouraging California legislators to learn from EU regulatory approaches. In May 2024, Umberg told CalMatters that the Senate Judiciary Staff had multiple meetings with EU officials while deliberating on California's definition of AI.[138] Beyond this, Umberg notably published an op-ed at the beginning of the 2025–26 legislative cycle that encouraged California legislators to 'follow the example of the European Union'.[139] Interestingly, California's private sector has also been calling for greater EU-California alignment. In August 2025, OpenAI publicly published its letter to Governor Newsom on harmonised regulation, calling for Governor Newsom

[136] AI. Van Hong Tran et al, 'Measuring Compliance with the California Consumer Privacy Act Over Space and Time', in *CHI '24: Proceedings of the 2024 CHI Conference on Human Factors in Computing Systems* (New York: Association for Computing Machinery, 2024).

[137] Anu Bradford, 'Exporting Standards: The Externalization of the EU's Regulatory Power via Markets', *International Review of Law and Economics* 42 (June 2015): 158–73.

[138] Khari Johnson, 'How California and the EU Work Together to Regulate Artificial Intelligence', *CalMatters*, 24 May 2024.

[139] Tom Umberg, 'Now that Trump has undone the AI Executive Order, California must lead on AI regulation', *Sacramento Bee*, 22 January 2025.

to introduce a safe harbour from California AI legislation if a California-based frontier developer has signed onto a 'parallel framework such as the EU's AI Code of Practice'.[140] While this drastic approach would effectively maximise alignment between the EU and California from the compliance perspective of California-based companies, it would also critically reduce the agency of California legislators to address unique concerns of Californians with new legislation and to take enforcement actions within California.

V. The Brussels-Sacramento Approach as a Lawmaking Alliance

AI will become a significant part of modern society. Alongside its potential to do good, the technology also poses a real risk of causing short- and long-term harms of many different kinds to citizens around the world. There appears to be a growing consensus that regulation is necessary, though opinions differ on how to achieve it – whether through strict legislation, self-governance, multi-stakeholder governance, soft law, or a combination of those. An Ayn Rand-style 'John Galt' logic of purely self-regulating AI, despite its emphasis on individual freedom,[141] will not work. The relationship between law and technology is twofold. Not only does new technology demand legal solutions, but law must also shape technology by defining what is permissible. Technologically, AI may make many new and beneficial things possible – one could even imagine a future where AI has cured cancer or solved world hunger. But the hope for this future does not mean that AI progress should be left to the market alone. We have experience with other free-market approaches that have failed for similar reasons, such as pharmaceutical regulation, environmental protection, and food safety. The same reasoning should be applied to AI, given its potential negative consequences – eg, algorithmic bias,[142] influence on due process,[143] risks to public health,[144] challenges to intellectual property,[145]

[140] OpenAI Global Affairs, 'OpenAI's letter to Governor Newsom on harmonized regulation', *OpenAI Global Affairs*, 12 August 2025.

[141] John Hocutt, 'Ayn Rand on Rights', *Essays in the Philosophy of Humanism* 17, no. 2 (2009): 1–12; Craig Biddle, 'Ayn Rand's Theory of Rights: The Moral Foundation of a Free Society', *The Objective Standard* 6, no. 3 (Fall 2011): 31–45.

[142] Reva Schwartz et al, *Towards a Standard for Identifying and Managing Bias in Artificial Intelligence*, NIST Special Publication 1270 (Gaithersburg, MD: National Institute of Standards and Technology, 2022).

[143] *State v Loomis*, 2016 WI 68, 371 Wis. 2d 235, 881 N.W.2d 74, regarding due process and the use of predictive systems on re-offending for sentencing. See Iñigo De Miguel Beriain, 'Does the Use of Risk Assessments in Sentences Respect the Right to Due Process? A Critical Analysis of the *Wisconsin v. Loomis* Ruling', *Law, Probability and Risk* 17, no. 1 (March 2018): 45–53.

[144] *Garcia v Character Technologies, Inc.*, 2025 WL 1461721 (M.D. Fla. 21 May 2025), regarding the death of Sewell Setzer after interactions with chatbots. The case is also directed against Google due to the technology behind Character AI (Google as a component part manufacturer) for aiding and abetting.

[145] It reveres mostly about the question of AI training with others' copyright. However, it seems that US court are willing to use the fair use doctrine on it due to its 'transformative' effect. See *Bartz v Anthropic*, No. 3:24-cv-05417 (N.D. Cal. filed 2024), or *New York Times Co. v Microsoft Corp. et al.*, No. 1:23-cv-11195 (S.D.N.Y. filed 27 Dec. 2023).

and concerns about data protection and privacy[146] – and the law can be used to minimise harms and facilitate a future where AI benefits society.

This approach has clearly been recognised by the EU and by the California government and legislature. The EU went furthest by adopting an omnibus regulation with clear prohibitions/obligations for providers, deployers, and others within the AI value chain. The AI Act prohibits certain types of AI systems and introduces obligations concerning transparency and explainability, data governance, risk assessment and management, fundamental rights impact assessments, human oversight, and certification. It also addresses general-purpose AI (GPAI) and GPAI with systemic risks, eg, copyright, watermarking, and deepfakes. The AI Act remains flexible. For instance, it applies only to high-risk AI systems and generative AI, while excluding national security, defence, and research activities.[147] It is based on an initial self-assessment, supplemented by third-party audits, standardisation, and industry-led codes of practice. The recently adopted General-Purpose AI Code of Practice[148] includes a robust risk assessment framework,[149] whereby compliance triggers a presumption of conformity.[150] Motivated by similar concerns, California legislators have introduced or adopted a broad range of AI laws. A significant portion of this legislation follows AI Act trends. There appears to be a consensus on regulating certain types of AI output (eg, deepfakes) and to require watermarking of AI output. Both legal systems have embraced the idea of self-certification reinforced by external oversight and have emphasised the importance of the pre-training and pre-deployment phases. Both share a strong concern regarding the risks of bias and algorithmic discrimination. Nonetheless, there are also clear limits to the consensus, as illustrated by the vetoed California SB 1047.

The EU, the US, and California share a common goal as democracies that are bound together in a globalised world. Neither the US nor the EU can face the challenges of the future – particularly in view of demographic trends – on their own.[151] At the same time, the development of large-scale generative AI is expensive[152] and energy-consuming.[153] It does not make sense to require companies to develop separate AI models for the EU and the US. Models

[146] CJEU, Case C-311/18, paras 90–92. See also Daniel J Solove, 'Artificial Intelligence and Privacy', 77 *Florida Law Review* 1 (2025).

[147] Article 2(3) and (6) AI Act.

[148] https://digital-strategy.ec.europa.eu/en/policies/contents-code-gpai.

[149] The final version corrected the third draft's differentiation between selected types of systemic risks and other risks, whereby fundamental rights were put in an optional second category.

[150] Article 53(4) AI Act. Similarly, California bill SB 813, if adopted, would establish third party independent certification by multi-stakeholder regulatory organisations (MRO) and a rebuttable presumption of compliance.

[151] The European population 65 and older will be in 2050 around 30 per cent of the population, and in the US around 23 per cent.

[152] Nikhil Kandpal and Colin Raffel, 'Position: The Most Expensive Part of an LLM Should Be Its Training Data', *arXiv*, 16 April 2025.

[153] International Energy Agency, 'AI Is Set to Drive Surging Electricity Demand from Data Centres While Offering the Potential to Transform How the Energy Sector Works,' IEA, 10 April 2025.

developed for Western markets – based on democratic values – will not be able to compete in countries that do not prioritise democracy and fundamental rights, as demonstrated by challenges faced by social media platforms and messaging services. In that regard, it is important that fundamental rights, at least to a certain extent, apply also to non-citizens (eg, the US Constitution). Conversely, AI systems developed in non-democratic states will be difficult to deploy in the EU and US markets. This has already been illustrated by concerns surrounding platforms like TikTok,[154] or the deployment of DeepSeek.[155] At the same time, fundamental differences between the EU and US approaches to data protection must be acknowledged. The EU conceptualises data protection as a fundamental right grounded in human dignity, protecting individuals against both private and public actors. By contrast, US law treats privacy more narrowly as a liberty interest, primarily focused on limiting state action.[156] Therefore, the EU protects personal data against both public and private actors, while US protections are sectoral and far narrower.

The EU and US legal frameworks are intertwined not only by shared values but also by market realities. It is in their mutual interest to develop compatible AI models that can be deployed across both markets. Hence, it is expected that most big tech corporations based in California will not take an intransigent position against EU regulation. Instead, companies will naturally seek harmonisation between the two jurisdictions and thus support a joint EU-US approach. Alternatively, if a federal US approach is not feasible, a Brussels-Sacramento (California) alliance may serve as a starting point. While California is by far the most influential US state in this area, the degree to which its laws will be adopted by other states remains uncertain. Despite certain limits, such cooperation is an opportunity for business: it would provide companies with a clear playing field to develop AI based on a robust, risk-based framework with oversight, protections against discrimination, and strong data protection standards. The success of such an approach is evidenced by the Brussels Effect and the same California Effect in the US. Regulation can shape global markets, without causing a race to the bottom. Despite doomsday predictions that the GDPR would cripple innovation, it provided a predictable environment for companies to develop privacy-by-design and privacy-by-default solutions and triggered a global shift in privacy regulation. In the same way, the EU and California have an opportunity to create a globally successful regulatory model for AI governance and AI data privacy. For success, several conditions have to be fulfilled, namely a significant domestic market, regulatory capacity, the enforcement of stringent standards based on the precautionary

[154] Protecting Americans from Foreign Adversary Controlled Applications Act, Public Law 118–50, Division H, 138 Stat. 955–960 (April 24, 2024), upheld by the US Supreme Court.

[155] *DeepSeek Blocked in Italy Due to Privacy Risks – Setting a Significant Precedent*, HIMSS, 25 March 2025.

[156] James Q Whitman, 'The Two Western Cultures of Privacy: Dignity versus Liberty', *Yale Law Journal* 113, no. 6 (2004): 1151–221.

principle, and the cost/benefit ratio of common standards.[157] The EU – US (or alternatively California market on high tech) can fulfil these conditions if they could agree to a common attitude towards precaution. Regulatory alignment should be welcomed by EU and California companies, as it would enable the creation of a huge common AI regulatory market and set a new global AI standard by merging the 'Brussels' and 'California' effects into a unified 'Brussels-California Effect'.

VI. Conclusions

While the EU and US share deep economic ties and democratic values, their diverging legal frameworks – most notably the EU's comprehensive GDPR and AI Act compared with the US's sectoral, fragmented approach – pose challenges to the continuation of data transfers and to the future of transatlantic AI cooperation. If the AI-data protection divergence continues, it may undermine the current EU-US DPF, given its fragility in the wake of past CJEU judgments (eg, *Schrems I* and *II*). The lack of clear integration of AI-related personal data concerns leaves the door open for a potential *Schrems III* challenge. The significant role of personal data in AI training data, and the question of the legal basis for using such data, call for a policy response. At the US federal level, no meaningful AI regulation related to privacy is foreseeable. Therefore, California emerges as a credible partner to bridge the transatlantic regulatory gap, due to its high-tech industry, central role in AI development, proactive legislature, and partial alignment with the EU approach. While recent legislative efforts such as AB 2013 and AB 1008 are steps in the right direction, further legislation is needed to ensure that AI systems developed in California can be deployed in the EU without legal obstacles or challenges.

The creation of a Brussels-Sacramento alliance – based on shared principles of fundamental rights and freedoms, transparency, data minimisation, and risk management – would not only safeguard the integrity of data protection and AI governance, but also provide for a globally competitive business model, ensuring interoperability, market access, global trend-setting, and public trust. Such success depends on three elements: inclusion of AI in the EU-US DPF; pursuing legislative AI convergence, especially between the EU and California; and creating a joint regulatory model that could serve as a sustainable, democratic, and innovation-friendly global AI model. The Brussels-Sacramento alliance is not only a political and legal necessity; it is an immense economic and ethical opportunity. By converging their regulatory approaches, the EU and California can set the world standard for safe, privacy-preserving AI.

[157] Bradford, *Brussels Effect*, 25–64.

Bibliography

AB 412, California, AI Copyright Protection Act, pending.

AB 1064, California, LEAD for KIds Act, pending.

AB 2885, California, Artificial Intelligence, 2023–24 Sess., ch. 843 (Cal. 2024).

AB 1008, California Consumer Privacy Act of 2018: personal information, 2023–24 Sess. (Cal. 2024).

AB 2013, California, AI Training Data Transparency Act, 2023–24 Sess. (Cal. 2024).

AB 2355, California, 2023–24 Sess., ch. 260 (Cal. 2024).

AB 2655, California, Defending Democracy from Deepfake Deception Act of 2024, 2023–24 Sess., ch. 261 (Cal. 2024).

AB 2839, California, Elections: Deceptive Media in Advertisements, 2023–24 Sess., ch. 262 (Cal. 2024).

AB 1831, California, 2023–24 Sess., ch. 926 (Cal. 2024).

AB 1836, California, Use of likeness: digital replica, 2023–24 Sess., ch. 258 (Cal. 2024).

AB 3030, California, Health Care Services: Artificial Intelligence, 2023–24 Sess., ch. 848 (Cal. 2024)

AB 853, California AI Transparency Act (2025-2026), pending.

An, Erin J. 'It's Finally Time for a National Data Privacy Law: A Discussion of the American Data Privacy and Protection Act (ADPPA)', *Brooklyn Journal of Corporate, Financial & Commercial Law* 18, no. 1 (2023): 229–46.

Alvarez, Daniel K, et al. *California Enacts 17 AI Bills in 2024*, Willkie Farr & Gallagher LLP (10 October 2024), www.willkie.com/-/media/files/publications/2024/10/california-enacts-17-ai-bills-in-2024.pdf.

Amarikwa, Melany. *Internet Openness at Risk: Generative AI's Impact on Data Scraping*, 30 *Rich. J.L. & Tech.* 533 (2024).

Anthropic Letter, 21 August 2024, https://cdn.sanity.io/files/4zrzovbb/website/6a3b14a98a781a6b69b9a3c5b65da26a44ecddc6.pdf.

Anthropic Letter, 23 July 2024, www.documentcloud.org/documents/25003075-sia-sb-1047-anthropic/.

Aslak Juliussen, Bjørn, Petter Rui, Jon, and Johansen, Dag. 'Algorithms That Forget: Machine Unlearning and the Right to Erasure', *Computer Law & Security Review* 51 (November 2023).

Bandi, Ajay, et al. 'The Power of Generative AI: A Review of Requirements, Models, Input–Output Formats, Evaluation Metrics, and Challenges', *Future Internet* 15, no. 8 (2023).

Bartz v Anthropic PBC, No. 3:24-cv-05417 (N.D. Cal.).

Berlain, Iñigo De Miguel 'Does the Use of Risk Assessments in Sentences Respect the Right to Due Process? A Critical Analysis of the *Wisconsin v. Loomis* Ruling', *Law, Probability and Risk* 17, no. 1 (March 2018): 45–53.

Bradford, Anu. 'The Brussels Effect', 107 *NW. U. L. REV.* 1 (2012), 1–64.

Bradford, Anu. *The Brussels Effect: How the European Union Rules the World* (Oxford: Oxford University Press, 2020).

Bradford, Anu. 'Exporting Standards: The Externalization of the EU's Regulatory Power via Markets', *International Review of Law and Economics* 42 (June 2015): 158–73.

Biddle, Craig. 'Ayn Rand's Theory of Rights: The Moral Foundation of a Free Society', *The Objective Standard* 6, no. 3 (Fall 2011): 31–45.

California Consumer Privacy Act of 2018, Cal. Civ. Code §§ 1798.100–1798.199.

California Online Privacy Protection Act of 2003, Cal. Bus. & Prof. Code §§ 22575–22579.
California Electronic Communications Privacy Act, 2015–16 Sess., ch. 651 (Cal. 2015).
Californians for Consumer Privacy, 'California Privacy Rights Act Executive Summary', *Californians for Consumer Privacy*, n.d., www.caprivacy.org/cpra-exec-summary/.
CJEU, Fact Sheet, Protection of Personal Data, July 2024, https://curia.europa.eu/jcms/upload/docs/application/pdf/2018-10/fiche_thematique_-_donnees_personnelles_-_en.pdf.
CJEU, Joined Cases C-293/12 and C-594/12, *Digital Rights Ireland and Others* [2014] ECLI:EU:C:2014:238.
CJEU, Case C-131/12, *Google Spain SL, Google Inc. v Agencia Española de Protección de Datos (AEPD), Mario Costeja González* [2014] ECLI:EU:C:2014:317.
CJEU, Case C-362/14, *Maximillian Schrems* [2015] ECLI:EU:C:2015:650.
CJEU, Case C-311/18, *Data Protection Commissioner v Facebook (Schrems II)* [2020] ECLI:EU:C:2020:559.
CJEU, Case C-413/23 P, *European Data Protection Supervisor v Single Resolution Board*, Opinion of Advocate General Spielmann [2025] ECLI:EU:C:2025:59.
CJEU, Case C-251/21, *Meta* [2023] ECLI:EU:C:2023:537.
Children's Online Privacy Protection Act (COPPA), 15 U.S.C. §§ 6501–6506 (1998).
Commission Decision 2000/520/EC of 26 July 2000 pursuant to Directive 95/46/EC of the European Parliament and of the Council on the adequacy of the protection provided by the safe harbour privacy principles and related frequently asked questions issued by the US Department of Commerce [2000] OJ L 215/7.
Commission Implementing Decision (EU) 2016/1250 of 12 July 2016 pursuant to Directive 95/46/EC of the European Parliament and of the Council on the adequacy of the protection provided by the EU-US Privacy Shield [2016] OJ L 207/1.
Commission Decision 2010/87 of 5 February 2010 on standard contractual clauses for the transfer of personal data to processors established in third countries under Directive 95/46/EC of the European Parliament and of the Council [2010] OJ L 39/5.
Commission Implementing Decision (EU) 2021/914 of 4 June 2021 on standard contractual clauses for the transfer of personal data to third countries pursuant to Regulation (EU) 2016/679 of the European Parliament and of the Council [2021] OJ L 199/31.
Commission Implementing Decision EU 2023/1795 of 10 July 2023 pursuant to Regulation (EU) 2016/679 of the European Parliament and of the Council on the adequate level of protection of personal data under the EU-US Data Privacy Framework [2023] OJ L 231/118.
Conner, Adam, 'The House Is Close To Passing a Moratorium on State Efforts To Regulate AI', *Center for American Progress*, 15 May 2025, www.americanprogress.org/article/the-house-is-close-to-passing-a-moratorium-on-state-efforts-to-regulate-ai/.
Council of Europe, CETS 225, 5.9.2024.
Coyle, Diane and Lucy Hampton, '21st Century Progress in Computing', *Telecommunications Policy* 48, no. 1 (2024).
EDPB, Opinion 28/2024 on certain data protection aspects related to the processing of personal data in the context of AI models, 17 December 2024.
EDPB Guidelines 1/2024 on processing of personal data based on Article 6(1)(f) GDPR.
European Strategy for Data; European Commission (COM/2020/66 final).
Executive Order (EO) 14110 on Safe, Secure, and Trustworthy Development and Use of Artificial Intelligence, 30 October 2023 (revoked).
Executive Order (EO) 14179 on Removing Barriers to American Leadership in Artificial Intelligence, 23 January 2025.

Executive Order (EO) 14192 on Unleashing Prosperity Through Deregulation, 31 January 2025.

Executive Order (EO) 14365 on Ensuring a National Policy Framework for AI, 11 December 2025.

Fair Credit Reporting Act (FCRA), 15 U.S.C. §§ 1681–1681x (1970).

Fechner, Holly, Shapanka, Mathew, and Klein, Samuel. 'Senate Nixes State AI Enforcement Moratorium, For Now', *Global Policy Watch*, 8 July 2025, www.globalpolicywatch.com/2025/07/senate-nixes-state-ai-enforcement-moratorium-for-now/.

Federal Trade Commission Act, 15 U.S.C. § 45 (1914).

Fleming, Anthony. 'The Sacramento Effect: State-Level AI Regulations', *Medium*, 27 April 2025, https://medium.com/@aflemingclt/the-sacramento-effect-state-level-ai-regulations-b7f4b9171b10.

Fredriksson, Per G, and Millimet, Daniel L. 'Is There a "California Effect" in US Environmental Policymaking?' *Regional Science and Urban Economics* 32, no. 6 (2002): 737–64.

Frazier, Kevin, and Thierer, Adam. 'Understanding the Proposed AI Moratorium: Answers to Key Questions', *R Street Institute*, www.rstreet.org/ai-moratorium-questions/.

Gadotti, Andrea, et al. 'Anonymization: The Imperfect Science of Using Data while Preserving Privacy', *Science Advances* 10, no. 29 (19 July 2024).

Garcia v Character Technologies, Inc., 2025 WL 1461721 (M.D. Fla. May 21, 2025).

George, Beth, et al. 'Compliance in a Global AI Market: Examining the Overlaps Between California's SB 53 and the EU AI Act', *Freshfields Blog*, 2 October 2025.

General Court, *Latombe v Commission*, Case T-553/23, judgment of 3 September 2025, ECLI: EU:T:2025:537.

Gluck, Justine. 'California's SB 53: The First Frontier AI Law, Explained', *Future of Privacy Forum*, 3 October 2025, https://fpf.org/blog/californias-sb-53-the-first-frontier-ai-law-explained.

Gray, David C, and Keats Citron, Danielle. 'The Right to Quantitative Privacy', *Minnesota Law Review* 98 (2013): 62–128.

Golda, Abenezer, et al. 'Privacy and Security Concerns in Generative AI: A Comprehensive Survey', *IEEE Access* 12 (2024): 48126–44.

G'Sell, Florence, Gillman, Zeke, and Ayer, Ashok. 'California's SB 1047 vs EU AI Act: A Comparative Analysis of AI Regulation', *Chaire numérique – Digital Governance and Sovereignty*, Sciences Po, 28 October, 2024, www.sciencespo.fr/public/chaire-numerique/en/2024/10/28/californias-sb1047-vs-eu-ai-act-a-comparative-analysis-of-ai-regulation/.

Health Insurance Portability and Accountability Act (HIPAA), 42 U.S.C. § 1320d (1996).

Hocutt, John. 'Ayn Rand on Rights', *Essays in the Philosophy of Humanism* 17, no. 2 (2009): 1–12.

Holland, Brian H. 'A Third-Party Doctrine for Digital Metadata', *Cardozo Law Review* 41, no. 4 (2020): 1549–600.

Huang, Mei-Lin. 'Digital Privacy in the Age of Surveillance: A Comparative Study of GDPR and CCPA', *OTS Canadian Journal* 4, no. 7 (2025): 65–74.

In re Clearview AI, Inc. Consumer Privacy Litigation, MDL No. 2967, No. 1:21-cv-00135 (N.D. Ill. Mar. 20, 2025).

Johnson, Khari. 'CA Proposes AI Regulations as Trump Signals Hands-Off Approach', *CalMatters*, 5 March 2025, https://calmatters.org/economy/technology/2025/03/ai-regulation-after-trump-election.

Johnson, Khari. 'How California and the EU Work Together to Regulate Artificial Intelligence', *CalMatters*, 24 May 2024, https://calmatters.org/economy/technology/2024/05/ca-eu-ai-regulation/.

Kaminski, Margot E. 'The Case for Data Privacy Rights (Or "Please, a Little Optimism")', *Notre Dame Law Review Reflection* 97 (2022): 385–99.

Kohler, Scott. 'All Eyes on Sacramento: SB 1047 and the AI Safety Debate', *Carnegie Endowment for International Peace*, 11 September 2024, https://carnegieendowment.org/posts/2024/09/california-sb1047-ai-safety-regulation?lang=en.

L., et al. v Alphabet Inc., US District Court for the Northern District of California; 3:23-cv-03440.

Lee, Peter. 'Synthetic Data and the Future of AI', *Cornell Law Review* 110, no. 1 (2025): 1–74.

LeBlanc and Felten v United States Privacy and Civil Liberties Oversight Board, No. 1: 25-cv-00542 (D.D.C. May 21, 2025).

LeBlanc and Felten v United States Privacy and Civil Liberties Oversight Board, No. 25-5197 (D.C. Cir. July 1, 2025).

Leffer, Lauren. 'Your Personal Information Is Probably Being Used to Train Generative AI Models', *Scientific American*, 19 October 2023.

Massey III, Theodore H. 'The Case for a Federal Data Privacy Law from a National Security Perspective – What the US Can Learn from Overseas', *Student Journal of Information Privacy & Policy* 3, no. 1 (2025): 99–132.

Mezei, Peter. 'Third European Court Decision on the General Purpose TDM Exception Is Out', *Kluwer Copyright Blog*, 8 May 2025.

McCarthy, Patrick, 'Infographic: The Growth of Computer Processing Power', *OffGridWeb*, 2 May 2017, www.offgridweb.com/preparation/infographic-the-growth-of-computer-processing-power/.

Murugesan, San. 'Understanding Web 2.0', *IT Professional* 9, no. 4 (July–August 2007): 34–41.

National Institute of Standards and Technology. 'AI Risk Management Framework (AI RMF 1.0)', January 2023, accessed 25 October 2025, www.nist.gov/itl/ai-risk-management-framework.

Novelli, Claudio, et al. 'Generative AI in EU Law: Liability, Privacy, Intellectual Property, and Cybersecurity,' *Computer Law & Security Review* 55 (2024): 1–16.

Nunez Duffourc, Mindy, Gerke, Sara, and Kollnig, Konrad. 'Privacy of Personal Data in the Generative AI Data Lifecycle', *Journal of Intellectual Property, Information Technology and E-Commerce Law* 13, no. 2 (8 July 2024).

NOYB, 'EU-US Data Transfers: First Reaction on 'Latombe' Case', 3 September 2025, https://noyb.eu/en/eu-us-data-transfers-first-reaction-latombe-case.

OpenAI Global Affairs, 'OpenAI's letter to Governor Newsom on harmonized regulation', *OpenAI Global Affairs*, 12 Aug 2025. https://openai.com/global-affairs/letter-to-governor-newsom-on-harmonized-regulation/.

Privacy Act of 1974, 5 U.S.C. § 552a (1974).

Proposal for a Regulation of the European Parliament and of the Council amending Regulations (EU) 2016/679, (EU) 2018/1724, (EU) 2018/1725, (EU) 2023/2854 and Directives 2002/58/EC, (EU) 2022/2555 and (EU) 2022/2557 as regards the simplification of the digital legislative framework, and repealing Regulations (EU) 2018/1807, (EU) 2019/1150, (EU) 2022/868, and Directive (EU) 2019/1024 (Digital Omnibus) [2025] COM(2025) 837 final.

Proposal for a Regulation of the European Parliament and of the Council amending Regulations (EU) 2024/1689 and (EU) 2018/1139 as regards the simplification of the implementation of harmonised rules on artificial intelligence (Digital Omnibus on AI) [2025] COM(2025) 836 final.

Regulation (EU) 2016/679 of the European Parliament and of the Council of 27 April 2016 on the protection of natural persons with regard to the processing of personal data and on the free movement of such data, and repealing Directive 95/46/EC (General Data Protection Regulation) [2016] OJ L 119/1.

Regulation (EU) 2024/1689 of the European Parliament and of the Council of 13 June 2024 laying down harmonised rules on artificial intelligence and amending Regulations (EC) No 300/2008, (EU) No 167/2013, (EU) No 168/2013, (EU) 2018/858, (EU) 2018/1139 and (EU) 2019/2144 and Directives 2014/90/EU, (EU) 2016/797 and (EU) 2020/1828 (Artificial Intelligence Act) [2024] OJ L 2024/1689.

Solove, Daniel J. 'Artificial Intelligence and Privacy', 77 *Florida Law Review* 1 (2025).

SB24-205: Consumer Protections for Artificial Intelligence Act, 74th Colorado General Assembly, 2024 Regular Session, https://leg.colorado.gov/bills/sb24-205.

SB 926, California, 2023–24 Sess., ch. 927.

SB 981, California, 2023–24 Sess., ch. 928.

SB 942, California, 2023–24 Sess., ch. 291.

SB 1120, California, Health Care Coverage: Utilization Review, 2023–24 Sess., ch. 879.

SB 11, California, AI Abuse Protection Act, pending.

SB 243, California, Companion Chatbots, pending.

SB 833, California, Human Oversight of AI in Critical Infrastructure, pending.

SB 53, Cal. Bus. & Prof. Code §§ 22757.10–22757.16 (2025); Cal. Gov't Code § 11546.8 (2025); Cal. Lab. Code §§ 1107–1107.2 (2025).

Schwartz, Reva, et al. *Towards a Standard for Identifying and Managing Bias in Artificial Intelligence*, NIST Special Publication 1270 (Gaithersburg, MD: National Institute of Standards and Technology, 2022).

Senior, Jennifer. 'How Companies Learn Your Secrets', *New York Times Magazine*, 16 February 2012, www.nytimes.com/2012/02/19/magazine/shopping-habits.html.

Shrivastava, Rashi. 'Forbes 2025 AI 50 List – Top Artificial Intelligence Companies Ranked', *Forbes*, 10 April 2025. www.forbes.com/lists/ai50/.

Solove, Daniel J, and Hartzog, Woodrow. 'The Great Scrape: The Clash Between Scraping and Privacy', Working Paper, *Boston University School of Law Faculty Scholarship Series*, 2024, https://scholarship.law.bu.edu/faculty_scholarship/3917.

State v Loomis, 2016 WI 68, 371 Wis. 2d 235, 881 N.W.2d 74.

Thompson, Neil C, Ge, Shuning, and Manso, Gabriel F. 'The Importance of (Exponentially More) Computing Power', *arXiv* (28 June 2022).

Tran, Van Hong, et al. 'Measuring Compliance with the California Consumer Privacy Act Over Space and Time', in *CHI '24: Proceedings of the 2024 CHI Conference on Human Factors in Computing Systems* (New York: Association for Computing Machinery, 2024).

Umberg, Tom. 'Now that Trump has undone the AI Executive Order, California must lead on AI regulation', *Sacramento Bee*, 22 January 2025, www.sacbee.com/opinion/op-ed/article298930455.html.

US Congress, *Rebuilding Economic Prosperity and Opportunity (REPO) for Americans Act*, H.R. 1, 119th Cong., enrolled March 27, 2025, enacted July 4, 2025 (Pub. L. No. 119-21).

White House Office of Science and Technology Policy, Blueprint for AI Bill of Rights, accompanied by a Technical Companion, October 2022.

White House, America's AI Action Plan, Winning the Race, July 2025, www.whitehouse.gov/wp-content/uploads/2025/07/Americas-AI-Action-Plan.pdf.

Whitman, James Q. 'The Two Western Cultures of Privacy: Dignity versus Liberty', *Yale Law Journal* 113, no. 6 (2004): 1151–221.

Working Party 29, Opinion 5/2014 on Anonymisation Techniques.

Zang, Dongsheng. 'The Privacy Act of 1974: The American Bill of Rights on Data and Its Unfinished Business', *University of Pittsburgh Law Review* 86 (2024): 85–160.

Zard, Alex, and Sears, Alan M. 'Targeted Advertising and Consumer Protection Law in the EU', *Vanderbilt Journal of Transnational Law* 56, no. 3 (2023): 799–851.

Zetter, Kim. 'California Now Has the Nation's Best Digital Privacy Law', *Wired Magazine*, 8 October 2015, www.wired.com/2015/10/california-now-nations-best-digital-privacy-law/.

Zhang, Chenshuang, et al. *Text-to-Image Diffusion Models in Generative AI: A Survey*, preprint, arXiv:2303.07909 [cs.CV], version 3.

Zwerdling, Daniel. 'Your Digital Trail: Does the Fourth Amendment Protect Us?' *All Tech Considered*, NPR, 2 October 2013, www.npr.org/sections/alltechconsidered/2013/10/02/228134269/your-digital-trail-does-the-fourth-amendment-protect-us.

8

Technical Standards: Co-Regulatory Pathways of Digital Policymaking for Artificial Intelligence

EMMA SEMAAN

Abstract

Technical standards play a central role in the new EU AI Act. Some of these standards are structured in a co-regulatory configuration, as they blend public and private governance to distribute regulatory duties across these spheres. This chapter explores the potential of adopting similarly co-regulatory technical standards for digital technology regulation in the United States, specifically given the legal context of the Supreme Court's 2024 judgment in *Loper Bright Enterprises v Raimondo* and the political context of the deregulatory priorities of the second Trump administration. It highlights the benefits of technical standardisation as a regulatory tool when it can be structured with the appropriate public oversight, particularly its adaptability, collaborative nature, and capacity to provide industry clarity on compliance.

Keywords

Artificial Intelligence Act; Co-regulation; Technical Standards; AI Regulation; Digital Policy

I. Introduction

After many years of anticipation, deliberation, and negotiation, the European Union's Artificial Intelligence Act (AI Act) officially passed in May 2024.[1] While

[1] Regulation (EU) 2024/1689 of the European Parliament and of the Council of 13 June 2024 (Artificial Intelligence Act), http://data.europa.eu/eli/reg/2024/1689/oj/eng. The AI Act is a legal

there are still questions of how the Act will play out in practice, its passage into law was a significant milestone for EU digital regulation and for AI regulation globally.[2] Within a month of this step forward for European regulation, the US Supreme Court released a series of judgments that will make regulation of digital technologies in the United States far more complicated in the decades to come.[3]

The June 2024 Supreme Court ruling in the case of *Loper Bright Enterprises v Raimondo* severely weakened the regulatory power of federal agencies in the US by overturning the long-established *Chevron* doctrine.[4] In the Supreme Court's landmark ruling in *Chevron U.S.A., Inc. v NRDC* (1984), executive agencies were accorded deference in determining how to implement ambiguous statutory authority, so long as their interpretations were reasonable.[5] The 2024 *Loper Bright* case repeals that practice of agency deference, leaving it to judges to determine whether regulatory activity falls within the scope of legislative intent.[6]

The ruling is expected to have an inordinate impact on administrative law – especially given that, per Supreme Court Justice Elena Kagan, *Chevron* has been cited as a legal precedent in more than 18,000 cases over the years since its inception.[7] *Loper Bright* has created significant obstacles to future regulatory efforts in the United States, and makes consumer-protective regulation like the EU's AI Act seem increasingly unlikely in the American context. Paired with a political climate that is both hostile to regulatory attempts and too chaotic to predict with accuracy, the United States faces severe challenges in regulating the digital sector.

Policymakers and legal experts working on mitigating digital harms in the United States will be seeking new avenues for regulation, especially as issues presented by digital technologies continue to emerge.[8] This chapter seeks to point out the benefits of technical standardisation as a pathway forward for American regulation in the digital space – specifically when structured as a co-regulatory tool and method, as illustrated in some respects by the EU AI Act. It focuses on the

framework that provides a uniform approach to address the issues that AI systems present across the EU. It delineates various categories of AI systems according to their risks, defining the requirements that 'high-risk' systems must satisfy to guarantee user safety; it then directs ESOs to develop technical standards for the concrete steps that can be taken to meet these requirements.

[2] Franz-Stefan Gady, 'EU/US Approaches to Data Privacy and the "Brussels Effect": A Comparative Analysis', *Georgetown Journal of International Affairs* (2014): 12–23.

[3] *Loper Bright Enterprises v Raimondo*, No. 22-451 (US, 28 June 2024); *Corner Post, Inc. v Board of Governors of the Federal Reserve System*, No. 22-1008 (US, 1 July 2024); *West Virginia v. Environmental Protection Agency*, No. 20-1530 (US, 30 June 2022).

[4] *Chevron U.S.A., Inc. v Natural Resources Defense Council, Inc.*, 467 US 837 (1984), https://supreme.justia.com/cases/federal/us/467/837/.

[5] *Chevron*.

[6] *Loper Bright*, 7–35.

[7] *Loper Bright*, 7–35 (Kagan, J., dissenting), *Loper Bright*, 26. Eli Sanders, 'A Supreme Court Justice Warned That a Ruling Would Cause "Large-Scale Disruption". The Effects Are Already Being Felt', ProPublica, 23 September 2024, www.propublica.org/article/supreme-court-chevron-deference-loper-bright-guns-abortion-pending-cases; *Loper Bright*.

[8] Ignacio Cofone, *The Privacy Fallacy: Harm and Power in the Information Economy*, 1st edn (Cambridge: Cambridge University Press, 2023), https://doi.org/10.1017/9781108995825.

potential for co-regulatory technical standards in digital policymaking, particularly for navigating the current legal and political context of United States.

While this chapter ultimately discusses one way in which the so-called 'Brussels Effect' might extend to the American context, it is also important to highlight that the EU is reciprocally affected by the digital policymaking of the United States. 'Big-Tech' firms, overwhelmingly headquartered on American soil, continue to make decisions that affect EU citizens. While efforts such as the General Data Protection Regulation (GDPR) and AI Act offer some measure of protection, cases such as the *Schrems* series are an indication that there are limits to what European regulation can accomplish in the face of an American '*carte-blanche*'.[9]

The United States is one of the most significant partners for the EU both politically and economically, and the effects of decisions made within its borders ripple across the pond. Given that the US now hosts a political environment that is hostile to regulatory function of any kind, but perhaps especially in relation to constraining the tech sector, European policymakers have a vested interest in the future digital regulatory efforts of this major global player.

This chapter begins with a brief background of technical standards in the EU AI Act and discusses the relevance of structuring them as co-regulatory in nature. It proceeds by making the argument for their use in digital policymaking the United States, given the legal context of the 2024 *Loper Bright v Raimondo Enterprises* US Supreme Court ruling and the current anti-regulatory political climate. Ultimately, this chapter finds that co-regulatory technical standards are specifically useful when it comes to regulating digital technologies in the US for three major reasons: they are typically developed through a highly collaborative process; they are flexible and can be adapted in response to technological advances; and they provide industry with clear guidance on how to comply with their legal obligations.

II. Background: Technical Standardisation in the EU AI Act

The Artificial Intelligence Act (AI Act) passed in May of 2024 is a tiered, risk-based regulatory structure that aims to protect safe and fair development and deployment of AI in the EU and beyond. It diverges from its predecessors within EU digital regulation like the GDPR, making use of harmonised technical standards: technical specifications developed by European Standardization Organizations (ESOs).[10]

[9] *Maximilian Schrems v Data Protection Commissioner*, Case C-362/14 (Court of Justice of the European Union, 6 October 2015), https://eur-lex.europa.eu/legal-content/EN/TXT/?uri=celex:62014CJ0362; "Schrems v. Data Protection Commissioner", *Global Freedom of Expression*, https://globalfreedomofexpression.columbia.edu/cases/schrems-v-data-protection-commissioner/.

[10] Mélanie Gornet and Winston Maxwell, 'The European Approach to Regulating AI through Technical Standards', *Internet Policy Review* 13, no. 3 (2024), https://doi.org/10.14763/2024.3.1784.

For this chapter, the consequential aspect of the approach to technical standardisation within the AI Act is their co-regulatory structure: or in other words, in the way technical standards can be configured to combine public and private governance mechanisms. Co-regulation is a form of 'regulated self-regulation', in which regulatory duties are distributed across both the public and private spheres.[11] The following section will discuss co-regulatory technical standards, and the utilisation of these standards in the EU's AI Act.

A. Co-Regulation in Technical Standardisation

Co-regulation is an 'alternative' regulatory configuration that is characterised by the cooperation of the state and private regulators in joint institutions, and therefore disperses regulatory duty among several stakeholders.[12] In its modern form, co-regulation originated in the context of Australian consumer protection law as a hybrid of state regulation and self-regulation.[13] It refers to the legal model in which the responsibilities 'of norm-drafting, implementation and enforcement are not under the sole authority of the sovereign ruler', and are instead spread among both public and private players.[14]

The relationship of private partners to the state is a key variable in self-regulation and co-regulation. It is also what most clearly differentiates the two from each other, although some scholars (Price and Verhulst, for example) view co-regulation as a form of 'regulated self-regulation'.[15] The extent of public or state involvement can be specifically tailored to fit the regulatory context and desired outcome, which we see clearly in the various iterations of co-regulation that have been implemented in European Member States.

Co-regulation can take many forms and has been used in European digital regulation since the 1990s. Co-regulatory codes of conduct, for example, were enacted in data protection in the EU through efforts such as the Data Protection Directive (1995) and continue to be included as part of modern regulatory efforts such as the GDPR.[16] They also found use through the US's efforts within

[11] Monroe Price and Stefaan Verhulst, 'The Concept of Self-Regulation and the Internet', *Departmental Papers (ASC)*, 1 January 2000.

[12] Christopher T Marsden, 'Co- and Self-Regulation in European Media and Internet Sectors: The Results of Oxford University's Study', in *Self-Regulation, Co-Regulation, State Regulation* (2005), 76, www.osce.org/sites/default/files/f/documents/2/a/13844.pdf.

[13] Marsden, 'Co- and Self-Regulation in European Media and Internet Sectors: The Results of Oxford University's Study'; Christopher T Marsden, *Internet Co-Regulation: European Law, Regulatory Governance and Legitimacy in Cyberspace*, 1st edn (Cambridge: Cambridge University Press, 2011), https://doi.org/10.1017/CBO9780511763410. State regulation and self-regulation are, as Marsden puts it, 'as old as markets'. Co-regulation is something of a hybrid, and in its modern form is relatively recent.

[14] Benoît Frydman, 'Coregulation: A Possible Legal Model for Global Governance', *SSRN Scholarly Paper No. 1980176* (Rochester, NY, 5 January 2012), 133–50, https://papers.ssrn.com/abstract=1980176.

[15] Price and Verhulst, *The Concept of Self-Regulation and the Internet.*

[16] Dennis D Hirsch, 'Going Dutch? Collaborative Dutch Privacy Regulation and the Lessons It Holds for US Privacy Law', SSRN Scholarly Paper no. 2393707, Rochester, NY, 1 November 2013, https://papers.ssrn.com/abstract=2393707.

digital privacy law, namely within the Children's Online Privacy Protection Act (COPPA).[17] Technical standards can be considered a form of co-regulation if they are configured to utilise aspects of both private and public governance. For example, if a public entity directs private or third-party entities to develop technical standards in order to fulfil specific statutory requirements, that collaboration would be considered co-regulatory.

Technical standards outline requirements, specifications, and procedures that are consistently applied to ensure the safety, reliability, and functionality of products or processes.[18] Standards have long been a regulatory tool in both the EU and US; they are currently used in the digital space for anything from data security, accessibility standards, and even hardware requirements that aim to prevent market fragmentation.[19] Standards have often governed the unseen specifics of the world: for example, the letters 'http' written before web addresses in a search bar refer to the HyperText Transfer Protocol (HTTP), the technical standard that defines how data is formatted and transmitted on the web.[20]

Technical standards can be mechanisms of purely private ordering, or self-regulation, when they are self-imposed by industry actors and unsupervised by public bodies. In these situations, the standards would be outside of the legislative ambit; self-regulatory mechanisms such as these often go unenforced and are therefore ineffectual, as there are typically no attached measures of public accountability or oversight.[21] However, if they were to be directed by public entities, such as executive agencies or other public regulatory bodies, the standards would be co-regulatory.[22]

Another opportunity for collaboration between private and public entities is within the accountability mechanisms of a regulatory regime. Private ordering can be structured alongside external oversight mechanisms, such as a duty to report compliance to the relevant public entity. The inclusion of public oversight is the feature that would make this arrangement co-regulatory, as it ensures that private industry is held accountable (by an external entity) for their role the regulatory process.[23]

[17] C Lee Peeler and Cobun Zweifel-Keegan, *Twenty Years Of Successful Co-Regulation Under COPPA* (BBB National Programs, Inc., 2019).

[18] Gornet and Maxwell, 'The European Approach to Regulating AI through Technical Standards'.

[19] US Department of Justice, Civil Rights Division, *ADA Standards for Accessible Design* (Washington, DC: US Department of Justice, 15 September 2010), www.ada.gov/law-and-regs/design-standards/; European Union, *Directive (EU) 2022/2380 of the European Parliament and of the Council of 23 November 2022 amending Directive 2014/53/EU (Radio Equipment Directive)*, OJ L 315, 7 December 2022, https://eur-lex.europa.eu/eli/dir/2022/2380/oj/eng.

[20] Roy T Fielding et al, *HTTP Semantics*, RFC 9110 (Internet Engineering Task Force, June 2022), https://doi.org/10.17487/RFC9110; Eric Rescorla, *The Transport Layer Security (TLS) Protocol Version 1.3*, RFC 8446 (Internet Engineering Task Force, August 2018), https://doi.org/10.17487/RFC8446.

[21] Neil Gunningham and Joseph Rees, 'Industry Self-Regulation: An Institutional Perspective', *Law & Policy* 19, no. 4 (1997): 363–414, https://doi.org/10.1111/1467-9930.t01-1-00033.

[22] For example, should a federal agency direct a private organisation to develop a 'code of conduct' based on a set of goals that agency is looking to fulfil, that would be an example of co-regulation.

[23] Guillermo Hernandez, 'Regulatory Oversight for Better Regulation', Penn Program on Regulation, The Regulatory Review, 8 December 2022, www.theregreview.org/2022/12/08/hernandez-regulatory-oversight/.

Typically, standards are developed via a collaborative process that relies heavily on technical expertise within the relevant industry.[24] Stakeholders from private industry and civil society are often invited to contribute to or comment on proposed standards, which further improves the specification and utility of the standards. If standard development is sanctioned or directed by a public entity, that would be an example of co-regulation, because of the formal integration of private-industry expertise with public-interest focused goals.[25] Through this avenue, the standards would be bound by the public interest in a way that self-regulatory standards are not, while retaining the same benefits of collaborative expertise and evaluation.

Technical standards, when sanctioned, directed, and/or overseen by public bodies, can be a form of co-regulation. As a regulatory tool, they have the advantage of being able to combine public oversight with private expertise, an approach which enhances accountability while maintaining regulatory flexibility. In some areas, the EU's AI Act supplies an example of how to build a co-regulatory structure for technical standardisation efforts in the tech regulation space.

B. Co-Regulation in the AI Act Technical Standards

There was already a strong ecosystem of AI-related standard-setting in place in the EU prior to the passage of the AI Act.[26] In 2018, the European Committee for Standardization (CEN) and European Committee for Electrotechnical Standardization (CENELEC), created a Focus Group on Artificial Intelligence at the direction of the European Commission, strengthening European participation in the International Standards Organisation (ISO) and International Electrotechnical Commission's (IEC's) AI technical committees.[27] Standardisation itself is not a new or novel tool, and indeed is not even particularly novel to the AI space.[28]

However, EU standardisation work, especially in the AI environment, typically has to do with product safety and is therefore geared towards the objectives of organisations. One reason the standards of the AI Act are considered 'novel' for the EU is that they are intended to address the risks that AI could pose to health, safety, and fundamental rights.[29] Principally, techniques that were previously used

[24] Irene Kamara, 'Co-Regulation in EU Personal Data Protection: The Case of Technical Standards and the Privacy by Design Standardisation "Mandate"', *European Journal of Law and Technology* 8, no. 1 (2017).

[25] Marsden, *Internet Co-Regulation*; Marta Cantero Gamito and Christopher T Marsden, 'Artificial Intelligence Co-Regulation? The Role of Standards in the EU AI Act', *International Journal of Law and Information Technology* 32, no. 1 (2024), https://doi.org/10.1093/ijlit/eaae011.

[26] Cantero Gamito and Marsden, 'Artificial Intelligence Co-Regulation?'.

[27] Cantero Gamito and Marsden, 'Artificial Intelligence Co-Regulation?', 5.

[28] J Soler Garrido et al., *Harmonised Standards for the European AI Act*, no. JRC139430, Science for Policy Brief (European Commission, 2024), https://publications.jrc.ec.europa.eu/repository/handle/JRC139430.

[29] Gornet and Maxwell, 'The European Approach to Regulating AI through Technical Standards'; Soler Garrido et al, *Harmonised Standards for the European AI Act.*

simply for product safety regulation have been expanded to cover the protection of fundamental rights.[30]

For the purposes of this chapter, the most critical facet of the EU's approach to digital regulation in the AI Act is the way in which the technical standardisation process is structured. There are two aspects of the AI Act's technical standardisation structure that make it co-regulatory in the view of this chapter: first, the process of norm-development by standards organisations which integrates public and private stakeholder expertise; and second, the use of accountability mechanisms that require external/public oversight of private regulatory implementation.

The AI Act lays out the essential requirements to the development and design of certain AI systems based on the tiered risk-categorisations, and then leaves further definition to take place through the development of 'harmonised standards' by the relevant ESOs.[31] The AI Act uses standards as a mechanism to operationalise legal obligations, particularly for high-risk AI systems, as they will detail the practical steps for compliance with statutory requirements.[32] The delegation of responsibility of standards development to ESOs, who will determine the specific procedures that should be carried out to achieve conformity with the legal obligations of the AI Act, is a good example of co-regulatory structuring.

This standardisation process integrates the expertise from external organisations, rather than centring regulatory rulemaking around a single legislative act or legal body. CEN, for example, is a member-driven organisation that includes national standardisation bodies from 34 European countries, as well as representatives from government, industry, and civil society organisations.[33] CEN provides a forum where these stakeholders work together to develop and approve standards for their respective industries, creating a multi-sectoral process of collaboration. This process bridges the public and private spheres within a joint institution to produce regulatory frameworks and goals, which makes it a strong example of co-regulation. ESOs, led by CEN and CENELEC, are currently in the process of drafting the necessary AI standards, following the request from the European Commission.[34]

[30] This is a particularly controversial aspect of the AI Act; for more on the use of standards for addressing normative or ethical questions see: Johann Laux et al, *Three Pathways for Standardisation and Ethical Disclosure by Default under the European Union Artificial Intelligence Act, Computer Law & Security Review* 53 (July 2024): 105957, https://doi.org/10.1016/j.clsr.2024.105957; Sandra Wachter, 'Limitations and Loopholes in the EU AI Act and AI Liability Directives: What This Means for the European Union, the United States, and Beyond', *SSRN Electronic Journal*, ahead of print, 2024, 691, https://doi.org/10.2139/ssrn.4924553.

[31] Soler Garrido et al, *Harmonised Standards for the European AI Act*; European Union, *Regulation (EU) No 1025/2012 of the European Parliament and of the Council of 25 October 2012 on European Standardisation*, OJ L 316, 14 November 2012.

[32] AI Act, Article 40; Cantero Gamito and Marsden, 'Artificial Intelligence Co-Regulation?', 7.

[33] European Standardization Organizations, 'European Standardization', CEN-CENELEC, www.cencenelec.eu/european-standardization/.

[34] The final version of the Code of Practice on General-Purpose AI (GPAI) models, for example, was officially published in July 2025. 'The General-Purpose AI Code of Practice', European Commission, July 2025, https://digital-strategy.ec.europa.eu/en/policies/contents-code-gpai.

Another important element of the new legislation, in a few specific instances, is its accountability mechanisms. A key requirement of the harmonised standards is that the oversight of AI systems must produce verifiable results, with their effectiveness ultimately tested. The specifications for harmonised standards and standardisation deliverables are set out in Article 40 of the AI Act.[35] Article 40(2) directs the Commission to issue standardisation requests covering obligations set out in Sections 2 and 3 of Chapter V of the AI Act to the relevant ESOs.[36] These requests must specifically ask for deliverables for reporting and documentation processes and be fulfilled in accordance with Article 24 of Regulation (EU) 1025/2012 on European standardisation.[37] The technical documentation needed to demonstrate compliance is a process outlined within the AI Act itself, designed to provide national supervisory authorities with the necessary information to assess compliance.[38] In instances where the reporting and compliance processes are ultimately overseen by public authorities, the accountability process can be considered co-regulatory.

Accountability is a key element of a successful regulatory regime. Self-regulation occurs when private industry is empowered to develop, implement, and assess their own systems and behaviour without public oversight.[39] The coercive ability of the state to further regulatory function is largely reliant on the ability to impose proportional consequences for non-compliance; without adequate public oversight ability, adherence to regulatory rules becomes difficult to measure and difficult to enforce. This is where self-regulation typically fails: there are no meaningful consequences for deviation from agreed-upon norms.[40] Co-regulation integrates the structures of private governance (such as norm-drafting) within a larger institutional setting of public oversight in order to ensure accountability, and this is one feature that distinguishes it from self-regulation.[41]

An important limitation of the AI Act is that in specific instances, it assigns responsibility to the manufacturer of the AI system, not a public authority, to

[35] AI Act, Article 40.

[36] AI Act, Article 40(2). Chapter V deals with General-purpose AI models; Section 2 enumerates the obligations for providers of general-purpose AI models, and Section 3 sets out the obligation of general-purpose models with systemic risk.

[37] ESOs are directed to provide evidence of their efforts to fulfil their obligations in accordance with Article 24 of Regulation (EU) No 1025/2012 on European standardisation.

[38] AI Act, Section 2, Article 11.

[39] Glen Hepburn, *Alternatives to Traditional Regulation* (OECD, n.d.), www.oecd.org/gov/regulatory-policy/42245468.pdf.

[40] In other words, self-assessment and self-reporting creates a clear conflict of interest. Edward J Balleisen and Marc Eisner, 'The Promise and Pitfalls of Co-Regulation: How Governments Can Draw on Private Governance for Public Purpose', in *New Perspectives on Regulation*, ed. D Moss and J Cisternino (Cambridge, MA: The Tobin Project, 2009), 127.

[41] Balleisen and Eisner, 'The Promise and Pitfalls of Co-Regulation: How Governments Can Draw on Private Governance for Public Purpose'. Cantero Gamito and Marsden, 'Artificial Intelligence Co-Regulation?', 9: 'Co-regulation ultimately depends on the credible threat of the government to intervene where a self-regulatory scheme fails to achieve its goals'.

conduct the conformity assessment for compliance.[42] For the majority of high-risk AI systems listed in Annex III, the AI providers may conduct conformity assessments themselves – and are not required to publicise the results thereof.[43] This includes systems such as those used for critical infrastructure, employment (recruitment, candidate evaluation), education, and more.[44] A reliance on self-reported industry adherence to the harmonised standards has the potential to create a 'presumption of conformity' for these high-risk AI applications, giving the impression of compliance with the requirements of the AI Act without true external oversight.[45] This chapter would define such practices as self-regulatory, given the lack of adequate public accountability or oversight mechanisms.

Therefore, while some accountability structures in the AI Act are co-regulatory in nature, those that utilise a self-regulatory regime are a significant limitation and are likely to weaken regulatory implementation and impact. It is necessary to distinguish between the two, in order to delineate which aspects of the AI Act might serve as a useful example for future technical standardisation efforts.

Article 40(3) of the AI Act notes that the purpose of the standardisation processes is to increase legal certainty; to contribute to global cooperation on standardisation; and to promote multi-stakeholder governance that is representative of all relevant stakeholders, through ensuring effective and balanced stakeholder participation.[46] These elements are all characteristic of standardisation as a regulatory tool, and are what make it particularly useful for the purposes of technology regulation, as the following section of this chapter will discuss.

III. Technical Standards for AI Regulation in the United States

While governance of digital technologies is increasingly necessary, the legal and political environment of the United States is currently hostile to regulatory efforts.[47] As mentioned previously, the recent judgment of the United States Supreme Court in *Loper Bright Enterprises v Raimondo* (2024) will echo in its negative effects on administrative law and policymaking in the United States for

[42] AI Act, Article 43.

[43] Artificial Intelligence Act, Art. 43(2): 'For high-risk AI systems referred to in points 2 to 8 of Annex III, providers shall follow the conformity assessment procedure based on internal control as referred to in Annex VI, which does not provide for the involvement of a notified body'. Citing Regulation (EU) 2024/1689 (AI Act).

[44] AI Act, Annex III(2–8).

[45] Mark McFadden et al, *Harmonising Artificial Intelligence: The Role of Standards in the EU AI Regulation* (Oxford: Oxford Information Labs, 2021), 1–42. Wachter, 'Limitations and Loopholes in the EU AI Act and AI Liability Directives', 692. 'This approach creates a major legal loophole in which those who are supposed to be regulated can testify to compliance with rules they have written for themselves'.

[46] AI Act, Article 40(3).

[47] Cofone, *The Privacy Fallacy*.

many years to come.[48] This section begins with a discussion of the implications of the *Loper Bright* ruling for future regulation in the United States, and an exploration of the political context within which this decision will be upheld. It goes on to discuss the usefulness of co-regulatory methods for technical standards in digital policymaking and concludes by evaluating the potential for co-regulatory technical standards for digital policymaking in the United States.

A. Legal and Political Context for Technology Regulation in the United States

There are some key environmental factors that must be taken into consideration when exploring the potential for the implementation of regulatory regimes in a particular jurisdiction.[49] Firstly, the political environment of the time and place where the regulation will be situated: what is realistic in the context of one presidential administration might be impossible in another. And secondly, the existing legal norms, principles, statutes, and case law that will shape the nature of the regulatory system. It is well-known that transplanting regulation from one jurisdiction to another is inadvisable, but the logics of particular regulatory systems (like co-regulation, or technical standardisation) are often applicable cross-jurisdictionally; the specifics of implementation will vary.[50]

i. Political Context

The 2025 inauguration of American president Donald Trump for his second term in office saw a slew of unprecedented guests: the power brokers of Silicone Valley. SpaceX and (formerly-Twitter) X's Elon Musk, Amazon's Jeff Bezos, Meta's Mark Zuckerberg, and Google's Sundar Pichai were among those seated front and centre in a move that made international headlines.[51] Since then, Trump has been vocal about his support for the 'Big Tech' heavy hitters, and has facilitated their strategic realignment with his administration; among other things, he has repealed Biden's

[48] *Corner Post, Inc.*; *Loper Bright*; *West Virginia*.

[49] An important caveat and disclaimer for this section is that I have re-written it (by necessity) several times in the last several months, as a result of the rapidly changing political ecosystem under the second Trump administration. The chaotic and often unpredictable actions and priorities of this administration have been difficult to navigate with any kind of foresight, but I have done my best to represent the political situation to the utmost accuracy as of the time that I am finalising this work for publication. This fact alone speaks volumes to the current political ecosystem.

[50] Bronwen Morgan and Karen Yeung, *An Introduction to Law and Regulation: Text and Materials*, 1st edn (Cambridge: Cambridge University Press, 2007), https://doi.org/10.1017/CBO9780511801112.

[51] Natasha Preskey, 'Jake Paul, Zuckerberg and Musk: Who's at Trump's Inauguration?', BBC News, 20 January 2025, www.bbc.com/news/articles/cgkjgmkn10ko. Apple's Tim Cook and Open AI's Sam Altman were also in attendance, but not captured in the now-famous photo of the front row behind Trump himself. In a jurisdiction now notorious for its propensity for regulatory capture, this was a clear red flag.

Executive order prioritising 'safe, secure, and trustworthy' AI development, framing this move as the liberation of innovation from 'bureaucratic overreach'.[52]

Trump has also rolled back a vast array of federal regulations and vowed to 'dismantle federal bureaucracy' with his restructuring of federal agencies. For President Trump, there seems to have been a strategic political investment in Silicon Valley's infamous 'move fast and break things' ethos, especially when it comes to the rapid development and deployment of AI systems.[53]

It is important to consider that Trump himself is something of a political outlier and does not always reflect the unified position of even his own party – indeed, the chaos of this administration has been brutally irreverent of most political convention. Despite the dominance of sensationalist headlines, the American political system is made up of more than just President Trump.[54] In Congress and within policy circles, there remains widespread discussion of implementing regulatory measures which would increase protection for children and minors online, and issues like age verification are still front and centre.[55]

There is also clear popular appetite and concern from citizens and citizen groups for stronger regulatory measures regarding digital privacy protection and other such common-sense technology regulation.[56] Individual states are often termed 'laboratories for regulation', as state regulation typically precedes federal measures and provides a blueprint for the successes and failures of regulatory attempts. States have long-since been developing their own protocols and measures for digital rights protection; jurisdictions as politically diverse as California, Colorado, and Texas have all instituted their own regimes of digital regulation.

[52] The White House, 'Removing Barriers to American Leadership in Artificial Intelligence', The White House, 23 January 2025, www.whitehouse.gov/presidential-actions/2025/01/removing-barriers-to-american-leadership-in-artificial-intelligence/. David Shepardson, 'Trump Revokes Biden Executive Order on Addressing AI Risks', Artificial Intelligence, *Reuters*, 21 January 2025, www.reuters.com/technology/artificial-intelligence/trump-revokes-biden-executive-order-addressing-ai-risks-2025-01-21/. The companies in turn are seeing a future of favourable government contracts and light-touch regulatory treatment.

[53] This is reflected in his administration's actions across the political arena, not just in regard to tech policy and regulation: David Smith, 'At Home and Abroad US Policy Chaos Has One Constant: Trump's Self-Interest', US News, *The Guardian*, 24 August 2025, www.theguardian.com/us-news/2025/aug/24/trump-policy-putin-summit; Martha Muir, 'US Shale Bosses Decry "Chaos" in Donald Trump's Energy Policy', Oil & Gas Industry, *Financial Times*, 24 September 2025, www.ft.com/content/5391ae3f-e87e-43d0-8e85-fc2fe3f99c21.

[54] The legislative priorities of Congress do not always have to reflect those of the president, though they are strongly affected by them. This is not to diminish at all the devastation that Trump's policies and executive orders have wreaked throughout the federal government and the country as a whole. The political system of the United States is one that favours measured decision-making and response, which is why it has been so difficult to react quickly to the moves that Trump has made. It is, however, an indictment of Trump's party, the members of which continue to bend to his whims, and of the Democratic party, which has yet to mount an effective opposition.

[55] The Supreme Court also recently ruled on a case upholding digital age verification measures in Texas: *Free Speech Coalition, Inc. v Paxton*, No. 23-1122 (US, 27 June 2025).

[56] Colleen McClain et al, *How Americans View Data Privacy: Tech Companies, AI, Regulation, Passwords and Policies* (Pew Research Center, 2023), www.pewresearch.org/internet/2023/10/18/how-americans-view-data-privacy/.

As of yet, states retain a greater degree of autonomy from federal pressure than executive agencies, though reliance on federal funding remains a barrier.[57]

An issue with relying on states for digital regulation is the inevitable fragmentation that occurs from state to state with varying regulatory regimes. There are now age-verification laws in Texas, for example, which prevent certain websites from showing content there; those same companies are allowed to continue distributing content without such verification in other states, like California.[58] Interstate commerce is one of the key priorities of federal government, precisely to prevent this fragmentation. However, given the current dearth of other viable political and legal options, state-based regulation might be a more readily available starting point for digital-age regulatory systems, including co-regulatory technical standardisation.

ii. Legal Context

Tech billionaire Elon Musk, who previously led the newly formed Department of Government Efficiency under the Trump administration, publicly detailed his intent to use the Supreme Court's recent *Loper Bright* (2024) judgment to further the administration's plans for 'regulatory rescissions'.[59] This section will discuss the impact of this case for federal executive agencies, and the barriers to regulation that have developed as a result.

The 2024 case *Loper Bright Enterprises v Raimondo* significantly diminished the regulatory authority of federal agencies in the US by overturning the long-standing *Chevron* doctrine. In the landmark *Chevron U.S.A., Inc. v NRDC* (1984) decision, the Supreme Court granted deference to executive agencies in interpreting ambiguous statutory language, as long as their interpretations were deemed reasonable.[60] However, *Loper Bright* eliminates this deference, shifting the responsibility to judges to assess whether agencies are acting within their legal authority to regulate.[61]

[57] Though the Trump administration has been known to put pressure on states through revoking federal grants and allowances, measures which threaten the sovereignty of states and will affect their willingness to adopt specific regulatory mechanisms. It is my hope that states will continue to hold their ground against the attempts of the current administration; but federal money, especially for universities and other centres of regulatory development and research, has become precarious.

[58] Though currently, both California and Colorado have age verification laws in the pipeline. Tyler Katzenberger, 'California Age Verification Bill Backed by Google, Meta, OpenAI Heads to Newsom – POLITICO', Politico, 13 September 2025, www.politico.com/news/2025/09/13/california-advances-effort-to-check-kids-ages-online-amid-safety-concerns-00563005.

[59] Vivek Ramaswamy and Elon Musk, 'Opinion | Elon Musk and Vivek Ramaswamy: The DOGE Plan to Reform Government', WSJ, 20 November 2024, www.wsj.com/opinion/musk-and-ramaswamy-the-doge-plan-to-reform-government-supreme-court-guidance-end-executive-power-grab-fa51c020. Musk has since resigned this position, and engaged in heated exchanges with President Trump over various social media platforms.

[60] *Chevron*.

[61] *Loper Bright*, § II(A).

Part of the reasoning of *Loper Bright*'s repeal of *Chevron*'s long-standing precedent is that 'the deference that Chevron requires of courts reviewing agency action cannot be squared with the APA [Administrative Procedure Act]'.[62] In section III(B)(1) of the Majority Opinion, Chief Justice Roberts writes that neither *Chevron* nor any following decision are reconcilable with the APA 'by presuming that statutory ambiguities are implicit delegations to agencies', as the dissenting Justices claim.[63] In his view, it is a court, rather than an agency, that should resolve interpretive questions resulting from statutory ambiguity, and that this approach better adheres to the APA.[64]

In her dissent, Justice Kagan refutes this approach: 'This Court has long understood *Chevron* deference to reflect what Congress would want, and so to be rooted in a presumption of legislative intent'.[65] Given that Congress does not (and in fact cannot) write perfectly complete regulatory statutes, there is an understood presumption that those statutes will have ambiguities that a different actor will have to resolve. In Kagan's view, and in the view of the Court when *Chevron* was decided, such interpretive prerogative can (and should) be delegated to the agency responsible for regulatory implementation, given their specific expertise. Agencies, in turn, report to a president, who answers to the public; courts have no such accountability and have no basis for making policy.[66]

While *Loper Bright* itself is not retroactive, the US Supreme Court's subsequent ruling in *Corner Post, Inc., v Board of Governors of the Federal Reserve System* extends the timeframe in which challenges to existing regulations can be reviewed by courts.[67] The *Corner Post* judgment therefore broadens the potential scope of Loper Bright.[68] This will likely increase the chances of a regulated entity successfully challenging an agency's action.

The *Loper Bright* ruling signals a major shift that could reshape daily life in areas that many Americans now take for granted, including clean air and water, safe food, and healthcare standards – especially taken in context with an incoming presidential administration that has been vocal in its aims to dismantle existing regulatory governance.[69] In the months that have passed since the judgment was

[62] *Loper Bright*, § III.

[63] *Loper Bright*, § III(B)(1).

[64] *Loper Bright*, § III. at 23: 'Perhaps most fundamentally, Chevron's presumption is misguided because agencies have no special competence in resolving statutory ambiguities. Courts do.'

[65] *Loper Bright* (Kagan, J., dissenting).

[66] *Loper Bright* (Kagan, J., dissenting) at 2.

[67] *Corner Post, Inc.*

[68] Susan C Morse, 'Corner Post Broadens Loper Bright, But Footnote 8 Offers a Limit | The Regulatory Review', 30 July 2024, www.theregreview.org/2024/07/30/morse-corner-post-broadens-loper-bright-but-footnote-8-offers-a-limit/.

[69] Robert Iafolla, 'GOP-Picked Judges Take Hard Line on Regulations Post-Chevron (1)', Bloomberg Law, 4 September 2024, https://news.bloomberglaw.com/daily-labor-report/gop-picked-judges-take-hard-line-on-rules-after-chevrons-demise. Morse, 'Corner Post Broadens Loper Bright'; Hoag Levins, 'Supreme Court's Chevron Reversal: A Seismic Shift for Health Care Regulation', Penn LDI, 11 November 2024, https://ldi.upenn.edu/our-work/research-updates/supreme-courts-chevron-reversal-a-seismic-shift-for-health-care-regulation/.

delivered, the United States has already seen its impacts on juridical practice. Long-standing federal regulations have faced a series of challenges by major corporations, including in a January 2025 ruling against net neutrality that specifically cited *Loper Bright.*[70] In August 2024, a decision by the United States District Court for the Northern District of Texas cited the case when they ruled against a Federal Trade Commission (FTC) rule banning non-compete agreements in employer contracts.[71]

Overturning *Chevron* has given judges far more discretion to overrule regulations instituted by federal agencies, thereby shifting decision-making from policy and subject-matter experts to the judiciary. When agencies are at constant risk of judicial scrutiny for even reasonable interpretations of the law, their purview of regulatory function is severely impeded.[72] There will likely be a chilling effect on the issuance of future federal regulations that would otherwise have been necessary to implement key priorities such as consumer protection or environmental protection. Federal agencies and policymakers must find different pathways forward for regulation in a post-*Chevron* world, in a political atmosphere that is hostile to regulatory rulemaking.

Federal agencies may now need an explicit, unambiguous statutory mandate to act, in order to withstand judicial scrutiny of their regulatory and enforcement efforts.[73] Legislation that includes specific delegation of authority for agencies to develop technical standards could provide the legal basis that their regulations need to survive in a post-*Chevron* system, ensuring that agencies have clear legislative mandates and preserving some of their regulatory autonomy.[74] A statutory directive to promulgate technical standards would be subject to *Loper Bright* review just like the direction to promulgate a rule, but the nature of technical standard-setting might make it a more palatable area for Congress to grant authority to agencies.

Assigning technical standards to agencies via explicit congressional direction reduces ambiguity about the legitimacy of agency action, which will be critical post-*Chevron*. For a divided Congress, it removes the burden of drawn-out argument on the specific contours of legislation; narrow and specific lawmaking

[70] *Ohio Telecom Association et al. v Federal Communications Commission*, No. 24-3449 (US Court of Appeals for the Sixth Circuit, 2 January 2025), www.govinfo.gov/app/details/USCOURTS-ca6-24-03449.

[71] *Ryan LLC, Chamber of Commerce of the United States of America v Federal Trade Commission*, No. 3:24-cv-00986-E (US District Court for the Northern District of Texas August 20, 2024). A note: the so-called 'Chamber of Commerce' is the largest lobbying organisation in the United States, not a government agency or affiliate, and advocates for 'pro-business' and 'free enterprise' growth.

[72] Thomas E Nielsen and Krista A Stapleford, 'What Loper Bright Might Portend for Auer Deference', *Harvard Law Review*, 5 July 2024, https://harvardlawreview.org/blog/2024/07/what-loper-bright-might-portend-for-auer-deference/.

[73] *Loper Bright*, § II(C).

[74] *Loper Bright*, § II(C). at 17: 'Congress has often enacted statutes [which] … expressly delegate to an agency the authority to give meaning to a particular statutory term … Other [statutes] empower an agency to prescribe rules to "fill up the details" of a statutory scheme, *Wayman v Southard*, 10 Wheat. 1, 43 (1825), or to regulate subject to the limits imposed by a term or phrase that "leaves agencies with flexibility," *Michigan v EPA*, 576 US 743, 752 (2015), such as "appropriate" or "reasonable".'

is difficult to achieve even on uncontested subjects, and technical standards have greater capacity for specificity because they are more easily updated than legislation. Technical standards provide a useful framework for agreement on specific, discrete subjects, while still allowing Congress to retain oversight of regulatory duties and purview.

The National Technology Transfer and Advancement Act of 1995 (NTTAA) defines the parameters for the use of consensus technical standards by federal agencies.[75] The Act defines the term 'technical standards' as 'performance-based or design-specific technical specifications and related management systems practices'.[76] Section 12(d) of the NTTAA requires that federal agencies use technical standards that are developed by voluntary consensus standards bodies as a means to carry out policy objectives or agency activities, and participate in the development of such technical standards when there is the scope and means to do so and when such participation aligns with the public interest.[77]

However, should a federal agency consider participation in external standard development to be inconsistent with applicable law or otherwise impractical (in situations where such standards do not align with what the agency deems to be the public interest, for example), Section 12(d)(3) empowers the federal agency or department to use technical standards that are not developed by voluntary consensus standards bodies.[78] Should an agency make this determination, they would then have purview to develop their own standards independently of external bodies; however, in a post-*Chevron* legal environment, agencies are at risk of scrutiny for any action that can be construed as an 'overreach' of their delegation of authority.[79]

Legislators have the purview to authorise standard-setting by including specific directives for federal agencies to develop technical standards within legislative packages. There is a key distinction to be made here: rather than directing the issuance of a specific regulation or rule, legislation that directs an agency to develop a suite of technical standards on an issue preserves a greater degree of autonomy and flexibility for the rulemaking agency and enables the incorporation of a wider range of subject-matter expertise. Pairing technical standards with legislation might help to shore up the role of executive agencies for better regulatory implementation. Ensuring a clear delegation of authority to agencies for this kind of rulemaking would be critical in preventing judicial challenges to statutory authority under the new *Loper Bright* framework.

The reason this chapter specifies that the structure of the technical standards should be co-regulatory is to indicate the need for: first, representative

[75] National Technology Transfer and Advancement Act of 1995, Pub. L. No. 104-113, 110 Stat. 775 (1996), as amended by Pub. L. No. 107-107, § 1115 (2001).

[76] National Technology Transfer and Advancement Act, § 12(d)(4).

[77] National Technology Transfer and Advancement Act, § 12(d).

[78] Office of Management and Budget, *Circular A-119: Federal Participation in the Development and Use of Voluntary Consensus Standards and in Conformity Assessment Activities* (Washington, DC: Executive Office of the President, rev. ed. 2023).

[79] *Loper Bright*, § C.

collaboration that is inclusive of public-interest perspectives; and second, external oversight of regulatory implementation that holds private industry accountable for upholding their role in the regulatory process. Without external mechanisms of oversight and accountability, industry would self-regulate; as discussed previously, self-regulation is well-known to be ineffective in constraining industry practices.[80]

There has been a historic reliance on self-regulatory regimes for digital regulation at the federal level in the United States.[81] That system has increasingly been augmented by individual state regulation which aims to protect things like consumer privacy online, but the protections granted by these individual states form a discontinuous patchwork. This has allowed for a '[regulatory] regime primarily concerned with ease of compliance for companies, and shielded from more consumer-protective modifications', in the scarce areas where it does exist.[82] Technical standards might seem promising as a prospective solution in these legal and political circumstances, but they must incorporate a representative development process and external accountability mechanisms to be an effective method of regulation.

Co-regulatory technical standards are specifically useful when it comes to regulating digital technologies for three major reasons: they are typically developed through a highly collaborative process that incorporates the expertise of stakeholders and technical specialists; they are flexible and can be adapted in response to technological advances without having to change the underlying statute calling for their development; and they provide industry with clear direction for how to comply with their legal obligations.

B. A Collaborative, Consensus-Driven Process

Standard-setting has potential as a tool for allowing appropriate expertise to be included in legislative and regulatory frameworks under the new status quo established by *Loper Bright*. The development of technical standards typically enlists a great deal of input from experts from a wide variety of backgrounds, making it an inherently collaborative and consensus-driven process.[83] This can

[80] Marsden, 'Co- and Self-Regulation in European Media and Internet Sectors: The Results of Oxford University's Study'.

[81] Michael Latzer et al, 'Comparative Analysis of International Co- and Self-Regulation in Communications Markets', SSRN Scholarly Paper no. 2134877, Rochester, NY, 1 September 2007, https://papers.ssrn.com/abstract=2134877.

[82] Laurent Crepeau, 'Responding to Deficiencies in the Architecture of Privacy: Co-Regulation as the Path Forward for Data Protection on Social Networking Sites', *Canadian Journal of Law and Technology* 19, no. 2 (2022): 411–55; Lindsey Barrett, 'Confiding in Con Men: US Privacy Law, the GDPR, and Information Fiduciaries', *Seattle University Law Review* 42, no. 3 (2019): 1057.

[83] IEEE Standards Association, 'Standards Collaboration'. International Organization for Standardization and International Electrotechnical Commission, *Information Technology, Cybersecurity and Privacy Protection – Cybersecurity Framework Development Guidelines*, Cybersecurity framework development guidelines 27110:2021, n.d., www.iso.org/obp/ui/#iso:std:iso-iec:ts:27110:ed-1:v1:en.

allow standards to be more comprehensive and more attuned to the reality of the regulated sector than what legislation can achieve alone, which is a feature that becomes especially relevant post-*Chevron*. This institutional collaboration is also a feature characteristic of co-regulation, as it is one of the mechanisms by which private-public interaction facilitates the regulatory process.

In the American legal context, technical standards can be set by federal agencies such as the Environmental Protection Agency (EPA), by non-regulatory federal agencies such as the National Institute of Standards and Technology (NIST), or by independent standards development organisations (SDOs) like the Internet Engineering Task Force (IETF).[84] Both NIST and IETF work with technical experts to develop actionable and relevant standards across sectors to support safety and innovation, and to prevent foreseeable problems from arising.

Through developing co-regulatory technical standards, agencies can effectively leverage expertise from both industry and civil society organisations to shape regulation and governance in ways that are more representative. NIST has just produced a set of technical standards to deal with the potential challenges of quantum computing and cryptography.[85] These standards aim to safeguard privacy and cybersecurity in the face of potential risks that would be associated with breakthroughs in quantum computing.[86] The standards serve as an example of how policy can begin to map a highly technical space, and were produced as part of holistic proceedings that gathered expert recommendations and evaluations over a two-year period. The incorporation of industry partner feedback, technologists' assessments, and the input of policymakers is emblematic of an inclusive and representative process of co-regulatory standard development.

In a congressional landscape that is actively prioritising deregulation and emphasising the role of the private sphere, co-regulatory technical standards might be a useful bridge between the public and private spheres and offer a path towards more inclusive governance, outside of the traditional regulatory ambit.[87] They might also take on outsized importance as an avenue for inclusive collaboration between private entities and civil society to take shape in governance efforts, in a context where the strong deregulatory position of a conservative administration might seek to roll back a range of protections for people and communities.

The tech sector is widely regarded as difficult to regulate precisely because of the high level of expertise required to understand the technologies themselves.

[84] 'Internet Standards Process', IETF, www.ietf.org/process/process/. 'National Institute of Standards and Technology', NIST, www.nist.gov/.

[85] NIST, *Post-Quantum Cryptography Standardization*, 13 August 2024, https://csrc.nist.gov/projects/post-quantum-cryptography/post-quantum-cryptography-standardization.

[86] Sydney Saubestre and Nat Meysenburg, 'Quantum Computing Is Coming. Better Encryption Helps Us Prepare for Its Arrival', New America, *Open Technology Institute*, 2024, http://newamerica.org/oti/blog/quantum-computing-is-coming-better-encryption-helps-us-prepare-for-its-arrival/.

[87] Jessica F. Green and Thomas Hale, 'New "Net Zero" Standards Could Transform the Climate – Unless They're Derailed', *Washington Post*, 4 October 2021, www.washingtonpost.com/politics/2021/10/04/iso-london-declaration-climate/.

Indeed, those with the greatest expertise in the field are frequently employed by the very companies that regulators aim to limit through more consumer-protective rulemaking. In this environment, technical standards can better use the expertise of practitioners to shape regulation and governance. Of course, regulators must also be diligent in ensuring that industry is not empowered to take advantage of a collaborative standard-setting process to further their own priorities at the expense of consumers.[88]

One of the major criticisms on the use of harmonised standards in the EU's AI Act is that, while standards bodies will be tasked with creating the regulatory frameworks that interpret the Act, most of the stakeholders included in the working groups of this process are industry representatives.[89] Even the civil society groups that are part of the relevant working groups often lack voting rights within those bodies, and are not always allowed to submit opinions or participate in the deliberative process.[90] The exclusion of civil society in this instance is a feature of the Act that may prove detrimental; what should have been an inclusive and collaborative process currently does not involve those who might be best positioned to advocate for the most robust public interest applications of the law.

In any future application of technical standards of the United States, it will be important to advocate for the active inclusion of civil society and other citizen-focused stakeholders in the standards development process. This would make the most of a co-regulatory framework that incorporates private and industry expertise with public-interest priorities. Regulatory capture is one major concern in the American context, however; given the level of influence of large corporate interests in politics via campaign finance and lobbying efforts, it is often difficult for the legislative process to be truly representative. This may be another reason why executive agencies are more suited to developing the technical specifics of regulatory efforts, as they may have more leeway than legislators dependent on corporate donors.[91]

C. Dynamic, Flexible Measures

Apart from the need for technical expertise, another often-cited challenge of regulating technology is the need for dynamic, flexible measures that can keep pace with

[88] Maximilian Laufer, *Democracy and Industry Capture of the Executive*, Georgetown Law: Denny Center for Democratic Capitalism, 21 September 2023, www.law.georgetown.edu/denny-center/blog/industry-capture-of-the-executive/.

[89] Wachter, 'Limitations and Loopholes in the EU AI Act and AI Liability Directives', 691; Martin Ebers, 'Standardizing AI – The Case of the European Commission's Proposal for an Artificial Intelligence Act', in *The Cambridge Handbook of Artificial Intelligence: Global Perspectives on Law and Ethics*, ed. L. A. DiMatteo, Cristina Poncibò, and Michel Cannarsa (Cambridge: Cambridge University Press, 2021), 340.

[90] Wachter, 'Limitations and Loopholes in the EU AI Act and AI Liability Directives', 691. Those civil society participants have so-called "observer status" within the working groups.

[91] Laufer, *Democracy and Industry Capture of the Executive*. The executive agencies are typically staffed by technical experts in the field.

the rate of technological innovation.[92] It is a frequent concern of policymakers and industry alike that tech regulation might become outdated too quickly to be effective, given the constant advancements in emerging technologies. While it is important to note that this concern is often used as a way for the tech sector to evade regulation altogether, there is a clear need for digital regulation to be highly responsive to rapid changes.[93] One key benefit of co-regulatory technical standards is that they can be routinely updated without affecting the legislation that directed their use, especially if a specified standards body were tasked with ensuring their continued relevance.

Historically, federal agencies have had the ability to establish technical standards that regulate how the United States approaches a variety of issues, to great effect. For example, the Clean Water Act's 1972 amendments gave the EPA the authority to implement the statute's outlined goals by setting standards for industry to follow.[94] The resulting pollution control programmes set water quality standards for all contaminants in surface water, as well as wastewater standards for industry. Though more than 50 years have passed since the Clean Water Act's 1972 amendments were originally enacted, the EPA has continuously updated its standards, allowing them to remain applicable today.

Because they can be updated as needed, technical standards are particularly suited to governing rapidly evolving technologies without needing to amend the legislation that initially called for their creation. In legislative environments that are frequently slowed by partisan gridlock, this adaptability proves especially advantageous.

It is important to note that standards are primarily effective for addressing specific issues within well-defined parameters. NIST's recent post-quantum cryptography standards, for example, are narrowly tailored and outline specific algorithms for encryption that attempt to safeguard cybersecurity against the potential dangers of quantum computing.[95] For broader issues that require more contextual judgments, such as algorithmic bias and discrimination, technical standards are likely *not* the most effective path forward in the United States.

The EU's AI Act attempts to utilise technical standards for the protection of fundamental rights, an approach that remains novel and controversial.[96] A major distinction between the US and EU jurisdictions is the vastly different legal approach and basis for fundamental rights and discrimination law; given this divergence, this is an aspect of European standard-setting that I do not find reasonable to compare within the scope of this chapter.[97]

[92] Wulf A Kaal, 'Dynamic Regulation for Innovation', *SSRN Electronic Journal*, ahead of print, 2016, https://doi.org/10.2139/ssrn.2831040.

[93] Harry Farmer, *Regulate to Innovate* (Ada Lovelace Institute, 2021), www.adalovelaceinstitute.org/report/regulate-innovate/.

[94] Clean Water Act of 1977, Pub. L. Nos. 95–217, 91 Stat. 1566 33 U.S.C. §1251 et seq. 233 (1977), www.epa.gov/laws-regulations/summary-clean-water-act.

[95] NIST, *Post-Quantum Cryptography Standardization*.

[96] Gornet and Maxwell, 'The European Approach to Regulating AI through Technical Standards'. Wachter, 'Limitations and Loopholes in the EU AI Act and AI Liability Directives', 686.

[97] Wachter, 'Limitations and Loopholes in the EU AI Act and AI Liability Directives', 689, 691.

There are clear limitations of technical standards for tackling broader and more complex regulatory challenges. It is critical to note that standards are not a replacement for regulation that prevents algorithmic discrimination, secures the protection of fundamental rights, or ensures effective consumer protection law (including anti-trust enforcement). The digital sector will require concurrent reform in these areas, alongside the use of standards for more technical issues.

Flexible, readily updated technical standards that are the product of expert collaboration are ideal for addressing specific and bounded issues. Standards are not a replacement for good lawmaking, but rather a tool that might help executive agencies enforce legislative goals and priorities in specific areas. In a legislative landscape that faces constant gridlock, the flexibility that standards provide can be particularly useful in effectively regulating technologies that are constantly evolving – and they also can serve to clarify compliance expectations for industry players, given that continuous evolution.

D. Clarifying Government Expectations, and the Importance of Accountability

In addition to protecting consumers, co-regulatory technical standards also provide benefits for regulated industries. When legislation is effectively paired with standard-setting to outline and specify the precise requirements of compliance with the law, industry implementation of Congress's objectives can be improved. A collaborative process of standard development that incorporates both industry expertise and the public interest provides much-desired clarity for industry in terms of regulatory implementation. Standards are intended to clarify and specify the details of implementation for legal instruments; they are also tools for producers and distributors to demonstrate that their products have been designed with the relevant legal requirements in mind.[98]

The creation of concrete guidelines for industry to follow facilitates compliance with the law and therefore can better achieve broader legislative goals and objectives. It is key, however, that industry involvement in standard-setting processes does not result in a system that has the appearance of regulatory scrutiny but is in fact simply industry-friendly. Incorporating industry expertise into standard-setting must be balanced by the incorporation of public-interest perspectives and expertise, and ideally the maintenance of oversight authority by public regulatory agencies.[99]

A defining feature that separates co-regulatory standards from self-regulatory ones is an accountability mechanism that ensures external or public oversight.

[98] Kamara, 'Co-Regulation in EU Personal Data Protection', 14.

[99] OECD, *OECD Regulatory Policy Outlook* (OECD, 2021), www.oecd.org/en/publications/oecd-regulatory-policy-outlook-2021_38b0fdb1-en/full-report.html.

For certain AI systems, the AI Act does incorporate co-regulatory accountability frameworks, within which oversight by an external body is mandated.[100] For example, in the case of AI systems that are themselves a product or are intended for use as a safety component of a product, a third party will conduct the relevant conformity assessments.[101] This collaborative effort that distributes the regulatory responsibilities between the public and private spheres, and maintains clear public oversight of private actors, is characteristic of well-structured co-regulation.

However, in some instances, it is the manufacturer itself, not a public authority, that is responsible for performing the conformity assessment, according to the AI Act.[102] This feature has been criticised by scholars as creating a 'presumption of compliance', while lacking legitimacy and transparency because the conformity assessments undertaken by providers themselves are not required to be made public.[103] As Wachter notes, 'This approach creates a major legal loophole in which those who are supposed to be regulated can testify to compliance with rules they have written themselves'.[104] As discussed in a previous section of this chapter, this assessment method falls within the category of self-regulatory practice, and is likely to prove inadequate for the purposes of accountability and regulatory efficacy.[105]

This chapter advocates specifically for a system of co-regulatory technical standardisation, which includes robust external oversight and accountability mechanisms, to avoid this very issue. While the AI Act incorporates co-regulation in many respects, it unfortunately fails to do so in all relevant areas, which has led to some specific loopholes and enforcement gaps.[106] The United States as a political context is known to be prone to regulatory capture; any standards-based legislation must be accompanied by public accountability and oversight to be efficacious in that context.[107]

E. Critiques and Alternative Perspectives

An often-cited counterargument to technical standardisation as a regulatory method is that it limits (or removes) democratic representation in decision-making, in comparison to a representatively elected legislature conducting rulemaking or norm-drafting processes.[108] However, as Justice Kagan notes in her dissenting

[100] As in, external to the provider or deployer of the AI system.

[101] AI Act, Article 43(3).

[102] AI Act, Article 48. Cantero Gamito and Marsden, 'Artificial Intelligence Co-Regulation?', 7.

[103] Wachter, 'Limitations and Loopholes in the EU AI Act and AI Liability Directives', 692. AI Act, Article 43(2).

[104] Wachter, 'Limitations and Loopholes in the EU AI Act and AI Liability Directives', 692.

[105] Price and Verhulst, *The Concept of Self-Regulation and the Internet*.

[106] Wachter, 'Limitations and Loopholes in the EU AI Act and AI Liability Directives'.

[107] Laufer, *Democracy and Industry Capture of the Executive*.

[108] Ebers, 'Standardizing AI – The Case of the European Commission's Proposal for an Artificial Intelligence Act', 20.

argument to the *Loper Bright* decision, 'Agencies are "subject to the supervision of the President, who in turn answers to the public"'.[109] *Loper Bright*'s relegation of policy-related decision-making to the courts, rather than to executive agencies with specific scopes of expertise and judgement, actually removes a mechanism of accountability by broadening judicial powers in this manner. The separation of government powers is already supported by administrative law such as the APA, which governs how administrative agencies of the US federal government may establish regulations and clarifies the function and purview of federal agencies.[110]

Another question to consider here is the scope for American regulators to utilise standards that were developed by international standards bodies, rather than developing them independently through domestic agencies. Of course, there are many international organisations responsible for developing standards and policy recommendations for the tech sector. Indeed, they are often critical contributors to the harmonisation of norms across countries. Various international standard-developing organisations, including the International Organization for Standardization (ISO), IEC, Institute of Electrical and Electronics Engineers (IEEE), and IETF, have long been working on standards for AI technologies.

While the US takes part in global standardisation efforts, political resistance complicates the adoption of international standards for domestic applications. Technical standards that are developed by American regulatory actors and agencies offer a more realistic path forward at this time, given a political context that is hostile to anything it views as 'foreign interference'.

The United States is a signatory of the World Trade Organization (WTO) and is therefore responsible for maintaining compliance with the WTO Technical Barriers to Trade Agreement (WTO/TBT), the international agreement that details how countries should use standards in regulation.[111] Section 2.4 of the TBT describes how externally developed standards should be used in technical regulations:

> Where technical regulations are required and relevant international standards exist or their completion is imminent, members shall use them, or the relevant parts of them, as a basis for their technical regulations except; when such international standards or relevant parts would be an ineffective or inappropriate means for the fulfilment of the legitimate objectives pursued, for instance because of fundamental climatic or geographical factors or fundamental technological problems.[112]

Essentially, it is a treaty requirement to harmonise technical regulatory standards as much as possible, which is useful for promoting collaboration and consistency

[109] *Kisor v Wilkie*, 588 US 571 (2019); *Loper Bright*.

[110] Administrative Procedure Act, Pub. L. Nos. 79–404, 551–559 5 U.S.C. (1946).

[111] Of course, digital technology regulation now takes centre stage in the discussion of TBT implementation, spanning issues from e-commerce to the regulation of disruptive technologies such as blockchain and artificial intelligence.

[112] World Trade Organization, *Agreement on Technical Barriers to Trade*, 1 January 1995, sec. 2.4, www.wto.org/english/docs_e/legal_e/tbt_e.htm.

in an increasingly globalised world.[113] While it likely would not be possible or wise to harmonise national legislation in this way, issues such as 'privacy by design', post-quantum cryptography and encryption, and other aspects of digital technologies that are more technical in nature are suitable areas for standardisation.

While there are a great many international standard-developing organisations working on developing standards for digital governance, the obstacles such organisations face in the current political context of the United States are significant.[114] President Donald Trump has a historically fraught relationship with the WTO and has previously threatened to remove the US from the list of signatories to the organisation entirely.[115]

The incorporation of internationally developed standards in this political context is therefore unlikely for the foreseeable future. A more realistic avenue for current regulatory progress is an analysis of the structural facets of other standards regimes, and the of the infrastructure required for their development and implementation in the US Domestic endeavours towards developing American-specific technical standards (even if some aspects of it are inspired by the EU's regulatory efforts) are likely a more feasible path forward at this time.

Finally, important to discuss is the limitations of this approach in a political and legal context that struggles with 'regulatory capture', as noted periodically throught this section. The United States is a political context that is sucesptiple to indistury interference within the legislative context, which has often meant that the commercial interests of industry are better represented than the interests of the broader citizenry or constituencies.[116] This is why this chapter has emphasised the 'co' aspect of 'co-regulation': functional systems of technical standardisation must be rooted in strong accountability mechanisms and practices, as well as collaboration with citizen groups and other representative parties in standard development processes.

Given the weakening of their regulatory purview post-*Loper Bright* alongside a hostile political context, it remains to be seen whether American federal

[113] World Customs Organization and World Trade Organization, *WCO/WTO Study Report on Disruptive Technologies* (Geneva: WTO, 2022), www.wto.org/english/res_e/booksp_e/wco-wto_e.pdf.

[114] Cantero Gamito and Marsden, 'Artificial Intelligence Co-Regulation?', 5.

[115] At the time of writing, this has not yet been initiated by President Trump, though it is unpredictable what may happen in the next few months (and indeed, the next four years). Another important note is that even President Joe Biden cemented the Trump-era steel and aluminium tariffs, a decision at odds with the WTO's decision that they violate international rules. 'Trump Threatens to Pull US out of World Trade Organization', US & Canada, *BBC News*, 30 August 2018, www.bbc.com/news/world-us-canada-45364150; Bhavna Dubey, 'Biden Cements Trump-Era Steel, Aluminum Tariffs in WTO Snub', *The Economic Times*, 13 December 2022, https://economictimes.indiatimes.com/small-biz/trade/exports/insights/biden-cements-trump-era-steel-aluminum-tariffs-in-wto-snub/articleshow/96187875.cms?from=mdr.

[116] This is in part due to campaign finance laws based on the *Citizens United v Federal Election Commission (FEC)*, 558 US 310 (2010) Supreme Court judgment, a ruling on campaign finance which cleared the way for corporate money to be involved in politics by classifying corporations as people ('corporate personhood') in order for their funds to be considered a manifestation of their right to 'speech'.

agencies will have the capacity or willingness to engage in the process of development (and supervision) of co-regulatory technical standards for technological regulation. The resources of these agencies have been severely depleted by extensive layoffs and funding cuts, and an unpredictable political environment renders more unforeseeable difficulties. But states may have an opportunity here to start paving the road for later federal implementation; should they successfully incorporate technical standards into their regulatory regimes, there may be a stronger case for executive agencies to later take up the mantle on the federal level, with a more cohesive strategy.

IV. Conclusion

The EU has sought to re-imagine a well-known regulatory tool, technical standardisation, and utilise it in a new way through the AI Act. Like the EU, there is already a robust system of standardisation in place in the United States. The US Supreme Court's 2024 ruling in the *Loper Bright* case, taken alongside the political context of a presidential administration that is clear in its aim for deregulation and dismantling of federal infrastructure, has presented an environment ripe for new imaginings of past ideas. This chapter examined the prospects of navigating digital regulation in the US using technical standards as a co-regulatory tool, taking forward some insights from the EU AI Act.

In the wake of the *Loper Bright* judgment, federal agencies – including those most responsible for protecting the interests of internet users, the Federal Communications Commission (FCC) and FTC – are decidedly vulnerable to challenges of their statutory authority. These agencies will face a higher burden of proving that their rulemaking and enforcement actions are justified; navigating this new judicial and regulatory environment in the absence of *Chevron's* dominant precedent will present significant challenges. Even the most 'inoffensive' regulatory rulemaking will be difficult to achieve in the political environment of the United States, for the foreseeable future.

Because *Loper Bright* in theory leaves intact deference to factual determinations made by agencies, it might be useful for agencies to look to technical standards to fortify their decision-making against judicial scrutiny. Standards are particularly useful as a tool for regulators in the continuously evolving tech sector because of their flexible and dynamic structure. With the sustained collaboration of experts and policymakers, technical standards can serve as comprehensive, specific tools that have the potential to evolve alongside the technologies they govern. For now, it may be up to individual states to show that there is popular investment and interest in technology regulation, and to pioneer systems that can later be adapted for federal or widespread use.

To remain useful and balanced as a tool, technical standards can be structured as co-regulatory tools, and must include mechanisms for public accountability and involvement to avoid industry-dominated outcomes. By combining public oversight with private expertise, co-regulation ensures adaptability, inclusivity, and accountability in standards development, which are key elements for effective digital governance. When used to pursue specific policy goals, co-regulatory technical standards can be a way to bridge regulatory gaps and accomplish legislative objectives in an era of evolving challenges.

Bibliography

Administrative Procedure Act. Pub. L. No. 79-404, 60 Stat. 237 (1946), codified at 5 U.S.C. §§ 551–559.

Balleisen, Edward J, and Marc Eisner. 'The Promise and Pitfalls of Co-Regulation: How Governments Can Draw on Private Governance for Public Purpose'. In *New Perspectives on Regulation*, edited by D Moss and J Cisternino. Cambridge, MA: The Tobin Project, 2009.

Barrett, Lindsey. 'Confiding in Con Men: US Privacy Law, the GDPR, and Information Fiduciaries'. *Seattle University Law Review* 42, no. 3 (2019): 1057.

BBC News. 'Trump Threatens to Pull US out of World Trade Organization'. *US & Canada*, 30 August 2018. www.bbc.com/news/world-us-canada-45364150.

Cantero Gamito, Marta, and Christopher T Marsden. 'Artificial Intelligence Co-Regulation? The Role of Standards in the EU AI Act'. *International Journal of Law and Information Technology* 32, no. 1 (2024). https://doi.org/10.1093/ijlit/eaae011.

Chevron U.S.A., Inc. v Natural Resources Defense Council, Inc., 467 US 837 (1984). https://supreme.justia.com/cases/federal/us/467/837/.

Clean Water Act (1977). Pub. L. No. 95-217, 91 Stat. 1566, 33 U.S.C. §§ 1251 et seq. (1977). www.epa.gov/laws-regulations/summary-clean-water-act.

Cofone, Ignacio. *The Privacy Fallacy: Harm and Power in the Information Economy.* 1st edn. Cambridge: Cambridge University Press, 2023. https://doi.org/10.1017/9781108995825.

Corner Post, Inc. v Board of Governors of the Federal Reserve System, 603 US ___ (2024).

Crepeau, Laurent. 'Responding to Deficiencies in the Architecture of Privacy: Co-Regulation as the Path Forward for Data Protection on Social Networking Sites'. *Canadian Journal of Law and Technology* 19, no. 2 (2022): 411–55.

Dubey, Bhavna. 'Biden Cements Trump-Era Steel, Aluminum Tariffs in WTO Snub'. *The Economic Times*, 13 December 2022. https://economictimes.indiatimes.com/small-biz/trade/exports/insights/biden-cements-trump-era-steel-aluminum-tariffs-in-wto-snub/articleshow/96187875.cms?from=mdr.

Ebers, Martin. 'Standardizing AI: The Case of the European Commission's Proposal for an Artificial Intelligence Act'. In *The Cambridge Handbook of Artificial Intelligence: Global Perspectives on Law and Ethics*, edited by Larry A DiMatteo, Cristina Poncibò, and Michel Cannarsa. Cambridge: Cambridge University Press, 2021.

European Commission. 'The General-Purpose AI Code of Practice'. July 2025. https://digital-strategy.ec.europa.eu/en/policies/contents-code-gpai.

European Standardization Organizations. 'European Standardization'. *CEN-CENELEC.* www.cencenelec.eu/european-standardization/.

European Union. *Directive (EU) 2022/2380 of the European Parliament and of the Council of 23 November 2022 amending Directive 2014/53/EU (Radio Equipment Directive).* OJ L 315, 7 December 2022. https://eur-lex.europa.eu/eli/dir/2022/2380/oj/eng.

European Union. *Regulation (EU) No 1025/2012 of the European Parliament and of the Council of 25 October 2012 on European Standardisation.* OJ L 316, 14 November 2012.

European Union. *Regulation (EU) 2024/1689 of the European Parliament and of the Council of 13 June 2024 (Artificial Intelligence Act).* http://data.europa.eu/eli/reg/2024/1689/oj/eng.

Farmer, Harry. *Regulate to Innovate.* Ada Lovelace Institute, 2021. www.adalovelaceinstitute.org/report/regulate-innovate/.

Fielding, Roy T., Mark Nottingham, and Julian Reschke. *HTTP Semantics.* RFC 9110. Internet Engineering Task Force, June 2022. https://doi.org/10.17487/RFC9110.

Free Speech Coalition, Inc. v Paxton, No.23–1122 (Supreme Court of the United States, 27 June 2025).

Frydman, Benoît. 'Coregulation: A Possible Legal Model for Global Governance'. *SSRN Scholarly Paper No. 1980176.* Rochester, NY, 5 January 2012. https://papers.ssrn.com/abstract=1980176.

Gady, Franz-Stefan. 'EU/US Approaches to Data Privacy and the "Brussels Effect": A Comparative Analysis'. *Georgetown Journal of International Affairs* (2014): 12–23.

Global Freedom of Expression. 'Schrems v. Data Protection Commissioner'. https://globalfreedomofexpression.columbia.edu/cases/schrems-v-data-protection-commissioner/.

Gornet, Mélanie, and Winston Maxwell. 'The European Approach to Regulating AI through Technical Standards'. *Internet Policy Review* 13, no. 3 (2024). https://doi.org/10.14763/2024.3.1784.

Green, Jessica F, and Thomas Hale. 'New "Net Zero" Standards Could Transform the Climate – Unless They're Derailed'. *Washington Post*, 4 October 2021. www.washingtonpost.com/politics/2021/10/04/iso-london-declaration-climate/.

Gunningham, Neil, and Joseph Rees. 'Industry Self-Regulation: An Institutional Perspective'. *Law & Policy* 19, no. 4 (1997): 363–414. https://doi.org/10.1111/1467-9930.t01-1-00033.

Hepburn, Glen. *Alternatives to Traditional Regulation.* OECD, n.d. www.oecd.org/gov/regulatory-policy/42245468.pdf.

Hernandez, Guillermo. 'Regulatory Oversight for Better Regulation'. *Penn Program on Regulation, The Regulatory Review*, 8 December 2022. www.theregreview.org/2022/12/08/hernandez-regulatory-oversight/.

Hirsch, Dennis D. 'Going Dutch? Collaborative Dutch Privacy Regulation and the Lessons It Holds for US Privacy Law'. *SSRN Scholarly Paper No. 2393707.* Rochester, NY, 1 November 2013. https://papers.ssrn.com/abstract=2393707.

International Organization for Standardization and International Electrotechnical Commission. *Information Technology – Cybersecurity and Privacy Protection – Cybersecurity Framework Development Guidelines (ISO/IEC TS 27110:2021).* www.iso.org/obp/ui/#iso:std:iso-iec:ts:27110:ed-1:v1:en.

Iafolla, Robert. 'GOP-Picked Judges Take Hard Line on Regulations Post-Chevron'. *Bloomberg Law*, 4 September 2024. https://news.bloomberglaw.com/daily-labor-report/gop-picked-judges-take-hard-line-on-rules-after-chevrons-demise.

IEEE Standards Association. 'Standards Collaboration'. https://standards.ieee.org/about/intl/standards-collaboration/.

Kaal, Wulf A. 'Dynamic Regulation for Innovation'. *SSRN Electronic Journal*, ahead of print (2016). https://doi.org/10.2139/ssrn.2831040.

Kamara, Irene. 'Co-Regulation in EU Personal Data Protection: The Case of Technical Standards and the Privacy by Design Standardisation "Mandate"'. *European Journal of Law and Technology* 8, no. 1 (2017).

Katzenberger, Tyler. 'California Age Verification Bill Backed by Google, Meta, OpenAI Heads to Newsom'. *Politico*, 13 September 2025. www.politico.com/news/2025/09/13/california-advances-effort-to-check-kids-ages-online-amid-safety-concerns-00563005.

Kisor v Wilkie, 588 US 571 (2019).

Latzer, Michael, Monroe E Price, Florian Saurwein, and Stefaan G Verhulst. 'Comparative Analysis of International Co- and Self-Regulation in Communications Markets'. *SSRN Scholarly Paper No. 2134877*. Rochester, NY, 1 September 2007. https://papers.ssrn.com/abstract=2134877.

Laufer, Maximilian. *Democracy and Industry Capture of the Executive*. Georgetown Law Denny Center for Democratic Capitalism, 21 September 2023. www.law.georgetown.edu/denny-center/blog/industry-capture-of-the-executive/.

Laux, Johann, Sandra Wachter, and Brent Mittelstadt. *Three Pathways for Standardisation and Ethical Disclosure by Default under the European Union Artificial Intelligence Act. Computer Law & Security Review* 53 (July 2024): 105957. https://doi.org/10.1016/j.clsr.2024.105957.

Levins, Hoag. 'Supreme Court's Chevron Reversal: A Seismic Shift for Health Care Regulation'. *Penn LDI*, 11 November 2024. https://ldi.upenn.edu/our-work/research-updates/supreme-courts-chevron-reversal-a-seismic-shift-for-health-care-regulation/.

Loper Bright Enterprises v Raimondo, No. 22–451 (Supreme Court of the United States, 28 June 2024).

Marsden, Christopher T. 'Co- and Self-Regulation in European Media and Internet Sectors: The Results of Oxford University's Study'. In *Self-Regulation, Co-Regulation, State Regulation*. 2005. www.osce.org/sites/default/files/f/documents/2/a/13844.pdf.

Marsden, Christopher T. *Internet Co-Regulation: European Law, Regulatory Governance and Legitimacy in Cyberspace*. 1st ed. Cambridge: Cambridge University Press, 2011. https://doi.org/10.1017/CBO9780511763410.

Maximilian Schrems v Data Protection Commissioner, Case C-362/14 (Court of Justice of the European Union, 6 October 2015). https://eur-lex.europa.eu/legal-content/EN/TXT/?uri=celex:62014CJ0362.

McClain, Colleen, Michelle Faverio, Monica Anderson, and Eugene Park. *How Americans View Data Privacy: Tech Companies, AI, Regulation, Passwords and Policies*. Pew Research Center, 2023. www.pewresearch.org/internet/2023/10/18/how-americans-view-data-privacy/.

McFadden, Mark, Kate Jones, Emily Taylor, and Georgia Osborn. *Harmonising Artificial Intelligence: The Role of Standards in the EU AI Regulation*. Oxford: Oxford Information Labs, 2021.

Michigan v Environmental Protection Agency, 576 US 743 (2015).

Morgan, Bronwen, and Karen Yeung. *An Introduction to Law and Regulation: Text and Materials*. 1st edn. Cambridge: Cambridge University Press, 2007. https://doi.org/10.1017/CBO9780511801112.

Morse, Susan C. 'Corner Post Broadens Loper Bright, But Footnote 8 Offers a Limit'. *The Regulatory Review*, 30 July 2024. www.theregreview.org/2024/07/30/morse-corner-post-broadens-loper-bright-but-footnote-8-offers-a-limit/.

Muir, Martha. 'US Shale Bosses Decry "Chaos" in Donald Trump's Energy Policy'. *Financial Times*, 24 September 2025. www.ft.com/content/5391ae3f-e87e-43d0-8e85-fc2fe3f99c21.

NIST. *Post-Quantum Cryptography Standardization*. 13 August 2024. https://csrc.nist.gov/projects/post-quantum-cryptography/post-quantum-cryptography-standardization.

National Technology Transfer and Advancement Act of 1995. Pub. L. No. 104-113, 110 Stat. 775 (1996), as amended by Pub. L. No. 107-107, § 1115 (2001).

Nielsen, Thomas E, and Krista A Stapleford. 'What Loper Bright Might Portend for Auer Deference'. *Harvard Law Review*, 5 July 2024. https://harvardlawreview.org/blog/2024/07/what-loper-bright-might-portend-for-auer-deference/.

Office of Management and Budget. *Circular A-119: Federal Participation in the Development and Use of Voluntary Consensus Standards and in Conformity Assessment Activities.* Executive Office of the President, rev. ed. 2023.

Organisation for Economic Co-operation and Development (OECD). *OECD Regulatory Policy Outlook 2021.* Paris: OECD, 2021. www.oecd.org/en/publications/oecd-regulatory-policy-outlook-2021_38b0fdb1-en/full-report.html.

Ohio Telecom Association et al. v Federal Communications Commission, No. 24-3449 (US Court of Appeals for the Sixth Circuit, 2 January 2025). www.govinfo.gov/app/details/USCOURTS-ca6-24-03449.

Peeler, C Lee, and Cobun Zweifel-Keegan. *Twenty Years of Successful Co-Regulation under COPPA.* BBB National Programs, 2019.

Preskey, Natasha. 'Jake Paul, Zuckerberg and Musk: Who's at Trump's Inauguration?' *BBC News*, 20 January 2025. www.bbc.com/news/articles/cgkjgmkn10ko.

Price, Monroe, and Stefaan Verhulst. *The Concept of Self-Regulation and the Internet.* Departmental Papers (ASC), 1 January 2000.

Ramaswamy, Vivek, and Elon Musk. 'Opinion | Elon Musk and Vivek Ramaswamy: The DOGE Plan to Reform Government'. *Wall Street Journal*, 20 November 2024. www.wsj.com/opinion/musk-and-ramaswamy-the-doge-plan-to-reform-government-supreme-court-guidance-end-executive-power-grab-fa51c020.

Regulation (EU) 2024/1689 of the European Parliament and of the Council of 13 June 2024 (Artificial Intelligence Act). http://data.europa.eu/eli/reg/2024/1689/oj/eng.

Rescorla, Eric. *The Transport Layer Security (TLS) Protocol Version 1.3.* RFC 8446. Internet Engineering Task Force, August 2018. https://doi.org/10.17487/RFC8446.

Ryan LLC, Chamber of Commerce of the United States of America v Federal Trade Commission, No. 3:24-cv-00986-E (US District Court for the Northern District of Texas, 20 August 2024).

Sanders, Eli. 'A Supreme Court Justice Warned That a Ruling Would Cause "Large-Scale Disruption". The Effects Are Already Being Felt'. *ProPublica*, 23 September 2024. www.propublica.org/article/supreme-court-chevron-deference-loper-bright-guns-abortion-pending-cases.

Saubestre, Sydney, and Nat Meysenburg. 'Quantum Computing Is Coming. Better Encryption Helps Us Prepare for Its Arrival'. *New America, Open Technology Institute*, 2024 http://newamerica.org/oti/blog/quantum-computing-is-coming-better-encryption-helps-us-prepare-for-its-arrival/.

Shepardson, David. 'Trump Revokes Biden Executive Order on Addressing AI Risks'. *Reuters*, 21 January 2025. www.reuters.com/technology/artificial-intelligence/trump-revokes-biden-executive-order-addressing-ai-risks-2025-01-21/.

Smith, David. 'At Home and Abroad US Policy Chaos Has One Constant: Trump's Self-Interest'. *The Guardian*, 24 August 2025. www.theguardian.com/us-news/2025/aug/24/trump-policy-putin-summit.

Soler Garrido, J, S De Nigris, E Bass Ani, et al. *Harmonised Standards for the European AI Act.* No. JRC139430, Science for Policy Brief. European Commission, 2024. https://publications.jrc.ec.europa.eu/repository/handle/JRC139430.

The White House. 'Removing Barriers to American Leadership in Artificial Intelligence'. 23 January 2025. www.whitehouse.gov/presidential-actions/2025/01/removing-barriers-to-american-leadership-in-artificial-intelligence/.

US Department of Justice, Civil Rights Division. *ADA Standards for Accessible Design.* US Department of Justice, 15 September 2010. www.ada.gov/law-and-regs/design-standards/.

Wachter, Sandra. 'Limitations and Loopholes in the EU AI Act and AI Liability Directives: What This Means for the European Union, the United States, and Beyond'. *SSRN Electronic Journal*, ahead of print (2024). https://doi.org/10.2139/ssrn.4924553.

Wayman v Southard, 23 US (10 Wheat.) 1 (1825).

West Virginia v Environmental Protection Agency, No. 20–1530 (US, 30 June 2022).

World Customs Organization and World Trade Organization. *WCO/WTO Study Report on Disruptive Technologies.* Geneva: World Trade Organization, 2022. www.wto.org/english/res_e/booksp_e/wco-wto_e.pdf.

World Trade Organization. *Agreement on Technical Barriers to Trade.* 1 January 1995. www.wto.org/english/docs_e/legal_e/tbt_e.htm.

9

Transitioning from Portability in the GDPR to Access in the Data Act: A Multidisciplinary Analysis of Data Access by Design

EMANUELA PODDA, NICOLA LESCHKE, PIERANGELA SAMARATI AND FRANK PALLAS

Abstract

Going beyond the dichotomy of personal and non-personal data, the Data Act introduces a paradigm shift in the right of access (and portability) as ingrained in the General Data Protection Regulation (GDPR). On that basis, and exploring this shift, this chapter compares the implementation of access and portability obligations under the GDPR and the newly introduced data access by design (and shareability) rights in the Data Act. Along this line, the chapter introduces a web-based data access process model tailored for continuous, real-time access under the Data Act.

This process model paves the way for soundly discussing technical implications and challenges to expect for the actual execution and enforcement of the new access obligations in practice. In particular, the continuous, real-time provision is only feasible, when the access request and provision process is automated. The chapter brings into fore design options for stream-like communication, automated queryable interfaces in the form of APIs, and an enhanced data management in the data holder's backend. Finally, the impact of the Data Act access obligations on users, data holders, and data recipients is discussed.

Keywords

Internet of Things; Commercial Confidentiality; Trade Secrecy; Access by Design; Process Model

I. Introduction

Being a core legislative component of the European Data Strategy, the Data Act complements other regulations such as the Digital Market Act, the Digital Services Act, or the AI Act with far-reaching provisions for manufacturers of connected products and related services as well as for providers of data processing services (such as cloud providers).

Besides other provisions on, eg, interoperability of different cloud services or obligations to provide certain data to public bodies in case of exceptional need, the Data Act[1] introduces data access rights beyond existing scopes of data access and data shareability rights in previous regulations like the GDPR or the DMA.[2] Structurally, the Data Act's right of access resembles, to a certain extent, the right to data portability from Article 20 of the GDPR,[3] opening up respective research as first points of reference for our analysis. In particular, the Data Act obligates responsible parties to implement them in a *by design*[4] fashion. In this regard, Article 4 of the Data Act obligates data holders and manufacturers of connected products to provide data generated from such products (Internet of Things (IoT) data) and related services (IoT service data) to the users in a machine-readable, continuous, and real-time fashion. Article 5 of the Data Act, in turn, extends this obligation to be also fulfilled towards third parties acting on behalf of the user, establishing a right to delegated access resembling the right to data portability. Thereby, a more open and versatile use of IoT (service) data so far locked into the data holders' data silos is facilitated.

The far-reaching expectable impacts of said access-related provisions for industry notwithstanding, it is so far only barely discussed – let alone understood – how they are to be implemented technically and what implications and challenges arise for the involved stakeholders. In particular, the newly established paradigm of *continuous, real-time data access by design* inevitably necessitates novel, technologically backed materialisations that meet regulatory particularities from the Data Act and are at the same time in line with established technical practices and the state-of-the-art. For any techno-legal discourse on data access under the Data Act to be well-founded, it is indispensable to understand these interrelations as well as the consequential technical options and challenges.

The primary goals of the chapter at hand are, thus, to provide a first techno-legal analysis of a) the right to access under the Data Act and b) the implications

[1] Regulation (EU) 2023/2854 of the European Parliament and of the Council of 13 December 2023 on harmonised rules on fair access to and use of data and amending Regulation (EU) 2017/2394 and Directive (EU) 2020/1828 (Data Act).

[2] Barbara Lazarotto, 'The Right to Data Portability: A Holistic Analysis of GDPR, DMA and the Data Act', *European Journal of Law and Technology* 15, no. 1 (2024).

[3] Paul De Hert et al, 'The Right to Data Portability in the GDPR: Towards User-Centric Interoperability of Digital Services', *Computer Law & Security Review* 34, no. 2 (2018): 193–203.

[4] According to Article 3(1) Data Act the obligation pertains to designers and manufacturers of connected products, as well as to designers and providers of related services.

for its technical implementation. Based on this analysis, we also aim to c) identify foreseeable challenges and conflicts to be addressed until full applicability of the Data Act and to d) sketch further implications for data holders, users, and data recipients.

Along these lines, our analysis unfolds as follows: In section II, we provide a comprehensive analysis of the right to data access by design as introduced by the Data Act in comparison to data portability from the GDPR, particularly comprising the scope of application, relevant roles, and covered data types. Section III then establishes a process-driven perspective to data portability and access under the GDPR and the Data Act, highlighting commonalities and differences even further and providing the so far largely missing link towards a technical implementation perspective. The latter is given in section IV and particularly discusses implementation options and identifies foreseeable challenges. Section V presents further general observations and implications for different stakeholders, while section VI concludes.

II. Data Access by Design: Transitioning from Access and Portability to Access and Shareability

The Data Act establishes novel harmonised rules concerning, on the one hand, the right of the user to access data and to share the aforementioned data with third parties to service switching (right to access and to share/to port data) and, on the other hand, the obligation to make product data and related service data accessible to the user (obligation to grant access).

The lexical choices of the European legislator seem to mirror, to some extent, the terminology used in the GDPR. In particular, for the right of access (*ex* Article 15 GDPR) while, only partially, for the right to data portability (*ex* Article 20 GDPR). The Data Act does not literally mention the right to portability, rather referring to the right to share data (*ex* Article 5 Data Act).

The regulatory approach impacts on the relation between these two rights as designed and ingrained in the GDPR. Scholars[5] investigated this relation, further clarifying that data portability – although interrelated with other 'control rights' among which the right of access – presents a narrower scope. The Data Act seems to reinforce this argument,[6] requiring designers and manufacturers of connected products and related services to implement the right of access in a *by design* fashion. Therefore, the scope of the right of access seems to broaden with respect to

[5] De Hert et al, 'The Right to Data Portability in the GDPR'; Orla Lynskey, 'Article 20 Right to Data Portability', in *The EU General Data Protection Regulation (GDPR): A Commentary*, ed. Christopher Kuner et al (Oxford: Oxford University Press, 2020), 497–507.

[6] Lazarotto, 'The Right to Data Portability'; Sarah Turner and Leonie Maria Tanczer, '*In Principle* Vs *in Practice*: User, Expert and Policymaker Attitudes Towards the Right to Data Portability in the Internet of Things', *Computer Law & Security Review* 52 (2024): 105912.

what was envisaged in the GDPR, integrating features of portability since its design phase. Apart from what is explicitly provided in the GDPR, the European Data Protection Board (EDPB, former Working Party 29)[7] provides interpretative guidance on these two rights.

Concerning their objective scope of application, both rights apply to personal data, but, more specifically, the right of access[8] relates to both inferred and derived data (also including personal data generated by a service provider). Differently, the right to data portability relates to data provided by the data subject only, covering only observed data and excluding inferred data.[9] In this regard, De Hert[10] emphasises that Recital 68 of the GDPR provides a further interpretation of the matter, supporting the argument that data collected in a non-written format (such as cookies and GPS data) could also be the object of portability.

Another element of differentiation refers to data format requirements. The right of access, along with the right to obtain a copy of data undergoing processing, does not require a machine-readable format, while the right to data portability imposes specific requirements instrumental to interoperability. De Hert[11] highlights that this difference clarifies the composition of the right to data portability as of three different rights: 1) the right to receive data concerning the data subject which he/she has provided; 2) the right to transmit those data to another controller; and 3) the right to have personal data transmitted directly from one controller to another. According to De Hert, especially the enforcement of the last right requires specific format requirements. Along this line of reasoning, the EDPB[12] clarifies that formats not appropriate for a data portability request can still be appropriate to a data access request.

Given these main features that characterise the two rights in the GDPR, it can be noted that the Data Act delineates an alternative regulatory approach emphasising the right of access while simultaneously integrating within several features inherent to the right of portability. Although in a by-design fashion, the Data Act provides clear regulatory shape and normative features of the right of access (*ex* Article 3 and Article 4 Data Act), without recalling any explicit reference to the right to data portability. In this last regard, the Data Act rather envisages a more

[7] European Data Protection Board, *Guidelines 01/2022 on Data Subject Rights – Right of Access*, 2023, www.edpb.europa.eu/system/files/2023-04/edpb_guidelines_202201_data_subject_rights_access_v2_en.pdf; European Data Protection Board, *2024 Coordinated Enforcement Action Implementation of the Right of Access by Controllers*, 2025, www.edpb.europa.eu/system/files/2025-01/edpb_cef-report-2024_20250116_rightofaccess_en.pdf; Article 29 Data Protection Working Party, *Guidelines on the Right to Data Portability*, 2017, https://ec.europa.eu/newsroom/article29/items/611233.

[8] European Data Protection Board, *Guidelines 01/2022 on Data Subject Rights – Right of Access*, 2023; European Data Protection Board, *2024 Coordinated Enforcement Action Implementation of the Right of Access by Controllers*.

[9] Article 29 Data Protection Working Party, *Guidelines on the Right to Data Portability*.

[10] De Hert et al, 'The Right to Data Portability in the GDPR'.

[11] De Hert et al, 'The Right to Data Portability in the GDPR'.

[12] European Data Protection Board, *Version 2.1*.

general 'right of the user to share data with third parties' (*ex* Article 5) that, according to Lazarotto,[13] adds specific nuances to portability as envisaged in the GDPR.

Perhaps with a vision driven by interoperability, the legislator seems to transition from portability to access only, enlarging the latter in favour of a collection-centric approach: users have direct access to data, exerting full control of it, whose design integrates *by default* portability features ingrained in the GDPR.

A. Portability: Features and Challenges in IoT Environments

Data portability has been one of the main novelties introduced by the GDPR,[14] laying the ground for a consumer rights-centric market.[15] In this context, data portability falls within the 'control rights' and grants the data subject with the right to 'receive the personal data concerning him or her, which he or she has provided to a controller' and to 'transmit those data to another controller without hindrance from the controller to which the personal data have been provided'. According to Article 20 of the GDPR, regulating the aforementioned right, when personal data have been provided a) on the basis of the data subject's consent, or b) the processing is necessary for the performance of a contract, and c) the processing takes place by automatic means, the data subject has the right to receive his/her personal data in a structured, commonly used, machine-readable, and interoperable format and to transmit them from one controller to another.

In time, the exercise of this right has been extensively discussed and empirically tested by scholars,[16] highlighting specific limitations and challenges in its actionability and technical implementation. Among the main challenges – recalled in institutional documents[17] – there are the constraints that data subjects face for direct, continuous, and real-time access to data generated in IoT environments. IoT environments rely on the integration of several technologies and communication solutions, creating a network infrastructure that allows intelligent objects

[13] Lazarotto, 'The Right to Data Portability'.

[14] De Hert et al, 'The Right to Data Portability in the GDPR'.

[15] Lazarotto, 'The Right to Data Portability'.

[16] Janis Wong and Tristan Henderson, 'The Right to Data Portability in Practice: Exploring the Implications of the Technologically Neutral GDPR', *International Data Privacy Law* 9, no. 3 (2019): 173–91; Sarah Turner et al, 'The Exercisability of the Right to Data Portability in the Emerging Internet of Things (IoT) Environment', *New Media & Society* 23, no. 10 (2021): 2861–81; Sophie Kuebler-Wachendorff et al, 'The Right to Data Portability: Conception, Status Quo, and Future Directions', *Informatik Spektrum* 44, no. 4 (2021): 273–73; Sophie Kuebler-Wachendorff et al, 'The Right to Data Portability: Conception, Status Quo, and Future Directions', *Informatik Spektrum* 44, no. 4 (2021): 264–72; Turner and Tanczer, '*In Principle* Vs *in Practice*'.

[17] European Commission, *Commission Staff Working Document, Impact Assessmennt Report Accompanying the Document Proposal for a Regulation of the European Parliament and of the Council on Harmonised Rules on Fair Access to and Use of Data (Data Act) SWD(2022) 34 Final Shaping Europe's Digital Future*, European Commission, 2022.

equipped with sensing, identifying, and processing capabilities to interconnect and communicate.[18] These environments generate a multitude of data that vary by consumer IoT segment, relevant for designing new services and enhancing innovation in the Digital Single Market. These new types of data challenge the legal semantic distinction between the two mutually exclusive definitions of personal and non-personal, as provided in the GDPR and in the Free Flow Data Regulation.[19]

Often IoT data generate constraints for data accessibility and portability/shareability, raising legal issues around commercial confidentiality, trade secrecy, and more generally, intellectual property protection.[20] To this extent, the GDPR clarifies that portability of data applies only to personal data and lists three exceptions to it,[21] among which is that the requested data are deleted or anonymised, rendered anonymous to the extent that it cannot be considered personal anymore. Scholars[22] have already debated on how the process of discerning personal data from non-personal data is 'fraught with difficulty' that, in IoT environments escalate. In this respect, the Data Act ensures full control of data users over their rights by overcoming the semantic distinction between personal and non-personal data, complementing the GDPR by shaping a new right of access.

B. Data Act and Data Access by Design

The Data Act moves beyond the two mutually exclusive semantic definitions of personal and non-personal data, and it regulates several types of data, falling under specific contexts listed with a denotation method.[23] Within different context, the Data Act recalls IoT data (referred to as data from connected products)[24] and IoT

[18] Luigi Atzori, Antonio Iera, and Giacomo Morabito, 'The Internet of Things: A Survey', *Computer Networks* 54, no. 15 (2010): 2787–805; Shancang Li, Li Da Xu, and Shanshan Zhao, 'The Internet of Things: A Survey', *Information Systems Frontiers* 17, no. 2 (2015): 243–59.

[19] Regulation (EU) 2018/1807 of the European Parliament and of the Council of 14 November 2018 on a framework for the free flow of non-personal data in the European Union.

[20] Ulla-Maija Mylly, 'Trade Secrets and the Data Act', *International Review of Intellectual Property and Competition Law* 55, no. 3 (2024): 368–93.

[21] Among the exceptions, there are the following cases: (a) if the request interferes with a task carried out in the public interest, and (b) if the portability of data affects the rights and freedoms of others.

[22] Michèle Finck and Frank Pallas, 'They Who Must Not Be Identified – Distinguish/Ing Personal from Non-Personal Data Under the GDPR', *International Data Privacy Law* 10, no. 1 (2020): 11–36; Emanuela Podda, 'Anonymization of Personal Data (Legal Perspective)', in *Encyclopedia of Cryptography, Security and Privacy* (Berlin: Springer, 2024), 1–3.

[23] Article 1(2) Data Act clarifies that the Regulation covers personal and non-personal data.

[24] *Ex* Article 2(5) Data Act a connected product is 'an item that obtains, generates or collects data concerning its use or environment and that is able to communicate product data via an electronic communications service, physical connection or on-device access, and whose primary function is not the storing, processing or transmission of data on behalf of any party other than the user'. Clarifying further, Recital 14 Data Act specifies that 'connected products' are those that 'obtain, generate or collect, by means of their components or operating systems, data concerning their performance, use or environment and that are able to communicate those data via an electronic communications service, a

service data (referred to as data from related services).[25] The Data Act refers to data at a syntactic level, defining it in Article 2(1), as of 'any digital representation of acts, facts or information and any compilation of such acts, facts or information, including in the form of sound, visual or audio-visual recording from connected products and related services'.

Recognising that not all data generated by IoT products and IoT related services are directly accessible by users,[26] the Data Act refers to: products designed for allowing direct data access (*on-device access/data storage*), regulated in Article 3 of the Data Act, and products not allowing direct access to data (access provided by electronic means), regulated in Article 4. Article 3 of the Data Act is beyond the scope of this chapter.

Article 4 of the Data Act clarifies that when direct access cannot be provided, the data holder should provide access by electronic means, engineering web-based access to data. In fact, data are often stored on the manufacturer's server or on the service provider's server (eg, cloud provider), requiring the design of new solutions striking a balance between involved parties and respective rights and obligations for enforcing rules and principles introduced by the Data Act. In this case, the Data Act imposes specific data requirements: data should be accessible easily, securely, free of charge, in a comprehensive, structured, commonly used and machine-readable format, and, where relevant and technically feasible, continuously and in real-time accessible, *through electronic means* (web-based access, as expressively mentioned in Article 4 of the Data Act).

i. *Data flow* ex *Data Act and Involved Roles*

The Data Act introduces a data flow that relies on the access and further sharing of IoT data and IoT services data with active participation of a few key actors (Figure 9.1). Apart from the respective roles of designers and manufacturers in granting direct access to data (direct access), as well as the role of public sector bodies requiring access on exceptional need, this chapter focuses on data access by design enhanced by electronic means (*ex* Article 4 of the Data Act). This section brings into fore the roles of the user, the data holder, and the data recipient; their

physical connection, or on-device access, often referred to as the Internet of Things, should fall within the scope of this Regulation, with the exception of prototypes'.

[25] *Ex* Article 2(6) Data Act it means 'a digital service, other than an electronic communications service, including software, which is connected with the product at the time of the purchase, rent or lease in such a way that its absence would prevent the connected product from performing one or more of its functions, or which is subsequently connected to the product by the manufacturer or a third party to add to, update or adapt the functions of the connected product'.

[26] European Commission, *Commission Staff Working Document, Impact Assessment Report Accompanying the Document Proposal for a Regulation of the European Parliament and of the Council on Harmonized Rules on Fair Access to and Use of Data (Data Act) SWD(2022) 34 Final Shaping Europe's Digital Future.*

features help clarify enhancing by electronic means access by design should encompass characteristics of portability since the design phase.

Article 2(12) of the Data Act foresees that, on the one hand, the user has the right to access data while, on the other hand, the data holder has the obligation to make the aforementioned data accessible to the him/her (or to a third party acting on behalf of the user) by rendering data available to a data recipient.[27]

The Data Act defines the user as 'a natural or legal person that owns a connected product or to whom temporary rights to use that connected product have been contractually transferred or that receives related services'. The Data Act creates a legal basis for providing access to personal data, or for making data available to a third party, only when the user is a data subject *ex* GDPR (Recital 7).[28] As anticipated, differently from the GDPR foreseen a set of 'control rights', the Data Act recalls only the right to access, clarifying the relation of complementarity between the two Regulations,[29] and that no provision of the Data Act should be applied or interpreted in such a way as to diminish or limit the right to the protection of personal data or the right to privacy and confidentiality of communications.

The data holder is defined as

> a natural or legal person that has the right or the obligation to use and make data available to the user, including, if contractually agreed, product data or related service data retrieved or generated during the provision of a related service.

A significant aspect of this role, which may influence the technical design of the access to data, is the safeguarding of commercial confidentiality, including trade secrecy, afforded to the data holder. To this aim, the Data Act envisages[30] that data holders should be able to require users (or third parties as data recipients) to maintain the confidentiality of data covered by trade secrecy. Along the same line, data holders should be able to identify trade secrets prior to their disclosure and to agree with users (or third parties) on the measures necessary to maintain

[27] These operations might require the involvement of the data process, improving the interoperability of data. In this regard, see extensively Recital 5 and Recitals from 80 to 99 of the Data Act: such services cover a very broad range different purposes, functionalities, and technical set-ups, falling into the three main data processing service delivery models and namely Infrastructure as a Service (IaaS), Platform as a service (PaaS), and Software as a Service (SaaS).

[28] The user might be a data subject as defined in Article 4 GDPR, but the terms differ in three respects: first, the user can also be a legal person; second, users do not necessarily share personal data, thereby not qualifying as data subjects; and third, a connected product or related service might only have one user (as defined in Article 2(12) Data Act), but several data subjects interacting with it. For example, in a flat with smart lights and with multiple persons in the household interacting with them via the same account but on their individual smartphones, the account owner would be the user, but all housemates might be data subjects in terms of the GDPR. Consequently, personal data related to other data subjects than the user need to be separated and de-identified or left out in the access request response, as long as there is no separate legal basis allowing their inclusion.

[29] Recital 7 clarifies that the Data Act complements the GDPR and it is without prejudice to it.

[30] The main reference is Recital 31 of the Data Act.

confidentiality, among which the use of model contractual clauses, confidentiality agreements, strict access protocols, technical standards, and the application of codes of conduct.

In fact, users promote competition by lowering barriers in the digital market, sharing accessed data with potential data holder competitors. Given the intersection between the right of access and the right to protect commercially valuable information, the Data Act seems to strike the balance in favour of commercial confidentiality, recognising it as a limit to the right of access. According to Article 5(11) of the Data Act, when the data holder providing access to data is also a trade secret holder and is able to demonstrate that it is highly likely to suffer a serious economic damage from the disclosure of trade secrets, a refusal to the request for access is legitimate.[31] Nevertheless, this does not preclude the possibility to explore further technical solutions tailoring a different proportional trade-off.

Although the Data Act requires data holders to disclose data to users (or third parties), even when such data qualify for trade secrecy protection, the disclosure should be interpreted in such a way as to preserve the protection afforded to trade secrets under Directive (EU) 2016/943, requiring the engineering of solutions striking a proportional balance between the right of access and the right to protect commercial confidentiality.[32]

Lastly, the data recipient is defined as 'a natural or legal person to whom the data holder makes data available'. The Data Act clarifies that this role includes a third party following an access request by the user (Figure 9.1). This confirms that the access request can be placed directly by the data user to the data holder, as well as by data recipients to whom the data user confers mandate of access. Moreover, the Data Act includes within this role also the data intermediation service provider *ex* Regulation (EU) 2022/868 (aka Data Governance Act).[33]

[31] To this aim, the Data Act clarifies that Directive (EU) 2016/943 of the European Parliament and of the Council on the protection of undisclosed know-how and business information (trade secrets) against their unlawful acquisition, use and disclosure provides that 'the acquisition, use or disclosure of a trade secret shall be considered to be lawful, *inter alia*, where such acquisition, use or disclosure is required or allowed by Union or national law'.

[32] IoT data and IoT related service data may disclose patterns that, relying on analytics and reverse engineering on retrieved data, may reveal commercially valuable information, or expose the data holder to potential trade secrets infringements. In this regard, disentangling the relation between Data Act and the Trade Secrets Directive becomes essential. In fact, the technical implementation of the aforementioned trade-off should take into account that, according to the Trade Secret Directive (namely Article 3(1)(b)), the practice of reverse engineering is considered a lawful acquisition of data. In any case, even if the Data Act clarifies that the data recipient is not allowed to use the accessed data to gain insight about the services of the data holders, particularly not to develop or enhance competitive products/services, this does not relieve the data holder of the burden of implementing technical measures to protect commercially valuable information in order to enforce its right to confidentiality on commercially valuable information and trade secrecy.

[33] In this regard, see extensively Recital 39 of the Data Act.

Figure 9.1 Involved Actors and Data Flow ex Data Act

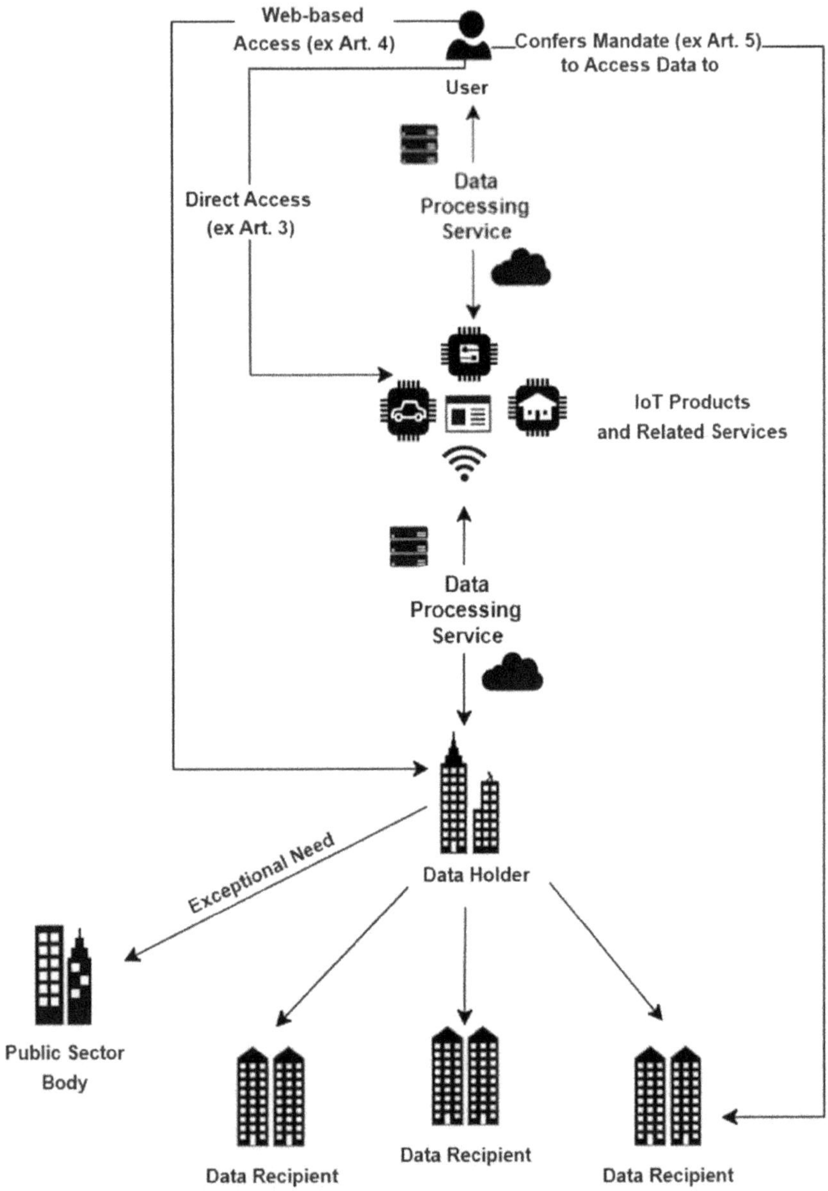

Given the legitimacy of a user access request (user that is a data subject *ex* GDPR, or by a third party under user's choice), and that the Data Act complements the GDPR, the design of the web-based access should not diminish or limit the right to the protection of personal data.

In instances where it is feasible to delineate personal data within the data streams generated by IoT products and related services, the user is endowed with all 'control rights' as outlined in the GDPR, including the right to data portability. This means that the right of access *ex* Data Act assumes a pivotal role in facilitating data portability as described in *ex* GDPR (data subject right), thus serving as a complement to it. Consequently, it becomes imperative to discern, not only from a regulatory point of view, the various categories of data that can be classified as IoT data and IoT services data.

ii. Modelling Data ex *Data Act: At the Intersection of Law and Computer Science*

The conceptual model (Figure 9.1) represents the potential data flow and relevant roles[34] depicted by the Data Act. It focuses exclusively on IoT data and IoT services data, as main data type considered by the Data Act. Further elaborating on this ground, this section undertakes a detailed examination of the relationship between this type of data and derives its potential sub-types according to the letter and the spirit of the law. It first elaborates on the objective scope of application of the Data Act and it further seeks to elucidate the extent to which such objective scope may be affected by its complementarity with the GDPR, namely with the enforcement of data portability.[35]

Recital 15 of the Data Act, clarifies that the concept of product data refers to 'data generated by the use of a connected product that the manufacturer designed to be retrievable from the connected product by a user, data holder, or a third party, including, where relevant, the manufacturer'. Differently, the concept of related service data refers to 'data which represent the digitization of user actions or events related to the connected product which are generated during the provision of a related service by the provider'.

According to the letter of the law, IoT product data and related services data include intentionally collected data, as well as data indirectly generated by the user's action and interaction with the IoT environment, among which those generated by the user interface, data generated by sensors or by embedded applications, either in periods of user inactivity.[36]

[34] Antoni Olivé, 'Introduction', in *Conceptual Modeling of Information Systems* (Berlin: Springer, 2007), 1–36.

[35] Recital 8 of the Data Act clarifies that technical and organisation measures should be implemented to grant data protection by design and by default, including not only pseudonymisation and encryption, but also 'technology that permits algorithms to be brought to the data and allow valuable insights to be derived without the transmission between parties or unnecessary copying of the raw or structured data themselves'.

[36] Accessibility should also be granted for relevant meta-data (including basic context and timestamp), combined with other data eventually reformatted into a commonly used format, or sorted and classified with other related data points.

The analysis of the legal text permits to derive further sub-types of data from connected products and related services. The Data Act mentions three data sub-types falling within its scope of application, namely: a) actively provided data, b) passively observed data, and c) pre-processed data.

Concerning actively provided data and passively observed data, Recital 35 clarifies that the rights of access should be granted regardless of the nature of data (personal/non-personal) as well as regardless of whether data is actively provided or passively observed. The same Recital follows clarifying that, contrarily to Article 20 of the GDPR on data portability, the Data Act ensures that technical obstacles no longer impede or prevent access to data. In this regard, with reference to the GDPR applicability and the large possibilities that digital economy gives to companies to obtain personal data in different ways, Malgieri[37] highlights the importance of determining the data 'source of production'. Malgieri[38] argues that personal data can be 'received, observed, inferred, or predicted by companies'.[39] Further developing Malgieri's line of reasoning, De Hert[40] clarifies the extent to which data portability applies: only to received and observed data (as supported by Recital 68 of the GDPR).

Concerning pre-processed data, Recital 15 of the Data Act clarifies that they fall within its scope of application, meant to be data that have been pre-processed for making them understandable and usable, prior to subsequent processing and analysis. The same Recital clarifies that the reference to the 'pre-processing' activity should not be interpreted as a means to impose to data holders the obligation to cleaning and transforming data, deploying substantial investments in such activity. This clarification supports further interpretation on the exclusion of the Data Act scope of application of information that are inferred or derived,[41] as an outcome of additional investment into generating value or insights from data (in line with what envisaged by Recital 15 of the Data Act, and contrarily to what envisaged by the right of access in the GDPR).[42]

In line with these considerations, according to the data model presented (Figure 9.2), data portability *ex* GDPR should be granted for actively provided data, passively observed data, and for pre-processed data if personal data or mixed data[43] may be identified in the stream of IoT data and related service data.

[37] Gianclaudio Malgieri, 'Property and (Intellectual) Ownership of Consumers' Information: A New Taxonomy for Personal Data', *Privacy in Germany* 4, no. 133 (2016).

[38] Malgieri, 'Property and (Intellectual) Ownership of Consumers' Information: A New Taxonomy for Personal Data'.

[39] Inferred or predicted data are usually generated by companies by data mining, while received and observed data are directly obtained by the data subject.

[40] De Hert et al, 'The Right to Data Portability in the GDPR'.

[41] This means that the Data Act restricts its scope of application to raw data, at syntactic level, data that has not yet evolved into meaningful information.

[42] Mylly, 'Trade Secrets and the Data Act'.

[43] European Commission, *Communication from the Commission to the European Parliament and the Council, Guidance on the Regulation on a Framework for the Free Flow of Non-Personal Data in the European Union*, European Commission, 2019.

Figure 9.2 Data Model ex Data Act

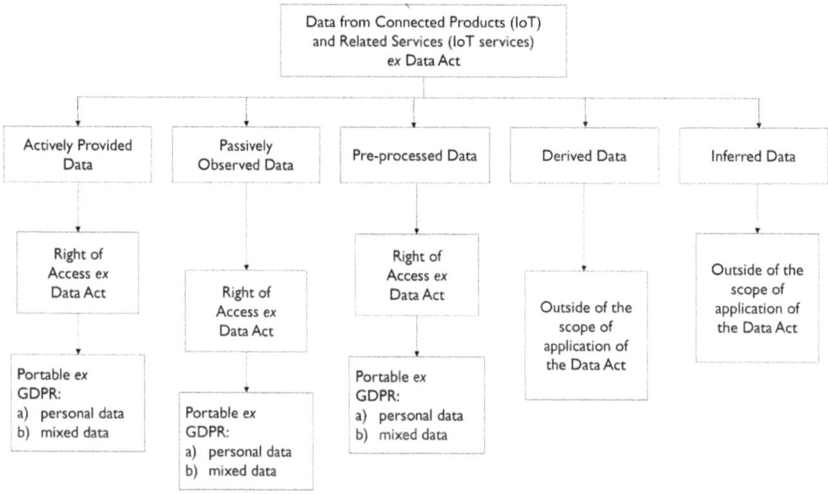

III. Data Access Process Models

In order to highlight similarities and differences in the practical implications of the GDPR's data portability and the Data Act's data access and sharing rights, we take a procedural perspective on the implementation of data access requests. From that procedural perspective, two-party data access and three-party data transfer tasks are overlapping.[44] Hence, we present a GDPR data access process (DAP) model suitable for data access and data portability, and extend it to continuous access processes under the Data Act.

A. The GDPR Data Access Process Model

The one-time access process as depicted by the GDPR data access and portability rights is well researched.[45] In practice, the process can be implemented in different modes, including web-based process mode. The process of a successful web-based

[44] In Section III.A.ii we show that GDPR data portability does neither change the tasks nor their order, but just the underlying data flow.

[45] Malte Hansen and Meiko Jensen, 'A Generic Data Model for Implementing Right of Access Requests', in *Privacy Technologies and Policy* (Cham: Springer, 2022), 3–22; Dominik Pins et al, 'Finding, Getting and Understanding: The User Journey for the GDPR's Right to Access', *Behaviour & Information Technology* 41, no. 10 (2022): 2174–200; Nicola Leschke et al, 'Streamlining Personal Data Access Requests: From Obstructive Procedures to Automated Web Workflows', *Web Engineering* 13893 (2023): 111–25.

DAP *ex* GDPR is shown in Figure 9.3. In the following, the involved tasks and roles are introduced.

Figure 9.3 Data Access Process ex GDPR

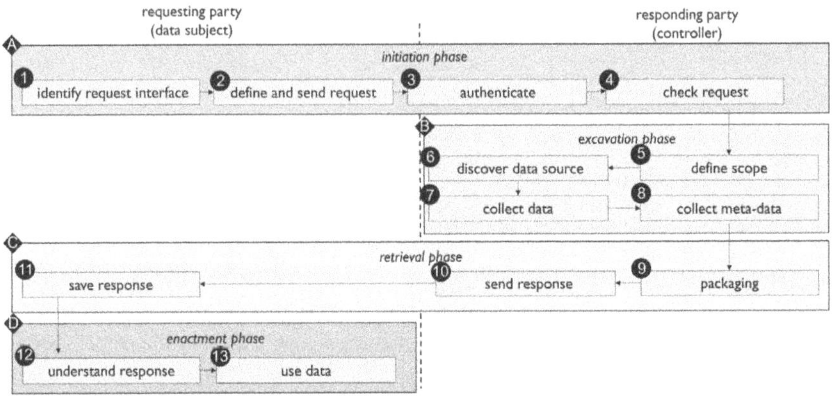

i. Involved Roles and Components

On an abstract level, there are at least two parties involved in a DAP: the requesting party and the responding party. In case of sole access according to the GDPR, the requesting party is the data subject and the responding party is the controller. In the case of data portability, there is an additional role for a third party receiving the request. However, as the request process itself remains unchanged, the receiving party is not considered in the model.

The web-based DAP rests upon three main components provided by the requesting party: First, the communication between data subjects and the interface of the controller usually happens via HTTPS or other common secure network protocols. Second, the interface is the entry point to the controller's internal systems and the endpoint data subjects can send their requests to. For example, the interface can be a contact or a request form, or an *application programming interface* (API).[46] The interface might also include descriptions of the expected response formats and contents.

Lastly, the controller's backend is composed of a number of internal databases which are queried for the requested information. The internal query answering is in practice the most challenging task of a DAP, as backends of modern complex systems are large and it is not always clear which internal systems hold information relevant for the specific access request. This complexity grows when some of the internal systems are provided and hosted by data processors.

[46] An API is a software that enables automated exchange of data between services through well-defined request response patterns.

ii. Process Tasks

The first phase of a DAP is the initiation phase (A). It starts with the data subject's task of *identifying the request interface*, which can be an e-mail address, a web form, or an automated, directly queryable interface. Then, data subjects *define and send the request*. The request can be refined in terms of data items requested, by asking for specific export formats or by specifying other relevant parameters to make a more tailored access request. To avoid access of unauthorised parties, next, the controller needs to *authenticate and authorise* the data subject. Lastly, the controller needs to *check the request* in terms of general applicability.

Next, in the excavation phase (B), the controller needs to first *define the scope* of the specific access request, ie, defining which data types and more fine granular sub-types are to be exported. Second, for all previously identified data items, the *data storage locations have to be discovered*. Finally, both the *content data* and, if applicable, *meta-data* items need to be collected.

In the retrieval phase (C), the collected data then needs to be *packaged* before the controller *sends the access response*. Upon retrieval, the data subject *saves the response*.[47]

Finally, in the enactment phase (D), the data subject needs to *understand the response* – both structure- and content-wise – in order to actually benefit from it. Then, the data can be *used*, eg, to make data driven decisions or to send the response to a third party in line with Article 20(1) GDPR (indirect transfer).

B. The Data Act Process Model

The DAP must be refined for connected products and related services according to the access obligations laid down in Article 4 and Article 5 of the Data Act, requiring web-based access. In particular, the adopted process has to acknowledge continuous and real-time access. In doing so, new challenges arise and need to be reflected both in the process (by adding endpoints and new sub-processes) and in the mode the process is carried out. In particular – and in contrast to the GDPR, where a subject's query can be manually answered within 30 days – Article 4(1) of the Data Act calls for real-time access, where technically feasible. This necessitates the DAP to be automated both in the initiation phase (by providing a queryable interface) and in the data excavation phase. Moreover, as introduced in section II, there are additional actors involved in the Data Act access process. Their roles in the DAP are briefly discussed in the following.

[47] To allow a more compact representation, we do not visualise the Article 20(2) GDPR scenario. In this case, the receiving party would be a third party appointed by the data subject.

i. Involved Roles and Technical Components

From the Data Act, we have identified the stakeholders in section II. We can map them to the roles in the DAP in the following way: the requesting party can either be a user or a data recipient, while the data holder is the responding party. Moreover, the obligation of the Data Act have implications for all three technical components implemented by the data holder. In particular, real-time access requires – different from the GDPR – completely automated processing. Moreover, the principle of continuous access converts the DAP from sporadic, isolated request-response interactions into a streaming scenario. This has consequences for both the API design and technical communication schemes and protocols. More specific technical implications are discussed in the following sections.

ii. Adopted Process Model

Based on the considerations outlined above, we now present a DAP model specifically tailored for Data Act access requests. Hence, this model includes the roles defined in the subjective scope and is tailored for continuous, real-time data access, while it respects the confidentiality of trade secrets (cf. Section II). The process is depicted in Figure 9.4. Tasks coloured in grey refer to tasks solely necessary in a DAP with a data recipient, while black coloured tasks are required in both, sole and delegated access scenarios.

Figure 9.4 Data Access Process ex Data Act

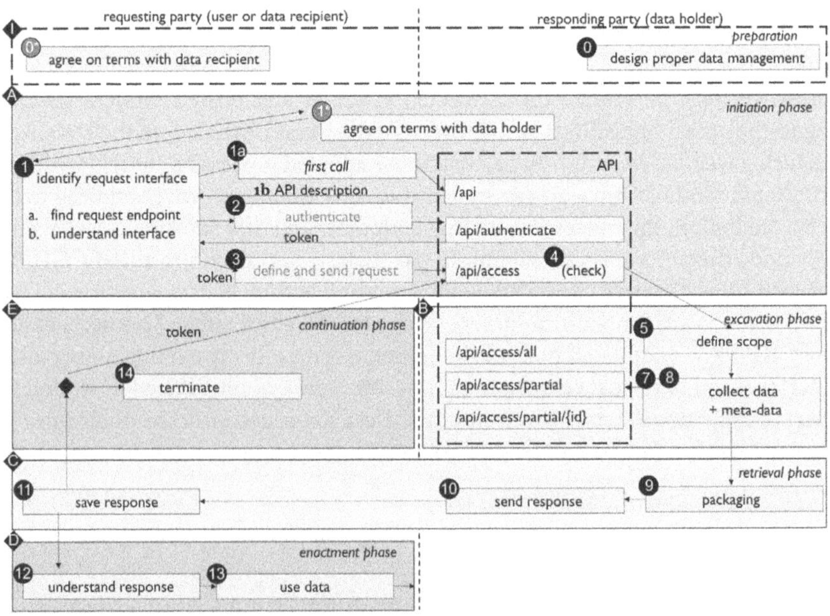

In contrast to the previous model, the Data Act DAP starts with a preparation phase (I), as the Data Act imposes the principle of *data access by design*, impacting the development of the connected product or related service. Hence, in contrast to on-demand access scenarios of the GDPR DAP, the internal systems of the data holder are already prepared for data provision. In particular, this means that the previous task 6, discovering the data sources, is replaced by an upstream task of carefully *designing proper data management* with data access in mind. This includes for example determining the data type(s) of collected data items and their storage locations. Moreover, if the access shall be delegated to a data recipient, the user needs to *agree on terms with the data recipient*.

Then, the initiation phase (A) starts like the GDPR DAP with the task of the requesting party to *identify the interface*. According to Article 3(2) of the Data Act, the data holder needs to inform the user about the access request modalities. Hence, the user can *identify the endpoint* of the interface by looking at the terms. Then, a first API call is made to retrieve the API description and the requesting party has to *familiarise with the interface*. In case the requesting party is the data recipient, the next task is to *negotiate terms between the data holder and the data recipient*.

Before *defining and sending the request*, the requesting party needs to be *authenticated*. The order of these tasks is switched in comparison with the general DAP because the access request is carried out as a call to the API, which, in turn, needs to be authorised and thus requires previous authentication.

Finally, the data holder receives the request via the API, *checks the request* for general validity and initiates the internal data excavation phase. The corresponding call to the internal system is defined in the interface and automatically triggered.

The next phase, the excavation phase (B), has changed the most from the GDPR to the Data Act-specific DAP due to task 0, design a proper data management. Hence, directly after *defining the objective scope* of the request, *the data items* and *corresponding meta-data* can be collected. Both tasks are combined, because with a careful data management with access in mind, the task of collecting all relevant data can be carried out with a single query.

Next, in the retrieval phase (C), the general tasks and their order have not changed between the GDPR DAP and the Data Act process. Still, the exported data needs to be *packaged*, now according to the format definitions in the Data Act, then *sent*, and finally *saved* by the requesting party. However, the underlying interface and communication channel have changed.

On a superficial level, the following enactment phase (D) also has not changed – the two tasks involved are still *understand response* and *use response*. However, on a semantic level the whole enactment phase is enhanced. Having a clearly defined API with information on expected response formats and content, and a response with meta-data, particularly including descriptions of the content, should facilitate the understanding and re-use of the data.

The newly introduced continuation phase (E) runs in parallel to phase D, as the access process under the Data Act goes into a loop. While it is not stopped, the DAP starts again, without the need of explicitly sending a new request. Moreover, some tasks might be faster in subsequent process runs. For example, in order to speed up task 7, collect the data items, the data holder might store the general scope of the request and the timestamp of the last iteration. Then, just the newly generated data has to be exported.

All three involved parties could *terminate* the DAP in this phase. The user can terminate the DAP at any point in time. In a delegated access scenario, the data recipient can stop the process, too. For the data holder, it is only possible to suspend the data sharing if trade secrets are affected by the access or the confidentiality of the response is no longer ensured.

IV. Technical Components in the Data Act DAP

A crucial point distinguishing data access under the Data Act from data portability is the *continuous, real-time* access mode. This transforms occasional data package flows into continuous data flows. Depending on the frequency with which IoT data is generated, this can result in constant data streams, event-driven, or repeated micro batch processing.[48] The envisioned data flow has an impact on the component designs. In the following, we highlight the impact of continuous processing on the technical components used in a Data Act DAP[49] (Figure 9.5).

Figure 9.5 Technical Components in a Data Act DAP

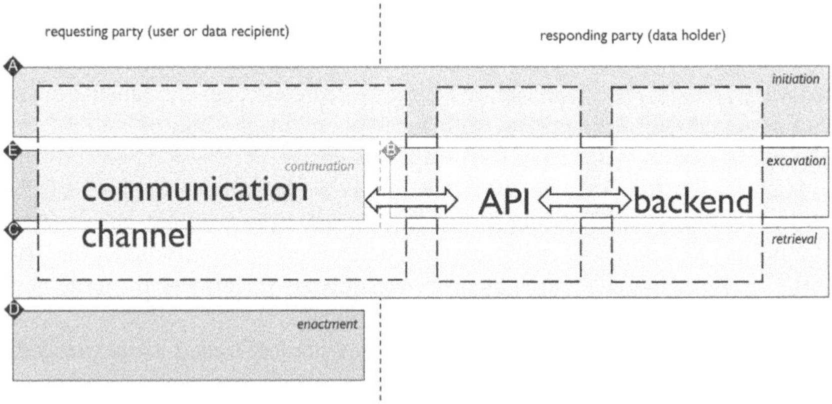

[48] Important for the Data Act definition of continuous and real-time access is the end-user view and not the computer systems view. Hence, sending data batches with an appropriate frequency is considered equal to a data stream.

[49] Note, that we look at a scenario where the data of connected devices is already transferred to the backend of the data holder. The interactions between connected devices and the data holder, and direct communication between the receiving parties and IoT devices are out of scope of this chapter.

A. Communication Channel: From Occasional Pickup to Continuous Flow

In contrast to occasional portability requests used for data portability, the communication component for data access under the Data Act needs to be able to handle stream-like data flows. The spectrum of stream-like data flows can be supported by different types of communication patterns. In a naïve synchronous approach, the request-response pattern used for occasional portability requests can just be repeated frequently. When adopting the paradigm of event-driven data flows, as generated by connected devices, a well-suited asynchronous communication pattern is publish-subscribe (pub-sub).

i. State-of-the-Art

To illuminate the spectrum of possible technical implementations (and without claiming comprehensiveness), we present one well-established implementation for each of the above-mentioned communication patterns, respectively. First, the request-response pattern can, for instance, be implemented using the commonly used and secure HTTPS[50] protocol. In the naïve setting, this can be implemented as frequent isolated request-response calls between the requesting party and the API. Such HTTPS-based communication is not only well-established in IoT scenarios,[51] but also widely used for data portability requests.[52] The pub-sub pattern, in turn, can for example be implemented with the MQTT[53] protocol.[54] However, MQTT messages are, per default, not encrypted. Hence, the specific MQTT implementation would need to add an additional, secure transport layer.[55]

ii. Challenges

Security and confidentiality are important to protect sensitive data included in an access request. The main security issues in stream-like communication regard authentication, authorisation, and confidentiality.

[50] HTTPS is the de-facto standard protocol used for encrypted transmission of data through the internet, eg used for websites, building on the Hyper Text Transfer Protocol, standardised by the IETF: https://datatracker.ietf.org/doc/html/rfc9110.

[51] Leonardo Babun et al, 'A Survey on IoT Platforms: Communication, Security, and Privacy Perspectives', *Computer Networks* 192 (2021): 108040.

[52] Leschke et al, 'Streamlining Personal Data Access Requests'.

[53] Message Queuing Telemetry Transport (MQTT) is a standard protocol for data transfer in IoT scenarios, introducing message brokers that broadcast published messages to a set of clients that subscribed to this kind of messages. Find the current standard here: https://docs.oasis-open.org/mqtt/mqtt/v5.0/mqtt-v5.0.html.

[54] Biswajeeban Mishra and Attila Kertesz, 'The Use of MQTT in M2M and IoT Systems: A Survey', *IEEE Access* 8 (2020): 201071–86.

[55] Sujitha Lakshminarayana, Amit Praseed, and P Santhi Thilagam, 'Securing the IoT Application Layer from an MQTT Protocol Perspective: Challenges and Research Prospects', *IEEE Communications Surveys & Tutorials* 26, no. 4 (2024): 2510–46.

First, the authentication of the data holder and the requesting party needs to be addressed, while the authentication of the requesting party is particularly critical. Users can, for instance, be authenticated through their user account. This includes at least a username and a password. However, in a continuous scenario, it is unsuitable to repeatedly ask for a password. Instead, it is more feasible to use access tokens generated upon a requesting party's initial authentication. To avoid token misuse, the token will have a limited live-time. Moreover, the token generation and validity span might need to be adopted to the shareability scenario. Here, two possible scenarios can be thought of: either the user generates a third party token and hands it over to the data recipient, or there needs to be an authentication process specifically tailored to authorised data recipients.

On the basis of the authentication, the requesting party needs to be authorised, ie the permissions to access specific resources are given. In particular, advanced token-based access control mechanisms can be used to address this challenge.[56] Still, the question of revocation of the token in case the user ends the sharing remains.

Finally, confidentiality in stream-like communication imposes additional challenges. In case the communication is HTTP-based, it must at least use encrypted connections, ie implement HTTPS. However, in event-driven architectures, message meta-data could also reveal confidential knowledge, particularly via timestamps or time-observed communication. Hence, the confidentiality of the message meta-data also needs to be preserved, for example through message indirection[57] or message delay.[58]

iii. Interrelations

The communication channel is the connection between the requesting party and the API of the data holder. That is, the communication channel needs to be known by the requesting party upfront. This is ensured by Article 3(2) letter b of the Data Act, which demands the data holder to communicate the access request modalities. Moreover, the chosen communication pattern has impact on the API design, which is introduced in the following section.

B. Interface: From Unstructured Web Requests to Structured APIs

As elaborated on in section III, continuous and real-time data access requests demand for well-defined and automated interfaces, contrasting standard GDPR

[56] Timothy Claeys, Franck Rousseau, and Bernard Tourancheau, 'Securing Complex IoT Platforms with Token Based Access Control and Authenticated Key Establishment', *2017 International Workshop on Secure Internet of Things*, 2017, 1–9.

[57] Lein Harn, Chingfang Hsu, and Zhe Xia, 'Mix Broadcast Network with User Untraceability for Resource-Constrained IoT', *IEEE Sensors Letters* 5, no. 9 (2021): 1–4.

[58] Wenjing Lou, Wei Liu, and Yuguang Fang, 'SPREAD: Enhancing Data Confidentiality in Mobile Ad Hoc Networks', *IEEE INFOCOM 2004* 4 (2004): 2404–13.

practices of free text requests via e-mail or web forms.[59] Hence, the interface has to be a structured API. Web APIs exposed to external parties (like users and data recipients) should be self-describing to allow for smooth and low-friction use. Of those API techniques meeting this requirement, REST and gRPC are commonly used. In the following, the API design considerations are exemplarily shown with both API technologies in their original, pure form. Other common API techniques, like for example Websockets, WS*, or GraphQL, follow similar principles and are therefore not discussed explicitly.

i. State-of-the-Art

RESTful APIs are based on HTTP(S) and aligned to the operations offered by the HTTP protocol, therefore, they are developer friendly. Hence, they are very common in IoT.[60] In particular, the commonly employed data exchange formats are well-known, like JSON or XML. Moreover, they are easy to extend and to maintain due to their 'loosely coupled' nature. In contrast, gRPC-based APIs are tightly coupled, ie, the requesting party and the data holder/API need to know the request specification in the Protobuf format. Protobuf is specifically designed for gRPC and encapsulates endpoints into a well-defined format. However, this format is not as commonly used as the exchange formats usually employed by REST APIs. Under the Protobuf abstraction layer, gRPC is based on HTTP 2.0 and particularly suited for streaming scenarios with high frequency data and bidirectional data streams.

ii. Challenges

In general, API calls need to be restricted to authorised parties only. Hence, on top of the tokens generated by the authentication mechanism of the communication channel, the API needs to deal with authorisation and access control. Primarily, specific API endpoints should only be queryable by legitimate requesting parties. This can be ensured by implementing token-based access control mechanisms.[61] On top of that, advanced access control measures can be implemented to enforce the terms and to ensure the confidentiality of the requested data. Such access models include, in particular, purpose-based access control,[62] attribute-based access control,[63] or advanced usage control.[64]

[59] Leschke et al, 'Streamlining Personal Data Access Requests: From Obstructive Procedures to Automated Web Workflows'.

[60] Mahda Noura, Mohammed Atiquzzaman, and Martin Gaedke, 'Interoperability in Internet of Things: Taxonomies and Open Challenges', *Mobile Networks and Applications* 24 (2019): 796–809.

[61] Pierangela Samarati and Sabrina De Capitani de Vimercati, 'Access Control: Policies, Models, and Mechanisms', *Foundations of Security Analysis and Design* (Berlin: Springer, 2001), 137–96.

[62] Karl Wolf, Frank Pallas, and Stefan Tai, 'Messaging with Purpose Limitation – Privacy-Compliant Publish-Subscribe Systems', *2021 IEEE 25th International Enterprise Distributed Object Computing Conference*, 2021, 162–72.

[63] Vincent C Hu et al, 'Attribute-Based Access Control', *Computer* 48, no. 2 (2015): 85–88.

[64] Aliaksandr Lazouski, Fabio Martinelli, and Paolo Mori, 'Usage Control in Computer Security: A Survey', *Computer Science Review* 4, no. 2 (2010): 81–99.

Moreover, the frequency and scalability of API calls needs to be considered. Specifically, developers need to think about the frequency of API calls to be expected and the envisioned number of simultaneous requests to define the performance requirements of the API. Noteworthily, a single user could authorise multiple data recipients to make repeated (continuous) access requests. In addition, in the envisioned scenario where the API is hosted at the data holder's side and not on-device, there might be many simultaneous user requests.

iii. Interrelations

The API is the interface between the requesting party and the data holder. Hence, it influences all other components. In particular, it interrelates with the data holder's backend and depends, for example, on the respective frequency of data generation. However, a malformed API with no semantic descriptions of the endpoints could have a negative impact on the whole DAP. Extensive API descriptions are crucial to understand the expected responses and to allow for data reusability.

C. Backend: From Ad-hoc Excavation to Automated Data Retrieval

While the backend is the most specific part of the data access components, it is also the component that is impacted by the data access by design obligations most.[65] In this section, the aim is to discuss the effects of the Data Act under the hood of the backend, but not to discuss specific implementations. In contrast to GDPR access and portability requests, which are often fulfilled on top of pre-existing infrastructures that evolved over time, connected products and related services must necessarily be designed with data access in mind. Hence, previously ad-hoc processes of discovering data storage locations and for formulating access requests on the fly are now replaced by an upstream task of designing the means of data management properly.

i. State-of-the-Art

For rather static systems the data model and fixed storage locations can be manually designed and documented. However, this is infeasible for evolving or complex systems. In case the backend itself operates in a streaming fashion, where the data is not necessarily stored but directly consumed and processed, the data model is implicit. Still, the internal data model needs to be defined such that data items

[65] As the backend holds the business logic of a service, it is specific to the IoT product or related service. However, as delineated in section III.B.ii, the upfront task 0 leads to significant changes in backend design.

within the scope are forwarded to the API for immediate provision to the requesting party.[66]

ii. Challenges

The most difficult task in the continuous provision is the automated definition of the request's scope. Besides the data source, the data model particularly has to include for every item an indicator whether this item conveys trade secrets or personal data. For requesting parties, the requester's role (user/data recipient) needs to be known. Then, based on pre-defined rules, it can be determined which data items are in scope of this specific access request.

However, the definition of the scope of access under the Data Act shall not interfere with the GDPR rights. While data access by design might also be beneficial for other access obligations, the definition of the request's scope needs to be adopted to the obligations of the specific regulation. This reinforces the need to have a complete data model and to not only manage the data affected by the Data Act.

While interoperability of the exported data is neither demanded by Article 4 nor Article 5 of the Data Act, it summarises all challenges related to the provision of data that is actually re-usable by the requesting party. Interoperability can be reached on different levels,[67] including the semantic layer. As mentioned in the previous section, semantic interoperability can be reached through extensive description of the data item's meaning, eg with the help of semantic web technologies for IoT.[68]

Lastly, for the provision of the exported data it will be necessary to narrow down the data formats fulfilling the Data Act obligations. While regulatory considerations on the formats are given in section II, it remains to be seen how these obligations are interpreted in practice.

iii. Interrelations

Automated processing in the backend is crucial for the continuous, real-time provision of data items. This is enabled by data access by design and upstream design of proper internal data models. However, without the provision of interoperable data exports, the reusability of the exported data items remains limited.

[66] Nesime Tatbul, 'Streaming Data Integration: Challenges and Opportunities', *2010 IEEE 26th International Conference on Data Engineering Workshops*, 2010, 155–58.

[67] Susanna Pantsar-Syväniemi et al, 'Situation-Based and Self-Adaptive Applications for the Smart Environment', *Journal of Ambient Intelligence and Smart Environments* 4, no. 6 (2012): 491–516.

[68] Andrea Cimmino, María Poveda-Villalón, and Raúl García-Castro, 'Ontologies and Semantic Interoperability', in *Springer Handbook of Internet of Things* (Cham: Springer, 2024), 407–25.

V. General Observations and Implications

This multidisciplinary perspective on the right of access *ex* Data Act, and the related obligation to render data accessible in a by-design fashion, proposes potential options on its technical implementation and enforcement. Compared with access and portability in the GDPR, in the Data Act the right of access integrates portability features as ingrained in the GDPR despite changing not only scope and formats of data, but requiring a process model relying on continuous and real-time access to data. This section provides a holistic view of the implications of the DAP *ex* Data Act for the roles introduced in section II: the data holder, the user, and the data recipient.

For data holders, the principle of data access by design relocates the task of discovering implicit data models tailored *ad hoc* for data shareability/portability requests upfront, to the product/service design phase. This impacts not only the design and implementation of the technical components analysed in section IV. In particular, the aim of providing requested data and corresponding meta-data to the requesting party in a quality that allows the re-use of data depends on the ability of the internal systems to automatically discover relevant data items and generate expressive descriptions. However, even in a single data holder's system the vocabulary to describe IoT (service) data might be very heterogeneous.[69] Consequently, the maintenance of a holistic semantically well-aligned data model ready for data export remains challenging. Moreover, the task of defining the request scope needs to be automatically performed by the backend system. While an automated system can never replace a legal analysis on a case-by-case basis, it is expected that some rule-based guidelines will facilitate this task. To this end, the EDPB and national Data Protection Authorities could assist in this effort and, with their advisory role, provide guidance on defining different scopes of specific access requests.

While the need to provide a public API is new to the DAP, it is already a well-established practice for connected services, and stream-like communication is already at the core of IoT designs. Consequently, the changes to these components go beyond the GDPR process, but are in alignment with IoT practices. Lastly, the newly introduced tasks of negotiating sharing conditions and the verification of confidentiality measures taken at the requesting party's also call for novel procedures.

For the user, with data access by design, obstructive access procedures are streamlined and with the provision of meta-data, the understandability of the data shall be enhanced. Hence, the data can be re-used in new contexts, thereby creating additional value. However, it remains to be seen if the new obligations

[69] Anderson Luis Szejka et al, 'Semantic Interoperability for an Integrated Product Development Process: A Systematic Literature Review', *International Journal of Production Research* 55, no. 22 (2017): 6691–709.

introduced in the Data Act effectively foster the users' right to access. In particular, the following challenges might still preclude users from exercising their right.

The continuous, real-time access mode fosters automation, which is only possible with machine-readability of the data and the access interface. In addition, the continuity also speaks against explicit human involvement in every act of data (re-)use. Instead, we expect automated technical tools on the side of users for Article 4 Data Act data access, too.

On top of the actual access process, data holders might ask the users to implement technical and organisational measures to protect the confidentiality of trade secrets and personal data. Hence, it must be known before the data access request to both the requesting party and the data holder, if the response is expected to include such sensitive data. At the same time, it cannot be expected that users implement and maintain advanced security measures. To what extent user-side precautions are actually to be considered demandable remains to be seen.

For the data recipient,[70] the main difference to a data portability scenario is the active role in the Data Act DAP. The automated processes are specifically tailored to data recipients that can automatically re-use the data. In particular, the obligation to provide not only the data, but also relevant meta-data to interpret and use those data, is a regulatory novelty that might have far-reaching implications, including a wider use of semantic technologies. However, without interoperability standards, the recipients need to implement translators for every data holder.[71]

Moreover, as the exported data may also convey trade secrets, the Data Act imposes additional safeguards to protect the commercial interests of data holders. In particular, the data recipient is not allowed to use the accessed data to gain insights about the data holders services, particularly not to develop or enhance competitive products/services.

In this regard, the data recipients have to prove the deployment of technical and organisational measures to protect the confidentiality of the exported data, as well as the compliance to the terms agreed with the user. In particular, this includes performing explicit risk assessments and aligning with standards such as ISO 27001, and on the technical side, stream- and IoT-specific confidentiality measures[72] will foreseeably play a particular role.

[70] Note that the data recipient is likely to provide a connected product or related service, too. Hence, given that data recipients themselves fall under the scope of the Data Act, they become data holders with all obligations imposed by data access by design.

[71] Such an architecture is, for example, implemented by the Data Transfer Initiative: https://dtinit.org/.

[72] Emanuel Onica et al, 'Confidentiality/Preserving Publish/Subscribe: A Survey', *ACM Computing Surveys* (New York) 49, no. 2 (2016); Frank Pallas et al, 'Redcastle: Practically Applicable Ks-Anonymity for IoT Streaming Data at the Edge in Node-Red', *Proceedings of the 8th International Workshop on Middleware and Applications for the Internet of Things*, 2021, 8–13; Poornima M Chanal and Mahabaleshwar S Kakkasageri, 'Preserving Data Confidentiality in Internet of Things', *SN Computer Science* 2, no. 1 (2021): 53.

VI. Conclusion

In the Data Act, data access by design goes way beyond existing data access and data portability rights as delaminated in the GDPR. The chapter provided a first discussion basis for further research on the enforcement of the right to access *ex* Data Act, as well as on how to make the trade-off between the right to access IoT and related services data of the user and the right to protect commercially valuable information of the data holder.

Moreover, and without claiming completeness, the chapter demonstrated the technical feasibility of the continuous, real-time mode of *data access by design*, envisaged in the Data Act. With a procedural approach that translated legal provisions into technical implications and challenges, the chapter provided an intermediate step of modelling a DAP *ex* Data Act.

By and large, the Data Act's newly introduced paradigm of continuous real-time access by design challenges concepts and technical designs, calling for completely novel approaches. The sooner manufacturers of connected devices and providers of complementary services recognise this need and adopt to the changed givens, the better will they be prepared for the paradigm shift that lies ahead.

Acknowledgements

Emanuela Podda's and Pierangela Samarati's work has been supported in part by the EC under project GLACIATION (101070141), by the Italian MUR under PRIN project POLAR (2022LA8XBH), and by project SERICS (PE00000014) under the MUR NRRP funded by the EU – NGEU. Nicola Leschke's and Frank Pallas's work has been supported by the EXDIGIT (Excellence in Digital Sciences and Interdisciplinary Technologies) project, funded by Land Salzburg under grant number 20204-WISS/263/6-6022.

Bibliography

Article 29 Data Protection Working Party. *Guidelines on the Right to Data Portability*. 2017. https://ec.europa.eu/newsroom/article29/items/611233.

Atzori, Luigi, Antonio Iera, and Giacomo Morabito. 'The Internet of Things: A Survey'. *Computer Networks* 54, no. 15 (2010): 2787–805.

Babun, Leonardo, Kyle Denney, Z Berkay Celik, Patrick McDaniel, and A Selcuk Uluagac. 'A Survey on IoT Platforms: Communication, Security, and Privacy Perspectives'. *Computer Networks* 192 (2021): 108040.

Board, European Data Protection. *2024 Coordinated Enforcement Action Implementation of the Right of Access by Controllers*. 2025. www.edpb.europa.eu/system/files/2025-01/edpb_cef-report-2024_20250116_rightofaccess_en.pdf.

Guidelines 01/2022 on Data Subject Rights – Right of Access. 2023. www.edpb.europa.eu/system/files/2023-04/edpb_guidelines_202201_data_subject_rights_access_v2_en.pdf.

Chanal, Poornima M, and Mahabaleshwar S Kakkasageri. 'Preserving Data Confidentiality in Internet of Things'. *SN Computer Science* 2, no. 1 (2021): 53.

Cimmino, Andrea, María Poveda-Villalón, and Raúl García-Castro. 'Ontologies and Semantic Interoperability'. In *Springer Handbook of Internet of Things*, edited by Sébastien Ziegler, Renáta Radócz, Adrian Quesada Rodriguez, and Sara Nieves Matheu Garcia. Cham: Springer, 2024.

Claeys, Timothy, Franck Rousseau, and Bernard Tourancheau. 'Securing Complex IoT Platforms with Token Based Access Control and Authenticated Key Establishment'. *2017 International Workshop on Secure Internet of Things*, 2017, 1–9.

De Hert, Paul, Vagelis Papakonstantinou, Gianclaudio Malgieri, Laurent Beslay, and Ignacio Sanchez. 'The Right to Data Portability in the GDPR: Towards User-Centric Interoperability of Digital Services'. *Computer Law & Security Review* 34, no. 2 (2018): 193–203.

European Commission. *Commission Staff Working Document, Impact Assessment Report Accompanying the Document Proposal for a Regulation of the European Parliament and of the Council on Harmonised Rules on Fair Access to and Use of Data (Data Act) SWD(2022) 34 Final Shaping Europe's Digital Future*. European Commission, 2022.

European Commission. *Communication from the Commission to the European Parliament and the Council, Guidance on the Regulation on a Framework for the Free Flow of Non-Personal Data in the European Union*. European Commission, 2019.

Finck, Michèle, and Frank Pallas. 'They Who Must Not Be Identified – Distinguish/Ing Personal from Non-Personal Data Under the GDPR'. *International Data Privacy Law* 10, no. 1 (2020): 11–36.

Hansen, Malte, and Meiko Jensen. 'A Generic Data Model for Implementing Right of Access Requests'. In *Privacy Technologies and Policy*, edited by Agnieszka Gryszczyńska, Przemysław Polański, Nils Gruschka, Kai Rannenberg, and Monika Adamczyk. Cham: Springer, 2022.

Harn, Lein, Chingfang Hsu, and Zhe Xia. 'Mix Broadcast Network with User Untraceability for Resource-Constrained IoT'. *IEEE Sensors Letters* 5, no. 9 (2021): 1–4.

Hu, Vincent C, D Richard Kuhn, David F Ferraiolo, and Jeffrey Voas. 'Attribute-Based Access Control'. *Computer* 48, no. 2 (2015): 85–88.

Kuebler-Wachendorff, Sophie, Robert Luzsa, Johann Kranz, et al. 'The Right to Data Portability: Conception, Status Quo, and Future Directions'. *Informatik Spektrum* 44, no. 4 (2021): 264–72.

Kuebler-Wachendorff, Sophie, Robert Luzsa, Johann Kranz, et al. 'The Right to Data Portability: Conception, Status Quo, and Future Directions'. *Informatik Spektrum* 44, no. 4 (2021): 273–73.

Lakshminarayana, Sujitha, Amit Praseed, and P Santhi Thilagam. 'Securing the IoT Application Layer from an MQTT Protocol Perspective: Challenges and Research Prospects'. *IEEE Communications Surveys & Tutorials* 26, no. 4 (2024): 2510–46.

Lazarotto, Barbara. 'The Right to Data Portability: A Holistic Analysis of GDPR, DMA and the Data Act'. *European Journal of Law and Technology* 15, no. 1 (2024).

Lazouski, Aliaksandr, Fabio Martinelli, and Paolo Mori. 'Usage Control in Computer Security: A Survey'. *Computer Science Review* 4, no. 2 (2010): 81–99.

Leschke, Nicola, Florian Kirsten, Frank Pallas, and Elias Grünewald. 'Streamlining Personal Data Access Requests: From Obstructive Procedures to Automated Web Workflows'. *Web Engineering* 13893 (2023): 111–25.

Li, Shancang, Li Da Xu, and Shanshan Zhao. 'The Internet of Things: A Survey'. *Information Systems Frontiers* 17, no. 2 (2015): 243–59.

Lou, Wenjing, Wei Liu, and Yuguang Fang. 'SPREAD: Enhancing Data Confidentiality in Mobile Ad Hoc Networks'. *IEEE INFOCOM 2004* 4 (2004): 2404–13.

Lynskey, Orla. 'Article 20 Right to Data Portability'. In *The EU General Data Protection Regulation (GDPR): A Commentary*, edited by Christopher Kuner, Lee A Bygrave, Christopher Docksey, and Laura Drechsler. Oxford: Oxford University Press, 2020.

Malgieri, Gianclaudio. 'Property and (Intellectual) Ownership of Consumers' Information: A New Taxonomy for Personal Data'. *Privacy in Germany* 4, no. 133 (2016).

Mishra, Biswajeeban, and Attila Kertesz. 'The Use of MQTT in M2M and IoT Systems: A Survey'. *IEEE Access* 8 (2020): 201071–86.

Mylly, Ulla-Maija. 'Trade Secrets and the Data Act'. *International Review of Intellectual Property and Competition Law* 55, no. 3 (2024): 368–93.

Noura, Mahda, Mohammed Atiquzzaman, and Martin Gaedke. 'Interoperability in Internet of Things: Taxonomies and Open Challenges'. *Mobile Networks and Applications* 24 (2019): 796–809.

Olivé, Antoni. 'Introduction'. In *Conceptual Modeling of Information Systems*. Berlin: Springer, 2007.

Onica, Emanuel, Pascal Felber, Hugues Mercier, and Etienne Rivière. 'Confidentiality/Preserving Publish/Subscribe: A Survey'. *ACM Computing Surveys* (New York) 49, no. 2 (2016).

Pallas, Frank, Julian Legler, Niklas Amslgruber, and Elias Grünewald. 'Redcastle: Practically Applicable Ks-Anonymity for IoT Streaming Data at the Edge in Node-Red'. *Proceedings of the 8th International Workshop on Middleware and Applications for the Internet of Things*, 2021, 8–13.

Pantsar-Syväniemi, Susanna, Anu Purhonen, Eila Ovaska, Jarkko Kuusijärvi, and Antti Evesti. 'Situation-Based and Self-Adaptive Applications for the Smart Environment'. *Journal of Ambient Intelligence and Smart Environments* 4, no. 6 (2012): 491–516.

Pins, Dominik, Timo Jakobi, Gunnar Stevens, Fatemeh Alizadeh, and Jana Krüger. 'Finding, Getting and Understanding: The User Journey for the GDPR's Right to Access'. *Behaviour & Information Technology* 41, no. 10 (2022): 2174–200.

Podda, Emanuela. 'Anonymization of Personal Data (Legal Perspective)'. In *Encyclopedia of Cryptography, Security and Privacy*, edited by Sushil Jajodia, Pierangela Samarati, and Moti Yung. Berlin: Springer, 2024.

Samarati, Pierangela, and Sabrina De Capitani de Vimercati. 'Access Control: Policies, Models, and Mechanisms'. In *Foundations of Security Analysis and Design*, edited by Riccardo Focardi and Roberto Gorrieri. Berlin: Springer, 2001.

Szejka, Anderson Luis, Osiris Canciglieri Jr, Hervé Panetto, Eduardo Rocha Loures, and Alexis Aubry. 'Semantic Interoperability for an Integrated Product Development Process: A Systematic Literature Review'. *International Journal of Production Research* 55, no. 22 (2017): 6691–709.

Tatbul, Nesime. 'Streaming Data Integration: Challenges and Opportunities'. *2010 IEEE 26th International Conference on Data Engineering Workshops*, 2010, 155–58.

Turner, Sarah, July Galindo Quintero, Simon Turner, Jessica Lis, and Leonie Maria Tanczer. 'The Exercisability of the Right to Data Portability in the Emerging Internet of Things (IoT) Environment'. *New Media & Society* 23, no. 10 (2021): 2861–81.

Turner, Sarah, and Leonie Maria Tanczer. '*In Principle* Vs *in Practice*: User, Expert and Policymaker Attitudes Towards the Right to Data Portability in the Internet of Things'. *Computer Law & Security Review* 52 (2024): 105912.

Wolf, Karl, Frank Pallas, and Stefan Tai. 'Messaging with Purpose Limitation – Privacy-Compliant Publish-Subscribe Systems'. *2021 IEEE 25th International Enterprise Distributed Object Computing Conference*, 2021, 162–72.

Wong, Janis, and Tristan Henderson. 'The Right to Data Portability in Practice: Exploring the Implications of the Technologically Neutral GDPR'. *International Data Privacy Law* 9, no. 3 (2019): 173–91.

PART 3

Practitioners' Corner

10

Unlocking DPO Happiness: Strategies for C-Level Executives and DPOs

PETER BERGHMANS AND JOLIEN GHYSELINCK

Abstract

How can organisations and Data Protection Officers (DPOs) work together to strengthen the DPO's critical function? A 2023 cross-sector survey identified five key determinants of DPO happiness and effectiveness: autonomy; positive relationships and collaboration; opportunities for growth and development; recognition and acknowledgement; and adequate resources. During CPDP.ai 2025, a dedicated DPO track curated by Peter Berghmans and Jolien Ghyselinck aimed to bridge practice and theory, connect DPOs with their organisations, and foster dialogue with academia. Building on the 2023 survey findings and insights from the DPO track's panels and workshops, this chapter proposes practical strategies to enhance DPO effectiveness through structural and cultural reforms within organisations.

Keywords

Data Protection Officers; Survey; Happiness and Effectiveness; Practice; Cooperation

At the 2025 edition of CPDP.ai, a significant milestone was reached: for the first time, the conference featured a dedicated track for DPOs. Through a series of interactive workshops and insightful panel discussions, experts explored the evolving challenges and opportunities facing DPOs across sectors. A recurring theme throughout these sessions was the complexity of the DPO's role in practice – both as a guardian of compliance and as a strategic actor within the organisation.

One particularly thought-provoking insight came from panellist Hielke Heymans, who captured the core tension at the heart of the DPO position:

> GDPR mandates that the DPO should not receive instructions and should be independent. Yet, for this independence to be meaningful, the DPO must also be effective. Effectiveness means having influence, which is why the GDPR requires access to top

> management. However, influence and independence are sometimes at odds. If you are too independent, no one listens. If you are too close to management, independence is compromised. There's a continuous balancing act, making the DPO role complex.[1]

This 'balancing act' is not just a theoretical dilemma. In practice, it reflects the daily reality of DPOs navigating between regulatory independence and organisational influence. Too much distance, and the DPO risks being marginalised. Too much integration, and their impartiality may be questioned. Meanwhile, organisations are increasingly aware that the effectiveness of the DPO is not only a legal necessity under the GDPR, but also a strategic asset – capable of enhancing trust, strengthening governance, and enabling responsible innovation. During CPDP.ai 2025, participants revisited a study of the French data protection authority CNIL (Commission nationale de l'informatique et des libertés) that highlighted the economic benefits of having a well-functioning DPO, ranging from improved corporate reputation to better access to data-driven business networks.[2]

Hence, how can companies and DPOs work together to strengthen this critical function – one that must remain both independent and influential? This chapter sets out to answer that question by directly addressing the tension highlighted by Heymans. We do so by exploring what an optimal balance between *influence* and *independence* looks like in practice – and how it can be actively shaped through deliberate organisational choices. Drawing on a 2023 study that surveyed DPOs across sectors,[3] we identify five core conditions that determine DPO satisfaction and effectiveness: autonomy; positive relationships and cooperation; opportunities for development; recognition and acknowledgement; and adequate resources. Each of these elements reflects deeper structural and cultural dynamics that affect the DPO's ability to function effectively and independently.

Building on these insights, this chapter presents a strategic playbook – offering concrete action points designed to strengthen the DPO function in a sustainable and balanced way. Each action is examined from two perspectives: that of the DPO, and that of the organisation. This dual approach aims to foster mutual understanding and shared responsibility in promoting data protection. Rather than treating the DPO as a compliance silo, this article advocates for a collaborative, integrated approach. By aligning organisational structures and cultures with the needs of DPOs, companies can foster a data protection environment that is not only legally compliant, but also resilient, adaptive, and human-centred. The remainder of this chapter is structured along five key action points of that playbook, followed by a reflection and conclusion:

I. **Promoting role clarity**: Establishing well-defined expectations and boundaries around the DPO role.

[1] Hielke Heymans, "The DPO Universales Crossing Borders on a Bumpy Road" (panel contribution, Computers, Privacy & Data Protection Conference, Brussels, 22 May 2025), available at https://www.youtube.com/watch?v=Hv5RxnRmbOw (accessed 1 September 2025).

[2] Commission Nationale de l'informatique et des libertés (CNIL), 'What are the economic benefits of having a DPO for a company?', 8 September 2025, available at https://www.cnil.fr/en/what-are-economic-benefits-having-dpo-company.

[3] Data Protection Institute, *Are DPOs Happy?* Version 13, 2023 (DP Institute, March 2024), www.dp-institute.eu/wp-content/uploads/2024/03/Zijn-DPOs-gelukkig_V13_EN.pdf.

II. **Embedding DPO independence into organisational structures**: Ensuring structural safeguards that protect the DPO's autonomy.
III. **Cultivating continuous learning and adaptation**: Encouraging professional development and responsiveness to regulatory change.
IV. **Fostering cooperation**: Building constructive relationships with key stakeholders across the organisation.
V. **Ensuring adequate resources**: Providing the necessary tools, time, and support for the DPO to do their job effectively.

I. Promoting Role Clarity

A substantial number of DPOs remain unsure if their role is adequately known within their organisation, this lack of visibility and recognition is particularly pronounced among DPOs in government organisations (especially law enforcement) and among those new to the role.[4] This disconnect is crucial: while DPOs are performing valuable work, its value or even its existence may not be adequately recognised or understood by the wider organisation. This could stem from a failure in internal communication, where the DPO's efforts and impact are not effectively conveyed to key stakeholders or the broader workforce.

To address this, C-level executives must proactively strive to clarify the precise scope of DPO tasks. This ensures that responsibilities align with legally defined duties and prevents DPOs from inadvertently performing tasks that rightfully belong to the data controller or processor. C-level executives should ensure that job descriptions for DPOs are clear and unambiguous, differentiating between advisory and operational roles. They should also provide guidance to department heads on when and how to engage with the DPO, establishing clear lines of communication and responsibility. Junior DPOs, in particular, often report experiencing unclear responsibilities. They are sometimes asked to undertake tasks typically assigned to the data controller or processor, such as drafting Data Protection Impact Assessments (DPIAs), rather than focusing on providing advisory input or monitoring data protection compliance. More experienced DPOs, conversely, appear more inclined to delineate their tasks in relation to those of the data controller or processor.

In tandem, DPOs must proactively communicate both their responsibilities and the tangible outcomes of their work to controllers and processors. This involves designing data protection programs with clear, measurable objectives that align with broader organisational goals, ensuring their contributions are both visible and quantifiable. These objectives should be regularly monitored and reported on, thereby demonstrating the concrete value and impact of the DPO's work. For example, a DPO might track the reduction in data breaches following

[4] Data Protection Institute, *Are DPOs Happy?*

the implementation of new policies or highlight the successful completion of DPIAs for new products. By articulating their value in a way that resonates with organisational priorities, DPOs can help foster a culture where data protection is fully integrated and genuinely appreciated.

Additionally, DPOs – especially those new to the role – should take initiative in seeking clarity around their responsibilities and should not hesitate to set boundaries when asked to perform tasks outside their advisory mandate. They should also take an active role in educating internal stakeholders on the distinct responsibilities of the DPO, the data controller, and the data processor to prevent misunderstandings and ensure compliance.

II. Embedding DPO Independence into Organisational Structures

Autonomy and independence are not just advantageous for the role of the DPO – they are legal requirements. These principles empower DPOs to perform their duties without interference or external pressure. The DPO Happiness Study of 2023[5] shows that the majority of DPOs feel free to carry out their responsibilities. However, a different picture emerges among more experienced DPOs: they report higher levels of pressure, including threats of dismissal or the withholding of information. This presents a paradox. With their deeper understanding of the GDPR and internal organisational dynamics, experienced DPOs are often more confident in offering firm advice and more likely to identify or challenge non-compliant practices. As a result, they may encounter greater resistance or friction from management or other departments.

C-level executives have a crucial role in safeguarding the DPO's independence. This involves creating a culture where the DPO's advice, even when challenging, is respected and considered thoughtfully. Executives should publicly affirm the DPO's independent status and establish clear reporting lines that minimise potential conflicts of interest.

DPOs, for their part, must actively assert and maintain their independence. This involves clearly communicating the boundaries of their role and the legal basis for their advice, even when it might be met with resistance. They should consistently document their recommendations and any instances where their advice is not followed, creating a transparent record that reinforces their independent position. They should also proactively communicate their duties and the results of their work to controllers and processors to enhance recognition and preserve their autonomy.

[5] Data Protection Institute, *Are DPOs Happy?*

By consistently demonstrating the value of their independent assessments and the risks associated with non-compliance, DPOs can strengthen their position within the organisation. Furthermore, DPOs must remain acutely aware of and adapt to ever-evolving scientific, technological, economic, political, legal, environmental, moral, and social changes. Viewing these shifts as opportunities for further education and active engagement within their networks will be essential for their continued effectiveness and well-being. This continuous learning helps DPOs to provide confident and accurate advice, thereby bolstering their independent standing.

III. Cultivating Continuous Learning and Adaptation

The dynamic nature of data protection necessitates a steadfast commitment to continuous learning and adaptation from both DPOs and the organisations they serve. The DPO role is not static; it is undergoing continuous transformation in response to a rapidly changing global landscape, influenced by significant evolutions in different domains. This continuous evolution demands that DPOs not only stay abreast of current regulations but also anticipate future challenges and adapt their expertise accordingly.

C-level executives play a pivotal role in fostering a culture of continuous learning by providing readily accessible and high-quality training opportunities for their DPOs. The vast majority of DPOs have a bachelor's degree or higher, and an equally high percentage have received specific training for the DPO role. The study emphatically highlights that training and education exert a 'great impact on the DPO's happiness'.[6] This is largely due to the intricate technical and legal aspects of the GDPR, which can be significantly challenging without specialised guidance. Therefore, executives should view investment in DPO training not as a mere compliance cost, but as a strategic investment in the organisation's overall data protection posture and the DPO's effectiveness and retention. This involves allocating dedicated budgets for ongoing professional development. This includes specialised courses on emerging technologies like AI, advanced cybersecurity measures, and new legal frameworks. Executives should also encourage DPOs to attend relevant conferences and workshops, facilitating their access to cutting-edge knowledge and networking opportunities. As the study shows, this also increases the happiness of the DPOs.

DPOs, for their part, must prioritise continuous learning through specific data protection training, as it significantly contributes to their happiness and confidence in navigating the complexities of GDPR compliance. This involves actively seeking out and engaging in specific training programs that address both current and anticipated challenges in data protection. They should embrace external

[6] Data Protection Institute, *Are DPOs Happy?*

review, seek inspiration from diverse sources, and utilise professional networks as a sounding board, which are all crucial for providing realistic and confident advice. During CPDP.ai 2025 this proved notably important for DPOs in law enforcement, where the EDEN Network strives to enhance a culture of support and information sharing amongst those DPOs.[7]

IV. Fostering Cooperation

Cooperation stands out as a paramount element for the well-being of the DPO, yet the landscape of these experiences remains varied, highlighting a critical area for concerted action from both C-level executives and DPOs themselves. A significant majority of DPOs experience feelings of isolation in their daily tasks, particularly those operating alone.[8] This sense of isolation is not merely a personal discomfort; it extends to the level of support DPOs perceive from organisational management and their cooperation with internal departments.

C-level executives bear a significant responsibility in cultivating an environment that champions cooperation and mitigates the isolation often experienced by DPOs. Their commitment has to include ensuring that DPOs hold appropriate authority within the organisational structure and promoting a culture that values collaboration over siloed operations. Executives should take deliberate steps to integrate the DPO into cross-departmental initiatives, where their insights are not only welcomed, but also embedded into strategic decision-making processes. This could involve structured, recurring meetings between the DPO and department heads to evaluate new projects with a data protection lens from the outset, rather than as an afterthought. Similarly, the DPO's participation in broader organisational strategy discussions should be normalised, recognising the strategic value that privacy and data governance bring to innovation and risk management.

For their part, DPOs must proactively engage in seeking and maintaining contact with all internal stakeholders and collaborating with internal experts such as (Chief) Information Security Officers ((C)ISOs). Such engagement serves as a vital 'sounding board', effectively mitigating feelings of isolation and offering invaluable opportunities for shared problem-solving and the validation of experiences. Cultivating robust cooperative relationships with all individuals involved in personal data processing is paramount to achieving a crucial integration of the tasks of the DPO. DPOs can initiate regular informal catchups with colleagues from various departments to demonstrate how data protection can be an enabler rather than a hindrance. They should actively participate in internal working

[7] The European Data Protection in Law Enforcement Network (EDEN) is a professional community supported by Europol that brings together DPOs in law enforcement to exchange expertise and foster best practices. See https://www.europol.europa.eu/activities-services/data-protection/eden (accessed 1 September 2025).

[8] Data Protection Institute, *Are DPOs Happy?*

groups, even if their primary role is advisory, to gain a deeper understanding of operational challenges and offer practical, integrated solutions. By proactively reaching out and demonstrating a willingness to collaborate, DPOs can transform perceived isolation into opportunities for impactful engagement.

V. Ensuring Adequate Resources

Regarding resource availability, opinions vary widely among DPOs. While a majority report sufficient access to information on personal data processing, particularly in private companies, a significant part perceives the feasibility of their diverse task package as insufficient.[9] This issue is predominantly observed in government organisations, where DPOs consistently score below average in almost all resource-related categories and frequently report being under pressure and pressed for time. In addition, organisations must provide sufficient space, time, and resources to enable DPOs to perform their duties effectively. This also entails addressing the frequently reported high workload experienced by DPOs, especially those who combine the DPO function with other roles. For instance, if a DPO is also a legal counsel or an IT manager, executives should ensure that these combined roles do not create an impossible workload or compromise the DPO's independence. This might involve re-evaluating staffing levels, redistributing certain tasks, or investing in tools that automate some of the DPO's more administrative responsibilities.

C-level executives in these sectors, particularly in government institutions and hybrid organisations, must conduct thorough assessments of their DPOs' workloads and allocate resources accordingly. This could involve increasing staffing, investing in specialised software or tools that streamline data protection processes, or providing access to external legal or technical expertise when internal resources are stretched. They should also consider whether the DPO function is being adequately resourced for the specific complexities of their organisational type, as public sector DPOs, for instance, often face more unique challenges in terms of bureaucracy and limited budgets.

DPOs, in turn, should proactively articulate their resource needs to management. This involves presenting clear justifications for additional resources, demonstrating how increased investment can lead to better compliance outcomes, reduced risks, and ultimately, greater organisational efficiency. They should also prioritise their diverse tasks, focusing on those with the highest impact on data protection and advocating for support in areas where resources are demonstrably insufficient. By effectively managing their workload and communicating their requirements, DPOs can help bridge the gap between perceived needs and actual resource allocation.

[9] Data Protection Institute, *Are DPOs Happy?*

VI. Reflection

While this chapter outlines practical strategies for improving DPO effectiveness through structural and cultural changes within organisations, the lived experiences of DPOs reveal that not all elements of professional well-being are within the immediate control of the DPO or the C-level executive. Two key factors – meaningful work and recognition (or acknowledgement) – stand out as critical yet underexplored dimensions of the happiness of the DPO.

Meaningful work is deeply subjective and rooted in the DPO's own perception of their contribution to data protection. Even in well-structured environments, a DPO may struggle to feel purposeful if their work is isolated, reactive, or disconnected from broader organisational goals. Similarly, recognition extends beyond internal performance reviews or management feedback. It can come from multiple actors: from the DPO themselves, through a sense of personal accomplishment; from colleagues and leadership who value their input; and even from data subjects, who appreciate the DPO's role in safeguarding their rights.

Additionally, external forces – most notably data protection authorities – play a significant role in shaping the DPO's experience. The study reveals that insufficient support or unclear guidance from supervisory authorities can negatively impact the DPO. When oversight bodies are seen as distant or punitive rather than supportive, DPOs may feel abandoned in their efforts to balance compliance with practical realities. In that sense, fostering DPO happiness is not solely an internal organisational task but a broader challenge involving multiple stakeholders. One of the objectives of the dedicated DPO track at CPDP.ai 2025 was uniting those oversight bodies and DPOs, eg during the workshop of the European Data Protection Board on their cookie audit tool and exploring the collaboration between the *Vlaamse Toezichtscommissie (VTC)* (Belgium) and DPOs. The high turnout for those workshops confirms the study's findings and underscores the need to expand such initiatives.

VII. Conclusion

This chapter has focused on several developed determinants of DPO happiness and effectiveness that lie within the sphere of influence of organisations and their leadership. Through deliberate action in these areas, organisations can move beyond a narrow compliance mindset and empower their DPOs as strategic partners. By safeguarding independence, nurturing collaboration, investing in professional development and ensuring that DPOs are properly resourced, C-level executives can build a strong foundation for resilient and effective data protection practices. However, further examination on the role of DPO in its entirety is needed, both for academic relevance and to help prepare DPOs and organisations for what's coming next!

Bibliography

Commission Nationale de l'informatique et des libertés (CNIL), 'What are the economic benefits of having a DPO for a company?', 8 September 2025, available at https://www.cnil.fr/en/what-are-economic-benefits-having-dpo-company.

Data Protection Institute. *Are DPOs Happy?* Version 13, 2023. DP Institute, March 2024. www.dp-institute.eu/wp-content/uploads/2024/03/Zijn-DPOs-gelukkig_V13_EN.pdf.

Hielke Heymans, '*International Data Transfers and Stakeholders on the Ground*'. Panel contribution, Computers, Privacy & Data Protection Conference, Brussels, 23 May 2025. Available at www.youtube.com/watch?v=ZtkF58NtP4s.

11

Empirical Methods for Supervising Algorithmic Profiling Systems[1]

Assessment Protocol for Examining Indirect Discrimination

JURRIAAN PARIE, YLJA REMMITS, BRINN HEKKELMAN AND MARK KATTENBERG

Abstract

When regulating algorithmic profiling systems, not only legal but also statistical information plays a key role. Using a Dutch public sector risk profiling algorithm as an example, we demonstrate that current frameworks, guidelines and soft law fall short in providing sufficient guidance for the interpretation of open norms within European non-discrimination law. We show that established methods from empirical science can help clarifying these norms. Building on a case-based example, we propose an assessment protocol designed to assist competent authorities in formulating targeted questions to examine indirect discrimination through algorithmic profiling systems used in the public and private sector. This approach builds upon existing legal frameworks, enabling authorities to effectively monitor algorithm-driven decision-making processes, even with limited resources.

Keywords

Non-discrimination; Statistics; Competent authorities; Algorithms and AI

[1] This chapter was written in collaboration with researchers from the Netherlands Bureau for Economic Policy Analysis (*Centraal Planbureau*), based on a joint Dutch article: Jurriaan Parie, Ylja Remmits, Brinn Hekkelman, and Mark Kattenberg, 'Praktische handvatten voor empirisch toezicht op profileringsalgoritmes', *Tijdschrift voor Toezicht* (TvT) 16, nos. 2–3 (2025): 73–81, https://doi.org/10.5553/TvT/187987052025016002005.

I. Introduction

Within the democratic rule of law, competent authorities play an important role in providing legal protection and legal certainty for citizens, consumers, and organisations. To fulfil this role with regard to the responsible use of algorithms and artificial intelligence (AI), new skills are required. Quantitative methods play an increasingly important role in this. For example, in research into a risk profiling algorithm in the College Grant Check (controle uitwonendenbeurs, abbreviated as CUB) process of the Netherlands Executive Agency for Education (DUO), indirect discrimination was established on the basis of a data study in which random samples, statistical hypothesis tests and the migration background of more than 300,000 students in the period 2012–23 were retrospectively analysed.[2] Building on this quantitative study, controlling state powers – both the judiciary and the Dutch Parliament – have been able to formulate a concrete normative judgement regarding the control process.[3,4]

However, it is the task of competent authorities to proactively prevent such fundamental rights violations. With ever-increasing digitisation and the limited extent to which organisations are able to manage the risks of AI systems, questions arise.[5] How is it possible that after the Dutch childcare benefits scandal 'very little has changed' to prevent discriminatory algorithms used by the Dutch public sector organisations?[6] Will the AI Act strengthen the supervision of algorithms by developing concrete standards for profiling algorithms? And how can competent authorities carry out their tasks more effectively with limited resources?

This chapter introduces an assessment protocol (Table 11.1) which supports competent authorities in conducting targeted supervision of indirect discrimination through algorithms and AI. In doing so, it builds on proposals formulated in the Risk Profiling Assessment Framework (Toetsingskader risicoprofilering) of the Netherlands Institute for Human Rights (NIHR) to use empirical methods to

[2] PwC, *Misusage College Grant* (2024), www.tweedekamer.nl/kamerstukken/detail?id=2024D07564&did=2024D07564; Algorithm Audit, *Preventing Prejudice* (2024), https://algorithmaudit.eu/algoprudence/cases/aa202401_preventing-prejudice/; Algorithm Audit, *Addendum Preventing Prejudice* (2024), https://algorithmaudit.eu/algoprudence/cases/aa202402_preventing-prejudice_addendum/.

[3] Rechtbank Overijssel, 29 October 2024, ECLI:NL:RBOVE:2024:5627, https://uitspraken.rechtspraak.nl/details?id=ECLI:NL:RBOVE:2024:5627.

[4] *Dutch Parliamentary Papers* 2023/24, D21614, www.tweedekamer.nl/kamerstukken/detail?id=2024D21614&did=2024D21614; *Dutch Parliamentary Papers* 2023/24, 24724, no. 229, www.tweedekamer.nl/kamerstukken/moties/detail?id=2024D11179&did=2024D11179; *Dutch Parliamentary Papers* 2023/24, 24724, no. 231, www.tweedekamer.nl/kamerstukken/moties/detail?id=2024D11181&did=2024D11181.

[5] The report *Focus op AI bij de Rijksoverheid* (Dutch Court of Auditors, 2024) shows that for 35 per cent of AI systems currently in use by Dutch public sector organisations, the performance is unknown. This outcome, among other things, led to 82 parliamentary questions from the permanent committee on digital affairs: *Dutch Parliamentary Papers* Z16114, www.rekenkamer.nl/publicaties/rapporten/2024/10/16/focus-op-ai-bij-de-rijksoverheid; www.tweedekamer.nl/kamerstukken/detail?id=2024Z16114&did=2024D40911.

[6] Interview with Aleid Wolfsen, chairman of the Dutch Data Protection Authority, *de Volkskrant* (2024), www.volkskrant.nl/tech/bij-zo-n-beetje-elke-tegel-die-we-lichten-ontdekken-we-discriminerende-algoritmen-bij-de-overheid-zegt-de-autoriteit-persoonsgegevens~b360ed6e/.

investigate indirect discrimination.[7] On the one hand, this is a topical and timely issue – the use of algorithms and AI systems will only increase in the near future. On the other hand, the DUO case shows that methods from empirical science, which have been established for decades, are only slowly finding their way into policy and supervisory practice.[8]

DUO's risk profiling algorithm illustrates how empirical methods can help informing normative value tensions, among others between effectiveness and unequal treatment. In hindsight, it turned out that the profiling characteristics from the risk profile (education level, age, and distance to parent(s)) were strongly related to students' migration background. Based on aggregated data provided by Statistics Netherlands (national bureau for statistics), it was possible to determine precisely at population level that in 2014, 63.3 per cent of the 16,023 vocational training (MBO 1–2) students and 13.2 per cent of the 104,814 university (WO) students had a non-European migration background. Since a higher risk score was assigned to MBO 1–2 students in the risk profile, a higher risk score was therefore indirectly assigned to students with a migration background. Based on these quantitative insights, it was possible to make an informed assessment of whether the distinction made by the risk profile was proportionate.

In March 2024, the Minister of Education, Culture and Science (OCW) came to a decision: on behalf of the cabinet, Mr Dijkgraaf apologised for indirect discrimination in the CUB process.[9] In November 2024, a compensation scheme for more than 10,000 students worth more than €61 million was announced.[10] At the same time, there remains parliamentary support for the use of profiling by the Dutch government. In the same debate in which the apologies were offered, Minister Dijkgraaf stated that: 'we are aware of the value of risk-based control procedures … Although, it is important that there are safeguards for risk-based approaches'.[11] Quantitative methods such as those discussed in this chapter will play an important role in validating it.

The DUO case is not an isolated one. Ill-considered risk profiling is exemplary of the broader use of algorithms by Dutch public sector organisations. 'With just about every tile we lift, we discover discriminatory algorithms', said Aleid Wolfsen in 2024 – chairman of the Dutch Data Protection Authority (AP).[12] Discrimination through profiling is also a risk in the private sector. In February 2025, journalists of Argos reported that Rabobank used discriminatory features in transaction

[7] Toetsingskader risicoprofilering – Normen tegen discriminatie op grond van ras en nationaliteit, the Netherlands Institute for Human Rights (2025), in particular 25–30.

[8] Since 2003, the Dutch national legislation enables government organisations to request specific population statistics for statistical research purposes. Drawing random samples and performing statistical hypothesis tests to measure effects, for example of medicines, has been a standard method since the 1950s.

[9] *Dutch Parliamentary Papers* 2023/24, 24724, no. 220, www.tweedekamer.nl/kamerstukken/brieven_regering/detail?id=2024D07562&did=2024D07562.

[10] *Dutch Parliamentary Papers* 2023/24, 24724, no. 243, www.tweedekamer.nl/kamerstukken/brieven_regering/detail?id=2024D43180&did=2024D43180.

[11] *Dutch Parliamentary Papers* 2023/24, D07566, www.tweedekamer.nl/kamerstukken/detail?id=2024D07566&did=2024D07566.

[12] Dutch Court of Auditors, 'Focus op AI bij de Rijksoverheid'.

monitoring systems and the NIHR ruled that Meta indirectly discriminated based on gender when showing advertisements for vacancies.[13,14] In this case as well, data analysis has played an important role in demonstrating unequal treatment.

Now that profiling algorithms are used in the digital fabric of society, it is important that competent authorities offer citizens, consumers, and organisations legal protection against discrimination. To this end, this chapter analyses the framework of European non-discrimination law (Section II). Subsequently, based on the DUO case, empirical methods are discussed that are helpful in testing profiling algorithms against legal frameworks (Section III). We will then introduce an assessment protocol based on which competent authorities can formulate targeted inquiries into algorithmic-driven risk profiling (Section IV). The chapter ends with a conclusion (Section V).

II. The Open Legal Norm: Who is Responsible for Interpretation?

Distinction is ever present. Both in classical antiquity and in today's society, distinction are made among other things for access to education, employment, and housing. Today, however, some forms of discrimination are prohibited. Constitutions, European treaties, directives, and national legislation prohibit direct discrimination based on protected grounds, such as ethnicity and nationality.[15] Prohibited discrimination can also occur indirectly through so-called *proxy characteristics*. In that case, distinction is not made directly on protected grounds, but on seemingly neutral selection criteria that lead to a disproportionate disadvantage for these groups. Examples of proxies for the protected grounds of ethnicity and nationality are postal code, level of income, licence plate, family member abroad, and low literacy.[16] Since correlations occur by definition in statistical modelling, profiling characteristics always have a proxy character to a greater or lesser extent. Making a distinction based on proxy characteristics is not necessarily

[13] 'Rabobank Discriminating Client Controles', *NPO Radio 1* (2025), www.nporadio1.nl/nieuws/onderzoek/acf57c37-6b5c-4f9c-b15a-fe03de8cff7c/rabobank-discrimineerde-bij-klantcontroles.

[14] Verdict: *Meta Platforms Ireland Ltd. Is Making Prohibited Discrimination on the Basis of Gender When Showing Job Advertisements to Users of Facebook in Nederland* (Netherlands Institute for Human Rights, 2025), https://oordelen.mensenrechten.nl/oordeel/2025-17; investigation that gave rise to the complaint: *New Evidence of Facebook's Sexist Algorithm* (NGO Global Witness, 2023), www.globalwitness.org/en/campaigns/digital-threats/new-evidence-of-facebooks-sexist-algorithm/.

[15] The prohibition of discrimination follows from the Treaties of the EU and the European Convention on Human Rights (ECHR). In the Netherlands, the prohibition of discrimination is laid down in Article 1 of the Dutch Constitution and elaborated in the Dutch Equal Treatment Act (*Algemene wet gelijke behandeling*, Awgb). Article 1 Awgb mentions the following protected grounds: 'religion, belief, political opinion, race, sex, nationality, heterosexual or homosexual orientation, or marital status'. Protected grounds listed in EU treaties vary by context. For example, age is a protected ground in the Employment Equality Directive (Art. 1, 2000/78/EC), https://eur-lex.europa.eu/legal-content/NL/TXT/PDF/?uri=CELEX:32000L0078, but not in the Racial Equality Directive (Art 2, 2000/43/EC), https://eur-lex.europa.eu/legal-content/NL/TXT/PDF/?uri=CELEX:32000L0043.

[16] *de Volkskrant*, 'Interview with Aleid Wolfsen'.

prohibited. However, it must be possible to objectively justify its use. European non-discrimination law provides a framework for this. This section analyses how the numerical world of algorithms and AI relates to the letter of the law, including developed *soft law* frameworks.

A. Legislation: Too General for Responsible Profiling Algorithms

The General Data Protection Regulation (GDPR), the Dutch Public Administration Law (Awb) and Dutch Equal Treatment Law (Awgb), among others, regulate the use of profiling algorithms. The most concrete standards for equal treatment come from non-discrimination law. The Awgb, treaties of the European Union and the Council of Europe (CoE) state that prohibited indirect discrimination occurs when an apparently neutral provision, criterion, or practice particularly affects persons in a protected group compared to other persons. There is no discrimination if the distinction made can be objectively justified. This justification test consists of three parts:[17]

Suitable: are the profiling characteristics sufficiently relevant and objective to contribute in a (more) effective way to the achievement of the legitimate aim pursued?

Necessary: are there other, less invasive, ways to achieve the aim pursued?

Proportionate: does the legitimate aim pursued carry enough weight to justify the distinctions made?

The above norms describe *what* the general legal frameworks are, *how* these open norms should be implemented for profiling depends on the context. In the DUO case, it is not immediately clear how the suitability, necessity, and proportionality of the three profiling characteristics can be tested.

The AI Act (AIA) does not appear to offer more concrete guidance. Product safety legislation ensures the responsible development and use of AI systems by public and private organisations, protecting the safety, health and fundamental rights of European Union (EU) citizens. According to the AIA, specific applications of AI systems that have been designated as 'high risk' must comply with harmonised standards – also known as CE marking.[18] The European Commission has therefore requested standardisation organisation CEN-CENELEC to develop 10 standards for high-risk AI systems that provide the presumption of conformity with the AIA, including a risk management and quality management system.[19]

[17] The objective justification test applies only if a legitimate aim is pursued. In the case of DUO, this condition is met, namely compliance with the College Grant Act 2000 (*Wet studiefinanciering 2000*, Wsf 2000).

[18] See, among others, Articles 1(2) and 40 of the AI Act.

[19] European Commission, *Draft Standardisation Request Amending Implementing Decision C(2023)3215 on a Standardisation Request in Support of Union Policy on Artificial Intelligence* (2023), https://ec.europa.eu/docsroom/documents/64114.

However, there are concerns among experts as to whether, under the considerable time pressure, useful standards for specific applications of AI systems, such as profiling, will emerge from this standardisation request.[20] The harmonised standards will primarily be procedural and will not provide prescriptive guidance for explainability, human intervention, and non-discrimination. In addition, many Dutch profiling algorithms, such as the DUO algorithm do not qualify as an AI system, which means that the AIA's requirements will not apply to this type of algorithm.[21] As a result, it is necessary for national legislators and regulators to continue to explore other initiatives to concretise open legal norms for the responsible use of profiling algorithms.

B. Soft Law Frameworks: Too Soft for Responsible Profiling Algorithms

The need for clearer guidance on the responsible use of profiling algorithms has not gone unnoticed by supervisors and policymakers. To provide more clarity on *how* open norms should be interpreted various institutions have developed *soft law* frameworks. The practical useful of these frameworks is demonstrated through the DUO case.

The Dutch Ministry of the Interior and Kingdom Relations has consolidated various guidelines, instruments, and frameworks that have been developed in recent years in an *Algorithm Framework*.[22] In the Algorithm Framework, reference is made *to* the Netherland Institute for Human Rights' Risk Profiling Assessment Framework for an 'explanation of how to carry out the objective justification test'.[23] The Algorithm Framework and Profiling Assessment Framework had not yet been published in the summer of 2023, when journalists reported a suspected overrepresentation of students with a migration background during the college grant control process of DUO. At the time, the researchers consulted other frameworks that offered little guidance to test the specific profiling characteristics against the applicable standards from non-discrimination law.[24,25] When unequal treatment is

[20] The authors affiliated with Algorithm Audit are active in various CEN-CENELEC working groups through the Dutch standardisation body NEN.

[21] Algorithm Audit, *Guidelines for AI Regulation Implementation – Definition of an AI System* (2025), https://algorithmaudit.eu/nl/knowledge-platform/knowledge-base/guidelines_ai_act_implementation/.

[22] *Algorithm Framework v2.1* (Ministry of the Interior and Kingdom Relations, 2025), https://minbzk.github.io/Algoritmekader/.

[23] *de Volkskrant*, 'Interview with Aleid Wolfsen'.

[24] 'Students with a Migration Background Remarkably Often Accused of Fraud, Minister Wants to Thoroughly Investigate System', *NOS* (2023), https://nos.nl/op3/artikel/2479700-studenten-met-migratieachtergrond-opvallend-vaak-beschuldigd-van-fraude-minister-wil-systeem-grondig-nagaan.

[25] *Impact Assessment Human Rights and Algorithms (IAMA)* (Ministry of the Interior and Kingdom Relations, 2021, www.rijksoverheid.nl/documenten/rapporten/2021/02/25/impact-assessment-mensenrechten-en-algoritmes; and *Research Framework Algorithms* (Central Government Audit Service, 2023), www.rijksoverheid.nl/documenten/rapporten/2023/07/11/onderzoekskader-algoritmes-adr-2023.

suspected, how to assess the suitability, necessity, and proportionality of the profiling features?

If there is a suspicion of unequal treatment, the next step is to investigate whether an apparently neutral profiling method disadvantages a person or group sharing the same characteristics. In the DUO case, this means checking whether students with a migration background have been disproportionately affected by proxy characteristics in the profiling algorithm. The Profiling Assessment Framework specifies that '"disproportionate" means that applying a risk profile increases the chance for an investigation due to a characteristic falling under "race" or nationality above the average chance of being selected for investigation in the case of random sample checks'. The reference to average probabilities and random sampling presupposes a quantitative methodology to examine this proportionality trade-off.

The next step is to carry out the justification test. This starts with assessing the *suitability* of profiling characteristics. The Profiling Assessment Framework explains that 'The essence of this test is to determine whether the use of risk profiling actually contributes to the identification of more violations of norms than if only random checks were used'. However, the framework does not prescribe how the 'effectiveness of each of the individual profiling characteristics' must be established. The Profiling Assessment Framework does state that this is 'in fact an empirical test'. In the DUO case the effectiveness of investigations that were randomly selected from 2014 and 2017 was 3.6 per cent (n=387) and 3.8 per cent (n=293) respectively. The effectiveness of the CUB process – of which the risk profile was a part – produced an effectiveness of 38.9 per cent and 35.3 per cent.[26] Due to the interconnectedness of the application of the risk profiling algorithm and manual selection in the control process, only the effectiveness of the entire control process could be determined in the DUO case. How the suitability of individual profiling features has been empirically tested is discussed in Section III, Empirical Methods.

When it has been demonstrated that the risk profile increases the effectiveness of investigations, the next step in the justification test is to examine its *necessity*. It must be motivated whether there are no less invasive alternatives for achieving the legitimate aim pursued. The Profiling Assessment Framework states that

> comparing alternatives is a matter of measuring and comparing effectiveness but also requires a trade-off: an alternative profile that has less or no (indirect) profiling characteristics also counts as a reasonable alternative if it costs marginally more and or is marginally less effective than the initial risk profile.

Compared to the random sample, the risk profile is effective, but DUO did not sufficiently investigate which alternatives were available during the development of the algorithm.[27] This does not sufficiently motivate the need for the use of the risk profile.

[26] See note 2.
[27] See note 2.

The Profiling Assessment Framework states that if the profiling method is considered suitable and necessary, the *proportionality* of the risk profile should be weighed: 'are the objectives of the risk profiling proportionate to the negative effects that this form of risk profiling causes'? To this end, all 'positive and negative effects of the risk profile should be carefully mapped out'. There is no standardised solution for resolving the trade-off between effectiveness and infringement of equality rights. Based on the DUO case, in Section III, Empirical Methods, we describe data analysis techniques that inform this proportionality assessment.

III. Empirical Methods

Digital information systems enable organisations to apply empirical methods at scale during the development and use of algorithms.[28] DUO's CUB process could be carefully examined because data on random samples and the migration background of students could be analysed retrospectively for the period 2012–22. The empirical methods used in this study are discussed in more detail in this section. In addition, it is explained how the methods can support the objective justification test.

A. Data Quality and the Random Sample

If empirical methods are used to inform the objective justification test, the available data must be reliable. At least the following questions must be answered positively: Are the data representative for the corresponding population? Are the data points objective and verifiable? Can manually assigned labels be trusted? Trust in data quality stands or falls with documentation standards. This includes documentation of the meaning, reliability, and topicality of the data. Organisations affiliated with the Dutch Ministry of Justice and Security (JenV), for example, have set up the JenV Data & Algorithms Scheme, which includes policy and protocols how data should be processed.[29]

During research into the DUO case, the available data on students living on their own were reliable. The values of the profiling characteristics (type of education, age, and distance to parents(s)) could all be determined unambiguously and objectively.[30] However, the data on the outcomes of the CUB process were not

[28] Jon Kleinberg, Jens Ludwig, Sendhil Mullainathan, and Cass R Sunstein, 'Discrimination in the Age of Algorithms', *Journal of Legal Analysis* 10 (2018): 113–74, https://doi.org/10.1093/jla/laz001.

[29] *JenV Data Standard Reference Data* (Judicial Information Service, 2023), www.justid.nl/producten-en-dienstencatalogus/informatieproducten/referentie-gegevens/jenv-gegevensstandaard-referentiegegevens.

[30] Education data (MBO 1–2, MBO 3–4, HBO, or WO) of students are collected by DUO from educational institutions; age is tracked via the Basic Registration of Persons (*Basisregistratie Personen*,

representative, because young MBO students were checked disproportionately often and this group is not representative of the entire population of students living away from home. Due to this so-called *magnifying glass effect*, the data on the results of the checking process is therefore not representative. The housing situation of young MBO students is usually different from the housing situation of university students.[31] As a result, there is insufficient information available about the effectiveness of the CUB process for higher professional education and university students.

In addition, the quality of the labels – in the DUO case the results of the inspection process ('lawfully' or 'unlawfully' received college grant) – must be trustworthy. It is a possibility that due to human bias or ambiguous work instructions, inspectors will more often judge certain students' grant receival as 'unlawful'. In that case, the collected labels are biased and possibly incorrect.[32] It is also important that successful objection procedures are corrected in the data. In the DUO case, the reliability of the labels and any bias in them was not investigated as such, because unequal treatment was the purpose of the study on the basis of a data study of all the different steps in the CUB process.[33]

Drawing a random sample combined with a carefully designed data collection process is therefore a best practice.[34] In a random sample, data subjects are selected for verification without a profiling method being used to select persons or organisations for an investigation. Preferably, a profiling method is designed solely on the basis of data drawn using a random sample. When this is not possible, the profiling method should be evaluated based on the results of a random sample drawn parallel to the algorithmic-driven selection process. In the DUO case, the CUB risk profile that had already been applied was not based on a random sample. The risk profile used was evaluated based on 387 and 293 randomly selected students for an investigation in 2014 and 2017.[35] Based on these random samples, assumptions in the risk profile were tested.

B. Testing Assumptions

If the data is trusted, empirical methods can be used to support the objective justification test. Based on the random sample, the appropriateness of profiling

BRP), and distance to parent(s) is determined internally based on the distance between the postal code of the parents' address and that of the student.

[31] *National Student Housing Monitor 2014* (Knowledge Centre for Student Housing), www.kences.nl/publicaties/landelijke-monitor-studentenhuisvesting-2014/.

[32] A so-called noise study can provide insight into the extent to which human assessments differ from each other; see Daniel Kahneman et al, *Noise: A Flaw in Human Judgment* (London: William Collins, 2021). See also 'Bias Experiment Influence Labels on Decision', *Parliamentary Papers II* 2023/24, 2024D17779, www.tweedekamer.nl/kamerstukken/detail?id=2024D17779&did=2024D17779.

[33] See note 2.

[34] *Report AI & Algorithm Risks Netherlands, Edition 3* (2024), www.autoriteitpersoonsgegevens.nl/system/files?file=2024-07/Rapportage%20AI-%20%26%20Algoritmerisico%27s%20Nederland%20-%20editie%203%20_%20voorjaar%202024.pdf.

[35] See note 2.

characteristics from a risk profile, the necessity of the entire model, and the proportionality can be investigated. The methods are applied to the DUO case.

On the basis of random samples drawn by DUO, it can be statistically investigated whether there is a link between profiling characteristics from the risk profile and unduly use of the college grant.[36] Assumptions from the profile can be tested by means of a hypothesis test: is it indeed the case that younger students are more likely to make unlawful use of the college grant than older students? What about older students who live far away from their parents? After applying the statistical hypothesis test (Z-test) to frequency counts observed in the random sample, only the characteristic 'distance to parent(s)' turned out to have predictive value.[37] The other characteristics are therefore considered not to be appropriate from this simple statistical test, regardless of possible qualitative justifications.

More advanced statistical methods can also be used to investigate the suitability of profiling features. This is necessary when different profiling characteristics are interrelated. This may be the case when there is no link between the feature and the outcome for individual profiling characteristics, while there is such a link within the risk profile used. The risk profile would then still use inappropriate characteristics.[38] This can be overcome by investigating the individual relationship between a characteristic and the outcome by testing conditional statistical significance.[39]

The random sample is also relevant to assess the necessity of a profiling method. The effectiveness of profiling characteristics considered appropriate should be compared with the effectiveness of the random sample. As mentioned earlier, the effectiveness of the random samples drawn by DUO from 2014 and 2017 was 3.6 per cent and 3.8 per cent respectively. The effectiveness of a risk profile must be compared to these figures. These results inform the proportionality assessment. This procedure must be repeated for each suitable characteristic added to the profiling method.

C. Population Statistics

One of the most complex aspects of mapping the effects of the risk profile is determining the proxy nature of the profiling characteristics. A sound methodology

[36] Algorithm Audit, 'Size Random Sample', (2024), https://algorithmaudit.eu/nl/knowledge-platform/knowledge-base/size_random_sample/.

[37] See note 2. Note that 'distance from parents' has predictive value only in the analysis of the 2014 sample and not in the 2017 sample. This is partly due to differences in the underlying population. In 2014, the population consisted of students in secondary vocational education (MBO), higher professional education (HBO), and university education (WO). In 2017, following the abolition of the college grant, the sample consisted only of MBO students. The predictive value of the characteristic 'distance to parent(s)' therefore depends on the specific purpose for which the profiling method is applied and must be examined and substantiated for each situation.

[38] The opposite can also be true, so that the risk profile is deprived of relevant variables and becomes less effective.

[39] In this way, two versions of the risk profile can be made – a model with and without the relevant characteristic – and it can then be tested whether there is a difference in both predictions.

to determine the proxy character is a data study based on population statistics. If the degree of indirect discrimination has been determined, this must be weighed against the necessity and appropriateness to distinguish based on this characteristic during the proportionality assessment. For the DUO case, we explain how the proxy nature of the profiling characteristics has been determined.

First of all, it must be determined in respect of which protected characteristic the proxy character is determined. European non-discrimination law states that 'race' and ethnicity are protected characteristics at all times.[40] This is not always the case for age.[41] Many public sector organisations, but also other institutions such as banks, have data at their disposal (such as nationality) based on which the proxy nature of profiling characteristics can be determined. However, these special categories of personal data may not always be processed according to the GDPR.[42] The GDPR itself offers some exceptions to be allowed to process this data for research into possible bias and the AI Act also offers an exception for this.[43,44] If these data are not available, or cannot be processed for this purpose, Dutch public sector organisations can submit a request to the Dutch national office of statistics Statistics Netherlands.[45] Based on population statistics, the proxy nature of profiling characteristics can be determined this way.[46]

During the DUO study, aggregation statistics provided by Statistics Netherlands were used to determine the proxy nature for the profiling characteristics (type of education, age, and distance to parent(s)) for the protected ground 'migration background'. The results are shown in Figure 11.1. The red line shows the proxy nature per profiling attribute. It follows that type of education has a strong proxy character: 13.2 per cent of university students have a non-European migration background, compared to 63.3 per cent of students in vocational education (MBO 1–2). In terms of age, older students are more likely to have a non-European migration background. The further away students live from their parent(s), the more often they are of Dutch origin. Note that for each profiling characteristic has a proxy nature to a greater or lesser extent. A detailed analysis of these aggregation statistics can be found in the report *Addendum Preventing prejudice*.[47]

[40] 'Race' is a legal term for personal characteristics such as skin colour, ethnicity, and national or ethnic origin; see *de Volkskrant*, 'Interview with Aleid Wolfsen', and Netherlands Institute for Human Rights, *Meta Platforms Ireland Ltd. Is Making Prohibited Discrimination on the Basis of Gender When Showing Job Advertisements to Users of Facebook in Nederland.*

[41] Netherlands Institute for Human Rights, *Meta Platforms Ireland Ltd. Is Making Prohibited Discrimination on the Basis of Gender When Showing Job Advertisements to Users of Facebook in Nederland.*

[42] Article 9, GDPR.

[43] M van Bekkum, 'Using Sensitive Data to De-Bias AI Systems: Article 10(5) of the EU AI Act', *Computer Law & Security Review* 56 (2025): 106115.

[44] Article 10, AI Act.

[45] Articles 41–42 of the Dutch Law on the National Office of Statistics. See *Maatwerk en microdata*, Statistics Netherlands (2025), www.cbs.nl/nl-nl/onze-diensten/maatwerk-en-microdata.

[46] Data can be processed securely by means of protocols drawn up by Statistics Netherlands. Data are analysed via a secure environment, and only aggregation statistics are shared rather than privacy-sensitive data of individual persons. Results for groups smaller than ten people are not published.

[47] See note 2.

Figure 11.1 Distribution of students with a (non-)European migration background and students with Dutch origin pre type of education, age and distance category in the college grant population 2014 (n=248,650)[48]

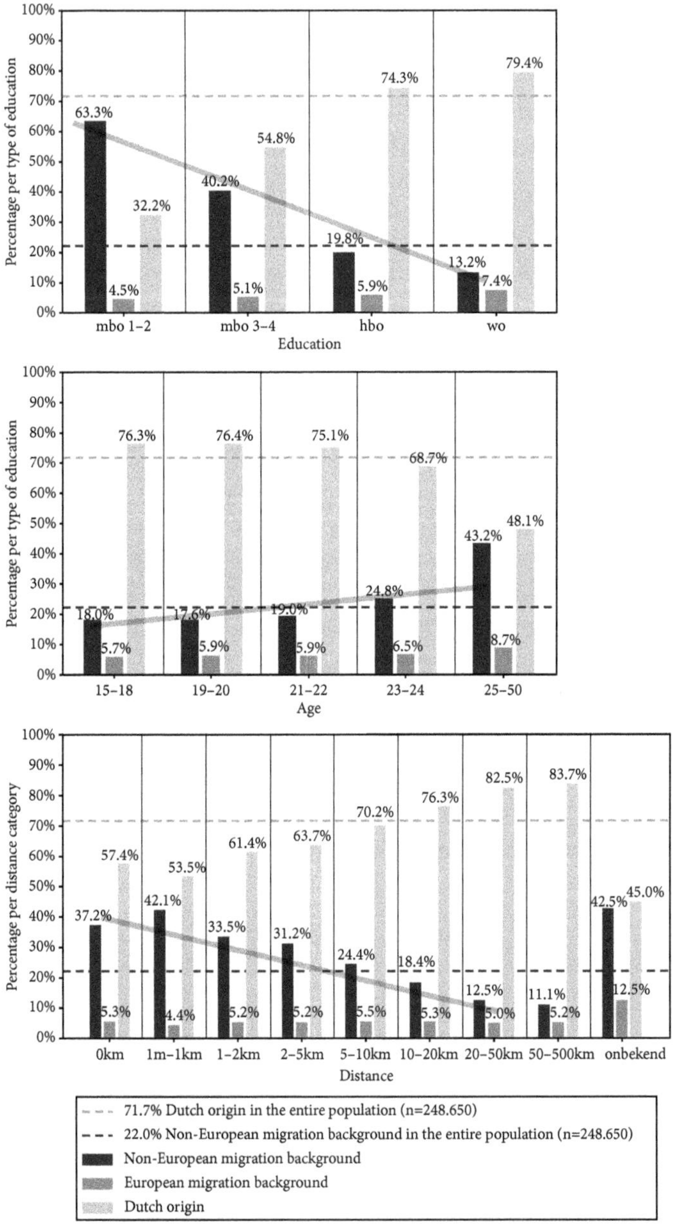

[48] Algorithm Audit, *Addendum Preventing Prejudice.*

Now that the proxy nature of the profiling characteristics is known, the proportionality of the risk profile can be weighed. Based on the statistical hypothesis testing, we know that the profiling characteristics type of education and age are inappropriate to use, as there is no statistical support for a relationship between the profiling characteristic and the aim pursued. These characteristics do not need to be considered in this step. How the profiling characteristic distance to parent(s) should be weighed in relation to its proxy nature is a value-driven consideration that must be settled transparently and in consultation with stakeholders.[49]

If data on the protected characteristic is available at the individual level, the effect of proxy characteristics on the outcome of the profiling method (who is or is not selected for an investigation) can be monitored. In this step, (un)equal treatment through proxy characteristics can be identified most directly. This is relevant because a risk profile based on multiple criteria can ensure that the proxy nature of an individual characteristic in combination with other proxy characteristics has a different effect than if the profile consists of only one characteristic. Based on the results, a link can also be established between the expected effectiveness of the profiling method and the extent to which the selection deviates from the representative sample. This link can be established, for example, by means of adjusted selection and helps to further inform the proportionality assessment. This technique is elaborated on in more detail in Section III.E, Adjusting Based on Characteristics.

How supervisors can gain insight into the choices made with regard to the proxy nature of profiling methods is described in Section IV, Assessment Protocol for Competent Authorities.

D. Demographic Groups not Available

Even if population statistics cannot be analysed, for example because internal data or Statistics Netherlands data are not available, there are still ways to investigate indirect discrimination. These methods are typically referred to as *unsupervised learning* or *anomaly detection*. Proven statistical methods can be used for this purpose, such as clustering.

In the context of scientific research, clustering was applied to the DUO case to investigate the degree of bias that could have been detected if Statistics Netherlands aggregation statistics on the migration background of students had not been available. Based on profiling characteristics (type of education, age, distance to parent(s)), students were grouped (in clusters) who were more often than average

[49] Anne Meuwese, Jurriaan Parie, and Anne Voogt, 'Algoprudence: Jurisprudence for Algorithms', *Nederlands Juristenblad* 10 (2024), https://algorithmaudit.eu/knowledge-platform/knowledge-base/white_paper_algoprudence/.

classified as 'high risk' by the profiling algorithm. The most disadvantaged cluster consists of MBO students who on average live relatively close to their parent(s).[50] Without access to students' migration background, this outcome could have served as a first signal for domain experts to further investigate a suspicion of unequal treatment in the CUB process.

E. Adjusting Based on Characteristics

By carefully monitoring the results of a profiling algorithm, unequal treatment can be mitigated by making adjustments.[51] Adjustment means that the producer of deployer of the algorithm adjusts the selection such that the proportion of people with a certain characteristic reaches a desired amount.[52] Adjusting offers a way to control unexpected and undesirable discrimination due to proxy characteristics. By taking the random sample as a reference point, unequal treatment can be prevented. An advantage of adjusting is that the loss in expected effectiveness of the risk profile is minimal.[53] However, this requires access to protected characteristics, such as migration background.

Adjustment is part of monitoring a profiling algorithm during use. After the allocation of risk scores, an extra step is introduced in which the selection is adjusted based on a specific characteristic. In the DUO case, this would mean that the students with a migration background with the lowest risk scores in the 'high risk' category would be replaced by the same number of students without a migration background with the highest risk scores who were not already in this category. As a result, the share of students with a migration background in the 'high risk' category decreases, while the expected effectiveness based on risk scores remains as high as possible. In this way, adjustments are made to obtain a selection that is more effective than a random sample (because a profiling algorithm is used), but that is very similar in composition to the sample (because it is adjusted accordingly). The challenge lies mainly in deciding when and to what extent adjustments should be made. This is a normative choice that relates to the justification test. In this way, adjustments contribute to weighing proportionality, because the relationship between effectiveness and unequal treatment is quantified.

[50] F Holstege, M Jorgensen, K Padh, J Parie, J Persson, K Prorokovic, and L Snoek, 'Auditing a Dutch Public Sector Risk Profiling Algorithm Using an Unsupervised Bias Detection Tool', *arXiv preprint* (2025), https://arxiv.org/abs/2502.01713.

[51] See Jon Kleinberg, Jens Ludwig, Sendhil Mullainathan, and Ashesh Rambachan, 'Algorithmic Fairness', *AEA Papers and Proceedings* 108 (2018): 22–27; or Brinn Hekkelman, MAC Kattenberg, and BJ Scheer, 'Eerlijke Algoritmes', *CPB Document* (2023), for an application to Dutch data and the term *bijgestuurde selectiemethode* ('adjusted selection method').

[52] It is possible to adjust selections on several characteristics; for an elaboration, see Brinn Hekkelman, MAC Kattenberg, and BJ Scheer, 'The Costs of Affirmative Action: Evidence from a Medical School Lottery', *CPB Discussion Paper* (2024).

[53] Kleinberg, Ludwig, Mullainathan, and Rambachan, 'Algorithmic Fairness', 22–27.

IV. Assessment Protocol for Competent Authorities

Table 11.1 Assessment protocol for examining indirect discrimination for competent authorities[54,55,56]

Organisational responsibilities	
1	Which algorithms and Al systems are used within the organisation?
	Note that algorithms and AI systems are not always recognised as such
Analysis of the problem	
2	Does the process in which the profiling method is used pursue a legitimate aim?
3	What problem is solved with the use of the profiling method?
4	Have vulnerable groups in the population been identified? Has the adverse impact on these groups been examined? If not, why not?
Data quality	
5	Was a random sample of the population drawn during the development phase of the profiling method? If not, was the used data during development analysed to assess its representativeness of the population?
6	To what extent are labels assigned by employees reliable?
7	Are profiling features excluded from the profiling method in advance, because they are subjective, subject to change or known as proxy features for a protected characteristic?
8	Has the proxy nature of profiling characteristics been established by analysis of population statistics? If not, why not?
9	Are selected profiling characteristics linked to aim pursued? Are the profiling characteristics objective and verifiable?
Profiling algorithm	
10	Was a random sample selected to compare against the results of the profiling algorithm? If not, why not?
11	Have assumptions in the profiling method been tested for suitability based on a statistical hypothesis test? If not, why not?
12	Is the necessity of the profiling algorithm evaluated by examining alternatives? If not, why not?
13	Has equal treatment of vulnerable groups been investigated by analysing population statistics? If not, have other analyses been carried out to identify possible unequal treatment?
14	Has the effectiveness of the profiling algorithm been determined? Are corrections, as a result of unequal treatment been investigated and are its effects on the expected effectiveness of the algorithm quantified?
15	How was the proportionality trade-off between equal treatment and effectiveness assessed?
Use	
16	Which portion of the conducted investigations was selected using the profiling method? What portion of the selected group was selected randomly?
17	Is the composition of the selected group for an investigation being monitored? Has correction of the selection been considered? If not, why not?

[54] Examples include protecting public safety, preventing crime, enforcing immigration policy, and combating fraud.

[55] Some examples of proxy characteristics for protected attributes such as race or nationality are zip code, level of income, licence plate, relative living abroad, and low literacy; see *de Volkskrant*, 'Interview with Aleid Wolfsen'.

[56] Algorithm Audit, *Public Standard Profiling Algorithms* (2024), https://algorithmaudit.eu/knowledge-platform/knowledge-base/public_standard_profiling/.

Supervisors – both internal and external – have an important function to safeguard that profiling algorithms are used responsibly. Especially when this technology is used for risk-based selections. Building on the applicable legal frameworks for equal treatment, including those described in the Profiling Assessment Framework of the NIHR, the assessment protocol in Table 11.1 supports supervisors in asking specific questions about the responsible use of profiling methods. The assessment protocol is empirical in nature and focuses on preventing undesirable indirect discrimination. The answers collected inform the objective justification test from non-discrimination law based on which prohibited indirect discrimination can be established. The questions relate to different phases of the algorithm lifecycle and help to prevent citizens, consumers, and organisations from being discriminated against. We encourage competent authorities to start asking questions from the assessment protocol to public and private organisations.

V. Conclusion

Forming a normative judgement about indirect discrimination is a complex task. Our analysis shows that non-discrimination law contains open norms that offer users too little guidance to use profiling methods responsibly in practice. Developed *soft law* frameworks are also of limited use for this purpose. This article describes empirical methods that can assist in determining whether indirect discrimination can be justified based on appropriateness, necessity, and proportionality. The use of random sampling, hypothesis testing, population statistics, and adjusting based on characteristics are central to this. Modern digital infrastructure makes it possible to analyse these data retrospectively at the population level. Based on practical experience, we have composed an assessment protocol that helps competent authorities to request relevant information about discrimination through profiling algorithms. This way, supervisors can improve their knowledge position without having to form a normative judgement directly. A question can easily be asked. Now that researchers have worked out examples, it is up to supervisors to scale up the practical use of these methods.

Bibliography

Algorithm Audit. *Addendum Preventing Prejudice.* 2024. https://algorithmaudit.eu/algoprudence/cases/aa202402_preventing-prejudice_addendum/.

Algorithm Audit. *Guidelines for AI Regulation Implementation – Definition of an AI System.* 2025. https://algorithmaudit.eu/nl/knowledge-platform/knowledge-base/guidelines_ai_act_implementation/.

Algorithm Audit. *Preventing Prejudice.* 2024. https://algorithmaudit.eu/algoprudence/cases/aa202401_preventing-prejudice/.

Algorithm Audit. *Public Standard Profiling Algorithms.* 2024. https://algorithmaudit.eu/knowledge-platform/knowledge-base/public_standard_profiling/.

Algorithm Audit. 'Size Random Sample'. 2024. https://algorithmaudit.eu/nl/knowledge-platform/knowledge-base/size_random_sample/.

Dutch Court of Auditors. *Focus op AI bij de Rijksoverheid.* 2024. www.rekenkamer.nl/publicaties/rapporten/2024/10/16/focus-op-ai-bij-de-rijksoverheid.

Dutch Parliamentary Papers. 2023/24, D21614. www.tweedekamer.nl/kamerstukken/detail?id=2024D21614&did=2024D21614.

Dutch Parliamentary Papers. 2023/24, 24724, no. 220. www.tweedekamer.nl/kamerstukken/brieven_regering/detail?id=2024D07562&did=2024D07562.

Dutch Parliamentary Papers. 2023/24, 24724, no. 229. www.tweedekamer.nl/kamerstukken/moties/detail?id=2024D11179&did=2024D11179.

Dutch Parliamentary Papers. 2023/24, 24724, no. 231. www.tweedekamer.nl/kamerstukken/moties/detail?id=2024D11181&did=2024D11181.

Dutch Parliamentary Papers. 2023/24, 24724, no. 243. www.tweedekamer.nl/kamerstukken/brieven_regering/detail?id=2024D43180&did=2024D43180.

Dutch Parliamentary Papers. 2023/24, D07566. www.tweedekamer.nl/kamerstukken/detail?id=2024D07566&did=2024D07566.

Dutch Parliamentary Papers. *Z16114.* www.tweedekamer.nl/kamerstukken/detail?id=2024Z16114&did=2024D40911.

Europese Commissie. *Draft Standardisation Request Amending Implementing Decision C(2023)3215 on a Standardisation Request in Support of Union Policy on Artificial Intelligence.* 2023. https://ec.europa.eu/docsroom/documents/64114.

Hekkelman, Brinn, MAC Kattenberg, and BJ Scheer. 'Eerlijke Algoritmes'. *CPB Document.* 2023.

Hekkelman, Brinn, MAC Kattenberg, and BJ Scheer. 'The Costs of Affirmative Action: Evidence from a Medical School Lottery'. *CPB Discussion Paper.* 2024.

Holstege, F, M Jorgensen, K Padh, J Parie, J Persson, K Prorokovic, and L Snoek. 'Auditing a Dutch Public Sector Risk Profiling Algorithm Using an Unsupervised Bias Detection Tool'. *arXiv preprint.* 2025. https://arxiv.org/abs/2502.01713.

JenV Data Standard Reference Data. Judicial Information Service. 2023. www.justid.nl/producten-en-dienstencatalogus/informatieproducten/referentie-gegevens/jenv-gegevensstandaard-referentiegegevens.

Kahneman, Daniel, Olivier Sibony, and Cass R Sunstein. *Noise: A Flaw in Human Judgment.* London: William Collins, 2021.

Kleinberg, Jon, Jens Ludwig, Sendhil Mullainathan, and Ashesh Rambachan. 'Algorithmic Fairness'. *AEA Papers and Proceedings* 108 (2018): 22–27.

Kleinberg, Jon, Jens Ludwig, Sendhil Mullainathan, and Cass R Sunstein. 'Discrimination in the Age of Algorithms'. *Journal of Legal Analysis* 10 (2018): 113–74. https://doi.org/10.1093/jla/laz001.

Meuwese, Anne, Jurriaan Parie, and Anne Voogt. 'Algoprudence: Jurisprudence for Algorithms'. *Nederlands Juristenblad* 10 (2024). https://algorithmaudit.eu/knowledge-platform/knowledge-base/white_paper_algoprudence/.

Ministry of the Interior and Kingdom Relations. *Algorithm Framework v2.1.* 2025. https://minbzk.github.io/Algoritmekader/.

Ministry of the Interior and Kingdom Relations. *Impact Assessment Human Rights and Algorithms (IAMA).* 2021. www.rijksoverheid.nl/documenten/rapporten/2021/02/25/impact-assessment-mensenrechten-en-algoritmes.

National Student Housing Monitor 2014. Knowledge Centre for Student Housing. www.kences.nl/publicaties/landelijke-monitor-studentenhuisvesting-2014/.

Netherlands Institute for Human Rights. *Meta Platforms Ireland Ltd. Is Making Prohibited Discrimination on the Basis of Gender When Showing Job Advertisements to Users of Facebook in Nederland.* 2025. https://oordelen.mensenrechten.nl/oordeel/2025-17.

Netherlands Institute for Human Rights. *Toetsingskader risicoprofilering (Risk Profiling Assessment Framework) – Normen tegen discriminatie op grond van ras en nationaliteit.* 2025. https://publicaties.mensenrechten.nl/publicatie/4093c026-ae41-4c1d-aa78-4ce0e205b5de.

NPO Radio 1. 'Rabobank Discriminating Client Controles'. 2025. www.nporadio1.nl/nieuws/onderzoek/acf57c37-6b5c-4f9c-b15a-fe03de8cff7c/rabobank-discrimineerde-bij-klantcontroles.

NOS. 'Students with a Migration Background Remarkably Often Accused of Fraud, Minister Wants to Thoroughly Investigate System'. 2023. https://nos.nl/op3/artikel/2479700-studenten-met-migratieachtergrond-opvallend-vaak-beschuldigd-van-fraude-minister-wil-systeem-grondig-nagaan.

Parie, Jurriaan, Ylja Remmits, Brinn Hekkelman, and Mark Kattenberg. 'Praktische handvatten voor empirisch toezicht op profileringsalgoritmes'. *Tijdschrift voor Toezicht* 16, nos. 2–3 (2025): 73–81. https://doi.org/10.5553/TvT/187987052025016002005.

PwC. *Misusage College Grant.* 2024. www.tweedekamer.nl/kamerstukken/detail?id=2024D07564&did=2024D07564.

Rechtbank Overijssel. Judgment of 29 October 2024, ECLI:NL:RBOVE:2024:5627. https://uitspraken.rechtspraak.nl/details?id=ECLI:NL:RBOVE:2024:5627.

Statistics Netherlands. *Maatwerk en microdata.* 2025. www.cbs.nl/nl-nl/onze-diensten/maatwerk-en-microdata.

Van Bekkum, M. 'Using Sensitive Data to De-Bias AI Systems: Article 10(5) of the EU AI Act'. *Computer Law & Security Review* 56 (2025): 106115.

de Volkskrant. 'Interview with Aleid Wolfsen'. 2024. www.volkskrant.nl/tech/bij-zo-n-beetje-elke-tegel-die-we-lichten-ontdekken-we-discriminerende-algoritmen-bij-de-overheid-zegt-de-autoriteit-persoonsgegevens~b360ed6e/.

12

Quo Vadis GDPR? Ex Orco Usque ad Coelum: A Call to Fundamentally Reshape GDPR Enforcement Mechanics

CHARLES-ALBERT (CHARLY) HELLEPUTTE

Abstract

The Pandora's box of (potential) General Data Protection Regulation (GDPR) simplification has been opened by the current European Commission. The debates as to what needs to be changed are fierce with many options being tested; a move to a multi-tiered threshold-based system, symbolic (and likely inoperative) changes targeting small and medium-sized enterprises (SMEs), encouraging non-GDPR enforcers to step in privacy or data protection matters. This chapter questions those changes to suggest that the only one reform that might be necessary at this stage is one focusing on enforcement mechanisms. Not to invent new ones, but to take inspiration from the patchwork that policymakers already designed for the digital ecosystem and come up with a system that is operative.

Keywords

Enforcement; GDPR; Reform; Regulatory framework; Consent or pay

I. A Fundamental GDPR (Enforcement) Reshape: Attraction or Attrition?

Privacy advocates are calling for a tougher stand against data-driven, consumer-focused companies[1] or support a dramatic shift on how GDPR is built;[2]

[1] noyb (European Center for Digital Rights), *GDPR: A Culture of Non-Compliance* (Report, January 2024), https://noyb.eu/sites/default/files/2024-01/GDPR_a%20culture%20of%20non-compliance.pdf.

[2] European Digital Rights (EDRi) and Access Now, *Position Paper on the EU Proposal for Additional Procedural Rules Concerning the GDPR*, 8 May 2024, https://edri.org/wp-content/uploads/2024/05/EDRi_GDPR-Procedural-position-paper.pdf; 'A View from Brussels: Size Matters, Say Voss, Schrems

politicians on both sides of the Atlantic are making innovation and adversarial enforcements against (US) tech champions their battlefields;[3] academics are addressing overlap of enforcement structures in the digital sphere[4] or questioning the nature of the enforcement gap;[5] while businesses are trying their best to work their ways towards accountability through pragmatic compliance, in an uncertain environment.

The antagonism does not, so far, translate to calls for an overhaul of the GDPR enforcement system by policymakers.[6] To the contrary, the European Commission[7] delivered a *satisfecit* to the current system, praising the increased use of the consistency mechanisms in GDPR (ie, European Data Protection Board (EDPB) opinions, EDPB dispute resolution, and the urgency procedure), confirming a trend towards increased enforcement and pledging that the procedural rules' changes[8] it proposed will deliver the right outcome. Hence, neither the Omnibus IV' simplification package, nor the upcoming Digital Omnibus are proposing the enforcement paradigm shift that GDPR may need if the European Union wants to keep its leadership (*dura lex, sed lex*) in privacy and data protection in the future.

There is however the need for an ambitious, fundamental change to reshape the GDPR enforcement's mechanisms. Not to change the GDPR itself; its principle-based nature, like the Napolean-inspired civil codes, fuelled by risk-based and proportionate approaches make GDPR fit for the digital age. But a change that is taking stock of the (multiple) existing enforcement frameworks that EU policymakers invented already and help fix some of the hinderances that the current model revealed to the world in the past years.

about GDPR Obligations'. *International Association of Privacy Professionals (IAPP)*, 6 March 2025, https://iapp.org/news/a/a-view-from-brussels-size-matters-say-voss-schrems-about-gdpr-obligations; Bureau Européen des Unions de Consommateurs (BEUC), *The GDPR Should Be Better Enforced, Not Reopened*, letter to Executive Vice-President Virkkunen and Commissioner McGrath, 24 April 2025, www.beuc.eu/sites/default/files/publications/BEUC-X-2025-037_The_GDPR_should_be_better_enforced.pdf.

[3] Elena Giordano, 'EU Resists Trump: Tech Regulation Is Our "Sovereign" Right'. *POLITICO*, 26 August 2025.

[4] Paul De Hert and Pawel Hajduk, 'EU Cross-Regime Enforcement, Redundancy and Independence: Addressing Overlap of Enforcement Structures in the Digital Sphere after Meta'. *Technology and Regulation* (2024): 291–308.

[5] Ido Sivan-Sevilla, 'Varieties of Enforcement Strategies Post-GDPR: A Fuzzy-Set Qualitative Comparative Analysis (fsQCA) Across Data Protection Authorities'. *Journal of European Public Policy* 31, no. 2 (2024): 552–85.

[6] The main focus in that regard seems to be given on a lack of harmonisation (something that the EDPB should be able to address with the tools GDPR gave it) or lack of resources at national levels (European Commission, *Second Report on the Application of the General Data Protection Regulation*, COM(2024) 357 final), but also the report from Letta (Enrico Letta, *Much More Than a Market: Speed, Security, Solidarity – Empowering the Single Market to Deliver a Sustainable Future and Prosperity for All EU Citizens* (Report, April 2024)).

[7] European Commission, *Second Report on the Application of the GDPR*.

[8] European Commission, *Proposal for a Regulation … Relating to the Enforcement of Regulation (EU) 2016/679*, COM(2023) 348 final.

II. What is not Working? The Misfortune of the Consent or Pay Peplum Says it All

The call to consider the need for fundamental enforcement reform can be supported in many ways. A powerful one comes from the Consent or Pay peplum, as it illustrates how an EU institution was weaponised, how enforcers sought to act like policymakers, and how the complex ecosystem of digital laws that the EU built is prone to diverging paths and hiccups as it is not sending a strong message, *dura lex, sed lex*; fundamental rights will be enforced seriously.

The culmination of the Consent or Pay misfortune is the opinion of the EDPB.[9] I have had the opportunity to write that this opinion is not one that the EDPB should have been tasked to issue; it was not its role. But it was trapped to do so. Why? Because Article 64(2) GDPR did not consider that national Data Protection Authorities would be using tactics similar to privacy activists for weaponising fundamental rights in a fight that had very little to do with privacy at its core.

Consent or Pay (or Consent and Pay, as I will explain below) is much more about the Internet we want. As much as 'free' doesn't exist, social media companies (but not only) helped come up with business models that attached value to personal data. It does not have any moral hazards to it; everyone realises it, users included. If this is a fundamental intrusion into privacy, it is up to policymakers to ban the practice completely. But they didn't. On the contrary, boundaries have been set in more recent market regulations, such as the Digital Markets Act (DMA) and the Digital Services Act (DSA) on the models. Profiling based on special categories of data (as defined under GDPR) are prohibited under the DSA, while, in practice, the DMA requires consent for gatekeepers' online advertising services.

The EDPB opinion questions not only existing regulations[10] or policy choices taken in the context of such regulations (such as the DMA and DSA), but also a ruling from the Court of Justice of the European Union,[11] as well as the fundamental right to conduct a business.

More importantly, the EDPB's opinion is unlikely to even adequately protect users' privacy. It might lead to an outcome that most users will not find themselves supporting. Access to social media may not yet be a fundamental right, but the opinion could lead to depriving users of what they want; content that they are interested in. The EDPB missed that 'Pay or Okay' is not binary. It is in fact 'Pay and Okay', as the underlying business models for each option is very different.

[9] European Data Protection Board (EDPB), *Opinion 08/2024 on Valid Consent in the Context of Consent or Pay Models Implemented by Large Online Platforms*, 17 April 2024, www.edpb.europa.eu/system/files/2024-04/edpb_opinion_202408_consentorpay_en.pdf.

[10] European Commission, "Commission Fines Meta €200 Million Following DMA Inquiry," press release, 23 April 2025, https://ec.europa.eu/commission/presscorner/detail/en/ip_25_1085.

[11] Court of Justice of the European Union (CJEU), *Meta Platforms Inc. v Bundeskartellamt*, Case C-252/21, judgment of 4 July 2023.

In the path towards enforcing against 'big tech', the EU got lost. It is unlikely because of bad faith; it might primarily be because it does not have the right architecture.[12]

III. A Brief Overview of What We have: The Myth of Perfect Enforcement versus the Flurry of Legal Theories

The piling of digital regulations came with attempts to either list[13] or structure[14] the unharmonised enforcement universe created by policymakers. Professor Paul de Hert and Pavel Hajduk's determination of a three-fold structure spread around (1) cooperative federalism; (2) centralised model; and (3) an intermediate ecosystem model[15] must be commended, even if the context of their work is different than one seeking to call for GDPR enforcement reforms.[16]

Appendix 1 seeks to highlight, in a summarised format, the variety of policy options that have been chosen along the way in the digital spaces, both in terms of structure and as far as the roles attributed to the EU or domestic 'boards' that have flourished in a recent past. Its reading may, hopefully, be a source of inspiration when investigating how to reshape enforcement mechanisms of GDPR. We should not reform in a vacuum; it should help answer the question: do we have a better option in the toolbox, suited to the needs of a strong commitment to privacy and data protection available out there to replace the current enforcement challenges and put GDPR back *ad coelum*?

A. *Quo Vadis* GDPR?

The EU normative capacity seems often to exceed its enforcement powers; is this the case in the field of privacy and data protection? While the GDPR has consolidated the EU authority as a global privacy standard, inconsistent enforcement is a major hinderance that may suggest that strong, centralised, or unified enforcement could be preferred to ensure the long-term viability of the GDPR.[17]

[12] Irish Council for Civil Liberties (ICCL), *European Enforcement Paralysis: ICCL's 2021 Report on the Enforcement Capacity of Data Protection Authorities* (2021), www.iccl.ie/news/2021-gdpr-report/.

[13] Kai Zenner, Scott Marcus, and Kamil Sekut, 'A Dataset on EU Legislation for the Digital World'. *Bruegel*, 16 November 2023, https://www.bruegel.org/dataset/dataset-eu-legislation-digital-world.

[14] De Hert and Hajduk, 'EU Cross-Regime Enforcement', 296.

[15] ibid, 296.

[16] The contribution suggests, using the Meta case as a trigger, that allowing other authorities than the DPAs to deal with data protection matters incidentally presents some advantages for cross-regime cooperation.

[17] Trine-Elise Straumøy, GDPR Enforcement and the EU's Digital Privacy Strategy (Bachelor's thesis, Norwegian University of Science and Technology, May 2025).

To those afraid of centralisation, let's consider models close to the one competition laws provide (see Appendix 1); a threshold-based central enforcement, combined with domestic powers. Such a system will still require cooperation to provide harmonised interpretation of key concepts; it will still give private right of action to data subjects to protect their fundamental rights; it might offer a good alternative to resources questions.

To those against some form of centralisation, consider this: what is a situation where one national data protection supervisory authority takes such a great share of the enforcement's powers or charge (eg, interactions with other relevant data protection authorities), as well as the correlated GDPR fine money. Between May 2018 and September 2022, one-fifth of all complaints referred among the DPAs were referred to the Irish DPA, and above 85 per cent of the data subjects' complaints are targeting 10 of the so-called 'tech giants'.[18] Maybe those numbers alone could work as a plea to consider the need for reform?

And, while we are at it, let's consider the introduction of a filtering mechanism in Article 64(2) GDPR, to avoid further weaponisation of EU bodies to the grocery reform list. GDPR deserves it.

Appendix 1. Digital Laws Enforcement Models

A. Competition Law (Articles 101–109 TFEU)

Enforcement follows a dual system. At EU level, the European Commission, through the Directorate-General for Competition, acts as the central authority. It investigates cartels, abuses of dominance, and mergers with EU dimensions, and can conduct dawn raids, request information, and adopt binding decisions, including fines and remedies. It ensures consistency across the EU and may take over cases of cross-border or EU-wide significance.

At national level, competition authorities apply both EU and national rules within their territory. They investigate anticompetitive practices, impose fines and remedies, and cooperate within the European Competition Network to exchange information and coordinate investigations, while ensuring alignment with EU law and Commission decisions.

B. Digital Markets Act (DMA)

The DMA also relies on a dual system but with centralised control. The European Commission, again via DG Competition, is the sole enforcer. It can adopt

[18] Yiran Lin, 'More Than an Enforcement Problem: The General Data Protection Regulation, Legal Fragmentation and Transnational Data Governance'. *Columbia Journal of Transnational Law*, 27 January 2024.

non-compliance decisions, carry out market investigations, update gatekeepers' obligations, and impose interim measures in urgent cases. In cases of systematic infringement, it may apply structural remedies, including divestiture.

National competition authorities support the Commission by providing local expertise, collecting information, and initiating investigations with prior notice. They operate within the European Competition Network and must coordinate closely with the Commission, whose decisions remain paramount.

C. General Data Protection Regulation (GDPR)

GDPR enforcement is decentralised. At EU level, the EDPB promotes consistency by issuing guidance, advising the European Commission, and resolving cross-border disputes through binding decisions.

At national level, Data Protection Authorities monitor and enforce GDPR, raise public awareness, handle complaints, and carry out investigations. Their corrective powers range from warnings and reprimands to bans on processing, suspension of data flows, and fines. Cooperation between DPAs is structured through the one-stop-shop mechanism to manage cross-border cases.

D. Data Act

The Data Act follows a decentralised model. The European Data Protection Supervisor supervises its application within EU institutions, the European Central Bank, and Union bodies.

National Data Protection Authorities enforce the Act at domestic level, raising awareness, handling complaints, investigating breaches, and imposing proportionate penalties. They also work with other authorities to ensure consistency across the EU.

E. Digital Services Act (DSA)

The DSA applies a mixed enforcement model. The European Commission, through DG Digital Services, has investigative and sanctioning powers. It may request information, demand access to data and algorithms, conduct interviews and inspections, and impose fines or suspend services for persistent infringements.

At national level, each Member State designates a Digital Services Coordinator or other authority to supervise platforms, conduct investigations, and ensure consistent enforcement.

F. Digital Operational Resilience Act (DORA)

DORA uses a mixed model. At EU level, oversight of critical information and communication technology (ICT) third-party providers lies with the European Banking Authority, European Securities and Markets Authority (ESMA), and European Insurance and Occupational Pensions Authority (EIOPA). They may investigate, conduct inspections, issue recommendations, and promote consistency across Member States. National competent authorities supervise financial entities under DORA, carrying out inspections and audits, imposing fines, remedies, or even criminal sanctions, and raising public awareness of the Regulation's requirements.

G. AI Act

Enforcement of the AI Act combines EU and national responsibilities. The European Commission, via DG CONNECT, evaluates measures against AI providers, investigates notified bodies, decides on high-risk AI authorisations, and may impose fines. The EU AI Office oversees implementation and supervises general-purpose AI models.

At national level, Market Surveillance Authorities monitor compliance, investigate complaints, and restrict or prohibit non-compliant systems. Notifying authorities supervise notified bodies, suspending or withdrawing their designation when necessary. Notified bodies themselves perform conformity assessments for high-risk AI and cooperate with each other and notify authorities through knowledge exchange and documentation.

Bibliography

BEUC (Bureau Européen des Unions de Consommateurs). *The GDPR Should Be Better Enforced, Not Reopened.* Letter to Executive Vice-President Virkkunen and Commissioner McGrath, 24 April 2025. www.beuc.eu/sites/default/files/publications/BEUC-X-2025-037_The_GDPR_should_be_better_enforced.pdf.

Court of Justice of the European Union (CJEU). *Meta Platforms Inc. v Bundeskartellamt*, Case C-252/21. Judgment of 4 July 2023.

De Hert, Paul, and Pawel Hajduk. 'EU Cross-Regime Enforcement, Redundancy and Independence: Addressing Overlap of Enforcement Structures in the Digital Sphere after Meta'. *Technology and Regulation* (2024): 291–308.

EDPB (European Data Protection Board). *Opinion 08/2024 on Valid Consent in the Context of Consent or Pay Models Implemented by Large Online Platforms.* 17 April 2024. www.edpb.europa.eu/system/files/2024-04/edpb_opinion_202408_consentorpay_en.pdf.

EDRi (European Digital Rights) and Access Now. *Position Paper on the EU Proposal for Additional Procedural Rules Concerning the GDPR.* 8 May 2024. https://edri.org/wp-content/uploads/2024/05/EDRi_GDPR-Procedural-position-paper.pdf.

European Commission. *Proposal for a Regulation ... Relating to the Enforcement of Regulation (EU) 2016/679*. COM(2023) 348 final.

European Commission. *Second Report on the Application of the General Data Protection Regulation*. COM(2024) 357 final.

European Commission. 'Commission Fines Meta €200 Million Following DMA Inquiry'. Press release, 23 April 2025. https://ec.europa.eu/commission/presscorner/detail/en/ip_25_1085.

Giordano, Elena. 'EU Resists Trump: Tech Regulation Is Our "Sovereign" Right'. *POLITICO*, 26 August 2025.

Irish Council for Civil Liberties (ICCL). *European Enforcement Paralysis: ICCL's 2021 Report on the Enforcement Capacity of Data Protection Authorities*. 2021. www.iccl.ie/news/2021-gdpr-report/.

Letta, Enrico. *Much More Than a Market: Speed, Security, Solidarity – Empowering the Single Market to Deliver a Sustainable Future and Prosperity for All EU Citizens*. Report, April 2024.

Lin, Yiran. 'More Than an Enforcement Problem: The General Data Protection Regulation, Legal Fragmentation and Transnational Data Governance'. *Columbia Journal of Transnational Law*, 27 January 2024.

noyb (European Center for Digital Rights). *GDPR: A Culture of Non-Compliance*. Report, January 2024. https://noyb.eu/sites/default/files/2024-01/GDPR_a%20culture%20of%20non-compliance.pdf.

Sivan-Sevilla, Ido. 'Varieties of Enforcement Strategies Post-GDPR: A Fuzzy-Set Qualitative Comparative Analysis (fsQCA) Across Data Protection Authorities'. *Journal of European Public Policy* 31, no. 2 (2024): 552–85.

Straumøy, Trine-Elise. *GDPR Enforcement and the EU's Digital Privacy Strategy*. Bachelor's thesis, Norwegian University of Science and Technology, May 2025.

Zenner, Kai, Scott Marcus, and Kamil Sekut. 'A Dataset on EU Legislation for the Digital World'. *Bruegel*, 16 November 2023. www.bruegel.org/dataset/dataset-eu-legislation-digital-world.

PART 4

EDPS Closing Remarks

13

The World is Watching

WOJCIECH WIEWIÓROWSKI

Ladies and Gentlemen, dear CPDP.ai guests (or survivors):

It is my pleasure, once again, to conclude the CPDP.ai 2025 conference. The Conference remains one of the most important international platform dedicated to privacy, personal data protection, and how to regulate technologies the digital age.

This year's edition titled 'The World is Watching' – apart from data protection, privacy, and AI – also focused on neurotechnology and neuroscience. All panels stressed the need for an interdisciplinary approach to AI and cooperation between public institutions, academia, industry, and civil society. On Wednesday, I was delighted to start my participation in this year's CPDP with a panel organised by the EU Fundamental Rights Agency, about the implementation of existing laws in the field of AI and how to ensure that the EU's fundamental rights are upheld in the realm of technological and societal developments. Discussions were fruitful; and I take this opportunity to salute the longstanding and close cooperation that the EDPS and FRA cultivate together.

Our partners at the panel were also the AI Office of the European Commission and the Council of Europe. Coming back to the broader goal of the Conference. A big part of our discussion at CPDP was devoted to the implementation of new legal instruments in the area of AI, and their respective requirements, when the development or deployment of an AI system impacts personal data processing.

I think it was stressed enough in these three days that the AI Act does not replace existing EU regulations and laws but constitutes additional safeguards to those stemming from the data protection frameworks. These frameworks already exist at the level of the EU with the GDPR, LED, and the EUDPR (Regulation 2018/1725), and at the level of the Council of Europe with the Conventions 108 and 108+. In other words, the requirements and safeguards established under data protection law, as well as under the sectoral law applicable to AI system deployed (eg, labour law, consumer protection law), must continue being respected. Against this background, both the AI Act and the Council of Europe Convention on AI should be welcomed as efforts to strengthen the rights of individuals subject to AI systems, but for this to happen, they must be considered as part of a broader legal framework that remains fully applicable. I would like to repeat the message I conveyed a year ago, concluding CPDP.ai 2024: *Data protection has not turned into 'everything AI'.*

Respect for data protection and privacy is the essential prerequisite to put people at the centre and ahead of technology. We must defend the identity of data protection in order to protect humanity. Data protection is a compass for the development of digital humanism, allowing for a smoother digital transformation that actually serves the interests of humankind. It should guide all of us in the digital age, or more precisely in the 'info sphere', described by Luciano Floridi as a special space 'that is seamlessly analogue and digital, offline and online'. Cooperation is the key word. The multiplication of regulatory frameworks is a response to the development of new technologies, which have profound implications on our societies, for better or for worse.

Their effective implementation requires a close and strong cooperation among all stakeholders. At EU level, we have launched the Digital Clearinghouse 2.0 (DCH 2.0) to foster collaboration among competent authorities. The DCH 2.0 aims to provide authorities with a forum to exchange and coordinate on issues of common interest and foster proactive and collaborative efforts to ensure a holistic application of EU law. The EDPS has also launched, in 2024, a key initiative named the 'AI Act Correspondents Network', in order to facilitate AI governance in public administrations. Even though the AI Act does not mention or require an AI correspondent, each EU institution has recognised the value of such a network and has voluntarily assigned one. More than ever, the data protection community from all over the world has a crucial role to play in the context of the implementation of AI: as long as personal data is used to fuel the development, training, and testing of AI systems, the data protection framework is often the 'first line of defence for other fundamental rights'.

It does not mean that it will be an easy task, especially in situations where individuals face threats to their lives and this is the work of humanitarian organisations and their data protection specialists, whom I would want to greet in a special way. In such extreme situations, the asymmetry of powers between those who are in need of protection and those who can give them such a support – either humanitarian organisations or other public or private entities – may lead them to renounce to the enjoyment of their fundamental rights. Moreover, the magnitude of digital problems on the horizon means that regulators from different fields and perspectives will have to work together to effectively prevent harm generated or amplified by AI. Synergies between consumer, privacy, competition, AI governance, sectoral laws, and digital services regulations will need to be explored, if we are to rein in the most troublesome use cases of AI.

Concluding the CPDP conference this year, I cannot forget about the sad anniversary we will observe this summer. In memory of Caspar Bowden, 10 years after his passing, we honour a visionary advocate for privacy and digital rights. His unwavering dedication to transparency, accountability, and the defence of individual freedoms shaped global debates on surveillance and technology.

Caspar – one of the founding fathers of CPDP – foresaw the risks of unchecked power in the digital age and stood firmly – even when it was inconvenient – against mass surveillance and for stronger privacy protections.

His legacy lives on in the work of countless activists, scholars, and policymakers inspired by his courage and intellect. We remember him not only for his insight, but for his integrity.

Thank you, Caspar. Thank you to all participants of CPDP for your courage and intellect.

See you next year.

INDEX

www.ingramcontent.com/pod-product-compliance
Ingram Content Group UK Ltd.
Pitfield, Milton Keynes, MK11 3LW, UK
UKHW020220041026
15470UKWH00012B/730

9 781509 993123